Where Do I Start? 3-Easy-Steps

CRASH COURSE

in Family History

FIFTH EDITION

How to Discover Your Family Tree and Stories

Step-by-Step Illustrated Guidebook
and Comprehensive Resource Directory

Paul Larsen

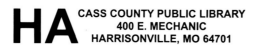

Publisher's Cataloguing-In-Publication Data

Larsen, Paul.
Crash course in family history : how to discover your family tree and stories : step-by-step illustrated guidebook and comprehensive resource directory / Paul Larsen. -- fifth ed.

   p. : ill. (chiefly col.) ; cm.

Includes bibliographical references and index.
ISBN: 978-1-937900-05-2

1. Genealogy. 2. Genealogy--Handbooks, manuals, etc. I. Title. II. Title: Crash course in family history.

CS16 .L37 2014
929/.1   20109

Published by
EasyFamilyHistory.com
1914 Pikes Dr, St George, UT 84770

EasyFamily History.com

The power to discover your family tree and story.™

To comment, or communicate with the author,
e-mail paul@easyfamilyhistory.com

Bulk Purchases / International Sales
To inquire about or arrange bulk purchase discounts for sales promotions, premiums, fund-raisers, or information on translations or book distributors outside the U.S.A., please contact the publisher at the above e-mail or mailing address.

Printed Book
ISBN 978-1-937900-05-2

Digital eBook
ISBN 978-1-937900-09-0

Printed in China

Table of Contents

To Peggy,

my sweetheart

and soulmate

forever.

From the bottom of my heart,
Thank you for
Your invaluable support,
Your unselfish patience,
Your true nobility,
Your unquenchable love, and
For being my inspiration and
Devoted companion for a lifetime.

Preface

I've written/ re-written this illustrated guidebook now five times over the last decade or so. It has been a tremendous effort to stay abreast of and report on the advancement of technology in this unique day-and-age. But also to present it in a simplified, user-friendly yet comprehensive format has taken great effort. No one can really grasp how much time and research it actually takes...except for my sweet wife. And perhaps other authors/ publishers.

Keeping things simple actually takes a lot of work. I've worked long and hard to make it the best it could be. At least the best I could do. I do it because I love family history and my beloved ancestors. And I love being able to use the talent I've been blessed with to help you also keep up on many advancements, and perhaps make it easier for you to discover your family tree and story.

Technology for family history keeps advancing dramatically. The quantity and quality of online data is dynamic, the ability for us to utilize sophisticated new tools to research and organize information, and the advancements to communicate and network with others is quite breath-taking.

Basically, each edition has been driven by what I know and have experienced about discovering my own ancestors and stories. I'm just portraying what I know. Each edition has progressed and developed immensely from the previous edition to a great extent because my knowledge and expertise has also progressed. And this Fifth Edition is no exception.

I estimate that this edition is about 80% totally new (or updated) and better content. There are many really good ideas, tips and material in previous editions that couldn't carry forward in this edition (even though I really wanted to) due to space limitations. You will find many great new resources and tools to assist you in this edition.

The New Face of Family History

We live in an unparalleled time. New technology plays such a big part in our lives today. iPads, smartphones, laptops, wifi, wikis, websites, etc. touching people. New technology to help us move from spending lots of time – as our parents and grandparents did – to finding, analyzing, evaluating things, and telling our story. We all have a story to tell, and with the new face of family history we can tell more of our story better, easier, faster than the previous generation.

We can upload our images, and download information to others instantly. Long-buried information from past generations is available for the first time in the history of mankind. Millions of books are available to search, view and download – both new and out-of-print yet valuable books. Even small collections in libraries worldwide are becoming available.

Technology to help us research better making information more available, more useful, more enhanced and valuable. We are able to quickly and easily access information at the touch of our finger, anytime we want, anywhere we go. Who would have imagined?

Our Fascinating Journey

You are about to embark on a fascinating journey that will take you back into history and forward into the eternities. Never has there been a more exciting time to discover your family tree and connect with your ancestors.

Family history is all about both family and history. It's about family and where they lived, how they survived, how they met life's challenges, what battles they fought, and what social and historical events brought changes into their lives.

How This Book Came To Be

Have you ever had a moment where you were given a thought or an idea that could change your life? You know, one of those moments where you were prompted by an unseen – but real force – to do something that you never really thought about doing before.

My wife and I were out one evening, and we ended up at a bookstore just browsing and enjoying the evening together when out-of-the blue a strong thought hit me. A strong feeling that

I should write a book about...family history.

I almost fell on the floor in the middle of the store because this was such an extremely foreign abstract thought. I had absolutely no inclination whatsoever about doing any such thing, as I was completely involved in a new business at the time – a new consumer product marketing company that I had recently started from scratch. I was essentially overwhelmed with this new business, and struggling to make it grow and become successful.

But this was a very strong feeling and I just couldn't shake it. The thought was: "You have the ability to write a book about family history, and there will be nothing like it in the marketplace." The thought even came to me for the title: Crash Course in Family History.

At first I was really taken back, but then I started thinking to myself. Well, I am involved in teaching classes about how to do family history using today's technology, and I have created lessons to teach these classes. I reasoned, these lessons could become the basis for the book, and there currently is no up-to-date book in the marketplace on how to do family history using today's technology.

I was quite aware of resources available in the marketplace at the time because I had been searching for aids to teach my class, and had come to the conclusion that there was no simple, convenient guidebook that provided information about what was available for family history and how to use it. I felt a great need and desire for people everywhere to easily learn how to do family history.

I reasoned with myself for a few moments, then I made an on-the-spot decision. "OK I'll do it! I'll write a book on family history. I'll make it easy to follow, a simple step-by-step approach, and in my own style with lots of colorful illustrations."

Family history is enjoying a worldwide revolutionary wave.

I don't know if I responded to myself out loud or just in my mind. In any case, I committed myself to do something I had never thought about before. I had written several small books before, but not on a subject that seemingly came "out-of-the-blue".

As we were driving home, I was going over in my mind how I could reorganize my time to be able to accomplish this. I decided that I would get up early each morning around 4 a.m. when my mind was fresh to try and fit it into my busy schedule. I did this and wrote until 8 or 9 a.m. then went to my day job.

It was an amazing experience – and a blessing – to write the book. It was such a refreshing time; no sounds or distractions and nobody around at that early hour. I was able to focus with a totally open mind. It was magic.

The words and thoughts just came into my mind and I could type as fast as they came to me. It was a wonderful and thrilling experience! It took me about a year to write the first edition of this book even though it had taken some months previously to create the class lessons.

I readily confess that I learned a lot about family history from writing the book that I didn't know before about how we are to connect to our ancestors today. And I was absolutely astounded at the many new technological tools and resources that are available to help us trace our family roots and stories. And that was more than a decade ago. It has since increased ten-fold.

A Family History Revolution

Alan Mann

"This decade is seeing the most dramatic change ever to occur in family history. New opportunities, greater access, collaboration, and social networking make family history a whole new world in this era of technology. We are at the dawn of a revolution in both interest in and ease of preserving our family's history."

Alan Mann
Senior British Research
Consultant at FamilySearch

Revolution in Genealogy

Dick Eastman

"We are in the midst of a computer revolution in genealogy.... The "islands" of genealogy data on individual hard drives are merging into very large online data bases, accessible to thousands simultaneously.... This is a very exciting time to be a computer-using genealogist!"

Dick Eastman,
author of the premium Eastman's
Online Genealogy Newsletter
www.eogn.com

Objectives of This Book

My main objectives for writing this book are to:

1 Describe and illustrate the new, easy, simplified process of how to do family history in an interesting step-by-step method that can be easily understood and followed by everyone.

2 Help people readily identify and link their ancestors, and work together or network as they identify names, and reduce duplication of the work.

3 Broaden the number of people connecting with their ancestors, and gain insight and strength by learning how ancestors met life's challenges.

How This Book is Organized

This is a fun "workbook" that tries to make it easier for you to connect to your ancestors, and hopefully fulfills a need in the genealogy community. It provides easily digestible bits of information throughout the book with guide lines, tips, and lots of resources that are visually appealing, easy to understand, and easy to follow. And the companion e-book provides one-click links to thousands of online resources.

You can skip around in the book to areas that interest you most if you want...and not skip a beat. For example, you can jump right into the *Best of the Internet* in chapter 5 and start surfing if you wish. It identifies Web sites that are **FREE** and those that require you to pay a fee. If some of the content on a Web site requires a fee, I've marked it with a dollar sign **$**.

Or you can start at the Introduction: Where Do I Start? followed by the 3-Easy-Steps to build your family tree and connect to your ancestors.

3-Easy-Steps
STEP 1: Plant Your Family Tree

Identify Your Ancestors Using Your Family and Networking with Others is the easiest part because you're actually planting your family tree and interacting with your family in the process.

STEP 2: Make New Discoveries

Add New Branches to Your Family Tree will help you see if someone has already found information on your family tree. No sense re-plowing a field that has been plowed. It will also help you discover lots of information on your ancestors.

STEP 3: Connect with Your Family

Discover Your Family Stories, Photos and Ancestral Village helps you connect with the lives and stories of your ancestors, discover your family heritage, enumerates the many benefits of connecting with your ancestors, and aids you in appreciating your heritage and honoring your ancestors.

Maybe you're curious about the idea of learning about your family history, but don't know where to start. Maybe you've listened to amazing stories from your grandfather, scoured old family photo albums, and attended family reunions. Now what? What records should you look for? What can they tell you about your ancestors and heritage? And what has already been done by others?

Get started today tracing your own family roots and stories, and discover new meaning in your life and the thrill of uncovering new-found treasures.

I hope that this new edition and our companion Web site www.EasyFamilyHistory.com are valuable resources and guides to assist you in planting your family tree, connecting to your ancestors, and discovering your family heritage and stories.

And benefitting you and your family in the process.

Paul Larsen
Author and Publisher

Where Do I Start?

Our Unique Opportunity

Using today's technology – the Internet, exciting, new computer tools, and new, readily available, rapidly-expanding databases of records from all over the world – genealogy and family history work is possible with ease and in record-breaking time. No people in history have ever had the opportunity to connect with their beloved ancestors, learn about their lives and challenges, and grow to appreciate our heritage as easily and readily as we do today.

The Most Beautiful Family Tree

"Through family history we discover the most beautiful tree in the forest of creation – our family tree. Its numerous roots reach back through history, and its branches extend throughout eternity. Family history is the expansive expression of eternal love." J. Richard Clarke

J. Richard Clarke

Suggested Activities

■ Begin to feel a "connection" to those who have gone before you.

■ Plant a seed in your heart for loving your ancestors that can sprout, and that you can nourish so it can grow and get root and bring forth fruit for you and your family for many generations.

■ Read, ponder and experiment upon the suggestions in this book; be persistent and patient.

■ Discuss ways your family can honor your ancestors.

■ Plan a special evening with your family to tell stories and enact a skit based upon your ancestors life.

Family History Insights - Introduction

Bruce C. Hafen
© by Intellectual Reserve, Inc.

A Bond that Ties Generations Together

"There really can be a bond and a sense of belonging that ties together generations. ... This bond gives us a sense of identity and purpose. Our ties with the eternal world suddenly become very real, sharpening our life's focus and lifting our expectations. ... We can discover within ourselves a reservoir of patience and endurance that we never will find without the deep commitment that grows from a sense of real belonging. Exerting such immovable loyalty to another person teaches us how to love.... Our sense of belonging to one another... foreshadows our belonging in the eternal family of God" Bruce C. Hafen

Abraham Lincoln

Man Was Made for Immortality

"Surely God would not have created such a being as man, with an ability to grasp the infinite, to exist only for a day! No, no, man was made for immortality."
Abraham Lincoln (1809-1865), *The Collected Works of Abraham Lincoln* edited by Roy P. Basler, p. 109.

Shakti Gawain

Guided by Intuition

"...we need to be willing to let our intuition guide us, and then be willing to follow that guidance directly and fearlessly."
Shakti Gawain, author

Alex Haley

A Hunger to Know Our Heritage

"In all of us there is a hunger, bone-marrow deep, to know our heritage—to know who we are and where we have come from. Without this enriching knowledge, there is a hollow yearning. No matter what our attainments in life, there is still a vacuum, an emptiness, and the most disquieting loneliness."
Alex Haley (1921-1992), Author of Roots

William Wordsworth

Where Do We Come From?

"Our birth is but a sleep
and a forgetting:
The Soul that rises with
us, our life's Star,
Hath had elsewhere its setting,
And cometh from afar:
Not in entire forgetfulness,
And not in utter nakedness,
But trailing clouds of glory do
we come From God,
who is our home."

William Wordsworth (1770-1850),
English Poet and Author.

Elaine S. Dalton
© by Intellectual Reserve, Inc.

We Did This For You

"...[As] my husband and I...walked through the Old Pioneer Cemetery searching for the grave of an ancestor... I was touched by the peaceful solitude and spirit I felt. I walked through the trees and read the names on the gravestones, many of them children and families. I wept as my heart was turned to our forefathers.... In my mind I asked many questions: Why did they leave their comfortable homes and families? Why did they suffer persecution, sickness, even death? Why did they sacrifice all that they had to come to this place? ... As I sat silently contemplating this scene, the answer came forcefully yet softly to my mind and heart: *'We did this for you.'* Those words...reminded me that our ancestors...sacrificed everything so that past and future generations would [receive] eternal blessings.... I know that if we [connect with our ancestors], the joyful day will come when we shall meet our ancestors once again and be able to say to them, *'We did this for you.'"*
—Elaine S. Dalton

Why Family History?

Unaware to some, *a quiet revolution* is sweeping the earth as millions of people worldwide are discovering new meaning in their lives. They are finding new meaning by simply connecting with their extended family and loved ones – whether it's a real life reunion or making a new connection with ancestors. Just the prospect of discovering one's family roots and heritage, and possibly reuniting with missing loved ones from long ago is absolutely *thrilling*. For many, it's a rewarding, deep-seated driving force.

Family history is about families. And it's changing how some people see life, and helping them gain a sense of identify and purpose in life.

People all over the world, of all faiths, creeds and races, are inspired to search for their family roots and stories. Thus, they are increasingly enabled to more fully appreciate and value their precious and unique heritage, and rightfully honor their forefathers who have gone before them.

As generations pass, people and their lives may be forgotten, but researching your heritage gives you the opportunity to discover who your ancestors really are. And helps bring your family together. As you do this, your knowledge of your forebears will increase, you will gain strength by

learning how your ancestors met life's challenges, you will gain a sense of identify and purpose in life, you will feel a sense of belonging that ties generations together, and your family will grow closer.

Connecting the Generations

Most people have an inner desire for the deep sense of love they feel for their family and loved ones to continue beyond the grave. Don't all of us long to feel bound together in love with the assurance that it will last forever?

To illustrate this yearning, in the famous sonnet entitled "How do I love thee?" Elizabeth Barrett Browning ponders the profundity of her love for Robert, and then concludes: *"If God chooses, I shall but love thee better after death."*

Elizabeth Barrett Browning

Tracing your family roots and stories helps establish a sense of belonging that bonds generations together. This bond gives you a sense of identity and purpose in life.

"Till We Meet No More to Part"

One such person was Major Sullivan Ballou who wrote one of history's most beautiful and moving love letters to his wife Sarah during the American Civil War.

Sullivan Ballou had overcome his family's poverty to start a promising career as a lawyer in Providence, Rhode Island. Sullivan and Sarah hoped that they could build a better life than they had known growing up for their two sons, Edgar and Willie. In addition to being

Sullivan Ballou

a successful lawyer, Sullivan also served twice as the Speaker of the Rhode Island House of Representatives.

At the age of thirty-two, being a strong opponent of slavery and devoted supporter of President Abraham Lincoln, Sullivan felt the need to serve the Union, leaving what would have been a very promising political career to enlist in the 2nd Rhode Island Volunteers in the spring of 1861.

On July 14, 1861, Major Ballou was stationed at Camp Clark, near Washington, D.C., while awaiting orders that led him to Manassas, Virginia. When he heard they were leaving, and that in the very near future they were to do battle with the Confederate Army, and not knowing if he would ever get another opportunity, he sat down and wrote a poignant letter to Sarah. A week later on 21st July, 1861, Major Sullivan Ballou was critically injured when a cannon ball shattered his leg and killed his horse during an attack by the Confederate Army at Bull Run, along with four thousand other Americans. He died July 29, 1861, eight days after the Battle of First Bull Run, Manassas, Virginia.

Though Sullivan had many noteworthy achievements to his credit, it was this letter to his wife for which he will always be remembered. His words professed his eternal love for Sarah, his unwavering belief in his cause, his heartfelt desire for the happiness of his sons, and his faith that they would be reunited after death. It is a truly moving and beautifully written piece which to this day, serves as a glowing testimonial to the love of a Father for his family. *Yankee* magazine published an article on the letter in which they stated "... his words of undying love brought millions to tears". His letter is on the next page.

When Sullivan died, his wife was age 24. She later moved to New Jersey to live out her life with her son, William, and never re-married. She died at age 80 in 1917. Sullivan and Sarah Ballou are buried next to each other at Swan Point Cemetery in Providence, RI. There are no known living descendants.

What Should We be Doing?

I believe that our family history opportunities may be to:

■ *Develop a Desire.* As we search out our ancestors, we grow to care more about those who have passed on, and feel a personal desire to connect with them. It all begins with a simple desire in our heart to connect with our ancestors.

We should allow a yearning for this marvelous blessing to take root in our hearts.

■ *Determine What to Do.* All of us can do something to search for our roots. It's not wise or necessary to attempt to do everything at once, but each of us can do something. Just what and how much we do depends on our own personal circumstances and abilities, and what our family may have already accomplished. We can, among other things:

• Complete family records as far as we can go

• Computerize our family history information and share with others

• Keep a personal journal and prepare personal and family histories, and

• Participate in family organizations.

■ *Continue to Be Involved.* We can be involved in some aspects of family history work throughout our lives. These are not necessarily activities we pursue for a brief time or put off until retirement.

Major Sullivan's Letter to His Wife Sarah

July 14th, 1861
Washington D.C.

My dear Sarah:

The indications are very strong that we shall move in a few days -- perhaps tomorrow. Lest I should not be able to write you again, I feel impelled to write lines that may fall under your eye when I shall be no more. ...

I have no misgivings about, or lack of confidence in, the cause in which I am engaged, and my courage does not halt or falter. ... I am willing -- perfectly willing -- to lay down all my joys in this life, to help maintain this Government....

Sarah, my love for you is deathless, it seems to bind me to you with mighty cables that nothing but Omnipotence could break; and yet my love of Country comes over me like a strong wind and bears me irresistibly on with all these chains to the battlefield.

The memories of the blissful moments I have spent with you come creeping over me, and I feel most gratified to God and to you that I have enjoyed them so long. And hard it is for me to give them up and burn to ashes the hopes of future years, when God willing, we might still have lived and loved together and seen our sons grow up to honorable manhood around us. I have, I know, but few and small claims upon Divine Providence, but something whispers to me -- perhaps it is the wafted prayer of my little Edgar -- that I shall return to my loved ones unharmed. If I do not, my dear Sarah, never forget how much I love you, and when my last breath escapes me on the battlefield, it will whisper your name.

Forgive my many faults, and the many pains I have caused you. How thoughtless and foolish I have oftentimes been! How gladly would I wash out with my tears every little spot upon your happiness, and struggle with all the misfortune of this world, to shield you and my children from harm. But I cannot. I must watch you from the spirit land and hover near you, while you buffet the storms with your precious little freight, and wait with sad patience till we meet to part no more.

But, O Sarah! If the dead can come back to this earth and flit unseen around those they loved, I shall always be near you; in the garish day and in the darkest night ...always, always; and if there be a soft breeze upon your cheek, it shall be my breath; or the cool air fans your throbbing temple, it shall be my spirit passing by.

Sarah, do not mourn me dead; think I am gone and wait for thee, for we shall meet again.

As for my little boys, they will grow as I have done, and never know a father's love and care. ... Sarah, I have unlimited confidence in your maternal care and your development of their characters. ... O Sarah, I wait for you there! Come to me, and lead thither my children.

Sullivan

(The Book of Love: Writers and Their Love Letters, by Cathy N. Davidson, Pocket Books, 1992; Brown University Alumni Quarterly (Nov. 1990): 38-42; Geoffrey C. Ward, The Civil War: An Illustrated History, New York: Alfred A. Knopf, 1990, 82-83.)

Begin with a desire in your heart to connect your ancestors. Plant a seed in your heart that can sprout and grow and bring forth good fruit for you for many generations. Learning and writing about your ancestors can help you better understand them and yourself. Family history work not only helps connect generations together, it also strengthens bonds between living family members.

Loving Your Ancestors

No previous experience is required to begin planting your family tree today. You don't have to become an expert, but you can and need to be an expert in loving your ancestors. Connecting with your ancestors, learning more about their lives, and honoring them is an expression of your love for them.

A Family Activity

Because family history is done *for* families, it is best done most efficiently *by* families. The blessings of tracing your family roots increase

when families work together to identify your ancestors. Family members usually have information to share, or they may be willing to help you look for information. If you do not have immediate family members who are able and willing to assist you, then perhaps friends and extended family members can help.

The Value of the Internet

One of my objectives for writing this book is to help describe the new, easy process to connect to your ancestors. And provide a simplified description—and easy access with one-click—to the sophisticated tools that are available to help us. The Internet is one of the essential tools today to help you discover your family roots and stories

and connect with your ancestors.

The Internet has become the easiest and fastest way to access vast resources of information about your family. It is an excellent tool to get started searching for your family roots; over one-third of the world's population currently uses the Internet. There are more records available every day, but keep in mind that even though the Web is huge (Google indexes over 26.5 billion public web pages), only a fraction of the records of the world have been digitized and available online today. In addition to using the Internet, you also need to search church, court, land, military, vital records, wills, probate, city directories, etc. which may not yet be found online.

iPads, tablet computers, e-Readers, and smart phones make it convenient for people to do family history from anywhere, anytime. Millions of people are taking snapshots of tombstones and other kinds of documents, and uploading them to "the cloud" where they are accessible on various web sites, such as: www.Find-a-Grave.com, www.BillionGraves.com, and www.RIPnav.com.

One of the most amazing things about using the Internet is the ability to network with others. For example, Facebook now has 1.2 billion people using the site each month, connecting both family and friends. *See the section "Networking with Others" on page 45 for more information.*

The Internet also provides a simple and inexpensive way for you to share your family history, stories and photos with others. By sharing information with each other, you help each other in your research, reduce the duplication of effort, and make the data more accurate. Sharing may help unite otherwise fragmented extended families. E-mail and texting help make the sharing of family data almost instantaneous.

We live in an exciting time. We are blessed with computers and the Internet to help us connect with our ancestors, and with people around the world.

> Interest in discovering your roots is exploding.

Family History is Booming

In the early 1800s there were no organizations dedicated to gathering family history. Beginning in 1837, England and Wales began mandatory recording of births, deaths, and marriages for everyone in their countries. Many countries around the world thereafter started recording more information in their census records. For example, Great Britain's censuses began recording names and ages of individuals in 1841, and the United States added names of family members in 1850 (previously only heads of household were named). In 1844 the New England Historic Genealogical Society was organized in Boston. Today, there are thousands of family history societies around the world.

In addition, many people began to publish their family histories. The results have been dramatic. Between 1450 and 1836, fewer than 200 family histories were published. Between 1837 and 1935, almost 2,000 more were published. Today more than 2,000 family histories are published each week. Genealogy and family history has become immensely popular worldwide. If you search for the term *genealogy* on the Web, you get over 81 million hits on Google.com, 160 million on Yahoo.com, and 40 million on Live.com.

Popularity in America

A 2005 survey by Ancestry.com showed that 73% of the U.S. population was interested in or actively researching their family history. (Market Strategies, Inc. 2005) A more recent survey, showed that **87% of Americans have an interest in their family history.*** This means that approximately 199 million adults in the U.S. are interested (ranging from either very interested or somewhat interested) in learning about their family history. Compare that to the voter turnout for the 2009 American presidential election of 131.2 million, the highest in at least 40 years.

*Based on a survey commissioned by Ancestry.com conducted by Harris Interactive interviewing a nationwide sample of 2,066 US adults aged 18+. http://sec.gov/Archives/edgar/data/1469433/000095012309058478/d68252b4e424b4.htm

Web-based technologies, online data, and collaboration using the Internet greatly enhances opportunities for engaging in family history research by enabling new ways of searching and organizing your information, as well as significantly easier communicating and networking. The dynamic growth of social networks and online communities on the Internet has demonstrated the strong desire of people to connect and share information with each other. All of this makes family history research more accessible to a broader group of people.

Alex Haley

Link to Your Past

"In every conceivable manner, the family is our link to our past, and the bridge to our future." Alex Haley

Alex Haley, American biographer, scriptwriter, author (1921-1992). In 1965 Alex Haley stumbled upon the names of his maternal great-grandparents, when he was going through post-Civil War records in National Archives in Washington, D.C. He spent years tracing his own family back to a single African man, Kunta Kinte, who was captured in Gambia and taken to America as a slave around 1767. That discovery led to Haley's epic book *Roots*, published in 1976 to wide acclaim. The next year the television miniseries *Roots* ran for a week on network TV and became a national phenomenon. *Roots* won a Pulitzer Prize and the National Book Award, and Haley is often credited with inspiring interest in family history. www.kintehaley.org

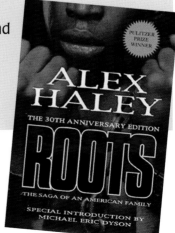

Do Your Ancestors Want to Be Found?

As you search for your family roots and stories, it's possible that you may make fortunate discoveries of significant information that you were not even looking for. This is called *serendipity or intuition* – the process of accidentally or coincidentally making meaningful family history discoveries while looking for entirely something else.

Most people that do family history have a healthy respect for serendipity and feel that the search for their family roots is often guided in mysterious, unexplainable, miraculous, coincidental ways. They usually have a similar story of an unlikely discovery falling into their lap, like a gift, which leaves them with a feeling of awe, as if their ancestors are helping with the search. It's almost as if your ancestors are standing behind you pushing you in the right direction.

This prodding may come in the form of inspiration, intuition, a dream, a thought that enters your mind, or *just being in the right place at the right time.* But in the end it's a little help from above that can lead you to information you may never find otherwise.

I believe that our forebears are deeply interested in our welfare. Clearly, as we do this work there is unseen but definitive help from those who have passed on before us.

Examples of Serendipity

- Running into a previously unknown cousin at a far-away cemetery, even though neither person had been there before *as if the meeting had been planned.*

- Effortlessly discovering an ancestor's grave that you shouldn't have easily found.

- Family photos and heirlooms that are reunited with their families under unexplainable circumstances.

- Mysterious discoveries of books that seemingly magically open to exactly the right page for long sought-after information.

- Having a book fall off the shelf and land on the floor to the page containing information you want.

- Several unacquainted people showing up at a library in a city where none of them live, on the same day, at the same time *each seeking the same common ancestor.*

Are Your Ancestors Gently Guiding You to Find Them?

In family history we call this Serendipity or Intuition. Some may also call it coincidence, hunch, synchronicity, fortuitous luck, paranormal, karma, ESP, providence, inspiration, psychic, sixth sense, inner voice, omen or just a 'miracle'. In any case, it happens to nearly everyone who is trying to build their family tree and connect to their ancestors over a long-time in one form or another. It's the process of accidentally or coincidentally making meaningful discoveries about one's ancestors while looking for something else entirely – as if your ancestors are pushing you in the right direction. It can be as simple as a thought or feeling. Many times it is manifest as extraordinary luck or fortuitous coincidence. People have experienced this guidance as simple as facts popping into their heads or as dramatically as an actual ancestral visitation from beyond the grave.

It was Found on the Gravestone

"One of my cousins was trying to locate our great-grandmother's grave in the cemetery in Garden City, Kansas while on their way to Colorado for a vacation. After searching for quite a while, they were unable to locate it and decided to go on down the road. When they went to get into the car, they noticed their daughter had lost a shoe so they went back into the cemetery to find it. It was found – on the gravestone of our great-grandmother!" Mere coincidence? Charles E. Templer, RootsWeb Review, Vol. 9, No. 43.

Something Kept Drawing Me Back

Dora Fisher had been searching all her life for more information about her father's youngest brother, believed by most to have been stillborn. An aunt told her she remembered her brother was born one evening about 1926 in Ontario, Canada. He died the following

morning. But no one living knew his name. Dora relates that she was working with *FamilySearch Indexing.* "I would download a

batch of 24 Ontario Death records, index them, and send them back. Then I would go do a load of laundry... but something kept drawing me back to the computer." After about 10 batches the names of her grandparents jumped off the page. They were listed as parents of a deceased boy: **John A. Taylor, Born: 20 Jan 1928, Died: 21 Jan 1928.**

She said, "I scared the heck out of my husband. I threw my arms in the air and hollered, 'I found him!' Then I cried. ...It was one month to the day since his next oldest sister had passed away. I can just see the two of them up there, screaming: 'Get back to that computer!' If I had stopped earlier in the day, someone else would have gotten this batch, and I still wouldn't have the information." Dora J. Fisher, http://archiver. rootsweb.com

The Last Remaining Evidence

After forty years, Edwin Cannon, Jr. decided to prune his old photographs from Germany. However, every time he planned to discard the

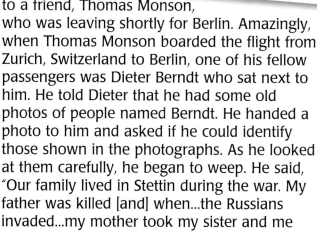

photographs of a family – a mother and father and their small children – he was impressed to keep them, although he was at a loss as to why. He knew their surname was Berndt but could remember nothing more about them. He decided to give them to a friend, Thomas Monson, who was leaving shortly for Berlin. Amazingly, when Thomas Monson boarded the flight from Zurich, Switzerland to Berlin, one of his fellow passengers was Dieter Berndt who sat next to him. He told Dieter that he had some old photos of people named Berndt. He handed a photo to him and asked if he could identify those shown in the photographs. As he looked at them carefully, he began to weep. He said, "Our family lived in Stettin during the war. My father was killed [and] when...the Russians invaded...my mother took my sister and me and fled from the approaching enemy. Everything had to be left behind, including any photographs we had. I am the little boy pictured in these photographs and my sister is the little girl. The man and woman are our dear parents. Until today I've no photographs of our childhood...or of my father." They had miraculously come into possession of the last remaining visual evidence of a couple who seemed to be calling from beyond the grave, saying to their children, "Remember us!" Was their meeting mere coincidence? Thomas S. Monson, CES Fireside, 11 January 2009

Courtesy of http://AncestryInsider.blogspot. com >Serendipity<

Ancestors Will Meet You Halfway

"We do indeed honor our ancestors when we search for them, and it seems, they return the favor. ... When one makes the effort to learn about the lives of ancestors, they will often meet you halfway." Megan Smolenyak, *In Search of Our Ancestors,* 2000, Adams Media Corp.

Megan Smolenyak

Valuable Intuition

"The only really valuable thing is intuition." Albert Einstein (1879-1955), physicist

Intuition and Inspiration

"I believe in intuition and inspiration; at times I feel certain I am right while not knowing the reason." Albert Einstein

Albert Einstein

Instinct is Worth More

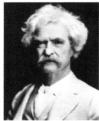

"For all the talk you hear about knowledge being such a wonderful thing, instinct is worth forty of it for real unerringness." Mark Twain (1835-1910). author, humorist

Mark Twain

Searching With an Open Heart

"I was amazed to find success in genealogy often comes from intuition, searching not with just the mind, but also an open heart, enjoying warm feelings with the deceased." George W. Fisk, author

Cosmic Fishing

"I call intuition cosmic fishing. You feel a nibble, then you've got to hook the fish." Richard Buckminster Fuller (1895-1983), inventor

RIchard Buckiminster Fuller

Looking for a Needle

"Serendipity is looking in a haystack for a needle and discovering a farmer's daughter." "Serendipity, the art of making an unsought finding." Pek van Andel

Intuition Discoveries

"It is through science that we prove, but through intuition that we discover." Jules Henri Poincaré (1854-1912), physicist, mathematician, philosopher

Jules Henri Poincaré

Inspirational Stories

Our forebears are anxious for us to connect with them. Here are some inspirational stories that will warm your heart and illustrate the point in tracing your family roots. Check out these books and Web sites for more stories.

Megan Smolenyak's Books - $

www.honoringourancestors.com

You can enjoy many inspirational stories in Megan Smolenyak's books of how people have experienced amazing incidents in the search for their roots. She was struck by the number of stories about random acts of kindness, coincidence, intuition, and serendipity. She found herself inundated with stories of distant cousins "coincidentally" meeting while visiting the cemetery of their ancestors, and she learned of family photos, papers, and Bibles that were reunited with their original families under circumstances that boggle the mind. $12.95

Hank Jones (caption)

Hank Jones' Books - Ⓢ
www.hankjones.com $16.95

Henry (Hank) Z. Jones, Jr. has written two books concerning the positive influence of coincidence and serendipity in family history research. Over a hundred respected researchers discuss their experiences in light of synchronicity, intuition, and genetic memory. *Psychic Roots: Serendipity & Intuition in Genealogy* and *More Psychic Roots* contains a collection of stories and experiences contributed by people the world over. As the author concludes: *"I do believe that our ancestors have no wish to be forgotten: they want to be found."*

Genealogy Today.com - ⒻⓇⒺⒺ
http://genealogytoday.com/family/ stories/serendipity.html

Joanne Rabun relates stories about people being led to certain information in some mystical way.

Ancestry Insider.com - ⒻⓇⒺⒺ
http://ancestryinsider.blogspot.com > *Serendipity*

The anonymous Ancestry Insider writes this popular blog that includes more stories about serendipity in genealogy for your enjoyment.

Ancestors at Her Fingertips

Kathleen had promptings at various times throughout her life. She sensed her Swedish ancestors were there, somewhere, waiting for her. She had searched for information for many years without success, but decided to try again. Before long she had the opportunity to go to Sweden, and found herself in the village church of her ancestors.

She followed the old, white-haired Swedish minister down a narrow flight of stairs into a small room where rows of brown leather-covered volumes lined the shelves from floor to ceiling. She told the minister her grandmother's birth date. He pulled a book from the shelf, opened it, and pointed to an entry. It was her grandmother's birth record. With excitement she watched as he pulled other books from the shelves showing the records of her grandmothers and great-grandparents families. In five minutes, she had in front of her information that she had not been able to find in ten years.

She quickly and happily copied all the records the minister had found for her, and wondered what she should do next. With only a short time to work in the church, she picked up the book for the next five-year period, but could not figure out the index in the front. She turned the page to where her family had been in the other book, but they were not there. She flipped through the book, trying to find some kind of pattern. With mounting panic and desperation, she gazed at the books lining the shelves. At her fingertips were the records she had been wanting for so long, but she didn't know how to use them! Each book was too thick to go through page by page.

She opened the book again and flipped a few pages. What could she do? She simply sat there, numb with disappointment. Gradually, she became aware of the book that she had just opened. The names on the page looked familiar. Despair gave way to joy as she recognized the names of her great-great-grandparents. There were 417 pages in the book, but completely at random, she had opened it to the one page that had the records of her family.

The Face on the Other Side

G.G. Vandagriff wanted to learn more about her great-grandmother. She had all the "data" about the dates and places, but wanted to really know her. She felt drawn to her in a way she couldn't explain, and the desire to know her grandmother consumed her. In a bold move, she knelt and prayed one night that she might become familiar with her in an intimate way. She wanted to know what she looked like, what her personality was, what her feelings were by following her husband to seven frontier settlements.

She knew that she was praying for a miracle, but the next morning she received a phone call that shocked her. The phone call was from her unknown third cousin, Joyce, also a descendent of her grandmother. Her cousin had obtained her phone number by coincidence and stated that she was the granddaughter of the favorite granddaughter of their grandmother and that she had her pictures, her quilts, and story upon story about her.

Within 36 hours of her prayer, she sat looking at her grandmother's face for the first time, and in the months that followed, she got to know her.

She now measures her character against her grandmothers, hoping that when they meet, that she will be worthy of her extraordinary heritage. www.meridian magazine.com/turninghearts/ 020919faceveil.html

One-Chance-in-a-Million

Cathy Corcoran was searching for information on her grandfather. She knew his birth date, but when faced with the daunting task of going through eleven thousand babies born in Boston in 1876 in someone's old handwriting, she was troubled. She randomly opened a dusty book and idly flipped to page 525. The name practically leaped off the page. What are the odds that she would open a book to that page and see that record? A million to one? It was amazing. It was a miracle. Read this story in Megan Smolenyak's book, *In Search of Our Ancestors*, p. 7-9.

My Ancestor Helped Me

Cheryl Bean went to the courthouse to view court records on her ancestor only to discover that the records had been misplaced during a recent move. After digging through book after book for some time in a huge basement room, she bowed her head in prayer, and then walked to the most remote row of books. She picked up the last volume on the shelf, but the title didn't look promising. She opened it anyway and discovered that the apparently mislabeled book had been used to record early territorial court hearings. She tried not to get her hopes up too high, but after some frantic page turning, there was the information she was seeking. She got an overwhelming feeling that she

wasn't alone, and prayed silently again to be led to any additional information about her ancestor. She found herself drawn to another row where she plucked out a book at random and found additional information. After that experience, she was convinced that she was not alone in the work of searching for her ancestors. Read this story in Megan Smolenyak's book, *In Search of Our Ancestors,* p. 10-11.

Their Families Finally Found Each Other with Help from the Other Side

Athena's Mother was suffering from terminal cancer, and she was near death. But her Mother said that she didn't want to go until she could find her family. Athena told her Mother that she would be with them soon, so why not send her back the information and she would see what she could do to help. Her father immigrated to the United States from Greece in 1915, and had changed his name, but they had never met any of his family, nor did they know any information about them, including their names.

Soon after her Mother passed away, Athena had some interesting things happen. In searching on the internet, she found a name that she thought was her father's true surname, but had never been able to verify it for sure. She wrote a letter and before long received a reply that his father was her grandfather's brother, and that they were living in Canada. Soon after that, she received a phone call from another man who told her that his wife was her mother's first cousin and they had emigrated from Greece to Canada and also been looking for them for many years. She came on the phone and cried and cried. She told her how they had come to Salt Lake many times trying to locate them, but they were never able to find them, due to the name change.

Not only were they able to associate with living members of the family as well as

learn about ancestors for the first time, but from the information she received, she went to the Family History Library and found over 100 names of relatives. When they had their very first family reunion, the love between them was immediate and it felt as though they had always been in their lives and there was an immediate bonding. They realized that their families had been looking for one another for 85 years. It seems there are times when family members can be more help to us in finding our roots from the other side. http://deseretbook.com

The Book Fell Open to the Right Place

Sherlene Hall Bartholome writes: "While living in New York...I had randomly chosen a book from among many about Ohio history. While thumbing through it, I remarked... that I sure would like to find the marriage of a certain couple from that state. No sooner did I name them than this book fell open to a page that had an entire paragraph about them, as their names practically jumped off the page to catch my attention! As the back of my neck went electric, and my eyes teared, I forgot any sense of reserve and demanded of the startled men: what names did I just mention to you? Look at this page — can you believe? Just look at this! This book fell right open to their names! Why, here's their marriage date! Do you know how long I've been looking for this? I tell you, there really are angels guiding this work! They inspected the open page, acknowledged that I spoke those same names

before I opened it, and seemed to be almost as excited and caught up in the moment as I." www.meridian magazine. com/turning-hearts/021122bookfell.html

I Hope You Remember Me

David Heyen awoke one morning with a strong feeling that he had left something undone in his family history and that *now* was the time to do it. The impression was so strong that he decided he should visit Rockport, Missouri, the place his father's family had lived. He hadn't visited there since he was young and was apprehensive about seeing long-lost family members, but the urgency he felt was strong so he decided to go anyway. His fears were soon put to rest as his relatives welcomed him with open arms. He became more and more astonished as piece after piece of his family's history fell into place. Family lines he had abandoned because of lack of information suddenly began to produce generous information. He found old photographs of grandparents four and five generations back whose information he had previously given up all hope of ever finding.

In reviewing the original documents his great-grandmother had given him, he happened upon a poem written in 1830 by John Brown, his fourth great-grandfather. It read, in part:

My Christian friends, both old and young, I hope, in Christ, you'll all be strong. I hope you'll all remember me, If no more my face you'll see. And in trust, in prayers, I crave That we shall meet beyond the grave. Oh glorious day, Oh blessed hope. My heart leaps forward at the thought! When in that happy land we'll meet. We'll no more take the parting hand, But with our holy blessed Lord, We'll shout and sing with one accord.

His eyes filled with tears as he felt impressed that these words from 1830 were written for him. He felt that his family members who had passed on were determined not to be forgotten and were urging him to discover who they were. He knew that someday he would have the chance to meet them in that joyous reunion John Brown wrote of so very long ago. By following the prompting he received, he found that a way was opened to him in his search, and now he knew we are never really finished with discovering our family roots and stories.

Sheer Dumb Luck?

Beth Uyehara found her great grandfathers grave and decorated it with flowers. The next morning

at the courthouse, while looking through deed indexes, she accidentally grabbed a book from the wrong shelf, and opened an index from the 1920s – decades after her family had left the area. Before noticing her mistake, she found two quit-claim deeds signed by her great grandfather's descendants and their spouses, showing their relationships and other valuable information. It was a bonanza of information. Was this just luck? In another city, while searching immigration and naturalization records for another great grandfather, she found his file and inside was not only his final certificate of citizenship, but also his personal copy of the Declaration of Intention. He must have left it behind at his swearing-in as a citizen. Since he died just twelve days after becoming a citizen, he had never returned to pick it up and there it sat for 120 years. As she and the clerk examined the file together, they discovered that the clerk's ancestor had been the character witness for Beth's ancestor when he applied for citizenship, so they had obviously been friends. Was their chance meeting just coincidence? Read this story in Megan Smolenyak's book, *In Search of Our Ancestors*, p. 3-5.

Our Ancestors are Close to Us

Reverend
Billy Graham

The Soul of Man is Eternal

The Reverend Billy Graham delivered a message entitled *What Happens When You Die?* published in *Decision* magazine in June 2003. He was referring to the April 2003 death of NBC journalist David Bloom who died in Iraq of a blood clot.

In the article, he stated that it's not possible *"that a Creator would...allow His highest creation... to become extinct at death."* He went on to say that while our body is temporary, our spirit or soul is eternal and will live forever. You can read the full article at http://billygraham.com/ourMinistries/decisionMagazine. Billy Graham, "The Reality of Eternity," Decision magazine, June 2003, Charlotte, N.C., BGEA

Boyd Packer
© by Intellectual Reserve, Inc.

Our Forebears are Close to Us

"It is a veil, not a wall, that separates us from the spirit world. ... Veils can become thin, even parted. We are not left to do this [family history] work alone. They who have preceded us...and our forebears there, on occasion, are very close to us. ..." Boyd Packer

John Taylor
© by Intellectual Reserve, Inc.

Forming an Alliance

"We are forming an alliance, a union, a connection, with those that are behind the veil, and they are forming a union and connection with us; and while we are living here, we are preparing to live hereafter, and laying a foundation for this." John Taylor, *Journal of Discourses,* 11:12/11/1864

Free Tutorials and Lessons

FamilySearch Help Center - FREE

https://familysearch.org/ask

What kind of help do you need? Click on an assortment of help options. *1. Product Support:* Get help with any of the family history tools provided by FamilySearch. *2. Research Assistance:* A community of researchers is ready to assist you

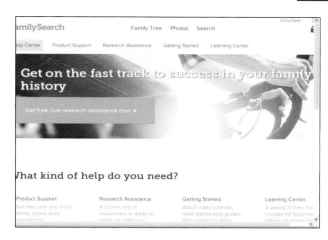

with your questions. *3. Getting Started:* Watch video tutorials, read step-by-step guides, and connect to other beginners. *4. Learning Center:* A variety of free, online courses for beginners to advanced researchers.

FamilySearch Learning Center - FREE

https://familysearch.org/learningcenter

Provides hundreds of online videos and genealogy classes to help you quickly discover your family history. You can learn the basic methods and key resources to start your family history, including: England, Germany, Ireland, Italy, Mexico, Russia and U.S. research.

FamilySearch Research Wiki - FREE

https://familysearch.org/learn/wiki

An incredible resource that provides links to record collections where your ancestor's information could be found, and research advice for how to approach research problems. Contains over 75,000 valuable articles providing thousands of links to websites and databases. *Beginning Genealogy:* start your family history, select computer software, organize your records, and research principles. *Find Records by Place:* click on 'All Countries' to browse alphabetically by country. *Research Tools:* research outlines/

guides, census records, forms, calendars, directories, migration routes, social media, etc.

BYU Independent Study -

http://ce.byu.edu/is > *Courses* > *Free Courses* > *Genealogy*

Free family history tutorials online, including: Introduction to Family History Research, Writing Family History, Family Records, Vital Records, Family Records, Military Records, German, French, Scandinavian and Huguenot Research.

Genealogy.com - www.genealogy.com

> *Learning Center* > *Free Genealogy Classes*

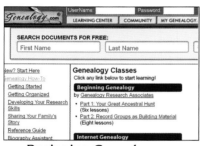

There are many different lessons under the following categories:

- Beginning Genealogy
- Internet Genealogy
- Tracing Immigrant Origins
- Researching with Genealogy.com

DearMyrtle.com -

www.dearmyrtle.com >*Lessons*

There are dozens of excellent lessons under the following categories:

- Beginning Genealogy
- Some Technology Won't Hurt
- For the Fun of It
- Critical Thinking

Ancestry.com - www.ancestry.com >

Learning Center

They offer videos by experts and a guide to all the key components for beginning your family history. They help you reach into the past and make meaningful connections with your forbears.

- What's New
- First Steps
- Next Steps
- Our Social Network

e-Newsletters / Magazines / TV Programs

The Latest How-to Info for Tracing Your Family Tree

Eastman's Online Genealogy Newsletter - www.eogn.com

A popular, daily newsletter summary of events, tips, reviews, and topics of interest from genealogist Dick Eastman, available in a *free Standard Edition* and a *Plus Edition* for $19.95/year.

Family Tree Magazine -

www.familytreemagazine.com

A leading how-to publication for those who want to discover, preserve and celebrate their roots. It covers all areas of potential interest to family history enthusiasts, reaching beyond strict genealogy research to include ethnic heritage, family reunions, memoirs, oral history, scrapbooking, historical travel and other ways that families connect with their pasts. Provides engaging, easy-to-understand instruction that empowers you to take the next steps in the quest for your past—with a beginner-friendly approach that makes family history a hobby anyone can do. The website has some free content, but the emphasis is on getting you to subscribe to the print edition of the magazine. $24.00/year

Family Chronicle Magazine -
www.familychronicle.com

 Bi-monthly magazine written for family researchers by people who share your interest in genealogy and family history. This "how-to" gene-alogy magazine has gained a reputation for solid editorial, presented in a highly attractive, all-color format. The website has some free content, but the emphasis is on getting you to subscribe to the print edition of the magazine. $25.00/year

GenealogyInTime.com -
www.genealogyintime.com

 An online genealogy magazine containing articles, how-to guides, listings of the latest online genealogy records as they become available on the internet, unique news stories, and the popular weekly column *Genealogy This Week*, a compilation of the best and most interesting new genealogy tools, resources and stories to help you get the most out of your family history research.

NGS Quarterly – *FREE*
www.ngsgenealogy.org/cs/ngsq

Since 1912, the National Genealogical Society Quarterly has published material concerning all regions of the nation and all ethnic groups including compiled genealogies, case studies, essays on new methodology and little-known

---

Here's some Things You Can Do Today to Get Started

10 Things You Can Do Today to Get Started

1. **Plant a seed in your heart** for a desire to connect to your ancestors; nourish the seed so it can grow; learn about the sacrifices they made to make your life better, prepare to receive help from your ancestors. (Pages 4-6)

2. **Take a free online "How To" lesson** (or tutorial). (Page 14)

3. **Subscribe to** a free e-newsletter or magazine; register for a free blog. (Pages 16-20)

4. **Review and purchase** a family history software program and get acquainted with the basics.

5. **Write down everything you know** about your ancestors; contact your family's "keeper of the flame" (your family's historian), and ask him/her to share their information. (Page 35)

6. **Search existing online family tree Web sites** and published family histories for information on your ancestor. (Pages 73-79)

7. **Scan your precious photos** and documents to a digital format to protect them and be able to easily share with others. (Page 201)

8. **Begin to write your family history;** gather your family stories; record the life stories of your parents/grandparents before its too late; record your own story while you can still remember; interview a relative; get grandkids involved to help establish a bond between generations. (Page 219)

9. **Collaborate with others** to add branches to your family tree using a social networking Web site; connect with your family, swap stories, and share photos, recipes and information. (Page 45)

10. **Hold a family reunion;** organize your family; reach out to your extended family members; start a family blog or online photo album; volunteer to help index public records at home.

resources, critical reviews of current books, and previously unpublished source materials. It emphasizes scholarship, readability, and practical help in genealogical problem solving.

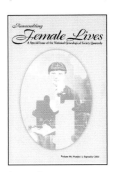

Articles show how to cope with name changes, burned courthouses, illegitimacies, and other stumbling blocks; how to interpret records that do not mean what they seem to say; how to distinguish among individuals of the same name; how to identify origins of immigrant ancestors; how to research a variety of ethnic groups; how to find a way through the maze of records at the National Archives; how to conduct research in specific states; and how to compile solid genealogies. Members of NGS receive the NGSQ four times per year. $65/year.

TheInDepthGenealogist.com – FREE
www.theindepthgenealogist.com

IDG is a digital community that provides a monthly digital magazine, a bi-monthly email newsletter, and active blog and forum providing articles and columns for genealogists and family historians of all levels to share, learn, grow and develop their skills. They provide an opportunity for all members of our community to come together, improve, and share their knowledge and experience in a friendly, approachable, and entertaining way. Filled with guest articles, regular columns and free resources it is a high-value publication for every genealogist, no matter the age, stage or focus of your research. Enjoy a new issue on 15th of each month.

Global Gazette - FREE $
http://globalgenealogy.com/ globalgazette/index.htm

An online family history magazine from Canada with helpful tips on researching

family history. Includes "how-to" articles and genealogy news as well as general genealogy information. There is some free content and a considerable amount of content that you can buy through their store at http://globalgenealogy.com.

GenealogyMagazine.com - FREE
www.genealogymagazine.com

A free online magazine with databases, photographs, articles and books for sell for tracing your ancestors. Free content just pay for the books you order.

Internet Genealogy - $
http://internet-genealogy.com

A bi-monthly magazine from the publishers of *Family Chronicle* and *History Magazine*. It deals primarily with doing genealogy research using the resources of the Internet. The rate at which new databases are coming online is staggering and many of these new records are linked to the original images, making them effectively original sources. $25/year

Family Research – FREE
www.lineages.co.uk

A free specialty online UK magazine for tracing your English, Scottish and Irish roots.

FamilyHistoryPlace.net - FREE
www.familyhistoryplace.net

Their mission is to make genealogy research fun and easy by providing a simple to use, fun, and informative website that helps you to do your research and get results quickly. Contains

articles, links to over 1000 genealogy societies and associations, book reviews, and a newsletter.

Topix.net - FREE

www.topix.net/hobbies/genealogy

News from thousands of sources, sorted geographically for US cities, as well as a wide variety of subjects.

RootsWeb Review - FREE

http://newsletters.rootsweb.ancestry.com

This free monthly e-zine provides news about RootsWeb.com, its new data-bases, mailing lists, home pages, and Web sites. It also includes stories and research tips from its readers around the globe.

WorldVitalRecords Newsletter - FREE

www.worldvitalrecords.com >Newsletter

A free weekly e-newsletter that provides how to articles and tips by industry experts, tutorials to help you make the most of technology, information about the newest collections on WorldVitalRecords and upcoming events.

GenealogyToday.com - FREE

http://news.genealogytoday.com

Articles and news releases from various resources around the Web.

Journal of Genetic Genealogy – FREE

www.jogg.info

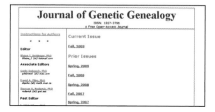

This is a technical scientific maga-zine that covers DNA testing for genealogy.

Forum - www.fgs.org >forum

The Federation of Genealogical Societies (FGS), consisting of more than 550 member societies and over 500,000 individual genealo-gists, publishes this quarterly magazine providing current information essential to the informed genealogist.

$18.00/year (non-member)

Who Do You Think You Are? TV Series - FREE

www.nbc.com/who-do-you-think-you-are
www.tlc.com/tv-shows/who-do-you-think-you-are

This TV program leads celebrities on a journey of self-discovery as they unearth their family trees – the quest to discover the genealogical roots of who they are – that reveals surprising, inspiring and even tragic stories that are often linked to crucial events in American history. Each episode exposes surprising facts and emotional encounters that will unlock your emotions – showing just how connected everyone is not only to the past, but to one another.

Book - Who Do You Think You Are?: The Essential Guide to Tracing Your Family History -

www.honoringourancestors.com

There is no such thing as an ordinary family. Each one has its own stories. No matter how plain you think your background is, chances are there is a saga just waiting to be discovered. This is the companion guide to the ground-breaking NBC TV series. You will learn how to chart your own journey into your past and discover the treasures hidden in your family tree. Features step-by-step instruc-tions from one of America's top genealogical researchers, Megan Smolenyak. $24.95

Faces of America TV Series - FREE

www.pbs.org/wnet/facesofamerica

What made America? What makes us? These two questions are at the heart of the new PBS TV series Faces of America with Henry Louis Gates, Jr. The Harvard scholar turns to the latest tools of genealogy and genetics to explore the family histories of 12 renowned Americans. Watch the fascinating episodes on their website anytime. They explore the making of America, becoming American, and American stories. A big part of the attraction, of course, is the celebrities and those irresistibly dramatic moments when we watch them learn of untold family histories.

Genealogy Roadshow – FREE

www.pbs.org/program/genealogy-roadshow

Everybody wants answers to questions about their own histories to help make sense of their lives today. This is a new genealogy television show in the U.S. – part detective story, part emotional journey – that combines history and science to uncover the fascinating stories of diverse Americans. Its aim to reunite people from all walks of life with their past, present and future. Expert genealogists uncover rich and surprising history about the people and places that make up our incredibly diverse and fascinating country.

Finding Your Roots – FREE

www.pbs.org/wnet/finding-your-roots

The basic drive to discover who we are and where we come from is at the core of the new PBS series with Henry Louis Gates that explores race, culture, and identity through the genealogies and family histories of notable celebrities.

The Generations Project TV Series - FREE

http://byutv.org/thegenerationsproject

A BYU TV reality series about discovering your roots. The show will help you solve unsolved mysteries about your family's history. Other family history series can be found at www.byub.org/new/genealogy.

Best Genealogy Blogs

Free-style, Interactive Web Sites with News, Commentary on Family History

Blogs are a very cool way to keep up with the latest stuff. A blog (short for "web log") is basically an easy way to post or view new information, photos, and web links online quickly, in an easy to read format with the most recent entry appearing first.

When a new article or tip is posted, it is sent automatically to you if you have subscribed to the blog. By subscribing to one or more genealogy blogs you can easily keep up with the latest techniques, tips and databases in family history in short order. Genealogy blogs are also a great source for locating genealogical data, networking with others, and much more. There are a lot of fun and interesting family history blogs. Check out my list below.

You can also easily create your own family blog just to connect with your extended family and others who share your interests if you wish.

The best way to read blogs is to use a *reader.*

Best Way to Read Blogs

Some people read genealogy blogs by visiting the Web page of each blog individually. But this can become a bit time-consuming and overwhelming. The best way to read blogs is to use a *reader.* This is a tool that brings all of the new posts in the blogs that interest you together into one place. Rather than visit a dozen different sites every day, you can visit just one.

A feed reader (or news aggregator) is a simple tool that maintains a list of the Web blogs and websites you're interested in, checks them at regular intervals for updates, and displays their contents in a readable format. All blog readers track what you've read previously and highlight new content for easy scanning. Here are some of the popular web-based readers or apps for your review. They are convenient because you can check your feeds from any computer or mobile device. Here are some popular readers.

Flipboard - www.flipboard.com (FREE)

A free app that helps you discover and share content in beautiful, simple, and meaningful ways. You can find everything that matters to you from world news to life's great moments. Just tap the [+] to save anything from the web – RSS feeds for all your favorite blogs, video channels, stories, photos, audio and more – into your own magazines to flip through later or share with friends. You can choose and arrange the sections you want then add your social networks like Facebook, Google+, Twitter and Instagram, if you wish. You get an informative and interesting reading experience customized just for you. Available for **iPad, iPhone, Android, Kindle Fire and NOOK.** Flipboard provides one of the best reading experiences on any platform, and is a great option.

Pulse - www.pulse.me (FREE)

Pulse is a fast and beautiful way to read your favorite blogs, magazines, social networks and newspapers. Choose from your favorite topics and interests, and customize your Pulse with unique pages and sources. Read your favorite blogs, newspapers, magazines, and more. Pulse won the prestigious Apple Design Award, and was named one of TIME's top 50 apps of 2011. Currently available for both Android and iOS (Apple) devices. To sync sources and settings, you must log into the same account on all of your devices. You may log in via Facebook or your individual Pulse account. Any changes you make to your sources, settings or Saved Stories on one device will sync to your other devices when you log in and refresh your application.

Feedly - www.feedly.com (FREE)

The better way to organize, read and share the content of your favorite sites. Organize your favorite blogs, news sites, podcasts and Youtube channels and access them all in one place. Multiple layout options, auto-mark as read, tagging, advanced sharing, keyboard shortcuts. Save articles across devices or share them on Twitter, Facebook, Google+, Evernote, Pinterest or LinkedIn. Named one of TIME Magazine Top 10 Smart-Phone Apps of 2011. Feedly is available on iPhone, iPad, Android devices and on the desktop.

MyYahoo! - http://us.my.yahoo.com (FREE)

Your own personalized version of Yahoo that combines your favorite parts of Yahoo and the Web into one place. You can choose what you want to see and hear: email, news, weather, photos, blogs, stock prices, sports scores, TV schedules, movie listings, and more. All content is updated frequently. Most of the content you add to My Yahoo are RSS feeds.

Bloglines Reader - www.bloglines.com (FREE)

A free online service that helps you subscribe to and manage lots of web information, such as news feeds, blogs and audio. Bloglines tracks the information you're interested in, retrieves new stuff as it happens, and organizes everything for you on your own personal web news page.

Almost every blog or website you visit will have what's called an RSS feed.

How To Subscribe To Blogs Using RSS Feed

RSS, an acronym for "Really Simple Syndication", is a standard distribution format that websites, such as news, sports, and blog sites, use to send updated headlines automatically to you. This is just a way for you to get the content delivered to you, instead of you going to the site to get to the content. Using the technology of RSS, you can save a tremendous amount of time, because once you subscribe to a site's RSS feed, you can receive feeds delivered in a feed reader, and read all your favorite sites in one convenient place, instead of going all over the Web. RSS is private; the sites you subscribe to know nothing about you.

After you have set up an account for your chosen reader, visit your favorite blogs and websites and look to see if they offer their content as a news feed. Look for the RSS icon. All you do to begin the subscribing process is click on the RSS icon or link. Select and copy the URL address from the address bar on the top, then go to your Reader and paste it into the "Add Subscription" field, and click the *Add* button.

When a new subscription is added, your news reader will go to the originating site and collect the most recent articles posted there. Your Reader checks each subscribed site regularly to see if new content has been added. If it has, that new content will be delivered to your reader. You can organize your subscriptions into categories by clicking on the *Settings* button.

Genealogy Blogs By Type – FREE

http://geneabloggers.com/genealogy-blogs-type

There are thousands of interesting and very valuable family history blogs. How do you find the blogs that most interest you? Thomas

MacEntee has a new feature at GeneaBloggers that allows you to view groups of genealogy blogs and blog posts organized by type to find those of most value to you. You need to check out GeneaBloggers and Geneabloggers Radio at www.blogtalkradio.com/geneabloggers.

Genealogy Blog Finder – FREE

http://blogfinder.genealogue.com

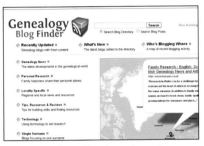

Tracks about 1800 genealogy blogs by category, such as: Genealogy News, Personal Research, Technology, Cemeteries, Podcasts, etc.

Ancestry Insider – FREE

http://ancestryinsider.blogspot.com

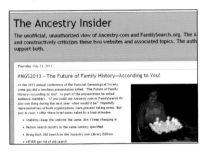

The unofficial blog of two big genealogy websites: Ancestry.com and FamilySearch.org.

Dear MYRTLE.com – FREE

http://blog.dearmyrtle.com

Pat Richley-Erickson's website is a fun, helpful family history site with a regular blog column of free news and tips. Currently, her blog is rated one of the top five in the industry. And Myrt is the host of the popular webinar series Mondays with Myrt viewed on her YouTube channel at www.youtube.com/user/DearMYRTLE.

Genea Musings – FREE

http://randysmusings.blogspot.com

Genealogy research tips, genealogy news items, genealogy humor, and some family history stories by Randy Seaver.

Genealogy Insider – FREE

http://blog.familytreemagazine.com/insider

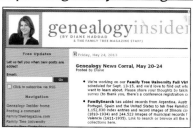

Diane Haddad's excellent genealogy blog at FamilyTree Magazine.

GeneaBloggers.com – FREE

www.geneabloggers.com

The genealogy community's resource for blogging by Thomas MacEntee. He keeps things humming with tech tips and advice for bloggers, industry news, geneablogger profiles, and blogging event calendars.

Kimberly's Genealogy Blog – FREE

http://genealogy.about.com

A popular blog by Kimerly Powell, the host of About.com's Guide to Genealogy, a professional genealogist, Web developer, and author of *Everything Family Tree*.

Check out FamilyTree Magazine's top 40 award-winning blogs listed under different categories.

Top 40 Genealogy Blogs FREE

www.familytreemagazine.com/article/Top-40-Genealogy-Blogs-2013

FamilyTree Magazine looked for those sites that deliver a dividend timely tech news, essential advice or simply the feeling of sharing a quest to part the curtains of the past. They categorized the top blog sites as follows:

• **Good Advice:** Heed the wise words of these bloggers to learn about resources, and discover tried-and-true techniques.

• **Tech Support:** Savvy bloggers to guide you to the best family tree tools for your search.

• **Gravestone matters:** Help you appreciate cemeteries for the genealogical havens they are: full of names and dates, historic statuary, and spots to contemplate the lives of ancestors committed to the earth long ago.

• **Heritage help:** These genealogists excel at sharing their ethnic roots research in informative, inspiring ways.

• **Shop talk:** Keeping up with genealogy news and resources.

• **Story time:** The family tales of these bloggers engage us with words and images, and offer useful bits of research wisdom.

Also see the Top Genealogy Blogs on page 235.

Genealogy's Star – FREE

http://genealogysstar.blogspot.com

A go-to site by James Tanner for the latest news along with tips on getting the most out of genealogy tech (and avoiding technological overload).

Moultrie Creek – http://moultriecreek.us

Denise Barrett Olson's long-running blog has broadened beyond its technology focus to also include tips on topics as diverse as cemetery artwork and archiving family keepsakes. But you'll also find plenty of plugged-in info on digital story-telling, creating great iPhone photos, family-cookbook apps, research management tools and other tech-y topics.

Armchair Genealogist – FREE

www.thearmchairgenealogist.com

A main focus of Lynn Palermo's blog is 'Writing your family history', but she has other interests, such as: Helpful Research Tips, Irish Genealogy for Beginners, Genealogy Conferences, Old Fashioned Recipe Collection, The Family History Blog to Book Project, Everyone Has A Story, Family History Writing Contests, Mind Mapping for Genealogists and Self-Publishing Tools for the Family History Writer.

4YourFamilyStory.com – www.4your-familystory.com > blog FREE

Caroline Pointer is a genealogist, family historian, writer, and blogger. She's also a coach to help you learn how to use technology to find your ancestors and get your family trees in shape, how to use technology to find your family story, how to use more than just Ancestry.com to find your ancestors, and how to use online and offline resources effectively. You can access her blog directly at www.blogginggenealogy.com.

She's the host of the *What's Up Genealogy?* show (a Google+ Hangout webinar). It airs on Friday nights 8PM CT, and it is focused on industry news that will affect your research, research tips, and interviews with genealogy experts.

Her informative 'Hangout' webinar shows are archived on her YouTube channel at www.youtube.com/user/4YourFamilyStory. You can also catch her Pinterest Family Stories boards at http://pinterest.com/familystories which feature tons of pins for research, photo and video tips, genealogy and social media apps, family reunion ideas, blogging, technology, recipes, and much more. http://www.4yourfam-ilystory.com. Also check out her Facebook page at www.facebook.com/4YourFamilyStory.

Ancestry.com Blog – FREE

http://blogs.ancestry.com/ancestry

Delivers the latest new offerings from Ancestry.com, plus research tips and articles.

Renee's Genealogy Blog – FREE
http://rzamor1.blogspot.com

Writing from the LDS family history perspective, Renee Zamora keeps readers up to date about online genealogy. Of course, she's a go-to blogger about the FamilySearch website, but you can also keep up with MyHeritage.com, Fold3.com, Ancestry.com and other sites here.

Graveyard Rabbits – FREE
www.thegraveyardrabbit.com

This blog is the headquarters for a network of bloggers around the world dedicated to transcribing tombstones and documenting local cemeteries in words and pictures.

Digital Cemetery Walk – FREE
http://digitalcemeterywalk.blogspot.com

Gale Wall shares cemetery stories as well as photos of her regular cemetery walks, backing up her belief that "Every stone has a story. And they are waiting to be told." There's something here for everyone who's fascinated by final resting places.

NARAtions – FREE
http://blogs.archives.gov/online-public-access

This is the U.S. National Archives and Records Administration (NARA) blog dedicated to providing better online access to NARA's treasures and the vast array of federal records (over 9 billion pages).

GHL Blog – www.ghlblog.org FREE

The Government and Heritage Library Blog (of the State Library of North Carolina) focuses on the collections, resources, and services of the library. The staff post news and information about the library's print and digital collections and resources, as well as the specialty research areas of state and federal government information, demographic and statistical information, Southern U.S. history, and genealogical research.

Jill Ball's Blog Videos – https://family-search.org/blog/en/rootstech-2013-video-interviews-jill-ball FREE

http://www.youtube.com/feed/UC5DuAhN0mixxlQKhlp7mRXAwww.youtube.com/user/bibliaugrapher/videos

Jill Ball is blogger for the popular Australian genealogy blog Geniaus - http://geniaus.blogspot.com. As an official RootsTech blogger, she had the chance to interview a dozen individuals at RootsTech in Salt Lake City. Her delightful videos are available on YouTube.

RootDig.com - http://rootdig.blogspot.com FREE

Michael John Neill's genealogy blog website with news and information. He also writes http://genealogytipoftheday.blogspot.com.

FREE

Olive Tree – http://olivetreegenealogy.blogspot.com

Updates and news about Olive Tree Genealogy and other websites free genealogy records. Helping you find your family tree and ancestry.

How Can I Find a Blog About My Ancestral Homeland?

http://familytreemagazine.com/article/learning-from-international-genealogy-blogs $

Here's some good ideas for learning research tips from inter-national blogs. FamilyTree Magazine also has a little e-book PDF that you can download called *Top 40 Genealogy Blogs Around The World* for $4.00. It also has tips to help you navigate the wide range of sources, so you can get cracking at your global genealogy hunt. www.shopfamilytree.com/top-40-genealogy-blogs-around-the-world-u4023

What are Podcasts? Vodcasts? Webinars? Hangouts?

Genealogy News, Views and Interviews at Your Leisure

http://genealogy.about.com/od/blogs/tp/podcasts.htm

Genealogy podcasts, vodcasts, webinars and Google+'s 'hangouts on air' are fantastic ways to learn research techniques and keep up with what's new in the world of family history. They are like TV or radio broadcasts but over the Internet. And they are becoming increasingly popular among family historians. You can learn from some of the most sought after genealogy experts from the comfort of your own home.

They cover a wide variety of family history topics that can be played back at your convenience. They offer an option for listening to or viewing lectures, interviews, discussions and tutorials when and where you want...

fascinating family history on demand. They can be interesting and entertaining, but also very useful for picking up some genealogy research tips. Most are free.

You can subscribe to them, much like you subscribe to blogs, so you're informed as new episodes become available. You can then listen to or view them on your computer, or digital mobile device from the comfort of your own home. You can ask questions online just as if you were attending a presentation in-person. You don't have to subscribe to them if you don't want, just visit the Web sites of your favorite podcasts/webinars/handouts whenever you wish to see what's new.

How To Attend A Genealogy Webinar -
www.archives.com/experts/macentee-thomas/how-to-attend-a-genealogy-webinar.html

An excellent article by Thomas MacEntee posted on Archives.com about how a webinar works, how to select a genealogy webinar, and how to get the most out of a genealogy webinar.

DearMyrtle Hangouts

http://blog.dearmyrtle.com *FREE*

DearMYRTLE was one of the first genealogy writers online, one of the first genealogy bloggers, one of the first genealogy podcasters, and one of the first web genealogy videocasters. She used a subscription service for many years and made many helpful and interesting webinars. Now Myrt is one of the first to use Google+ Hangouts for her weekly videocasts. They are free, watched by thousands of persons live, and archived on her YouTube channel for viewing at your convenience. They are informal conversations, not structured lectures or presentations. They discuss how to do family history online, genealogy software, issues of the day, etc.

Podcasts

A podcast is a multimedia digital file (audio radio, video, PDF, or ePub files) made available on the Internet for downloading to a computer or mobile device (laptop, iPad, iPod, smartphone, etc.). A vodcast (or video podcast) includes video clips. Web TV series are often distributed as video podcasts, and have become extremely popular online. Some of the most popular podcasts are: DearMyrtle, Genealogy Guys, Genealogy Gems, Dick Eastman, FamilyTree Magazine, and Geneabloggers, in no particular order. More information below. The Family History Show, a monthly video podcast from the UK, is a good example of a vodcast. Here are some of the more popular podcasts.

Genealogy Guys – **FREE** www.genealogyguys.com

George Morgan and Drew Smith have been at this quite a while and have over 260 genealogy podcasts awaiting your listening pleasure. They are entertaining, informative, and include news from the world of family history research. They discuss new databases, the latest genealogy news, genealogy resources, and technologies of interest to genealogists, highlight interesting Web sites, answer listener email, and throw in plenty of other interesting nuggets to help you with your research. Topics have included interviews with top genealogical experts, software programs, book reviews, and more.

FamilyTree Magazine Podcasts – **FREE** www.familytreemagazine.com/info/podcasts

In this monthly online radio show, host Lisa Louise Cooke takes you behind the scenes to learn more about the topics covered in the current issue of the magazine. Each episode features interviews with genealogy experts and Family Tree Magazine editors on using genealogy Web sites, records and resources. Plus, editor Allison Dolan gives you sneak previews on upcoming issues, and

managing editor Diane Haddad delivers the scoop on the latest genealogy news. They have a huge number of online archived podcasts, webinars and seminars. Some of these are free and others have a fee.

Genealogy Gems – **FREE** http://lisalouisecooke.com/podcasts

Host Lisa Cooke shares research strategies and inspiration for anyone researching their family history. New podcasts are generally published on a weekly basis and are approximately 25 minutes long. There are over 170 archived podcasts available to keep you busy. Topics include: genealogy 'how-to', resources, Google searches, and top genealogy experts.

Dick Eastman's Podcasts – **FREE** http://blog.eogn.com > Podcast

Genealogy tech guru Dick Eastman posts a number of interesting podcasts to his online blog at Eastman's Online Genealogy Newsletter. From any page on his site, scroll down in the right-hand column and click on the "podcasts" category. The majority are interviews with world-renowned genealogy experts conducted at various genealogy conferences and events and are definitely interesting to listen to. This newsletter is a terrific resource, and includes many resources and the latest news.

Geneabloggers Radio – **FREE** www.blogtalkradio.com/geneabloggers

This live 1.5-hour Internet genealogy radio show, hosted weekly by Thomas MacEntee, brings in a number of wonderful genealogy guests from around the world. The discussion is lively, interesting and informative. Archived shows are well worth listening to.

You also need to check out her archived Hangouts on her YouTube channel at www.youtube.com/user/DearMYRTLE.

How do Hangouts Work?

http://blog.dearmyrtle.com/2013/02/how-do-google-hangouts-on-air-work.html

Here is the location of DearMyrtle's genealogy community https://plus.google.com/u/0/communities/104382659430904043232 where live Hangouts are viewed.

What's Up Genealogy?

http://www.4yourfamilystory.com

www.4yourfamilystory.com/whats-up-genealogy-show

Caroline Pointer is the host of the informative, free *What's Up Genealogy?* webinar show. It airs on Friday nights 8PM CT, and it is focused on

Here's the best way to find a comprehensive schedule for genealogy webinars.

GeneaWebinars.com – FREE
www.GeneaWebinars.com

The GeneaWebinars blog is the best place to find upcoming genealogy webinars. GeneaWebinars is a calendar and blog devoted exclusively to coordinating online genealogy seminars. Their calendar uses Google Calendar, allowing you to add the event to your own Google Calendar. This site also maintains a list of sites that host webinars, as well as links to the sites with webinar archives. DearMYRTLE maintains this awesome resource.

Webinars

A webinar (i.e. Web seminar or online workshop) refers to a service that allows conferencing – voice and video chat – that can be shared with people everywhere. Typical features may include: Slide show presentations, live or streaming video, VoIP (real time audio communication through the computer via use of headphones and speakers), text chat for live question and answer sessions, polls and surveys, and screen sharing. As an attendee, you merely need to register with the host, then click on the link in your confirmation email at the time of the event to attend.

Some of the Most Popular Webinars

Legacy Family Tree - FREE
www.familytreewebinars.com

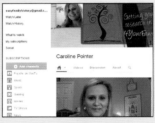

DearMyrtle - http://blog.dearmyrtle.com

RootsTech - www.rootstech.org

What's Up Genealogy? - www.youtube.com/user/4YourFamilyStory

Relative Roots - www.relativeroots.net/webinars

Ancestry.com - www.ancestry.com/cs/us/videos

Family Tree Magazine - www.familytreemagazine.com/interactive/webinars

So. California Genealogical Society - www.scgsgenealogy.com > Programs > Webinars

RootsMagic - www.rootsmagic.com/webinars

industry news that will affect your research, research tips, and interviews with genealogy experts. The shows are archived on her YouTube channel at www.youtube.com/user/4YourFamilyStory. Also check out her Facebook page at www.facebook.com/4YourFamilyStory. Need help with your family history research? Need help learning how to use technology? Receive exclusive tips on technology and research to help you get your research in shape. Sign up for these great hangout webinars.

Legacy Family Tree Webinars –
www.familytreewebinars.com   *FREE* $

All live webinars are free for everyone, and for 7 days after the live event. You can watch via your computer or mobile device. There are usually 3-5 new webinars each month. You can view the schedule on the website. To view a webinar after 7 days, you need a membership

to get on-demand access to their entire video archives. Membership is $9.95 monthly, $49.95 yearly - includes 1 year unlimited access to their recorded webinars, access to the instructors' handouts, and 1 year of 5% off anything in their store. You can also purchase any of their library of webinar CDs or digital downloads for $9.95.

RootsTech Videos – www.rootstech.org *FREE*

RootsTech is an opportunity unlike any other to discover the latest family history tools and techniques, connect with experts to help you in your research, and be inspired in the pursuit of your ancestors. It is an annual conference in Salt Lake City with a unique emphasis on helping you learn and use the latest technology to get started or accelerate your efforts to find, organize, preserve and share your family's

Hangouts

Regular *Hangouts* are free video chats that you can have with friends, relatives and colleagues over the Internet up to 10 people. They are great for chatting with family members all over the world, hosting team meetings, or just catching up with a bunch of friends. One touch to call the whole family.

But with *Hangouts On Air,* live discussions are shared with everyone – broadcast to

the world. The live broadcast is posted on the hosts Google+ home page as well as their YouTube channel. The archived broadcast can be viewed by anyone, anytime. Up to 10 people can actually participate in the live discussion, but thousands can view the live broadcast, and thousands more the archived broadcast at their convenience.

Unlike a webinar, the link for a 'G+ Hangouts on Air' isn't created until just before the event is to go live. Participants must have a Google+ account, which is as simple as activating it with a Gmail account, and register with the host who will notify you of the event. Hangouts work the same everywhere – computers, Android, and Apple devices – so nobody gets left out.

connections and history. Attendees will learn key skills from hands-on workshops and interactive presentations at the beginner, intermediate, and advanced level. You can view the informative, valuable session videos online for free.

Relative Roots –

www.relativeroots.net/webinars

Relative Roots was among the first to take genealogy education into the 21st century by offering quality, affordable webinars. The core of their webinar schedule is DNA/Genetic Genealogy, but they periodically offer webinars on additional genealogy topics.

Ancestry.com – FREE

www.ancestry.com/cs/us/videos

Ancestry is not currently doing live webinars, but you can access their webinar archives for free. It's worth your time.

Family Tree Magazine – FREE

www.familytreemagazine.com/interactive/webinars

Get live genealogy hints and help from genealogy experts in our webinars! These interactive events will teach you how to improve your research skills and make new family history discoveries. Each webinar lasts about an hour and includes a Q&A session where you can get answers to your specific genealogy questions on the workshop topic.

So. California Genealogical Society – FREE

www.scgsgenealogy.com > Programs > Webinars

Their webinar broadcasts are free and open to the public as part of SCGS's mission to provide an outreach of educational services. These one-hour webinars are live broadcast presentations given by professional genealogical speakers and expert lecturers. Now offered twice monthly (the first Saturday and third Wednesday), don't miss out on this valuable educational resource.

Google Hangouts App

https://itunes.apple.com/us/app/hangouts/id643496868?mt=8
https://play.google.com/store/search?q=hangouts

The new Google Hangouts app is a free over-the-top mobile messaging service. It's a universal app for **iOS (Apple), Android and for Chrome** and allows you to share text, photos and live video with each other. You can chat, like you would in a normal messaging app; include photos, which are automatically stored in albums; and you can also jump in on a multi-person video hangout. It eliminates the need to hop between different apps — a messaging app for texting, a photo album for checking out photos that have been sent and saved, and a video chatting app for seeing the person you're talking to. You also have the option to delete conversations, or save them — because some conversations are important or memorable, and you don't want them to disappear forever.

Marketplace: Charts, Forms, Books, Supplies

Online Store
FamilyRoots Publishing - FREE $

www.FamilyRootsPublishing.com

Over 3500 great genealogy guidebooks can be found on the website, including regional guide-books for most countries, American states, and Canadian provinces. Guides on writing, and recording genealogy, photography, DNA research, genealogy dictionaries, computer use, immigration, migration, etc. are found here. The items come from many different publishers around the world, with a good number being published by their own company. They also publish a free, twice-weekly, email genealogy newsletter. Owned by Leland and Patty Meitzler, best-known for having started Heritage Quest in 1985, and as a popular speaker at conferences.

Expos / Networking FREE $
FamilyHistoryExpos – www.fhexpos.com

This website and service helps you understand the new tools, techniques and technology to trace your roots in today's ever-changing techno-logical environment. They manage the premier *Family History Expos* held each year around the country which teach beginners true methods of research and help experienced researchers improve their results by introducing them to new tools. Podcasts and TV/Videos feature interviews with family history professionals, software devel-opers, and product/service providers, including expert advice from some of the country's most successful genealogists. Founded by Holly Hansen, author, lecturer, former editor of *Everton's Genealogical Helper* magazine and the *Handybook for Genealogists*.

Books / eBooks
EasyFamilyHistory.com – FREE $

www.easyfamilyhistory.com/store

Your convenient online store for the popular family history books and e-books by Paul Larsen to guide beginners and empower experts using today's technology. The website also provides a *free* Learning Center with how-to articles, guides, and tips; *free* Teaching Aids, and an LDS Center.

Charts
Free Genealogy Fan Chart – FREE

https://createfan.com

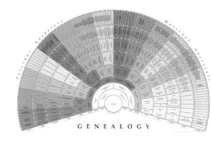

See your family tree like never before. This site allows you to create a 9-generation colorful fan chart for *free* using your own family tree information as found in FamilySearch FamilyTree. You log into FamilySearch from this site, and it extracts your family tree automatically and creates a PDF fan chart of your tree. [Note: Be patient while it gathers all your information. It may take awhile.]

You can easily print an 8 ½ x 11" chart on your home printer, but if you want to print a beautiful wall chart, simply email the PDF file to www.gen-erationmaps.com/familychartist or www.genealo-gywallcharts.com. You may want to merge possible duplicates of your ancestors and check for accuracy in FamilySearch *before* you print it. It's nice to have a working chart to review your information, or a large beautiful wall chart for your family to enjoy.

Charts
GenealogyWallCharts.com – FREE $
www.genealogywallcharts.com

They create/print amazing wall charts from your genealogy. They accept all genealogy file formats and convert them to selected charts, excluding PDF charts.

Charts
Family ChartMasters – FREE $
https://familychartmasters.com

Inexpensive charts to get your information onto paper where you can see everything. They offer personalized working charts, beautiful decorative charts, and custom heirloom charts. Just send your computer file and digital photos, and it arrives on your doorstep for a very reasonable price.

A web application that makes creating and designing beautiful genealogy charts easier and faster than ever before. With beautiful graphics and embellishments it is easy to create something personalized for your family. You choose the layout, information to be included, size, paper, color, pictures, borders, backgrounds and artistic design. You can create an 8.5 x 11 chart *free* and save it to your computer to print whenever you choose. If you decide you want to print a larger size for your home, just order from the same menu and your chart will be printed and shipped to you promptly for a small fee.

Charts and Forms
About.com – FREE
http://genealogy.about.com/cs/freecharts

Free downloadable family tree charts, pedigree charts, research logs and other free forms to help you in your genealogy research and keep your family tree organized.

Online Store
RootsBooks – www.rootsbooks.com $

A one-stop online genealogy bookstore for books, computers, software, and more.

Online Store
Global Genealogy – www.globalgenealogy.com $

Shop online for family history supplies, maps, forms, software, books, etc.

Online Store
Alibris.com – www.alibris.com > *genealogy* $

They connect people who love books, music, and movies to more than 100 million items from thousands of sellers worldwide since 1998 – supporting thousands of independent sellers.

Online Store
HeritageBooks – www.heritagebooks.com $

Over 4,900 titles of genealogy books, maps, and CDs.

Online Store
PictonPress – www.pictonpress.com $

A publisher for over 40 years, specializing in genealogical and historical research material of the 17th, 18th, and 19th centuries.

Online Store
TheFamilyHistoryStore – $
www.thefamilyhistorystore.com

International online retailer of a growing line of genealogy and history related products & gifts since 2003.

CHAPTER 1

3-Easy Steps
Follow These 3-Easy Steps to Build Your Family Tree and Connect to Your Ancestors

STEP 1 –
Plant Your Family Tree

Identify Your Ancestors Using Your Family and Networking with Others

1 Use Your Family

Suggested Activities

■ Start writing down what you know about your family.

■ Fill-in a *pedigree chart* and *family group sheet*.

■ Call relatives to find out if someone has already compiled a family history or other records that might contain the information you're looking for. Ask them to e-mail a GEDCOM file of their information. This is a great head start.

■ Look around your house for documents that might provide new information or verify the information you already have. Keep copies of everything you find in your search.

The success of tracing your family roots and stories increases when families work together. Family members will often have information to share, or they may be willing to help you look for information.

Your relatives may remember important events and dates that have not been recorded. They may have family heirlooms, records, mementos, photographs, and other valuable items. They may have interesting family stories to tell, and they can sometimes direct you to others who knew your ancestors or to other relatives you may not know.

Family History Insights - 1

Collect Everything About Your Life

Boyd K. Packer
© by Intellectual Reserve, Inc.

"Get a cardboard box. Any kind of box will do. Put it someplace where it is in the way, . . . anywhere where it cannot go unnoticed. Then, over a period of a few weeks, collect and put into the box every record of your life..... Collect diplomas, all of the photographs, honors, or awards, a diary if you have kept one, everything that you can find pertaining to your life; anything that is written, or registered, or recorded that testifies that you are alive and what you have done." Boyd K. Packer

A Light From Our Ancestors

Gaius Sallustius Crispus

"Distinguished ancestors shed a powerful light on their descendants, and forbid the concealment either of their merits or of their demerits." Gaius Sallustius Crispus (86-34 BC), Roman historian

An Inheritance From Our Ancestors

Samuel Adams

"The liberties of our country, the freedom of our civil constitution, are worth defending at all hazards... We have received them as a fair inheritance from our worthy ancestors... [they] transmitted them to us with care and diligence." Samuel Adams (1722-1803), Founding Father

Benefits From Ancestors

"What task could be more agreeable than to tell of the benefits conferred on us by our ancestors, so that you may get to know the achievements of those from whom you have received both the basis of your beliefs and the inspiration to conduct your life properly?"
– William Malmesbury, 1125 A.D.

Traits from Ancestors

Ralph Waldo Emerson

"A man finds room in the few square inches of the face for the traits of all his ancestors; for the expression of all his history, and his wants." Ralph Waldo Emerson (1803-1882), Poet and author

A Quotation from Ancestors

"Every book is a quotation; and every house is a quotation out of all forests, and mines, and stone quarries; and every man is a quotation from all his ancestors." Ralph Waldo Emerson

Made from Our Ancestors

"...a man represents each of several of his ancestors, as if there were seven or eight [ancestors] rolled up in each man's skin ... and they constitute the variety of notes for that new piece of music which his life is." Ralph Waldo Emerson

Feel A Special Connection

Gordon B. Hinckley
© by Intellectual Reserve, Inc.

"As you look into the [computer] you may be surprised to find names of your parents, of your grandparents, of your great-grandparents, and your great-great-grandparents, who have bequeathed to you all you are of body and mind. You will feel a special connection to those who have gone before you and an increased responsibility to those who will follow." Gordon Hinckley, National Press Club Speech, March 8, 2000

Identify Your Ancestors Using Your Family

The information you gather about your ancestors gives you a greater appreciation of your heritage, the sacrifices your ancestors made for you, and a better understanding of what their life was like. Your knowledge of your forebears will increase, your family will grow closer, families will be strengthened, and the opportunity to learn more about your kindred dead will bless lives.

As you gather information about your ancestors, you are welding family links, and drawing yourself and your family closer to God. Your ancestors want to be found as much as you want to find them.

> Follow the 3-Easy-Steps to begin building your family tree and connect to your ancestors.

QUICK TIPS ON GETTING STARTED

1. Begin with a pedigree chart. It will be a road map for your Family history search. Create your own four generation pedigree chart. From memory, begin to fill in information on the lines indicating your father, your mother, your grandparents, and so on.

2. Start with yourself and what you already know about your parents and grandparents.

3. Work back one generation at a time, from the known to the unknown.

4. Be as complete as possible when you record information.

5. Don't be overwhelmed by the process.

6. Choose one of the commercially available family history software programs.

Write Everything You Know About Your Ancestors

Identifying your ancestors is fun and so much easier today. You can begin right now by picking up a pencil and writing down information on a piece of paper.

Begin with what you already know by writing information on yourself and work back one generation at a time. The most important family history information you already posses – your memories and the memories of your loved ones. Gather information about yourself, your siblings, your parents, your grandparents, and your great grandparents. Make a list of each member in your family that can help you identify your ancestors. Typically, information about your close relatives is readily available simply by talking to them, and searching through information in your home.

Write down specific information, such as: names, dates and places of important events such as birth, marriage, and death, ancestral village, occupation, etc. Try to gather 3-4 generations (or more) of information on your ancestors. Don't be concerned if you're missing information because you can go back and fill it in later.

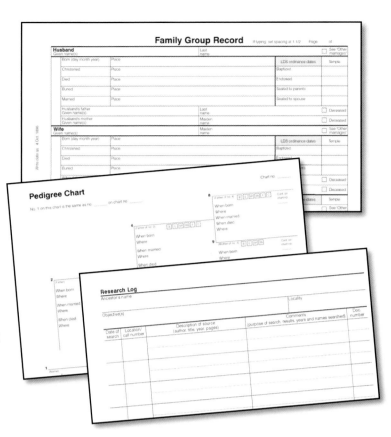

A *research log* is a comprehensive list of what you have already searched and what you plan to search next for an ancestor.

Why Keep a Research Log?

A research log is like a treasure map outlining your progress and documenting your search for your own family roots and stories. It can tell you what you have searched, what you found or didn't find, and save you time because you don't need to search the same source again. You can also tell your family or others what you have already searched, and help you decide on the next steps. Your family or others may want to look at the same sources as you did, so it's a quick way to provide confidence to others, and your records will be more complete. You can easily photocopy or print out a copy of your log. Don't go hunting for family history treasures without your map.

Forms and Computers Make It Easier

You can start just by writing information on paper. However, it's best to obtain a family history software program to help you keep things organized and print forms you can use to record your family information. These programs make the task of recording and organizing your information much easier.

There are many useful forms, but the first forms of most value to you are a *Pedigree Chart, Family Group Record,* and *Research Log.*

Pedigree Chart

(Family Tree Chart) Lets you list your pedigree – your parents, grandparents, great grandparents, and so on.

Family Group Record

A tool to help you organize your research by families. Because information about an individual ancestor is most often found with information about your ancestor's siblings or parents, this form is a helpful organizational

Free Charts and Forms

You can download free blank family tree charts, pedigree charts, fan charts, research logs, timelines, internet research logs, census worksheets, to do lists, immigration forms, checklists, etc. from various web sites. These different forms help you keep your information organized and help you stay on track. You can also print forms using your family history software program. *For resources, see below plus "Marketplace" on page 31.*

FamilySearch Research Assistance -
https://familysearch.org/ask/researchAssistance.

 Use the Search box using the keyword "forms" to locate numerous charts and forms. **FREE**

Ancestry.com - **FREE**
www.ancestry.com > *Get Help*

 Ancestry is a subscription website, however excellent blank family history forms and charts can be downloaded for free without subscribing. Click on 'Get Help' in the upper right corner, then use the search box to search for forms and charts.

Cyndi's List - www.cyndislist.com/free-stuff/printable-charts-and-forms **FREE**

 Cyndi's List has links to over 150 family history forms and charts that are available on-line.

Family Tree Magazine - **FREE**
www.familytreemagazine.com/FREEFORMS

 Family Tree Magazine has created forms that can help you access and organize your family history information. They're available in two formats: text and PDF. The text versions give you the basic form structure in files you can open in your word-processing software. You can print, edit or even type your information right in the file. The PDF versions are read-only files with snazzier designs—they're suitable for displaying or sharing your research with others.

tool. It includes room to write information found about a husband, his wife and their children.

Research Log

Helps keep track of the information you find. Include the name of the ancestor you are researching, the information you find, and the sources. This will help you remember what records you have searched and what information you found.

Look for More Information in Your Home

Look for sources in your home that might contain the missing or incomplete family

Suggested Activities

- Look at your pedigree chart and make a list of the records you need to verify the information you have gathered. You probably have some blank spots on your chart; think about what kinds of records you need to help you fill in those blanks.

- Look around your house for photographs, documents, old letters, journals, newspaper clippings, family Bibles—anything that might provide new information for your pedigree chart or verify the information you already have. Document your own life first by gathering records and information about your birth, marriage, graduation, military service, and so on. It is the same process you will eventually use to document the lives of your ancestors.

- Make copies of your original documents and organize your materials in labeled file folders. Enter any new information on your pedigree chart.

Family Checklist

http://learn.mocavo.com/family-history-toolkit/internal-sources-checklist

Your home, and the homes of other family members, will be rich in resources to help you discover the who, what, where, when, why, and how of your family history. This checklist provides many of the relevant items and records to look for. Do not get discouraged if you do not find all of these items, not every family has all of them. Just try your best to locate a few that will be most relevant for your personal research project. Use these items to help add to or validate the information that you have in your pedigree chart and family group sheet.

information you're seeking. Useful sources include: birth, marriage, and death certificates, family bibles, journals, letters, photo albums, funeral programs, obituaries, wedding announcements, family registers,

Remember that records are created because of important life events.

Research Tip

Look for two kinds of records:

■ Original (primary) records created by eyewitnesses at the time an event occurs.

■ Compiled (secondary) records created by genealogists and historians, sometimes many years after an event has occurred.

First, check compiled records because someone may have already done much of the research you are trying to do. However, when using compiled records, try to verify the information you find there by then obtaining the original records and documenting the information.

church records, military records, legal papers, newspaper clippings, etc.

Add this information to your pedigree charts and family group records. It's important to record the sources of the information. This helps you and others know where the information came from. To do this, it's easier to use the *Notes / Sources* (or citations) function on your family history software program.

Choose a Family or Ancestor You Want to Learn More About

After gathering names, dates and perhaps some stories about your family, the next step is to choose a specific ancestor, couple, or family line on which to focus your search. Look for missing or incomplete information on your pedigree chart and family records. You could choose to learn more about your grandparents, or an ancestor you were named

after. Start with the generations closest to you, and work your way back. The key here isn't who you may choose to study; just that it is a small enough project to be manageable. This is especially important if you're just starting out building your family tree. People who try to do too much all at once tend to get bogged down in details. Identify questions you want to answer about your ancestor, such as: "When and where did he die?" Select one question at a time as the objective.

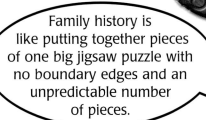

> Family history is like putting together pieces of one big jigsaw puzzle with no boundary edges and an unpredictable number of pieces.

The Family History Jigsaw Puzzle

People like solving puzzles. But with the family history puzzle, you have to show that new pieces actually belong to your puzzle. It's fun! The first pieces you start with are *yourself* and *your spouse.* Then, hopefully, you will have both sets of your parents (4 pieces) and grandparents (8 pieces) that have at least some records of their birth and marriage dates and places. Then find the next 16 pieces − your great grandparents − to fit next to them. If you don't put the pieces together in just the right way, then you'll never get to see the final picture. To make sure your puzzle pieces end up in the proper positions you should use pedigree charts and family group sheets to record your research data and keep track of your progress.

> Call relatives to find out if anyone has already compiled a partial or complete family history that might contain the record(s) you are looking for.

1 Use Your **Family**

You can also check with local libraries, historical societies and genealogical societies to see if family histories are on file there.

Ask Relatives for Information

Make a list of relatives and the information they may have. Contact them − visit, call, write, or e-mail them. Be sure to ask specifically for the information you would like. Add the information to your pedigree charts and family group records. Record your relatives names, addresses, phone numbers, email addresses, relationship, and the date of your interview(s) in the *Notes* or *Sources* function of your family history software program.

Is Your Family Tree Naked?

Noted genealogist Helen Leary, CG, CGL, says, publishing or sharing your genealogy without citing sources is like sending it into the world naked. You should tell others where you obtained your information. The hundreds of hours you spent putting your family history together won't be respected unless you document your sources. Sources establish credibility. Citing and documenting sources is no longer important, it is *essential*.

Documenting Your Information

Citations and Sources

Information technology has been a great boon to tracing your own family roots and stories today. When tracing your family it is very important that you keep track of every piece of information. Taking time to document where you got your information will save you time later in your research and help prevent duplicating the research that you or others have already done.

This is important not only as a way to verify your data, but also as a way for you and others to go back to that source when future research conflicts with your original assumption. It helps you to easily go back to your previous source to see if you may have missed information or you want more details. It's also a way to let others know on which records you based your facts, i.e. did the birth date you have for your great-grandmother come from a published family history, a tombstone, someone's

Cite Your Sources

The six elements of a good source citation include:

■ Author (who provided the information)

■ Title

■ Publisher (including location)

■ Date of the information (usually the year)

■ Location of the source you used (page number, library or archive) and the call number

■ Annotations: These are optional comments by you about the source. [Place your comments in square brackets.]

Consistent formatting is useful, helpful, and even required in some cases, but for now, don't get hung up on the commas and colons. Just begin citing your sources, and cite them well enough that others can understand what you searched. *(See web sites below on where to find standardized formatting styles.)*

Here's an important point you should know about citing sources.

Citing Online Sources

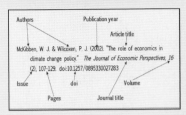

Authors · Publication year · Article title

McKibben, W. J. & Wilcoxen, P. J. (2002). "The role of economics in climate change policy." *The Journal of Economic Perspectives, 16* (2), 107-129. doi:10.1257/0895330027283

Issue · doi · Volume · Pages · Journal title

When citing websites, emails, scanned image files, CD files, or other electronic media sources, the basics still apply but you must include instructions to help others find the work. Consider an annotation from you to help understand the source.

Here a sample annotation: This website <www.123456789.com> contains numerous hyperlinks to other websites. On this date [xx/xx/xxxx] these sources were checked and found to be active and additional data on my grandpa's (Jack Austin's) will was found.

Whenever material in a citation is not obvious, an explanation in the annotation is appropriate.

memory, or a birth certificate. With your sources documented, you and others can retrieve the same data bringing credibility and traceability to your family history.

Whether the source is a probate court record, a tombstone, an email, a website, a yellowed newspaper clipping, grandfather's diary, or a conversation with your grandmother, cite your sources. It doesn't matter if you take notes by hand, use a computer, make copies on a copier or dictate them into a recorder; you need to carefully cite your sources.

You should provide quality citations for your sources so you can remember where you found the information. This will also guide you to where to look for more information, and provide a trail for others to follow. Besides your own posterity, others with whom you share your information have the same desire and need to verify the facts which you have researched.

Any statement of fact, whether it is a birth date or an ancestor's surname, needs to have its own individual documented source. You should consider documentation of an information source just as important as finding and recording the information itself. Record enough information about the source, and tie it to the information in your history so someone else can retrieve it. Today's family history software will do this for you.

Cite Your Own Source

A citation must cite the source *you* used, not the one that someone told you existed in their citation. Another person's research, even cited, is hearsay until you can verify the source for yourself. For example, if a cousin tells you that she extracted your grandfather's birth information from his birth certificate, then your cousin is your source for the information, unless he/she provided you a photocopy, a scanned copy, or you actually verified his/her copy of the certificate.

EasyBib.com - www.easybib.com (FREE)

A free web tool that automatically formats citations and bibliography based on your input.

> Here's a book that is the best single source of information for documenting your family history.

Evidence Explained

This must-have book for every genealogist conveys the principles behind source citation, the formats in which citation should be cast, and the fundamentals of evidentiary analysis itself. Whatever the source of information – courthouse land records, family Bibles, cemetery markers, microfilmed census registers, unpublished manuscripts, electronic e-mail, or a videotaped family reunion – you will find multiple examples of each in this book. It offers13 concisely explained points of genealogical analysis,

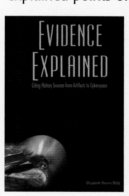

including: the distinction between direct and indirect evidence, and between quality and quantity, and the importance of custodial history. Elizabeth Shown Mills, published by Genealogical Publishing Company $59.95. www.genealogical.com

www.historicpathways.com

> Organizing and documenting as you go is smart because it keeps the best information at your fingertips and saves time.

Organize and Document As You Go

One of the most fundamental and important principles of family history research is to organize and document AS YOU GO! Good documentation lays the groundwork for easier correlation and evaluation of sources. If you put off documentation until later, you may never do it.

This results in information clog-ups. Failure to document starts a chain of confusion, redundant searches, missing or overlooked evidence, and uninformed linkage decisions.

Source citations should become a habitual part of all of your research. Include notes, sources, facts and complete information in the original file so that the information posted is complete and adequately documented. Not only do you want to document all of your evidence and sources, but others reading your family history may want to retrace your path as well. They may want to visit the same places, access the same web sites, documents, books or microfilm, and experience the thrill of the trail that you enjoyed.

Where do you put your notes and source citations? If you're writing a family history, citations may be embedded in parentheses within the text, shown as footnotes (at the bottom of each page) or as endnotes (at the end of a chapter or the work). If you're keeping your genealogy in a computer software program, it allows for recording your notes and sources under each individual and event. Good documentation includes:

Research Logs –

Fill in the purpose of each search, and source data on logs *before* looking at the source because repository catalogs often describe the source better than the source itself which makes your trail easier to follow. It also helps to keep track of unsuccessful searches (negative evidence). After success, list where you file the copy. Good research logs serve as a guide to all the sources on a family researched successfully or unsuccessfully. They help avoid repeated searches of the same unproductive sources. Good logs help you pick up research after a pause. They assist in evaluation by starting your thinking about a source as you describe it on the log. Research logs are also the best place to document your thinking and research strategies. Write lots of comments to yourself about your search strategies, suggestions, questions, and discrepancies you have noticed.

Family Group Records –

Compile a good family group record right at the start. Keep up-to-date with source footnotes for every event. Cite ALL the known sources for that family in footnotes tied to the events they document. Add more than just birth, marriage, and death events on the family group record. Add all events like census, military service, and migrations to the family group record. Well-documented and up-to-date family group records are the best source of ideas about where to search next. They show all the clues and background information needed to guess name variations, guess dates and places of events, and guess the most likely sources to document those events.

Photocopy Source Documents –

If the repository will allow it, *always* make a photocopy. Photocopies are better than handwritten copies because photocopies show ALL the clues, including things you would ignore if you copied by hand. Cite the footnote information in the margin on the front of the copy. This starts your thinking about and evaluation of the source. On the back of the copy write the name of the file and file number where you will store this copy.

Stay organized by completing paper work and filing before starting another search.

Well-Organized Files –

Start research on a family by preparing a new research log for the family and a well-footnoted family group record. Start each individual search by filling in part of your research log BEFORE the search. Give the date of the search, repository, purpose of the search (person and event you seek), and the source you will search. If the source does not have useful information put nil on the research log. Keep everything up-to-date. Don't start more research before doing all the paperwork and filing from the previous search.

Online Source Citations - $

www.dianehacker.com/resdoc

An excellent booklet about creating source citations particularly electronic media. $9.95

About.com Citing Sources - FREE

http://genealogy.about.com/cs/citing

Tips on documenting your research and formats for citations, including citations for electronic genealogy sources and maps.

A Cite For Sore Eyes - FREE

www.oz.net/~markhow/writing/cite.htm

An article on quality citations for electronic sources such as web pages, email, mailing lists, and CD-ROMs by Mark Howells.

Creating Worthwhile Genealogies - FREE

http://rwguide.rootsweb.ancestry.com/lesson12.htm

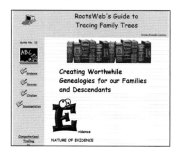

An interesting lesson on evidence, sources, documentation, and citation from RootsWeb's *Guide to Tracing Family Trees.*

How to Share Your Information Using GEDCOM

What is a GEDCOM?

A GEDCOM (**GE**nealogical **D**ata **COM**munications) is a type of file that takes family history information from one computer program and compresses it into a standard format which can be transferred into any other program. Importing and exporting a GEDCOM file is usually the best way to receive or send your information anywhere in the world via e-mail. You can receive from (import) or share (export) your information with other people, even if they use a different family history program. It was created by FamilySearch and The Family History Library in the mid-1980s to make it possible for people with different brands of software and computers to share their information.

To Create and Export a GEDCOM File

In most software programs, go to *File > Export to GEDCOM* and create a new file with a ".ged" file extension after the name. GEDCOM files can be uploaded to genealogy sites on the Internet, and can be adjusted for privacy and copyright concerns.

Steps to Import GEDCOM Files

When you import a GEDCOM file, all of the information from the GEDCOM file is added into your database file. To preview the data, you could import the GEDCOM file into an empty file. From there, you can correct or change information or select specific individuals and family lines to import into your actual database file. If you change information in the new file, you need to create a new GEDCOM file to import the information into your actual database.

- From the *File* menu, select *Import.*
- Select the drive and folder where the file is located.
- Select the file.
- Click *Import.*
- Choose the import options that you want.
- To import the file, click *OK.*

When receiving a new GEDCOM file, rather than merging the data back into your actual database file directly; always transfer it to a new, empty database file which you create.

After examining the new data, you can then import the records you wish into your primary family history database file. Even then, before you merge the new GEDCOM data, make a backup of your original database first.

GEDCOM (FamilyTree) Web Sites

There are many GEDCOM database web sites you can search for matches on names, dates, and locations; download the information; and share (or upload) your information.

FamilySearch.org - *FREE*
www.familysearch.org

Ancestry.com - *FREE* *$*
www.ancestry.com

RootsWeb.com - *FREE*
www.rootsweb.ancestry.com

Archives.com - *$*
www.archives.com

GenCircles.com - *FREE*
www.gencircles.com

One Great Family.com - *$*
www.onegreatfamily.com

MyTrees.com - *$*
www.mytrees.com

GeneaNet.org - *FREE*
www.geneanet.org

Evaluate the Evidence

Family historians must also learn to weigh and evaluate evidence, especially conflicting evidence. Don't assume that if several pieces of information agree, the data must be correct. Such assumptions may lead to erroneous pedigrees which may create a dead-end to your family tree.

Remember to cite the specific sources *you actually used* in compiling your family history. "Source notes have two purposes: to record the specific location of each piece of data and to record details that affect the use or evaluation of that data." *(Evidence! Citation & Analysis for the Family Historian).*

If you have conflicting information, carefully examine it and sort it into either primary or secondary evidence. Primary sources are usually written records created at or near to the time of the event. Secondary sources are second-hand information that has come from some other person or record. Get as close to the original documents as you can as they are more likely to be correct. And don't blindly accept information you find in a book, CD, on the Internet, or from someone's memory.

One of the most important skills you can acquire will be learning to evaluate the accuracy of primary records and the relative reliability of secondary sources. Remember that most of the family history information you discover online is from a secondary source. You should consider it a *clue* to check out.

James E. Faust
© by Intellectual Reserve, Inc.

A Joy to Know Our Ancestors

"Unlock the knowledge of who you really are by learning more about your forebears.... We can have exciting experiences as we learn about our vibrant, dynamic ancestors. They were very real, living people with problems, hopes, and dreams like we have today.... It is a joy to become acquainted with our forebears...and can be one of the most interesting puzzles you...can work on."
– James E. Faust

Networking with Others

Stay Connected

Connecting families to each other and to your roots and stories

People everywhere are hungry to learn more about their ancestors and family stories. The dynamic growth of social networks and online communities on the Internet has demonstrated the strong desire and need of people to connect and share information with each other. All of this makes family history research more accessible to a broader group of people, as well as more accurate.

Family history is all about collaboration – sharing information and working together. Networking with others who share the same family tree is perhaps the best and easiest way to discover and share your family roots and stories. You can work together with close and (currently) unknown relatives to share your stories, photos, heritage, and sources; jointly analyze the data; and come to the most accurate information concerning your ancestors.

Most likely you won't even know the person who may be the one that has the family tree information and photos you need or want. Perhaps it's a distant cousin that you know nothing about that has the photos and stories you're seeking.

> Many people are discovering their family stories and photos just by using FamilySearch's *FamilyTree* and Ancestry's *Member Connect.*

1 Use YOur **Family**

Two Excellent Ways to Connect

These two giant companies provide a simple means for you to connect with others who may share your family tree.

Using some of the latest, exciting networking tools and apps allows you to build your family tree easier, faster, and more accurately. You can safely use email, social networking sites, mailing lists, newsgroups, family associations, and queries to establish very beneficial and friendly connections with others. Here's some information about the best networking tools and apps to assist you.

FamilySearch FamilyTree - *FREE*
www.familysearch.org

After registering, click on FamilyTree, and connect yourself to your (hopefully) existing family tree for *free*. FamilySearch has billions of records in their databases, but the FamilyTree feature is new so your family tree may or may not already exist there. Upon searching, if a part of your family tree does not already exist, then you have the opportunity to add your information and start your family tree so others can collaborate with you. Overtime, this "family tree for everyone" will dynamically grow and become one of the greatest family history resources on the Internet.

When you view the detail page of any individual in your family tree, it provides the email address of the person who contributed the information – and possibly stories, photos, documents, etc. – of your ancestor. You can also be notified when new information is added about your ancestors. *See more information beginning on page 245.*

Ancestry's Member Connect -
http://landing.ancestry.com/memberconnect

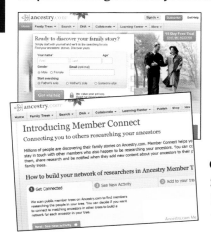

Ancestry's Member Connect feature helps you stay in touch with other members who may also be researching your ancestors. You can contact them, share research and be notified when they add new content about your ancestors to their public family trees. Member Connect not only shows you the member activity on the ancestors in your family tree, it also shows you who has saved or commented on records featuring your ancestors. You need a subscription to Ancestry to connect with others. U.S. $12.95/month for 6-month membership. World $24.95/month.

Social Networking

One of the Best Tools to Stay Connected

Social networking refers to a class of web sites and services that allow you to connect with friends, family, and colleagues online, as well as meet people with similar interests or hobbies. With these web sites you can connect with your family, swap stories and recipes, share family photos, and build collaborative family trees. You and your extended family and distant cousins can collaborate and share information on your shared family tree.

Some of the sites use advanced technologies like wikis (type of website that allows you to add, and perhaps edit the available content), RSS (timely updates or web feeds from favored websites that you subscribe to), mapping, and online family tree building to help you connect with your family and ancestors. All of these family history social networking sites have great appeal, wonderful capabilities, and are private and secure.

Here are some of the most popular social networking sites to explore.

MyHeritage.com -
www.myheritage.com

A family-oriented social network service and genealogy website. It allows members to create their own family websites, share pictures and videos, organize family events, create family trees, and search for ancestors. With over 64 million users, it is one of the largest sites in the social networking and genealogy field with more than 1 billion online profiles. There are more than 24 million family trees and 151 million photos on the site, and the site is accessible in 38 languages.

It allows you to search for your ancestors online using a metasearch engine, which searches its own database, and queries 1,526 other databases. **Family pages** are online profiles for entire families. Members can use their family pages to invite other family members, share photos and videos, schedule birthday parties and events, and stay in touch with their family. *See page 262 for more information.* Basic (250 people in tree) Free, Premium (2500 people) $5/month, Premium Plus (Unlimited people) $7.50/month.

Facebook

Facebook.com - www.facebook.com FREE

A social networking website where you can add family and friends and send them messages. It currently has more than 850 million active users worldwide, and has become so ubiquitous that the generic verb "facebooking" had come into use to describe the process of browsing others' profiles and news or updating one's own.

Facebook is a great tool for family history. You can share your genealogy research finds, ask for help, stay in touch with family, find resources and family connections, and share photos. You can join a host of Facebook networks organized by city, workplace, school, region, plus genealogy communities, and even tap into *free* apps.

One of the most popular applications on Facebook is the *Photos* application where you can upload an unlimited number of photos; 300 million photos are uploaded daily. You can also "tag", or label users in a photo.

Article: Set up a Facebook Page for Your Ancestors - FREE

https://familysearch.org/techtips/2012/03/facebook-page-ancestors

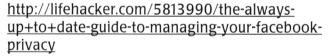

There are several ways to enhance your chances of finding genealogy-minded relatives through Facebook Pages. Two of those ways are setting up a Facebook Page for your ancestor, or starting a family organization Facebook Page. James Tanner describes some of the ins and outs of doing this in this article.

Article: How Facebook Opens the Door to Family History - FREE

https://familysearch.org/techtips/2011/03/facebook-opens-door-family-history

Robin Foster provides tips on how to find your family using Facebook.

Guide to Keeping Your Facebook in Control - FREE

http://lifehacker.com/5813990/the-always-up+to+date-guide-to-managing-your-facebook-privacy

Up-to-date information about Facebook's privacy changes, including details for how to tweak your privacy settings to keep your information safe.

Facebook Communities

FamilySearch - www.facebook.com/familysearch FREE

Provides access to global family history records and services to people around the world.

Research Communities on Facebook

https://familysearch.org/learn/wiki/en/Research_Communities_on_Facebook FREE

Lists and links to FamilySearch-sponsored Genealogy Research Communities on Facebook.

GeneaBloggers - www.facebook.com/geneabloggers FREE

Helps genealogy and family history fans blog about their passion.

1 Use Your Family

> Here are just a few of the many Facebook family history communities and apps you can join or download.

Facebook Communities

FamilyTree Magazine - *FREE*
www.facebook.com/familytreemagazine

A publication about genealogy and family history; includes resource guides, technology how-to articles, history and genealogy news.

We're Related - *FREE*
www.facebook.com/myrelatives

See who you are related to on Facebook. It allows you to find your relatives on Facebook and build your family tree. Much like the current Facebook profile design, each user has a profile page, a wall, info, photos, and relatives in lieu of friends. You can see your relatives' news on a filterable page that is similar to the Facebook home page. It allows you to communicate with and focus on a subset of your Facebook friends.

Unclaimed Persons - *FREE*
www.facebook.com/unclaimedpersons

A person dies. No one knows how to reach the family. The coroner's investigators have exhausted their resources. That's when Unclaimed Persons starts to work. Volunteers use their genealogical and investigative skills to locate the next of kin.

FamilyBuilder's Family Tree
- http://livefamily.com   *FREE*

Building family connections on social networks.

GenealogyWise - *FREE*
www.facebook.com/GenealogyWise

A social network especially for genealogy created by the National Institute for Genealogical Studies. You can connect with new found cousins, share resources, and learn more about genealogy. You can join or create surname, locality, or topic groups. The Group feature allows you to collaborate, share, and ask questions of other members.

Family Village - *FREE*
www.facebook.com/appcenter/myfamilyvillage

Lets you build your own town populated by your family. As your village grows, it works behind the scenes to find real documents about your heritage: newspaper article, yearbook photos, census records, maps, and anything else that could enrich your knowledge of your personal genealogy.

Relative Finder App - *FREE*
https://apps.facebook.com/relativefinder

Connects a Facebook account with FamilySearch FamilyTree to connect families.

Here's a great way to create a free wiki page for your ancestors using WeRelate.

WeRelate

WeRelate Wiki - www.werelate.org

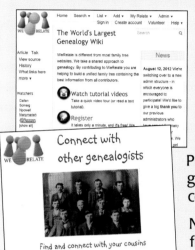

A free public-service wiki for genealogy sponsored by the Foundation for On-Line Genealogy in partnership with the Allen County Public Library, and a great way to collaborate.

Not only can you find information to help your family history research, but you can also create wiki pages for your own ancestors. You can gather together the records of a person's life, plus tell his story. On each person and family page you can write the history of that person or family, provide proof documents (e.g. birth, marriage, death certificates, etc.), and all your collected sources are always right there. This is a great way to collaborate with others easily, receive notifications by e-mail whenever changes are made to pages you are working on, and view family trees, maps, and timelines.

Another great thing is to create your own personal profile or wiki page. This can be your genealogy 'headquarters' – an expandable, desktop work space for all of your family tree research efforts that can be shared with others to collaborate and work

together. You can provides links to your family trees, people, family and place pages, photos, articles, personal archived original documents, and research guides that all support your research.

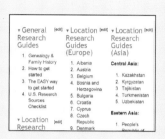

Their 'Research Guides' contain information about doing family history research in particular places or on particular topics. Click on

www.werelate.org/wiki/Category:Research_guides. It cross references with two of the best external sources: FamilySearch Wiki – an extensive and growing wiki of family history research guides, and USGenWeb – an excellent compilation of user-contributed resources for genealogical research.

When you upload a family tree (GEDCOM) file, it automatically checks for duplicates already in the database. If a potential duplicate is found, the information may be merged with the person already in the database which means that you may be automatically connected to new branches of your family tree. The data from your GEDCOM will be used to create person, family and source pages within WeRelate for you. *Learn more:* http://moultriecreek.us/gazette/resources/werelate/

Something Greater than Ourselves

"When our hearts turn to our ancestors, something changes inside us. We feel part of something greater than ourselves. Our inborn yearnings for family connections are fulfilled when we are linked to our ancestors..."

Russell M. Nelson
© by Intellectual Reserve, Inc.

Russell M. Nelson (1924-   ), Internationally renowned cardiothoracic surgeon and religious leader

Pinterest

Pinterest - http://pinterest.com *FREE*

Pinterest is an online pinboard to organize and share things you love, and has become one of the most popular social networking sites. Unlike other social media sites (like Facebook and Google+), what you

share on Pinterest stays on your boards as 'pins'. The pins are images, videos and photographs you select from your own hard drive or a variety of websites you like, which make a highly visual and engaging experience. You can enjoy sharing genealogy and technology resources, but you can also share great recipes, home decorating ideas, etc. And you can follow only the boards with pins that interest you.

Pinterest is linked to both Facebook and Twitter so you have the option of adding in your Facebook family and friends. Anything you add into a board will then be shared with all of your followers and contacts. If you want more control over the content, simply limit the number of people with whom you are connected. You are not limited to the standard pinboards, you can delete those you do not want, rename them, or add your own boards. For example, you could create your own board for a particular ancestor, a surname, or post old photos of people you can't identify. Perhaps someone can identify the people in the photo.

It's simple to organize, access and store all your favorite genealogy databases, blogs, census records, YouTube videos, websites and projects. It's kinda like clipping coupons or interesting articles out of a magazine or newspaper. When you click on any of the pins, it links you directly to the original website. This means that your family photos, pictures of gravestones, maps, etc. can be organized into pinboards which can be easily accessed by anyone. It's an interesting way to organize, preserve, and share your photos and documents with others. And get young people involved. What could be better?

Pinterest is also a way to do family history research on a given topic. If you search for a particular topic, the results will show all of the pins relating to that topic, which in turn links you to that website.

Here are some excellent sample pinboards to get started or give you some ideas.

Family History Sample Pinboards

Family Tree Creative Ideas -
http://pinterest.com/myheritage pins/the-creative-family/

Family tree creative ideas and family-related pinboards.

Family Stories -
http://pinterest.com/familystories

Caroline Pointer's family stories boards feature tons of pins for research, photo and video tips, genealogy and social media apps, family reunion ideas, blogging, technology, recipes, and much more. Learn more about bringing technology and genealogy together at www.4yourfamilystory.com.

Check out her free video on **OneNote Research Plan,** an effective organizational system to help you keep track of all the research for your ancestors which syncs with your computer and all your mobile devices. Caroline is a coach to help you learn how to use technology to find your ancestors and get your family trees in shape, how to use technology to find your family story, how to use more than just Ancestry.com to find your ancestors, and how to use online & offline resources effectively.

You should also check out her excellent YouTube videos on *What's Up Genealogy?* at http://www.youtube.com/user/4YourFamilySto ry/videos.

http://www.youtube.com/watch?v=M_kn36bt8L Y&feature=youtube

Google +

Google+

http://plus.google.com **FREE**

Google Plus is a free social networking program from Google that allows you to connect and share information with others. *Circles* are organized lists of your family members, friends, business associates, etc. You can hover over their name and see which Circle you put them in. *Hangouts* are meet-ups with friends. It lets your buddies know you're hanging out and see who drops by for a face-to-face-to-face chat. *Huddle* (or group chat) lets everyone get on the same page. Sparks looks for videos and articles it thinks you'll like.

Finding the Genealogy Community on Google+ **FREE**

https://familysearch.org/techtips/2011/10/finding-genealogy-community-google-plus

James Tanner has written a good article in FamilySearch that explains how to use Google+.

If you already have a Google account (Gmail, Alerts, Picasa, etc.), you are already registered and just need some minimal information for your G+ profile.

Google Blog - **FREE**

http://googleblog.blogspot.com

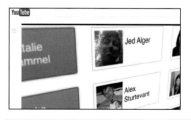

Learn more about Google. Insights from Googlers into products, technology, and the Google culture.

You Will Have Strength

"[Your ancestors] hearts are bound to you. ... You will have more than your own strength as you choose to labor on to find them."

Henry B. Eyring
© by Intellectual Reserve, Inc.

Henry B. Eyring, American educational administrator, author, and religious leader

Circles - Groups (like the 'friends' function in Facebook) for the people in your life: family, friends, business and social contacts. You can define Circles in any way you want and make them as expansive or limited as you choose. Just drag-and-drop to the Circle you choose. Use circles to share with only the people you choose.

Hangouts - A virtual meeting place where up to 10 people can participate in an online video chat at the same time. For example: family members, family tree research cousins, cooking classes, music concerts, prayer groups, people with certain medical conditions, game shows, etc. There's even G+ mobile apps for your smartphone so you can hang out at any time, from just about anywhere. It's a way to create instant webcasts and share documents, videos, and computer screens with others.

Free 2-Minute Video:
Google+: A Quick Look **FREE**

ww.youtube.com/watch?v=1JagF4t0tJk&feature=rellist&playnext=1&list=PLF3DFB800F05F551A

Free 4-Minute Video:
How to use Google+ **FREE**

http://www.youtube.com/watch?v=2zXjvQSuZYA&feature=related

GenealogyWise

www.genealogywise.com

A free social network especially for genealogy that combines community interaction with tools and resources for people who are interested in researching and sharing their family history with others. It's an open network that allows anyone to join and create social groups within the genealogy-focused community. The innovative and easy-to-use platform opens the doors of social networking to millions around the world who are interested in sharing their passion for family history and in meeting new people that share that passion. The free service allows users to join surname groups, explore ancestral records, share photos, video, and family trees. You can create a profile to tell others about your research interests, receive and respond to emails from other users without publishing an email address, create online family trees and personal research pages, and collaborate with other users.

MyFamily

www.myfamily.com

In a secure, password-protected environment, you can create online family photo albums, share family news, maintain a calendar of family events, and more. Everyone gets their own personal profile page, where you can share more about yourself, access any of the family groups you belong to, set your profile picture, update your status and receive notes from your family members. Privacy settings allow you to control who can see the contents on your profile page, so you can feel safe

adding your phone number and email address. $29.95/year total.

Twitter

https://twitter.com

Twitter is a 'microblog' where you can make short posts (140 characters or less) to give links to photos, websites, blog posts, or just ask questions and hold conversations. Twitter posts (tweets) are searchable so you can find people interested in the same things as you. So many people and organizations use Twitter to let us know what they are doing so you can learn something useful. Twitter isn't for everyone, but if you like to learn the latest about genealogy, or want to share short bits of your research with friends and family, it's a great platform.

Twitter Genealogy -

https://twitter.com/search?q=%23genealogy&src=hash

Go to this weblink to search for tweets about the latest on genealogy.

https://twitter.com

Tweetdeck- www.tweetdeck.com

An app that allows you to manage multiple accounts and synchronize your configuration when you use TweetDeck from different computers. It allows you to read all of ones Twitter, Facebook, MySpace, LinkedIn, Foursquare, Google Buzz messages on one page. TweetDeck is currently available as a desktop app, a web app, or a Chrome app.

Genes Reunited

www.genesreunited.com

Every family has a story. This site will help you discover yours. One of the UK's largest genealogy websites with over 12 million members. It's free to build your family tree online, search for your ancestors in 850+ million names in family trees, census, birth, marriages, death and military records, and send messages to other members to discover a shared family history and find new relatives. A subscription allows you to build your family tree by posting it on the site and investigating which ancestors you share with other members. You can also search historical records, such as census records from England, Wales and Scotland and birth, marriage and death records dating from 1837 to 2006. Online community boards give you the opportunity to chat and share advice. You can also upload and share family photos and documents. £1.67 ($2.56)/month/year

Sample Video Stories from Genes Reunited -

www.youtube.com/user/GenesReunitedYT

Our Story

www.ourstory.com FREE

Allows you to create a visual timeline, colla- borate with family and friends, and document every moment of your

loved ones' life with video, pictures, and sto- rytelling. The site also offers ways to share with anyone you want and backup these memories on CD, DVD and books.

KinCafe.com FREE

www.kincafe.com

A free social networking site to connect, bond and cherish loved ones. You can build and link family trees together, remember birthdays and anniversaries, share your photo albums, family calendar, blogs and other family treasures with all who care most. You man- age whether to allow your friends and relatives to see your family's content. It allows you to build a family tree and then collaborate with family to expand the tree. Share family photos, keep with family events and activities via the family calendar, or post the latest news in the family blog.

eFamily.com FREE

http://www.famiva.comhttp://efamily.com

This free social network for families offers a secure, password protected place for you and your relatives to connect and collaborate. You can share photos and stories, work together to build an online family tree, explore family maps, and more. Enjoy great collaboration features such as shared calendar, events, newsletters, status updates and more. You can also add tags or keywords to photos so others can find them easily, and you can also choose the privacy settings of who will be able to view your photos.

Flickr.com
www.flickr.com

A popular photo-sharing website

that offers a cost-effective way to archive and share your treasured photos. It offers strong features such as a large community of users and many photo editing tools. You can share stories and discuss the photos available on the site, and build relationships. You can also explore the world's most interesting photos. Flickr is home to over 8 billion of the world's photos (and growing) with about 90 million users. It can be used not only to protect your ancestral photos, but for actual genealogical research. Many people are discovering their ancestors images online.

Many archives are using Flickr to present some of their unique collections called *The Commons.* There are more than 50 archives, libraries and museums presenting their collections, including: the Library of Congress, Smithsonian, New York Public Library and U.S. National Archives.

YouTube FREE
www.youtube.com

A popular video-sharing site that allows you

to upload videos and share them with a few people or with everyone. You can search for videos on family history and other topics from archives, libraries, genealogy record companies and many other organizations.

Skype www.skype.com FREE

A free program that allows you to make

secure voice and video calls to other Skype users any-where in the world

You can search the entire Flickr database in a number of ways.

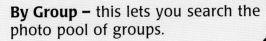

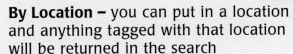

Flickr Database Searches

By User – this lets you search the photostream of individual users.

By Group – this lets you search the photo pool of groups.

By Location – you can put in a location and anything tagged with that location will be returned in the search

Their *Groups* feature is a fabulous way to share content and conversation, either privately or with the world. Check out their *genealogy* group at www.flickr.com/groups/genealogy. There are over 10 million groups, or you can start your own, such as your family or friends. You can create your own photo sets and collections and have control over who is viewing your photos. This is a great way to share certain photos with family and friends while sharing other photos with public users.

For mobile users, Flickr has an app for iOS (Apple), Android, and Windows Phone 7 operating systems. Their *free* photo storage limits the number of photos uploaded each month to 2 videos (90 second time limits) and 300MB, and the number that can be displayed (only the 200 most recent images). The *pro* service offers unlimited storage, uploads, sets and collections, and archiving of high-resolution original images. $24.95/year

http://www.flickr.com/groups/genealogy

over the internet. You just need an internet connection and a computer or Smartphone with a microphone, speaker (or an inexpensive headset), and video camera. You can also buy a Skype phone to use like a regular phone, and make calls to regular phones, although they charge for this service.

Mailing Lists
*Exchange e-Mails with Others
with a Common Interest*

RootsWeb Mailing Lists - FREE

http://lists.rootsweb.ancestry.com

Mailing lists are free discussion groups where individuals with a common interest share information with each other by e-mail. All subscribers can send e-mail to and receive e-mail from the list.There are thousands of family history/ genealogy mail lists. This is the oldest and largest index of family history mail lists (over 32,000 currently) which is organized in categories: Surnames, USA, International, and Other. You can use the search for information that has already been posted to the mailing lists. Enter names or keywords and click "Search" to search their archives for information that matches.

Cyndi's List - FREE

www.cyndislist.com/mailing-lists/complete

This page links to the website from Rootsweb 'Genealogy Resources on

1 Use YOur Family

Message Boards

You can post any information about a lost relative on relevant message boards, look for others researching the same family lines, swap research tips, help others look up records to find living relatives in your area, search for hard-to-find data, and enjoy the great benefits of working together. You'll find message boards on the following websites:

> Internet message boards allow you to post a question to be viewed by large groups of people.

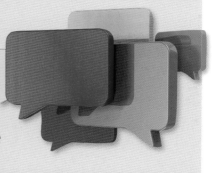

over 17 Million posts on more than 161,000 boards. You can search for content by surnames, localities, and topics.

Genforum Message Boards - FREE

http://genforum.genealogy.com

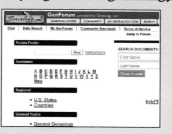

You can search for content by surnames, localities, and topics.

CyndisList Message Boards - FREE

www.cyndislist.com/queries

Cyndi's List provides hundreds of links to queries, message boards, and mailing lists indexed by: General Resources, How To, Locality Specific, and Military.

Networking

A great way to find and perhaps contact your lost relatives is to use social networking websites which are huge. *See Social Networking starting on page 45.*

Ancestry Message Boards - FREE

http://boards.ancestry.com

It may be the world's largest online genealogy community with

the Internet by John Fuller' which is currently being updated. Note that mailing lists for various topics are linked on appropriate category pages all throughout Cyndi's List. Surname mailing lists are listed individually on each of the Surname category pages on Cyndi's List as well.

Yahoo Groups - http://groups.yahoo.com/search?query=genealogy&type=combined

A gathering place on the Internet for many genealogy groups to send and receive emails, schedule meetings, share files and photos, or have private group chats.

How to Use Genealogy Mailing Lists to Further Your Research - *FREE*
http://genealogy.about.com/od/mailinglists/a/mailing_lists.htm

An article by Kimberly Powell providing tips on how to best use mailing lists ranging from the RootsWeb lists to individual mailing lists sponsored by genealogical societies, genealogy software publishers, etc.

Newsgroups

Discussion Groups with Common Interest

A Newsgroup (or a Discussion Group) is a forum for sharing information that are stored on the Internet until you request the messages. They allow you to post messages and reply to other users. There are dozens of newsgroups and tools that will search these messages. For more information and links, see the following web pages:

www.cyndislist.com/newsgroups

www.newsdemon.com/genealogy-newsgroups.php

Surnames and Family Associations

Individual Family Surnames

RootsWeb Surname List -
http://rsl.rootsweb.com

Allows you to register the surname you are researching. By checking these lists, searchers often find others looking for the same surnames. Every day, dozens of connections are made between relatives using these lists. Currently contains over 1,242,000 surnames.

Cyndi's List -
www.cyndislist.com/newsgroups/queries
Numerous links to surname web sites.

Finding Your Ancestors -
http://genealogy.about.com/library/weekly/aa041700a.htm

A guide to internet search techniques for the surnames in your family tree. There

are many wonderful family history Web pages on the Internet which remain undiscovered because people just don't know how to locate them. These pages may contain just the valuable information that you are looking for – family trees, stories, photographs, cemetery transcriptions, wills, etc.

Surname Finder - www.surnamefinder.com

Providing easy access to resources for 1,731,359 surnames.

Queries

Requests for information about a specific ancestor, couple, or family. Besides accepting queries, most sites allow you to search the queries left by others. These include www.usgenweb.org and www.genforum.com.

How To Write a Successful Query - http://genealogy.about.com/cs/surname/ht/surname_query.htm

Make the most out of online genealogy message boards and mailing lists by learning how to write a clear and effective query.

Help (or Lookup) Lists

USGenWeb.org - www.usgenweb.org

Provides e-mail addresses of people for each county in the U.S. willing to look up information for you at no charge. These are volunteers who do quick searches in various local record books, records, and record offices as a public service. The same is true of local historical societies, libraries, and other organizations.

5 Tips on How to Find 'Lost' Living Relatives/Friends

And connect with your ancestors at the same time

Family history is one of the most interesting, pleasurable, and gratifying hobbies. Following the trails and life-challenging trials of your fore-bears can lead you to many exciting tales of successes, triumphs, failures, loves, and the passion of true-life stories, as glamorous as any from Hollywood.

Relatives and friends can become separated for so many reasons – adoption, divorce, relocation, disasters, war are just a few. Just as great as discovering your family roots and stories is the prospect of connecting with living relatives from long ago – siblings, grandparents, distant cousins, aunts, uncles, even parents and children. This is an absolutely *thrilling* experience that you will

not want to miss if you're searching for lost relatives.

The search may sometimes seem difficult, but these tips and resources for finding lost relatives (and missing friends) can lead you on the right trail to finding that certain someone you've been yearning so much to locate. By doing so, you will discover a new and unbeliev-able joy that you may not have anticipated.

The Joy of Finding Living Relatives

Oscar-winning actress Helen Mirren was thrilled when she discovered her Russian relatives. She took an extraordinary emotional journey back to the country estate that was the family home until the Bolsheviks drove them out. She said it was more exciting than her Oscar night. She returned to a tiny hamlet to rediscover her roots and meet the relatives she never knew existed. She and her elder sister Kate dug into the rich soil and planted three roses in memory of their great-grandmother. It was a moving moment. Read about it here... www.dailymail.co.uk/femail/article-470030/Helen-Mirren-reveals-joy-meeting-Russian-relatives.html

The Simplest Things

Sometimes the simplest things are very effective when looking for living relatives. Simply type the information you have about the person you are looking for (e.g. full name, address, etc.) into the *Google* (www.google.com) or *Mocavo* (www.mocavo.com - scours millions of hard-to-find genealogy Web pages) search engines and in a matter of seconds, you may get exactly what you are looking for. If the surname is fairly common, you may want to use the Advanced Search options located at www.google.com/advanced_search and www.mocavo.com/search.

One of the obvious choices is to simply look in the local phone book for the area you remember them last living in. You can find most white pages online and some of them are free. You can also interview key living relatives to learn about family stories, and to have relationships explained to you to find details that will assist you in finding other living relatives.

Searching for lost relatives may require a generous investment of your time, but its worth it. Set aside some time to make some calls if you don't find your relative immediately. You may have to telephone a few people with the same surname, but in doing so you might locate someone who knows your relative and would be happy to pass on a message.

There are challenges to finding lost living relatives that may require you to become both a  family historian and a private investigator. Here are 5 tips and numerous resources on how to find living relatives and friends.

Webinar on CD
Reverse Genealogy: Finding the Living 💲

www.legacyfamilytreestore.com/ProductDetails.asp?ProductCode=W_REVERSE

Megan Smolenyak's webinar presentation covers proven techniques for tracing 20th and 21st century friends and relatives from the past to the present. She is a popular writer, speaker and TV guest on national shows. 1 hour 45 minutes, plus 4 pages of handouts. $9.95

How to Find Living Relatives
1. Start Here

Prepare a list of all the names, locations and dates of key events such as births, marriages and deaths. Old address books are a great source of information. The more detail you can collect at this point, the easier and more successful you will be. Focus on a single relative or family at a time, and record every bit of new information you find, including where and when you found it. You can't research everybody. You need to focus where you're more likely to have the most success. Make a calculated decision and choose one family to research first.

If you come across details about a family member in another line of the family, put it aside in a safe place but don't get sidetracked. Concentrate on one family line until you can fill in everything you can going back at least 4 generations or until you reach a real dead-end. When this happens, then begin researching another family as far back as you can go.

Even if the relative you're looking for has re-located, you may be able to trace them through their last known address. It is possible that the current residents of their former habitation have a forwarding address that may enhance the chances of a successful outcome to your ancestor search for free. Otherwise neighbors may have remained in contact with them and can tell you where they have moved to.

Search Social Security Death Index

It may be a good idea to see if a person is actually alive before starting an extended search for living relatives. In the US, one of the best ways to do this is to search the Social Security Death Index (SSDI), an Internet file that contains records of deaths for those who had social security numbers and the death was reported to the US Social Security Administration.

Most records start in 1962, but the file does contain some records of deaths beginning in 1936. The absence of a particular person in the SSDI is not proof that this person is alive. Additionally, there is a possibility that incorrect records of death have been entered.

Each of the following websites offer different search features for the SSDI.

FamilySearch FREE

https://familysearch.org/search/collection/1202535

https://familysearch.org/learn/wiki/en/Social_Security_Death_Index_%28SSDI%29

You can also search FamilySearch's Historical Records Collection for free.

https://familysearch.org/search/collection/list#uri=http://familysearch.org/searchapi/search/collection/1202535

Continued on next page.

Free Guide to Finding People

www.searchsystems.net/free-find-people-guide.html FREE

1. Use their People Search Service at http://publicrecords.searchsystems.net/people-search.html

2. Search Using Public Records

• Property records

• Recorded documents: deeds, mortgages, liens judgments, military discharges, bonds, trusts, child support enforcement, dbas, power of attorney filings, financing statements, trusts, partnership documents, leases, and wills.

• Voter Registration

• Professional Licenses (contractor, accountant, attorney, doctor, security guard, or other licensed professional)

• Are they Deceased? (Social Security Death Index)

• Did they get Married? Divorced? (state or county marriage and divorce databases)

• Relatives, Roommates, Neighbors

• Post Office (use 'Address Service Requested')

• Other Avenues: Unclaimed Property, court and criminal records, business filings (corporations, fictitious business name filings, LLCs), Uniform Commercial Code filings, building inspection databases, utility information.

Check out SearchSystems **Free Guide to Finding People**. Detailed information can be found on their website.

3. Social Networking Sites

Very useful tools to find and connect with people.

www.Facebook.com - the most popular social networking service worldwide; you can communicate with friends and other users through private or public messages and a chat feature.

www.Twitter.com - a real-time information network that connects you to the latest stories, ideas, opinions and news about what you find interesting.

www.LinkedIn.com - connects the world's professionals to make them more productive and successful.

www.MyLife.com - make valuable personal and professional connections, plus pull together your social and email communications to help simplify your life.

www.MySpace.com - a social networking service with a strong music emphasis; simply start typing and a search display screen appears with the most relevant hits for that search

www.Classmates.com - find old high school friends

www.Plaxo.com - online address book, hosting over 50 million address

Ancestry.com - *FREE*

http://search.ancestry.com/search/db.aspx?dbid=3693

GenealogyBank - *FREE*

www.genealogybank.com/gbnk/ssdi

FamilyTree Legends - *FREE*

www.familytreelegends.com/records/ssdi

SteveMorse.org - *FREE*

www.stevemorse.org/ssdi/ssdi.html

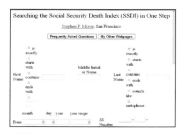

Using this web site allows you to search 6 different SSDI websites by typing the information once and switching between the different sites.

2. Search Directories

Online telephone and historical directories are some of the best sources for finding living people. A *telephone directory* usually lists the person in whose name the phone is listed, and an *archived city directory* may list more information and people in a particular household.

You may want to search several telephone directories because each site has a different list of names. Search for the name with and without initials. You may need more information than just full name and the place, especially if the person has a common surname and lives in a big town or city. Check the telephone directory for *similar names* in areas the missing person may be living.

Best Telephone Directories

ZabaSearch.com - *FREE*

http://zabasearch.com

You get telephone numbers and addresses in the US for free, and it has three times more residential listings than white pages phone directory. No registration required. Instant results.

WhitePages.com - *FREE*

www.whitepages.com

Offers to find people, businesses, reverse phone and reverse addresses with over 50 million monthly users. Their award-winning apps help millions of people find people and places, manage their communication, block spam and identify incoming calls and texts.

US 411 - www.411.info *FREE*

A free online information service for US.

Canada 411 - http://411.ca *FREE*

Canada's online directory service with more than 12 million annual visitors.

USSearch.com - $

www.ussearch.com/consumer/index.jsp

They pioneered the concept of providing information about people via the Internet to locate hard-to-find friends, relatives and others and they have a huge database. They also provide optional detailed information about a person's background and criminal records from social networking profiles and public records. Search by name, phone, or address.

Intelius.com - www.intelius.com $

A leading information commerce company. They provide consumers and businesses with predictive intelligence for important everyday decisions about people, businesses and assets. They offer products and services ranging from basic people search to comprehensive HR background checks and identity theft protection. Membership includes unlimited people searches and reverse phone lookups with instant results. 2-Day no obligation free trial. $19.95/month.

InfoSpace.com - *FREE*

www.infospace.com

Web search that brings together top results from all leading search engines. The search engine for Dogpile, MetaCrawler, WebCrawler, and WebFetch,

The New Ultimates White Pages - *FREE*

www.newultimates.com/white

A centralized, fast, and common interface to 14 different directories. Just type your search criteria into the first search engine and it is automatically copied to the other directory forms.

PeopleFinders.com - $

www.peoplefinders.com

A source for locating family members, friends, classmates, military buddies or anyone you want to get in touch with. Few things compare to the joy of reconnecting with people you haven't seen in years, and they're ready to help you find anyone using a name, address, email or most any other information you have. $14.95/first 30 days.

AnyWho.com - *FREE*

www.anywho.com/whitepages

A free online white pages directory where you can find people by their name, address or you can do a reverse lookup by phone number.

1 Use Your **Family**

NetrOnline.com - *FREE*
www.netronline.com/public_records.htm

A portal to official state web sites, and those Tax Assessors' and Recorders' offices that have developed web sites for the retrieval of available public records over the internet. An excellent source for a name, street address, city, state, zip code, and usually a phone number for any person involved in a real estate transaction.

VirtualGumshoe - *FREE* $
www.virtualgumshoe.com

A leading public record resource among private investigators, researchers, and journalists. It contains over 4000 links to public information databases and informational sites useful to investigators of all types, including a large directory of free links.

The Phone Book UK - *FREE*
www.thephonebook.bt.com

Free telephone directory for all of the UK.

192.com UK - www.192.com *FREE* $

Free UK telephone directory for UK after registration. Name and location (city) is required. More information for a fee.

Best Archived City/ County Directories

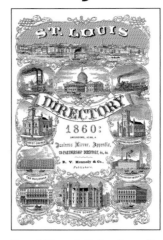

City and county historical directories are similar to present day telephone books and are useful records for locating people. They typically contain information for working family members, including name, occupation, and home and business addresses. Essentially every city in the US published a directory usually annually since the early 1800's. They are helpful in placing your living relative or ancestor in a specific location in a particular year. Directories can also be used to follow an individual's occupation, place of employment, and place of residence, as well as potentially identify life events such as marriages, deaths, and migrations.

City directories are found in the local public library or historical society of the city of interest. They may also be found at a state university library or the state library or historical society. The Library of Congress has the largest collection of city and county directories on microfilm. An increasing number of directories are being digitized and made available online.

Online Historical Directories - *FREE*
https://sites.google.com/site/onlinedirectorysite

An ongoing project to provide a complete online listing (both free and subscription) for historical alumni, business, city, county, farm, Masonic, rural, social, and other types of directories for the United States and Canada, as well as international directories. There are also lists of resources, articles, and ideas of where to find offline historical directories.

Directory Search Tips

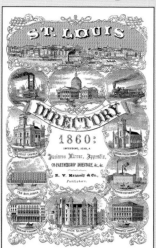

If you can't find a city directory for the small town where your ancestor or relative lived, try checking directories of larger nearby cities to see whether your ancestor's smaller town might have been included there.

Only search for your ancestor's surname. Since the entries are alphabetical you'll see all of the people with that surname and you don't run the risk of missing your ancestor if his given name is abbreviated.

Check every available city directory for the time period when your ancestors were living in the area. People overlooked in one directory may be included in the next. Names were also often misspelled or standardized, so be sure to check name variations. If you can locate a street address for your family from a census, vital, or other record, then many directories also offer a street index.

In collections that contain directory images, be sure to use both the browse and search functions. Browsing lets you view a directory page-by-page as you would if you were looking at the actual book. Check the table of contents to see what types of information were included. You may find street directories, lists of advertisements (which may include your

> City directories are very useful in tracking your ancestors' and living relatives' residences in between census years.

ancestor's business), lists of government officials, charitable organizations, churches, cemeteries, hotels, maps, and much more.

Remember that many people share the same names, so when you find your ancestor in a city directory, be sure to use other sources like censuses or family records to confirm that the address and occupation match.

Once you've found your ancestor in a directory, take the time to look at the addresses and occupations of other people who share their surname. You might find relatives living in neighboring houses or working in the same industry.

Make a note of the name, date, and publisher of the city directories you review, and also the names you checked for. In some cities, multiple directories may have been published for the same year. If your ancestor isn't listed in one directory, you may find them in another, so it's important to keep a record of which directories you've already searched to keep from duplicating your research.

Widows are often noted as such, so by locating the last directory in which the husband appeared and the first directory listing the wife as "widow of" it's possible to narrow down the husband's date of death.

Once you've located an ancestor in a city directory, enter the street address (using quotes) into the keyword field. This will bring up other residents of that address, which may include in-laws and other family members.

Don't miss the late listing of names received too late for inclusion in the alphabetical portion, generally located just before or after the alphabetical list of residents. This may include people who had recently moved to the area (including those moving within the city limits), as well as individuals the canvasser missed on his initial visit.

US City Directories - *FREE*
www.uscitydirectories.com

This web site attempts to identify all printed, micro-filmed, and online directories, and their repositories, for the United States. They have a clickable map of the United States showing where all known city directories are throughout the country. This is an ongoing project.

DistantCousin - *FREE*
www.distantcousin.com/directories

A free online archive of city directory records and scanned images.

FamilySearch - *FREE*
https://familysearch.org/learn/wiki/en/United_States_Directories

A Wiki article that provides links to directories by state. The Family History Library Catalog also lists a large collection of city directories, most of which can be borrowed on microfilm for viewing at your local Family History Center. View the catalog at www.family-search.org/catalog-search.

Ancestry.com - $
http://search.ancestry.com/search/db.aspx?dbid=2469

This database is a collection of directories for U.S. cities and counties in various years from 1821-1989. It currently contains directories for all states except Alaska.

Fold3 - $
www.fold3.com/s.php#query=City+Directories

Includes directories for thirty large metro-politan centers in twenty U.S. states.

WorldVitalRecords.com - $
www.WorldVitalRecords.com

A collection of directories for U.S. cities and counties.

WorldCat.org - *FREE*
www.worldcat.org

A portal to the collections and services of more than 10,000 libraries worldwide. You can determine what city directories a particular library may hold by accessing their website through WorldCat.

USGenWeb - *FREE*
http://usgenweb.org

Provides resources and queries for every state and country in the US. Clicking on a state link takes you to the state's website and a listing of directories for each county.

Library of Congress - *FREE*
www.loc.gov/rr/microform/uscity

The Library of Congress has a large collection of city directories on microfilm in their Microform Reading Room indexed by state. These directories are not available via interli-brary loan. However, they provide a list of free-lance researchers in the greater Washington D.C. area who perform research for a fee.

3. Browse the Internet

You can use the Internet to help locate a lost family member or friend with sites that help you link to other sites, or search their databases.

CyndisList.com - *FREE*
www.cyndislist.com/finding-people

Includes a category about Finding People; the index of categories provides dozens of links to sites to help locate living people, including: Criminal & Prisoner Resources, E-Mail Addresses, General Resources, Military, Postal Addresses, Professionals, Volunteers & Other Research Services, Publications, Software & Supplies, School & Classmate Resources, Telephone Directories, and United Kingdom Resources.

ProGenealogists.com - *FREE*
www.progenealogists.com/genealogysleuthb.htm

Their Genealogy Sleuth links you to web sites that professional genealogists use daily to do US genealogy research. Check out their Find Living People section.

SearchSystems - *FREE* $
www.searchsystems.net

The largest and best directory of hard-to-find public record databases around the world to help you locate businesses and people featuring over 55,000 links to public record databases. It's a portal to these searchable databases containing billions of names. The links are organized by geographic location and by type of public record with helpful descriptions. They add new databases each day, and continually evaluate each link to determine if it's working. Their basic searches are free, and their Premium searches are pay-per-search databases, such as Criminal Records ($6.95 statewide, $14.95 national), Bankruptcy, Judgment & Tax Lien databases ($5.00).

More Free Public Record Sites - *FREE*
www.publicrecordsources.com
www.brbpub.com

Links to thousands of free public record sites in US listed by state and category (births, deaths, marriage, etc.), civil records, criminal records, driving records, real estate records, public record vendors, record retrievers, and more.

Ancestry.com - www.ancestry.com $

Ancestry has numerous databases, including: directories, public records, church, military, census, marriage records, etc. that you can search for your relatives. You can search for free, but you need a membership to view detailed records. Consider adding a life event (birth, marriage, etc.) to your search criteria and define a range of years (e.g. the last 10 or 20 years) to narrow down the hits.

PeopleFinders -

www.peoplefinders.com

Find people by name, phone number, address, or email. They search billions of records to help you easily locate people, retrieving results almost instantly. No sign up required to see a preview of actual records. $0.95/search or $14.95/month.

411Locate - www.411locate.com

A tool for locating the friends, family members, and acquaintances that you have lost touch with over the years. Initially formed with the intent of compiling all of the information found in Yellow Pages, White Pages, and Public Records.

PeopleTracer UK - FREE $

www.livingrelativesearch.co.uk

Ancestry.co.uk has added this new service to find living people in the UK, and is free for up to ten searches per day. The free searches provide "preview pages" that contain basic information sourced from the Edited Electoral Rolls, telephone directory records, land registry records and even Google Maps to provide up-to-date details of people's whereabouts. You'll see a preview with name, city/town and telephone number. The type of information that's available within the full results will also be displayed. If you want to access more detailed information and enjoy unlimited free result previews, you can purchase a credit package to suit your needs. £11.95-£29.95 ($18.75-$47.00)

USA People Search - $

www.usa-people-search.com

Includes current and past addresses, phone numbers, age, full names & aliases, and relatives. Premium Membership options include unlimited searches with public records regarding people, property, marriage, divorce, death and unclaimed money. $2.95 3-day trial, $24.95/ month

4. Check the Newspaper Archives

Obituaries may also include information about living relatives or other useful clues. You need to know the full name of the deceased person, approximate date of death and the place where the person passed away/lived at the time of death. *See 'How to Bring Your Ancestors to Life Using Newspapers' on page196.*

5. Create a Family Blog

A free family blog is a great and easy way to connect to and keep-in-touch-with your relatives. Extended family members can give

you valuable information about your family history and stories which in turn can be of major help when looking for lost living relatives. This also is an easy and efficient way to keep family members up-to-date on your findings.

You don't have to be a geek to create a simple blog or web page. Dozens of services will host it at no charge.

Making First Contact

When you decide to reach out to your newly discovered living relatives – whether by e-mail, phone, or in person – be prepared for any questions they may have. They may be suspicious of your motives at first. Fears of identity theft and scams are common. Make clear that this isn't a scam. Try to contact them in the least intrusive way as possible. And offer to provide them with copies of your research.

20 Tips to Help Keep You on the Right Track

Some practical Do's and Don'ts

The following suggestions may be helpful to keep you on the right track, and hopefully prevent misfortune when planting and growing your family tree. You need to be aware of some potential pitfalls (unforeseen or unexpected difficulties) when researching your family roots and stories. Here's some practical Do's and Don'ts for pulling everything together, saving you valuable time, and making your journey fun.

■ **Begin with yourself** and your parents

> Don't get sidetracked with multiple goals. Organize your overall search strategy and focus your efforts. Plan where you are going and keep track of where you have been.

and work backwards on your pedigree, building on the supporting evidence you find, one generation at a time. Research is usually not difficult, but it does require understanding the basics. Basics are easily learned, and, with experience, productive and efficient research will become easier. Don't overwhelm yourself by taking on too much all at once. Take baby steps. Focus on one small step at a time, like one single family, or a single surname in a particular place.

■ **It is important for you to understand the difference** between building your family tree through actual research in appropriate records vs. that of merely collecting names without supporting evidence to verify that your family tree is correct. Don't assume something is correct just because someone says so, or it's in print, or on the Internet. Verify it with documented research from multiple sources (when possible) for every name, date, and place in your records.

■ **Research is finding clues to lead you to records that prove relationships.** You build your case one or two facts at a time, and base continuing research on those proven facts. If the information you are working with is incorrect, then you are wasting your time. Do your research thoroughly as you go so that you can recognize your family among errors, misspellings, and various other imperfections.

■ **Create a time line** of your ancestor's life listing all events in chronological order to view the whole picture. Then, log your progress. Write down supporting evidence for each event in the time line and the source of the evidence to keep you from duplicating the research. Make a *To Do* list of information you are seeking and the records that are available for the Surname or location you are searching.

- **Realize that you will encounter spelling variations of names.** Assuming that there is only one way to spell your family name can cause you to bypass good information. Consider anything remotely close to the name you are looking for. And be alert for the use of initials and nicknames. The older the time period in which you are researching, the less consistent your ancestors were about the spelling of their surnames. Some of them may have been illiterate, and could not tell the record keeper how their names were spelled.

- **Don't assume that "Jr" and "Sr" are father and son.** Usually they are, but sometimes they are not. They may be uncle and nephew, grandfather and grandson, cousins, or even no relation. These are merely titles to distinguish an older man from a younger one with the same name. To add to the confusion, these titles shift as "Sr" dies and "Jr" becomes "Sr", and a younger person often becomes "Jr". Without sufficient research in official records, one cannot detect these changes and identities. It only takes one misidentification to cause you to spend years researching the wrong people.

- **Beware of compiled family data that does not support** documented names, dates, and places. Without evidence, one

Do NOT enter surnames (last names) in all uppercase letters into your database. Enter women using their maiden name. If you don't know their maiden name, just use their first given names, i.e. "Grandma" is not a first name. Do not use titles (Dr., Mrs., Mr., Colonel, Rev., etc.) in name fields, but you can enter suffixes like Jr., Sr., III, etc.

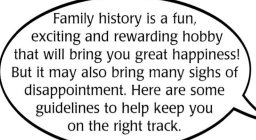

Family history is a fun, exciting and rewarding hobby that will bring you great happiness! But it may also bring many sighs of disappointment. Here are some guidelines to help keep you on the right track.

has nothing more than possible clues with which to try and find proof. However, even if existing Internet family trees contain likely errors, they may provide valuable clues – such as a date or place you had not known about – that can give you new ideas for searching.

- **Always note the source of any material you copy.** Obtain copies of your proof documents as you find them. Finding information from multiple sources strengthens your case if it agrees, or indicates the need for deeper research if it disagrees. Studying the documents periodically often reveals clues previously missed.

- You may often encounter **conflicting information** that you will have to weigh against other evidence. Try to determine which is the most likely to be true. Periodically review and verify the conclusions you have reached concerning each of your ancestor's lives; this will help to prevent wasting time following blind alleys.

- **Try not to let your organizing get behind.** Establish a filing system for your papers from the start (using file folders, 3-ring binders, and your computer) and file each page of notes, photocopy, etc. as you acquire it. It's disheartening to rummage through a high stack of unfiled papers to find that copy of a birth certificate you desperately need.

- **Don't assume modern meanings** for terms used to describe relationships. For example, in the 17th century a stepchild was often called a "son-in-law" or "daughter-in-law", and a "cousin" could refer to almost any relative except a sibling or child.

- **Remember that indexes** to books rarely include the names of all persons mentioned in the book and, moreover, occasionally contain errors. If it appears that a book is likely to have valuable information, spend some time skimming its contents rather than returning it immediately to the shelf after a quick look at the index.

- **Collaborate with others searching the same names.** Advertise the surnames you are researching by submitting them to genealogical directories and surname lists on the Internet, such as RootsWeb Surname List at http://rsl.rootsweb.com. This will put you in touch with others who are researching the same surnames.

- **Learn who the siblings of your ancestor were** because it can often lead to the desired information you need. Example: Perhaps a death record is not available for your grandmother, but if you have documents that prove who her siblings were, then maybe their death records might give parent information, etc. There might also be a biography about some of them that would give family background information. Knowing who the siblings and in-laws were can help sort out individuals with the same name.

- **Pay attention to your ancestor's neighbors,** witnesses to their legal transactions (marriages, deeds, etc.), guardians or godparents of their children, and other close associates. All persons in these categories may be potential relatives of your ancestor, and investigating them can provide clues for you to work with in developing your family tree. Your ancestors were part of networks of social acquaintances, business contacts, military comrades-in-arms, extended family, in-laws, neighbors, and, of course, family members. Use those

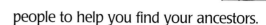

Make frequent backups of your computer disks. Consider long-term storage of all your computer information with a secure online, automatic-backup company, such as www.mozy.com or www.carbonite.com.

people to help you find your ancestors.

- ***Death records*** usually contain parent information and various other important data. Death records usually are found in the county in which death occurred. Examples would include death while traveling, visiting, hospitalized, in prison, etc. outside his or her county of residence. ***Probate records*** can prove family relationships that may be found nowhere else. If there was property to be distributed, probate records would be found in the person's county of residence. It's also possible that additional probate records might be found in other counties/ states where the deceased owned property.

- **Wills don't always mention all children** of a deceased person. Often a child has already been given property and it simply does not specify that in the Will. If the gift was real estate or other personal property, then there likely would be a deed. Wills are only a small part of probate records. Much, much more can be revealed in *estate records, inventories, bills of sale, administrator bonds, order books, etc.;* all heirs are likely to be named in estate settlements. Law suits among family members often occurred and these can be a goldmine of factual information on which to build. Knowing the names of siblings and in-laws helps you to recognize key people in the indexes. Develop your family group sheets so the information will be handy.

- **Don't assume that family stories are completely true;** often there is partial truth in them but details have become distorted through the years. A common one might be "great-great grandma was an Indian". Someone may have said "she looked like

> At times, if you feel like you're on your own in putting together your family history puzzle, remember that you're not alone. Your ancestors really are there pushing you in the right direction and cheering for you.

an Indian", or, "she might have been an Indian", or "she lived near Indians". Always seek out official records that can prove or disprove components of the story.

■ **Don't assume that children** in a pre-1880 census household (when relationships were stated) are children of the head of the household: They may or may not be. They may be nieces, nephews, step-children, grandchildren, or no relation. Study the ages and birthplaces of all household members. Other year's census records, probate, guardianships, deeds, etc. may help identify relationships and reveal the true children of the head of household. Understanding these relationships can be crucial to building your family tree and can unlock pieces of the puzzle. Census records through 1840 can be very helpful when analyzed with other records, but they can also be misleading if you insist on "accounting" for everyone; various circumstances affected household members.

The Greatest Happiness

Gordon B. Hinckley
© by Intellectual Reserve, Inc.

"God is the designer of the family. He intended that the greatest of happiness, the most satisfying aspects of life, the deepest joys should come in our associations together and our concerns one for another as fathers and mothers and children". Gordon B. Hinckley (1910-2008), American religious leader

Footprints On the Sands of Time

Henry David Thoreau

"The lives of great men all remind us we can make our lives sublime and departing leave behind us footprints on the sands of time." Henry David Thoreau, (1817-1862) American writer, philosopher and naturalist

We Can Take Comfort

M. Russell Ballard
© by Intellectual Reserve, Inc.

"No matter how difficult the trail…we can take comfort in knowing that others before us have borne life's most grievous trials and tragedies by looking to heaven."

M. Russell Ballard (1928-   ), businessman and religious leader

You Will Find a Way

Richard G. Scott
© by Intellectual Reserve, Inc.

"I don't need to tell you the details of where to go and who to see. When you determine you are going to succeed, you will find a way. You will discover those who can help you. I promise you the Lord will bless you in your efforts...and He will guide your... efforts to [find] your ancestors."

Richard G. Scott (1928-   )

3-Easy Steps
Follow These 3-Easy Steps to Build Your
Family Tree and Connect to Your Ancestors

STEP 2 – Make New Discoveries

Add New Branches to Your Family Tree

Help From beyond the Veil 2

Computers, technology, and the Internet have revolutionized the way we do family history and genealogy today. We can search farther and faster than ever before, and we can record everything we find with just a few keystrokes. Computers allow us to discover, store, access, and share family history information with speed and convenience.

The Internet is an excellent and powerful tool for you to gather your family history information and share it with others. It's made up of millions of sites which are just files stored on computers around the world. Each site can contain any number of associated pages – each of which has an unique electronic address, i.e. *about.com.* It's estimated that more than two million separate web sites are devoted to genealogy / family history.

Family History Insights - 2

Decide to Do Something Significant

"Set aside those things that don't really matter in your life. Decide to do something that will have eternal consequences. Perhaps you have been prompted to look for ancestors but feel that you are not a genealogist. Can you see that you don't have to be anymore? It all begins with love and a sincere desire. ... This is...a monumental effort of cooperation on both sides of the veil where help is given in both directions. It begins with love. Anywhere you are in the world, with prayer, faith, determination, diligence, and some sacrifice, you can make a powerful contribution. Begin now. I promise you that the Lord will help you find a way. And it will make you feel wonderful." Richard Scott

Richard G. Scott
© by Intellectual Reserve, Inc.

2 Make New Discoveries

Finding Joy in Family History

"Thirty-five years ago I was... in England. My mother had been pursuing her grandmother's family history, but she knew nothing more than that her grandmother had been born in a little place called Philly Green, England. My mother had never been able to locate this town. ... As I was driving...I saw a little sign that said "Philly Green." Several weeks later, I returned and drove down a winding country lane until I came to a quaint little village with a church that had been built in 1174. I went out into the cemetery and looked at each headstone. During the next few hours, I had the privilege of finding the headstones of my great-grandmother's family members. I'll never forget how I felt that day standing in that cemetery in that beautiful place in England. I felt a connection with my ancestors, particularly with my great-grandmother, who as a seventeen-year-old girl left her family in England and moved to [America]. What a great experience! This kind of joy really can come to every[one]." Monte J. Brough

Monte J. Brough
© by Intellectual Reserve, Inc.

Creating Memories

"Each day of our lives we make deposits in the memory banks of our children." Charles R. Swindol,

pastor of the First Evangelical Free Church of Fullerton, California (1971-1994); radio host for *Insight for Living;* www.oneplace.com

Nature's Masterpiece

"The family is one of nature's masterpieces." "Those who cannot remember the past are condemned to repeat it." George Santayana (1863-1952), Philosopher & poet.

George Santayana

Tend Your Roots

A family tree can wither if nobody tends it's roots. Unknown

Become Acquainted with Ancestors

"It doesn't matter whether your computer is able to compile all the family group sheets for everyone that every lived on the earth, it remains the responsibility of each individual to know his kindred dead...[it is] each person's responsibility to study and become acquainted with his ancestors." J. Fielding Smith

J. Fielding Smith
© by Intellectual Reserve, Inc.

Lemons and Bad Apples

Any family tree produces lemons, nuts, and a few bad apples. Unknown

A Tree Without Roots

"To forget one's ancestors is to be a brook without a source, a tree without a root." – Chinese Proverb

Digging in Dirt/Facts

The difference between a geologist and a genealogist is that one digs in the dirt and sometimes finds artifacts, while the other digs in facts and sometimes finds dirt. – Unknown

Jump Start Your Family Tree

When you're tracing your family roots and stories, why re-plow a field that has already been plowed? You are most likely not the only nor the first person searching for and building your family tree. So see if someone has already found information on your ancestors. You can save yourself hours of work, verify information that you already know, make connections between generations, and help you determine which ancestors to search for. Most web sites allow free searches, but some may require a fee or just to register. If you don't have a computer or an Internet connection at home, you can use one at a Family History Center, or your local library or university.

Some of the most useful websites offer invaluable databases of existing family trees, vital information and transcribed census records, such as _FamilySearch.org_ and _Ancestry.com_; others are collections of links to other sites, such as _Cyndi'sList.com_ and _Linkpendium.com_; some are more specific with genealogies from people or about a specific group of people, such as _GenServ.com_ and _AfriGeneas.com_; others offer useful data such as land records, like _The Bureau of Land Management (BLM.gov)_, and some specifically help you to learn how to do family history, such as _DearMYRTLE.com_ and _Genealogy.About.com_.

We are living in exciting times because old records are being indexed to electronic formats at an ever increasing rate. This is changing family history dramatically. An enormous number of old records still exist which are very difficult to research right now because they have not been digitized, but sometime in the future essentially all old records will be converted to electronic

formats. This means that we will most likely be able to connect with ancestors and solve family history problems in the near future that may still be very difficult today.

Many people think that family history is nothing more than a hunt for an already completed family tree.

2 Make New **Discoveries**

How Reliable Is the Information Found in Online Family Trees?

Some may think that their family tree already exists. Something like... "I'm double-parked. Can you please quickly give me my family tree?"

Of course, that's a fantasy and an unrealistic expectation. But millions of existing family trees are on the Internet and growing, and your chances of locating quality information – for at least a portion of your family tree online – are better than you might think. Check out the many fine family tree resources below.

However, common sense tells you that the information freely uploaded to the online databases may or may not be substantiated, or of questionable validity. For example, the handwriting of previous centuries, even where documents have been well preserved, is often difficult to read and may have been transcribed incorrectly.

You need to regard the online family tree data as a clue or a starting point for further research, verification and documentation. For this reason, you should never just download a family file you find online and add it directly to your own research without first verifying the accuracy of the information.

First, Search Existing Family Trees Online

There are many wonderful web sites with existing family tree databases to help you determine if someone has already found information on your ancestor. These are valuable 'lineage-linked' or pedigree databases linking each generation together. Think of them as numerous pedigree charts connected together that people submit to the database using many different sources of data and images.

FamilySearch FamilyTree -

www.familysearch.org

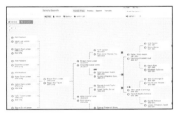

Free family history, family tree, genealogy records and resources from around the world. A web site that provides access to the world's largest collection of free family history information all in one

> Here's a tip when searching family trees online.

Be sure to track the footnotes and sources if they are included in the online family trees you find. These sources often lead to additional information about your ancestors and also help you evaluate its accuracy.

5 Steps to Verify Online Sources

http://genealogy.about.com/od/basics/a/verifying.htm

Read Kimberly Powell's steps about how to verify online family history information.

> Many who have built family trees on the Ancestry.com Web site have been frustrated about not being able to export or download their family tree (including images, documents, historical records, etc.) to their computer.

How to Export Your Family Tree from Ancestry.com

To download a family tree from Ancestry.com online family trees, you must be the owner of that tree. Open the Family Tree Pedigree View of your tree on Ancestry.com. Just above the dark green header, on the right side, click on the link for "Tree Settings" and you see your "Tree Info". On the right side is a section for "Export your tree"; click on the light green button for "Export tree", and Ancestry will prepare your GEDCOM file for downloading to your computer. If you want to save your file to your desktop or a file folder on your computer, click "Save". You can import the GEDCOM file into your own database later using your family history software.

place—from U.S. census data to the parish records of tiny European villages. It's a powerful computer software system to help you learn about your ancestors. You can do significant research online and also discover what records you need to search to find your ancestors in record-breaking time. It provides easy access for the gathering and sharing of family history information. *See more information in Chapter 5.*

FamilySearch Community Trees -

http://histfam.familysearch.org *FREE*

Community Trees are genealogies from specific periods and localities that have been linked according to family lineages. Many trees include associated documents and images. Each community tree is a searchable database that allows views of individuals, families, ancestors, and descendants and gives various options for printing. *See more information on page 257.*

To use these comprehensive Web sites and indexes, think about what you know about a specific ancestor or surname and then look in the appropriate categories.

Research Tip

If you are trying to find information on a Quaker couple married in Virginia in 1766, you could look in categories for marriages, Virginia, Quakers, or Colonial records. They can also help locate information about an ancestor's culture, traditions, homeland, and history.

Rootsweb WorldConnect - FREE
http://wc.rootsweb.ancestry.com

Rootsweb WorldConnect is a free collection of user-submitted GEDCOMs (family trees). The database contains more than 710 million names in family trees submitted by users.

Ancestry has over 5 billion names in more than 50 million family trees. They can help you identify how ancestors are related and give you clues about birth, marriage, and death information. You can expect to find names, ages, places, dates, family relationships, and more. You can also often find contact information for someone researching the same name.

Ancestry Private Member Trees -
824 million, updated Mar 2009 $

This database contains family trees submitted to Ancestry by users who have indicated that their tree can only be viewed by Ancestry members to whom they have granted permission to see their tree. These trees can change over time as users edit, remove, or otherwise modify the data in their trees. If you would like to view one of these trees in its entirety, you can contact the owner of the tree to request permission to see the tree.

Ancestry Public Member Trees - $

2.1 billion updated Mar 2009

This database con-tains family trees

submitted to Ancestry by users who have indicated that their tree can be viewed by all Ancestry members. You can contact the owner of the tree to get more information.

Ancestry Millennium File - $
921k updated irregularly

A database created by the Institute of Family Research that contains linked family records with lineages from throughout the world, including colonial America, the British Isles, Switzerland, and Germany. Many of these lineages extend back to nobility and renowned historical figures. A good way to have success in using this database is identify at least one Gateway Ancestor, an early American immigrant who has been identified as having roots in British or European nobility. In this database there are about 300 individuals who have proven ties to nobility or royalty. Source information is also provided making it easier to verify the accuracy of the research done.

MyHeritage World Tree - $
www.myheritage.com

A large, multinational site that focuses on connecting families, through family tree website building, photo storage, and tools for discovering and connecting with distant relatives. They have over 72 million paid members and offer more than 27 million family trees, containing 1.5 billion people. Their Record Detective™ technology helps generate new findings and discoveries from your family tree dead-ends.

WeRelate.org - www.werelate.org FREE

A free public-service wiki for genealogy offering a large wiki with pages for over 2,400,000 people with a unified family tree containing the best information from all contributors.

Make New Discoveries 2

GenCircles Global Tree - $

www.gencircles.com/globaltree

A popular place for searching and submitting family trees. Surnames from over 90 million ancestors can be searched for free, and if you've submitted your own GEDCOM file you can use their "matching technology" to pair the people in your pedigree with those already on file.

One Great Family.com - $

www.onegreatfamily.com

A family history program that allows everyone to combine their knowledge and data to build one huge, shared database. Using sophisticated, patented technology, OneGreatFamily is linking all of the family trees together into one shared, worldwide database with shared multimedia, notes, research, biographies and citations. They have about 241 million linked names. 7-day free trial. $14.95/month.

MyTrees.com - $

www.mytrees.com

Contains a pedigree-linked database with over 370 million names, share your family tree world wide, build your own family tree on-line, and store family history pictures online for display with your family tree. 31-day free trial. $10/10 days.

Geni.com - www.geni.com FREE $

Using their basic free service, you can create a small tree and share an unlimited number of photos, videos, and documents with your families. A paid sub-

scription allows you to find matching trees and merge those into the single world family tree, which currently contains over 70 million living users and their ancestors. Additional pay services include enhanced research tools and premium support.

Geneanet - www.geneanet.org $

A French pedigree database in 9 different languages with about 2 million members and more than 400 million entries in their Family Trees, Archival Records, Indexes, and Family Pictures. It is useful for searching family trees from continental Europe. Membership offers enhanced search options and other features, but the family trees can all be searched and accessed free of charge. A handy e-mail alert notifies you when new trees are added that match your criteria.

GenesReunited - FREE $

www.genesreunited.co.uk

A UK site where you can register free and search over 787 million names in over 13 million trees to see if anyone has information about the people you are looking for. Pay-per-view £5.00 (about $8)/50 credits.

WikiTree - www.wikitree.com FREE

A free, collaborative project to create a single worldwide family tree with over 5 million profiles.

Family Tree Searcher.com - FREE

www.familytreesearcher.com

Enter your ancestor information just once to search existing family trees at nine online family tree data-bases.

Next, Find Vital and Civil Records

Records of births, marriages, deaths, divorces and adoptions kept by most countries are one of the best resources for helping you build your family tree. Death records are especially helpful because they may provide important information on a person's birth, spouse, and parents. Some researchers look first for death records because there are often death records for persons who have no birth or marriage records.

Best Resources for Vital Records	
State & County Archives	page 190
Newspapers (& Obituaries)	page 196
Cemeteries & Obituaries	page 208
Court, Property & Probate Records	page 213

Search the U.S. Social Security Death Index

https://familysearch.org/search/collection/list

https://familysearch.org/learn/wiki/en/United_States_Social_Security_Death_Index_(FamilySearch_Historical_Records)[photos: social security 3&4]

Contains information about persons whose deaths were reported to the Social Security Administration from about 1935 through current. The majority of the death records are from 1962 and later. It provides birth and death dates and identifies the person's last place of residence and the place the death payment was sent. The Social Security number and the state of residence when the Social Security number was issued are also provided.

This index currently contains vital statistics for over 93 million deceased individuals. A number of websites provide the database.

https://familysearch.org/search/collection/1202535

https://familysearch.org/learn/wiki/en/United_States_Social_Security_Death_Index_(FamilySearch_Historical_Records)

www.genealogybank.com/gbnk/ssdi

http://ssdi.rootsweb.ancestry.com

http://search.ancestry.com/search/db.aspx?dbid=3693

http://stevemorse.org/ssdi/ssdi.html

Then, Search for a Family History That has Been Published

Published family histories are usually books that give genealogical information about one or more generations of a particular family. Currently, FamilySearch has over 100,000 digitized family history publications available online and growing.

Libraries and genealogical societies have been collecting published family histories for years. You can often find family histories in libraries in the area where your ancestors lived. Your family's stories might be among them. Compiled stories and histories can be an amazing source of information about the lives of your ancestors. They provide stories and interesting information that help you really connect with your ancestors.

10 Places to Find a Published Genealogy -

www.familytreemagazine.com/article/finda-published-genealogy

A FamilyTree Magazine article about where to search for a published genealogy.

 Backwards Progress

Only a genealogist regards a step backwards as progress. Unknown

 Invited to Great Things

"He is invited to great things who receives small things greatly." Cassiodorus (c. 485 - c. 585), Roman statesman, writer

Cassiodorus

Published Family Histories Online

Published family histories are usually books that give genealogical information about one or more generations of a particular family. Search these resources for published histories.

Name	Address	Description
FamilySearch Family History Library	www.familysearch.org >Search >Books **FREE** https://familysearch.org/catalog-search	Family, society, county, and town histories. Nearly a million publications in its library, and is working with many affiliate libraries to create the largest digital collection of published histories on the Web.
Internet Archive	http://archive.org **FREE** http://archive.org/mediatypesbrowse.php?mediatype=texts	A digital library offering about 3m public domain books. Free to read, download, print, and enjoy.
Allen County Public Library	www.genealogycenter.org **FREE**	One of the largest research collections available, with records from around the world: over 350k printed volumes, over 513k items of microfilm and microfich, and over 55k volumes of compiled genealogies.
Ancestry	www.ancestry.com > Stories, Memories, History Collection **$**	A collection of histories that profile families from all fifty U.S. states, Canada, and the British Isles going back to the 1700s.
BYU Library	http://sites.lib.byu.edu/familyhistory http://lib.byu.edu/digital **FREE**	Includes histories of families, county and local histories, how-to books on genealogy, genealogy magazines and periodicals, medieval books, and gazetteers.
Clayton Library for Genealogical Research	www2.houstonlibrary.org/clayton **FREE**	One of the top Genealogy Research Libraries in the United States containing about 100k books, 3k periodical titles, 70k microfilm, and numerous electronic databases
Mid-Continent Public Library	www.mymcpl.org/genealogy **FREE**	A wealth of resources for genealogy.
Library of Congress	www.loc.gov/rr/genealogy **FREE** http://memory.loc.gov/ammem/index.html	One of the world's premier collections of U.S. and foreign genealogical and local historical featuring more than 50k genealogies and 100k local histories.
Genealogy Branches	www.genealogybranches.com/countyhistories.html **FREE**	Online County Histories, Biographies and Indexes

Name	Address	Description
HeritageQuest Online	www.heritagequestonline.com > Search Books **FREE**	Over 23k family and local histories. See if your library subscribes; you can use your library card at home to access the Web site.
Google Books	http://books.google.com **FREE**	Find millions of great books you can preview or read for free. If the book is out of copyright, or the publisher has given permission, you'll be able to see a preview of the book, and in some cases the entire text. If it's in the public domain, you're free to download a PDF copy.
Open Library	http://openlibrary.org **FREE**	Seeks to include a web page for every book ever published. It holds 23m catalog records of books, in addition to the full text of about 1.6m public domain books, which may be read and downloaded.
Online Books	http://onlinebooks.library.upenn.edu **FREE**	Over 1 million free books online.
Genealogical Book Links	http://genealogybook-links.com **FREE**	Links to digital biographies, histories, and history books organized alphabetical and by state and subject.
LDS Church History Library	http://churchhistorycatalog.lds.org **FREE**	Access to records and images of people, places, and events in LDS Church (Mormon) history.
Cyndi's List	www.cyndislist.com/us/state-level-records-repositories **FREE**	Extensive links to state libraries, archives, genealogical and historical societies.
UK Dictionary of National Biography	www.oxforddnb.com **$** $29.95/month	The national record of those who have shaped British history and culture from the Romans to the 21st century. It offers some 60k books and over 11k images of concise, up-to-date biographies.
WeRelate	www.werelate.org **FREE**	A large genealogy wiki with pages for over 2.4m people and growing.
Making of America	http://quod.lib.umich.edu/m/moagrp **FREE**	A digital library of primary sources in American social history containing about 10k books and 50k journal articles.
Paper Trail	www.paper-trail.org **$** $19.95/month	The 19th Century migration on the overland trails to the far West is illuminated by the writings of thousands of pioneers who took this long and dangerous journey.
Linkpendium	www.linkpendium.com **FREE**	A directory of more than 10m genealogy links by location and surname.
1000 Years of Family History	www.broughfamily.org/family_history_video.html **FREE** www.youtube.com/view_playlist?p=BD2585B808562AAB	Video documentary on 1000 years of history of a well-known family surname in England.

Make New 2 Discoveries

What is a Family History Center?

Typical Family History Center

Family History Centers are local branches of the Family History Library located in Salt Lake City, Utah, and there are some 4,600 centers worldwide. The library houses a collection of genealogical records that includes the names of more than 3 billion deceased people. It is the largest collection of its kind in the world, including: vital records (birth, marriage, and death records from both government and church sources); census returns; court, property, and probate records; cemetery records; emigration and immigration lists; printed genealogies; and family and county histories.

Since many people are not able to travel to Salt Lake City to use the library, local Family History Centers make the library's resources accessible to those interested in finding their family roots. They enable you to research the vast holdings of the library including its computerized indexes.

Free Website Access

In addition to FamilySearch.org, Family History Centers also offer access to the following popular subscription or fee-based websites for free.

> www.Fold3.com
> Godfrey Memorial Library - www.Godfrey.org
> www.WorldVitalRecords.com
> www.HeritageQuestOnline.com
> www.Ancestry.com

Join thousands of volunteers around the world who are helping to make more free records available online through www.FamilySearch Indexing.org.

Everyone is welcome at a Family History Center at no cost to use their resources. When you want to look at actual records of the people you are researching, you can visit the Family History Center nearest you and order copies of the records from the main library in Salt Lake City. They provide friendly, knowledgeable volunteers at the centers to assist you without cost or obligation.

To locate the nearest family history center, click on: www.familysearch.org, then click on: *Get Help > In-Person Help Find a Family History Center;* or you may call 1-800-346-6044 in the United States and Canada.

Free Research Outlines

http://sites.lib.byu.edu/familyhistory/research_outlines

Years ago, FamilySearch developed dozens of valuable Research Outlines on different topics to help you in the process of researching your family tree. They were published for decades, and provided detailed instructions in genealogical techniques, research strategies, and listed the best resources to use in family history research. Although the printed guides are out-of-print and in the process of being updated which will be available in FamilySearch Wiki, the current Outlines are still available for free online as PDFs. And they are still valuable because they contain enormous amounts of information and resources. They are specific for most countries, US states, and selected topics.

Geographical (by country and state)

Africa	Latin America
Asia	Pacific & Polynesia
British	IslesCanada
Europe	Scandinavia
United States	

Selected Topics

Jewish Genealogy	Native American
Quaker Genealogy	Tracing Immigrant Origins
Tracing LDS Families	US Military Records

Where to Search Chart (Types of Records)

OBJECTIVE	RECORD TYPES	
To obtain information about the following...	Look in the Family History Library Catalog, Locality and Subject sections for these type of records...	
	First look for:	**Then look for:**
Age	Census, Vital Records, Cemeteries	Military Records, Taxation, Obituaries
Birth date	Vital Records, Church Records, Bible Records	Cemeteries, Obituaries, Census, Newspapers, Military Records
Birthplace	Vital Records, Church Records, Census	Newspapers, Obituaries, Military Records
City or parish of foreign birth	Church Records, Genealogy, Biography, Obituaries, Naturalization & Citizenship	Emigration and Immigration, Vital Records*, History
Country of foreign birth	Census, Emigration and Immigration, Naturalization and Citizenship, Vital Records*	Military Records, Church Records, Newspapers, Obituaries
County origins & boundaries	History, Maps	Gazetteers
Death	Vital Records, Cemeteries, Probate Records, Church Records, Obituaries	Newspapers, Military Records, Court Records, Land and Property
Divorce	Court Records, Divorce Records	Newspapers, Vital Records*
Ethnicity	Minorities, Native Races, Societies	Church Records, Emigration and Immigration, Naturalization and Citizenship
Historical background	History, Periodicals, Genealogy	Church History, Minorities
Immigration	Emigration & Immigration, Naturalization & Citizenship, Genealogy	Census, Biography, Newspapers, Church Records
Maiden	Vital Records, Church Records, Newspapers, Bible Records	Military Records, Cemeteries, Probate Records, Obituaries
Marriage	Vital Records, Church Records, Census, Newspapers, Bible Records	Biography, Genealogy, Military Records, Probate Records, Land and Property, Nobility
Occupation	Census, Directories, Emigration and Immigration, Civil Registration, Occupations, Probate Records	Newspapers, Court Records, Obituaries, Officials and Employees
Parents, children, & other family members	Vital Records, Church Records, Census, Probate Records, Obituaries	Bible Records, Newspapers, Emigration and Immigration, Land and Property
Physical description	Military Records, Biography, Court Records	Naturalization, Civil Registration, Church Records, Emigration & Immigration, Genealogy, Newspapers
Place-finding aids	Gazetteers, Maps	Directories, History, Periodicals, Land & Property, Taxation
Place of residence when you know only the state	Census, Genealogy, Military Records, Vital Records, Church Records, Directories	Biography, Probate Records, History, Land and Property, Taxation
Places family has lived	Census, Land and Property, History	Military Records, Taxation, Obituaries
Previous research	Genealogy, Periodicals, History	Biography, Societies, Nobility
Record-finding aids	Archives and Libraries, Societies, Genealogy	Periodicals
Religion	Church Records, History, Biography, Civil Reg.	Bible Records, Cemeteries, Obituaries, Genealogy

2 Make New Discoveries

© 2001 Intellectual Reserve, Inc.

Find Your Ancestors Using Census Records

Census Records

A Unique Snapshot of Your Ancestors, and a Building Block of Your Research

Beginning in 1790, federal censuses were taken in the United States every decade. They cover most of the population. The census has proven to be a great resource for family historians. There are few other records that help you track your ancestors throughout their lifetime. They can place entire families at a specific point in time, help establish family relationships, and are one of the best sources to explore.

You also use the U.S. census to identify the country of birth for your immigrant ancestor, and birthplaces of all family members. Use these birthplaces and ages to trace where the family lived and when. There is a 72-year privacy cap on census and military records so the records that are now available for research span the years 1790-1940.

From 1790 to 1840, the census takers asked few questions, thus limiting the value these records have for us today. Starting in 1850, however, more

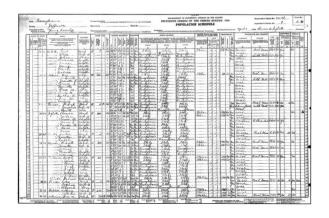

information was gathered by the census takers. For example, enumerators listed the names, ages, and gender for all persons living in the house, whereas prior censuses only listed the heads of household.

After 1850 censuses also identify an individual's country of birth. Beginning in 1880 censuses identify the country of birth for the individual's parent. From 1900 to 1930 censuses list the year the individual immigrated to the United States. The 1870, 1900, 1920, and 1930 censuses indicate whether the individual was a naturalized citizen of the United States. The 1920 census identifies the year of naturalization. The census records are searchable by name, birth year, city and more.

One of the basics of family history research is to start with yourself and work backward in time, moving from the known to the unknown. So you may want to consider starting your search with the most current 1940 census. For questions about the US 1940 census go to http://1940census.archives.gov/faq.

Overview of the U.S. Census -
www.ancestry.com/wiki/index.php?title=Overview_of_the_U.S._Census

Ancestry.com interesting article about census background, uses of, strengths, limitations, problems, etc.

AccessGenealogy - www.accessgenealogy.com

A free search center that offers links for searching many different types of records, such as census reports, newspapers, periodicals, emigration and immigration forms, vital records, voting records, military records, Native American genealogy, library archives, cemeteries, churches, and courts; plus Native American and African American essentials. It includes tons of links to other web sites.

Census Web Sites

Ancestry.com - www.ancestry.com $

> *Search* > *Census and Voter Lists*

This site offers all of the US, Canadian, and UK census records available. It also provides links to selected State census records, Mortality Schedules, Slave Schedules, Veterans Schedules, Indian Census Rolls, and more. Free access to the1940 Census. The information details more than just names or population numbers. It includes people's moves across the country, their race, marital status, assets, residence, schooling and other personal information. The 1890 census was largely destroyed in a fire, but they have compiled a "substitute" with various other records (e.g. veterans schedules) to help bridge the gap. Canadian census records include the schedules for 1851-1916. Preview available for free, but you must subscribe to see any details. $22.95/month. Free at some Family History Centers.

Archives.com - www.archives.com/census $

This site is owned and operated by Ancestry.com and also provides the complete US census schedules. 7-day free trial, $7.95/month.

FamilySearch - www.familysearch.org

> *Search* > *Browse All Published Collections* **FREE**

FamilySearch provides *free* family history, family tree, and genealogy records and resources from around the world, including census records. Many new and updated census records become available regularly with increasing frequency with many on-going indexing projects by 170,000 volunteers. The historical record collections are updated frequently as new records are indexed or digitized. In addition to census records, you can also search other worldwide record collections (birth, death, marriage, pension, church, tax, military, baptism, christening, burial, funeral, and civil registration records). Millions of new records are being added every month. Find out more at www.familysearchindexing.org.

When you are looking through the Historical Record Collections and are looking at a collection list (e.g. census records), you will see some collections with a camera icon next to the collection and some without the camera icon. The camera icon tells you that this record collection has digitized images of each record within that collection. If no icon is shown, the images are currently not available but will be in the future.

To the right of the collection title, you will see either the words 'Browse Images' or you will see a number. If you see a number, that means the collection has been indexed and that the number indicates how many records are in the collection. If you see the words Browse Images, this means that the collection has not been indexed yet. But the images are grouped together according to locality, record type, and year range. This makes it so you don't have to look through the entire collection, but can narrow your search the time and place you are interested in searching.

HeritageQuestOnline - **FREE**

www.heritagequestonline.com

Contains U.S. Census indexes and images, but only indexes "Head of Household". It is available free through your local library if they subscribe (you can log-on at home) with your library card.

World Vital Records.com - $

www.worldvitalrecords.com

Many countries took periodic censuses to keep track of various aspects of the population. Where available, these records often include helpful details about your ancestors and their families and allow you to pinpoint their location at a particular point in time. You can now search all of the US census records with ease on this site, as well as other selected countries, such as: England, Wales, Canada, and Australia. $16.25/month, $89.99/year.

Make New Discoveries 2

MyHeritage - www.myheritage.com

MyHeritage has the complete set of US census records from 1790 to 1940, with a total of 650 million names. You can also search their vast collection of UK records from England and Wales.

They recently added all England and Wales Census records between 1841 and 1901. Free access to the1940 US Census.

Find My Past - www.findmypast.com

They offer a complete set of US, UK, Australian, New Zealand, and Irish census, military, land, newspaper,

vital records, and more. Their census, land, and substitute records currently total over 906 million. Free access to the US 1940 Census. Search for free, but subscribe to view records. Pay-as-You-Go $13.95/100 credits, $5/month (1-year subscription) for US, $16.66/month (1-year subscription) for world records. Free at some Family History Centers.)

CensusRecords.com -
www.censusrecords.com

This is a FindMyPast website with identical records. Free access to the1940 Census. Search for free, but subscribe to view records. Pay-as-You-Go $7.95/1000 credits, $12.95/month, $34.95/year.

2 Make New Discoveries

Top 10 Search Tips for Census - FREE
http://genealogy.about.com/od/census/a/census_search.htm

Kimberly Powell has compiled some good census search tips that you need to read. Many new and updated census records are becoming available regularly with increasing frequency due to on-going indexing projects, and are now available mostly on FamilySearch.org and Ancestry.com.

Links to State Census Records Census Online.com - www.census-online.com FREE
https://familysearch.org/learn/wiki/en/United_States_Census

Links to all US state and Canadian province census records.

Free US Census Forms - FREE
www.ancestry.com/download/Forms

These US, UK, and Canada free census extraction forms allow you to see the format and column headings

One of the most well-known uses of Soundex indexes is for some of the federal censuses of the US.

Searching Census Records

Not all of our ancestors appear in Soundex indexes because they could have been overlooked or misread by the Soundex indexer, or the enumerator may have misspelled the person's name so badly that the Soundex was thrown off. These old microfilm indexes have been largely replaced today by online search engines. Although census records exist in Europe, Africa, Asia, and Latin America, they generally do not have indexes as do US census records.

for various census years, and provide a convenient method for extracting and filing important information you find. You can also view what information is available for each census schedule.

Year-by-Year Census Questions - *FREE*

www.census.gov/history/www/through_the_decades/index_of_questions

Through the decades, the census has collected data on personal information, residency, employment, education, military, nativity and citizenship. An examination of the questions asked during each census illustrates changes in our nation's understanding of race, the impact of immigration, growth of the Hispanic population, and computer usage. If you have any questions about the 1940 census go to http://1940census.archives.gov/faq.

Census Ancestry Map - *FREE*

www.census.gov/population/www/cen2000/census atlas/pdf/9_Ancestry.pdf

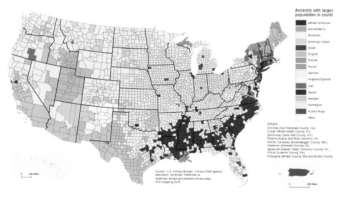

The question about ancestry first appeared on the census form in 1980 which allowed respondents to give attributions of their "ancestry or ethnic origin" and enabled people to identify an ethnic background, such as: German, English, Italian, etc. This PDF (15mb) is a series of maps of the US which shows the results (the most frequently reported ancestry) by geography (city, county, state, region). It is interesting to see the geographic patterns of ancestry even though the largest immigrations occurred many decades ago.

For some ancestries, continuity in geographic distribution is very evident. For instance, in 1900

Norwegians were a large share of the population in Wisconsin, Minnesota, and the Dakotas. One hundred years later, census data in 2000 still indicated high percentages of Norwegian ancestry in these states population. Look for the geographic distribution of your ancestry.

Genealogy.com -

www.genealogy.com/genealogy/uscensustxt_popup.html

Detailed introductory summary of each U.S. Census 1790-1930 (not 1940).

U.S. Census Bureau.gov - www.census.gov

Census dates for countries and areas of the world. Shows the dates of census enumerations over the past half century, as well as projected or scheduled enumerations in the near future for countries around the world. Also view an enhanced U.S. and world population clock.

Census Links.com - www.censuslinks.com

Links to worldwide census records.

Census research is usually very rewarding and provides a snapshot of an individual or a household at a specific time and place in history.

Census Tutorial

It can also be frustrating if you don't understand how to effectively search the census. Learn how to search the census and acquire valuable tips to ensure your success using the article found on page 83.

using the article found on page 83.

2 Make New Discoveries

Search Immigration & Nationalization Records

Immigration

Immigration (coming in), Emigration (exiting) Naturalization (rights of citizenship), & Migration (moving)

If you don't know your ancestor's name, start with a more recent generation. Records of recent ancestors usually lead to records of earlier generations.

Remember, your ancestor's name may not be listed the same way in all records. Look for variations. When using online family trees, if footnotes and sources are given, copy them onto your research log. These may lead to additional information about your ancestor.

Historical Background

Millions of people have immigrated to America from all over the world. Historians estimate that fewer than one million immigrants crossed the Atlantic during the 17th and 18th centuries. And over half of all *European* immigrants to Colonial America during the 17th and 18th centuries arrived as *indentured servants* – a person who was placed under contract to work for another over a period of time, usually seven years, especially during the 17th to 19th centuries.

In the early years, immigration was fewer than 8,000 people a year. After 1820, immigration increased. From 1836 to 1914, over 30 million Europeans migrated to the United States. The death rate on the transatlantic voyages was high, during which one-in-seven travelers died.

In 1875, the nation passed its first immigration law, followed by the Emergency Quota Act in 1921, and the Immigration Act of 1924 aimed at restricting the Europeans, who were entering the country in large numbers beginning in the 1890s.

Emigration records list the names of people leaving, and immigration records list those coming into the United States. There are passenger lists for ships coming into the US and border-crossing records of people leaving Canada or Mexico for the United States.

These immigration and naturalization records tell the story of your ancestor making that life-changing decision to immigrate and become an American citizen. Earlier immigration records typically don't contain as much detail, but 20th century immigration records can be very rich in detail, including the names and addresses of other family members, in both the old country and new. Some of the details you may find in immigration records include: emigrant's name, age, occupation, destination, place of birth or last residence in their country of origin, names of other relatives, immigration details, and in some cases, photographs.

The resources herein document the journey of your immigrant ancestor and their steps towards becoming a citizen of their new country. They include passenger ship records, border crossings, immigration and emigration records, passports, and naturalization records.

Indentured Servants Database

www.pricegen.com/immigrantservants/search/simple.php

This ongoing project aims to identify all indentured servant immigrants in American and European sources from 1607-1820. To date, there are over 20k immigrant servants listed in the database.

Historical Immigration Trends

 There are more than 100 different ethnic backgrounds among America's population today, and not every group immigrated at the same time. Here are some general historical trends than may affect the direction of your family history research. Each period brought distinct national groups, races and ethnicities to the United States.

Time Period	General Historical Immigration Trends
1500's-1776: Colonial Period	English, African, Spanish, French, Dutch, German, Welsh, Finnish, Scottish, and Scotch-Irish
1776-1820	Continuation of the same groups but in decreasing numbers due to wars and early attempts at immigration restriction.
1820-1880	Catholic Irish, German, Norwegian, Swedish, Danish, Chinese, Japanese, French Canadian
1880-1920	Italian, Polish, Austrian, Czech, Slovak, Yugoslav, Romanian, Russian, Hungarian, Greek, Arabs, Jews and Japanese
1920-1945	German, Italian, Polish, Czech, British, Irish, Canadian and Mexico, plus refugees from Nazi Germany
1945-today	Canadian, Mexican, Central & South American, Caribbean, Korean, Vietnamese, Laotian, Cambodian, Middle Easter Arab, Soviet Jewish

Early Colonization

Two main regions of early colonization were New England and Virginia. Nearly all of 14,000 pre-1624 Virginia settlers came from the London area.

England's Civil War of 1642-1649 and the subsequent Interregnum years up to 1660 significantly impacted the New World settlements. Royalists, at the be-heading of King Charles I, fled England and found refuge in the Virginia Colony.

Because King Charles' war-like campaigns so terrorized the Nonconformists (i.e. Puritans), it likewise caused thousands to flee England for Leyden, Holland and North America.

Plymouth Colony, created in 1620, by English Separatists (Pilgrims), had by 1650, become populated with numerous Puritans and other English Nonconformists who crossed the ocean seeking religious freedom.

The First Thanksgiving at Plymouth (1914)
By Jennie A. Brownscombe

The Massachusetts Bay Colony began around this period, with its first inhabitants who came from counties Devonshire, Dorset and Somerset. Later, during the Civil War, this colony was comprised of emigrant 'refugees' from England's cradle of Puritanism – counties Suffolk, Norfolk, Cambridgeshire, NW Essex and east Hertfordshire.

Make New 2 Discoveries

Tracing Immigrant Origins - (FREE)

https://familysearch.org/learn/wiki/en/Tracing_Immigrant_Origins

http://net.lib.byu.edu/fslab/researchoutlines/NonGeographic/TracingImmigrantOrigins.pdf

FamilySearch Wiki pages and a *Research Outline* (133-page PDF) from FamilySearch (essentially the same info in different formats) introduces the principles, search strategies, and various record types you can use to identify your immigrant ancestor's original hometown.

Part 1. **Search Strategies** describes the five basic steps in detail you can use to find an immigrant's place of origin.

1. Identify what you know about the immigrant
2. Decide what you want to learn
3. Select the records to search

4. Find and search the records
5. Use the information

Part 2. **Country of Arrival** describes tactics and record types for records created in the immigrant's new country. The general strategy is to search family sources first, then records of previous research, and finally original records about the immigrant. Certain types of original records are more likely to give immigration information than others. See the "Record Selection Table".

Part 3. **Country of Origin** describes the tactics and record types from his or her homeland.

1. Survey Records of Previous Research
2. Search Nationwide Records: Census, Civil Registration, and Taxation
3. Search Departure Records
4. Localize the Surname
5. Search Regional Records
6. Search Local Records

Make New Discoveries 2

How to Find Your Ancestor's Birthplace or Place of Origin

If you have an ancestor who came from Europe, you need to identify their birthplace before you can find more generations of your family. Except for a few areas that have censuses, it is virtually impossible to do research in Europe unless you know the place of origin.

You should have already gathered as much information as possible from your home and your family, and filled out a pedigree chart. As you find the place of origin of one ancestor, you may also find information about other members of the family. Be sure to copy all the information you find about the family onto your research log.

1. Search a U.S. census to find the country your immigrant ancestor came from and, if possible, the year of immigration.

2. Next, search these records in this order:

- Passenger arrival lists for a U.S. port
- U.S. naturalization records
- Passenger departure lists for a European port
- Other record collections

If you don't find your ancestor in any of the records described here, you may be able to identify the place of origin in U.S. vital records, cemetery records, funeral-home records, or obituaries.

3. Then, look for that birthplace in a gazetteer.

A gazetteer is a dictionary of place-names. Remember that place-names and jurisdictions change. If possible, use a gazetteer that was published near the time when your ancestor was born. Old gazetteers are often called "historical" gazetteers. A gazetteer will help you identify the jurisdiction (the empire, kingdom, or country) that may have kept the records when your ancestor was there. A historical gazetteer may also help you identify the church records for your ancestor's birthplace. Knowing the church may be useful because births, marriages, and deaths were usually recorded in the Catholic registers, especially before the 1850s. Once you have identified the place of origin for your ancestor, you have opened the door to the world of records in Europe.

Here are some tips for identifying your immigrant ancestor.

Immigration Search Tips

- Search for your ancestors by name, narrowing the search with their age, dates of arrival, ports of departure or arrival, or country of origin.

- Keep in mind that your immigrant ancestor may not have used the English version of his or her given name and that the surname may also have ethnic variants. This is most likely to be the case in records created when he first immigrated (e.g., passenger arrivals). Learn the ethnic equivalents and try searches in the immigrant's native language.

- Learn about pronunciation in your immigrant ancestor's native language. In some cases clerks may have recorded the name as they heard it.

- Try searching for other variations of your ancestor's name in case it was spelled incorrectly.

- When you find an immigration document, it's important to look at the original image, which may contain information such as the name and address of the immigrant's nearest relative, their intended destination in their new country, or names of other relatives traveling with them.

- Be sure to note and research the names of witnesses and fellow passengers from the same place in immigration records. They were often relatives, employers, or friends from the immigrant's previous home. Tracing these individuals in census, directory, or immigration records may help you learn about your ancestor's life before and after they arrived in their new country.

- If your immigrant ancestor in the U.S. was alive after 1900, locate them in the 1900, 1910, 1920, or 1930 census and look for immigration and naturalization details that can help narrow your search.

Identifying Your Immigrant Ancestor - **FREE**

www.ancestry.com/cs/Satellite?c=Learning_C&childpagename=USLearningCenter%2FLearning_C%2FPageDefault&pagename=LearningWrapper&cid=1265125549325

An Ancestry article by Juliana Smith that shows an overview of identifiers to help locate your ancestor.

LDS Emigration and Immigration - **FREE**

https://familysearch.org/learn/wiki/en/LDS_Emigration_and_Immigration

In the early years of the LDS Church, all faithful members were encouraged to gather to Zion. The records showing these early Saints' faith and endurance are of great interest to their descendants. By learning about an ancestor's immigration to Zion, you may find records that provide clues to births, marriages, and deaths that occurred along the way. You may also find names of children and other relatives in these records, and clues that will help you identify the family's place of origin.

Passenger Arrival Records

Our ancestors came to America mostly on ships. In 1620, it took the Mayflower 66 days to cross the Atlantic. By the 1840's, the average

2 Make New Discoveries

length for sailing ships from the British Isles was 5-6 weeks. From the European continent it took a week or so longer. After the civil war, the majority of immigrants arrived on steamships. Initially, the voyage time fell to 2 weeks and then continued to decline into the 20th century. Steamships remained the primary means of travel until after WWII. Most immigrants now arrive by plane.

Passenger arrival records can help you determine when an ancestor arrived and the ports of departure and arrival. They can also be used to identify family and community members who arrived together as well as the country they came from.

Official passenger lists began in 1820 when the government began to regulate immigration. Before then, most passengers were considered 'cargo', not passengers. Most ships coming to America did not document who was on board. Many people traveled on uncomfortable, rat-infested cargo ships – usually only 5, 10, maybe 30 passengers suffered together.

But travelers recorded fellow passengers in diaries, journals, and letters. And cargo manifests and lists have been found in museums and archives. To find passenger arrival records for immigrants arriving before 1820, you must rely on published lists of immigrants' names taken from newspapers, naturalization oaths, indenture lists, headright grants, and other records. These types of records are listed in the *Place Search* of the Family History Library Catalog.

FamilySearch Wiki Resource Site -
https://familysearch.org/learn/wiki/en/US_Immigration_Passenger_Arrival_Records *FREE*

A valuable wiki page providing information and links to passenger arrival records pre-1820 and after 1820.

One-Step Web Pages - *FREE*
http://stevemorse.org

Dr. Stephen Morse developed his own specialized search form that enables us to search all of the immigration databases (Ellis Island, Castle Garden, etc.) in more ways that are faster and in some cases more useful: by passenger, "sounds-like" using the last name, town search, Jewish passengers, ancestor's village, date, and damaged images which are not indexed. If at first you don't succeed, try using different names (or spellings) your ancestor may have used, last-name only searches, switching the first and last names in your search, and by approximating their arrival date.

Ancestry Immigration Records - $
http://search.ancestry.com/search/category.aspx?cat=40

A vast collection of searchable Passenger Lists, Citizenship & Naturalization Records, Border Crossings and Passports, Crew Lists, Immigration and Emigration Books, and Ship Pictures and Descriptions. It provides a name index and image for the records of Ellis Island and Castle Garden from 1820 to 1957. $22.95/month. Free at libraries that subscribe and some Family History Centers.

FamilySearch Passenger Records - *FREE*
http://www.familysearch.orgwww.familysearch.org/catalog-search *(Search by Keyword)*

The Family History Library has copies of over 12,000 microfilms of passenger arrival records and indexes from the US National Archives. These microfilms are

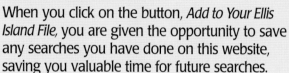

The small passenger list manifest page showing your ancestor's name in the Ellis Island Archives can be enlarged by clicking on the small magnifying glass icon to the side of the photo.

available for viewing at your local FamilySearch Center. The film numbers of these records are most easily found in the *Place Search* of the Family History Library Catalog under [State], [County], [Town] - Emigration and Immigration.

OliveTreeGenealogy Records - *FREE*

www.olivetreegenealogy.com

This excellent website provides free links and information about genealogy records to help you find your brick-wall ancestors and build your family tree, including: Passenger Lists, Ships Search, Immigration Tips, Canada, Military, Genealogy Guide, Loyalists, New Netherland, Native American, Palatine Genealogy, Photo Albums, Almshouse, Orphan Records, Huguenots, Mennonites, Quakers, UK Ireland, Genealogy Secrets! & Odds 'n Ends. It also offers genealogy tutorials, help files, and resource guides to help find your ancestors in census records, land records, ships passenger lists, birth, marriage and death records, and more.

CastleGarden Records - *FREE*

www.castlegarden.org

Free access to an extraordinary database of information on 10 million immigrants from 1830 to 1913 (which overlaps Ellis Island from 1892 to 1913). Over 73 million Americans can trace their ancestors to this early immigration period.

Ellis Island Records - *FREE*

www.ellisislandrecords.org

This site indexes nearly 25 million records for immigrants, passengers, and crew members that arrived through the port of New York

When you click on the button, *Add to Your Ellis Island File*, you are given the opportunity to save any searches you have done on this website, saving you valuable time for future searches.

between 1892 and 1924. There are an estimated 100 million Americans who have at least one ancestor who entered the U.S. through Ellis Island. On this site you'll find: *Passenger records* (giving passenger name, date of arrival, ship of travel, age on arrival, and more); *original manifests* showing passenger names and other information; and *ship information,* often with a picture, giving the history and background of each ship that brought the immigrants.

Canadian Genealogy Centre - *FREE*

www.collectionscanada.gc.ca/genealogy

Canada's documentary web site offers immigration and naturalization databases in both official languages, as well as vital, census, military, and land record databases.

Filby's Passenger and Immigration Lists Index *FREE* $

If you are seeking immigrant ancestors prior to the 1820s, this important work is the only place to go for tracing relatives to early colonial America and beyond. It contains listings of over

The Soundex Indexing System

Soundex is a phonetic index that groups together names (last name) that sound alike but are spelled differently, *for example*, **Smith** and **Smyth**, as pronounced in English. This helps searchers find names that are spelled differently than originally expected, a relatively common family history research problem. In the Soundex code, all surnames are reduced to a letter followed by three digits.

The easiest way to obtain the Soundex code for a name is to use one of several online Soundex converter programs as listed below. Simply type a name, and at the click of a button, the converter will divulge the corresponding Soundex code. There may be subtle differences between programs.

The most well-known genealogical use of Soundex is on parts of the 1880, 1900, 1910, 1920, and 1930 United States Federal Censuses. It is also used by the federal government for selected ship passenger arrival lists, certain Canadian border crossings, and some naturalization records.

The Soundex was a boon to many researchers in earlier days, but it does not work well with non-European surnames and is not as useful in today's technology. For more information you can go to:

National Archives - FREE
www.archives.gov/publications/
general-info-leaflets-55.html

Search your local library catalog online to see if they have a copy. You can also search it at www.ancestry.com which is free to preview, but you must subscribe to view the details. You can use Ancestry for free at a Family History Center.

You can also go to this WorldCat site (worldwide library catalog) to locate the library in your area that carries the index.
www.worldcat.org/title/passenger-and-immigration-lists-index-a-guide-to-published-arrival-records-of-about-500000-passengers-who-came-to-the-united-states-and-canada-in-the-seventeenth-eighteenth-and-nineteenth-centuries/oclc/7385897?referer=brief_results

ImmigrantShips FREE
www.immigrantships.net

14,000+ Passenger Manifests in 14 volumes plus numerous other passengers listed in special projects.

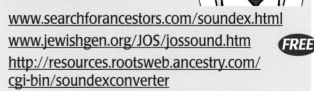

Here are some websites that will automatically convert any name you type into the Soundex code for that name.

Soundex Converter

www.searchforancestors.com/soundex.html
www.jewishgen.org/JOS/jossound.htm FREE
http://resources.rootsweb.ancestry.com/
cgi-bin/soundexconverter

4.7 million individuals who arrived in US and Canadian ports from the 1500s through the 1900s, and is updated annually, and makes finding your immigrant ancestors easier than ever. Thousands of different records have been used to compile this index, from original passenger lists to personal diaries.

Here are some tips to help find the arrival record for your immigrant ancestor.

How to Find Your Ancestor in Passenger Arrival Records

Embarking on a sometimes hazardous voyage, moving to a strange new country, and beginning life anew requires a special kind of courage. For many, leaving their plush homeland meant saying goodbye to family and possessions, knowing that they would never see some of them again. Most certainly, many lived a life of deprivation and hardship so they and their descendants could have a better life.

Determine full name, approximate date of arrival, approximate age, and likely port of arrival.

If the year of arrival is unknown and they were still living in the early 1900's, try searching the 1900, 1910, 1920 and 1930 census records as they each have a 'Citizenship' column with the year of immigration and place of birth.

Search Multiple Ports of Entry. While about 22 million immigrants pass through Ellis Island, many arrived through other U.S. ports, and through Canada, which was often a cheaper route.

Search for 'Ethnic' names because many passenger arrival records were created before they arrived in the U.S.

Try to locate a record of them leaving the old country - emigration records.

Check fellow passengers. Immigrants often traveled with other family members and neighbors from their home-towns. When they arrived in their new home, they may have lived near these people, too. So take a quick look to see who traveled with your ancestor – look a few pages forward and back. And pay close attention to surnames that seem familiar. You may discover that a traveling companion's surname is the same surname of a witness to your ancestor's marriage, a sponsor at a baby's baptism, a business partner or a neighbor.

Look for country of origin, not country of departure – since immigrants often had to travel to major ports to board their ship, these may not be one and the same.

Look for details about the immigrant's destination. It could be the home of a friend or another family member – use city directories and other local resources to help you learn more.

European Passenger Departure Lists

Use European passenger departure lists to identify an immigrant ancestor's birthplace or last residence in his or her country of origin. This makes them an enormously valuable source for family history research.

FamilySearch Wiki – FREE Hamburg Departure Lists

https://familysearch.org/learn/wiki/en/Hamburg_Passenger_Lists

This Wiki page provides detailed explanations and links to records. The Hamburg Lists are available on microfilm from the Family History Library, which means they can be ordered from your local Family History Center. All lists are indexed by name.

The Hamburg passenger lists contain the names of about 5 million who departed Europe from Hamburg, Germany between 1850 and 1934 (except 1915–1919). Approximately one third of the passengers were from Germany, while nearly two thirds came from Eastern Europe. The records also include about 750k Jewish immigrants from Russia, and are in German.

The Direct Passenger Lists include passengers who sailed directly to their destination without stopping at other European ports. The Indirect Passenger Lists include passengers who stopped at another European or British port before sailing to their final destination. About 20% of the immigrants leaving Europe took indirect routes because it was less expensive.

You need to know your ancestor's name (remember that you may need to also look for variant spellings), and your ancestor's approximate age at the time of departure. The year and age will help you distinguish between two individuals with similar names. Most other departure ports in Europe have few or no records available.

2 Make New Discoveries

Joe Beine Links - FREE
www.germanroots.com/hamburg.html

The Hamburg Passenger Departure Lists 1850-1934

A large number of German emigrants left from the German ports of Bremen and Hamburg (as well as other European ports). Most of the Bremen passenger departure records were destroyed. But the Hamburg lists survive. They are available online at Ancestry, and on microfilm from the Family History Library, which means they can be ordered from many local Family History Centers (although there may be restrictions on ordering these records in Europe). Here you will find links to online Hamburg indexes and digitized images, and sites with offline research tips. At the bottom of the page is a brief guide to help you read the German language passenger lists after you find them.

Provides information and links to the Hamburg Passenger Departure Lists.

Ancestry.com Hamburg - $
http://search.ancestry.com/search/db.aspx?dbid=1068

ancestry.com   Subscribe Sign In

Search > Immigration & Travel

Hamburg Passenger Lists, 1850-1934

Hamburger Passagierlisten, 1850-1934

This online database contains passenger lists of ships that departed from the port of Hamburg, Germany from 1850-1934 (with a gap from 1915-1919 due to World

> Over 82% of immigrants arrived through New York (Manhattan wharfs, Castle Garden, Ellis Island), but there were other entry ports.

Ports of Arrival

New York was not always the leading port, even though it was established by the Dutch in 1625. It was not until the Erie Canal opened in 1825 that New York became the busiest port of entry.

Boston was founded in 1630 and was the leading trading and passenger port from the Colonial period until 1750.

Baltimore, founded in 1729, is the best protected deep-water port and closest East coast port to the Midwest. Inspectors boarded ships at the mouth of the Chesapeake and completed inspections on board as the ship sailed north to Baltimore.

Philadelphia was founded in 1682 and rivaled Boston for a short time. It was a leading port of immigration until New York rose to prominence. During the Irish potato famine, Philadelphia failed to establish adequate shipping lines to receive the influx of immigrants and fell behind the other major ports.

New Orleans was founded by the French in 1718 and controlled by Spain from 1762 until sold to the US in 1803 as part of the Louisiana Purchase. It then grew to the 4th largest city in the US by 1840. Travel up the Mississippi River made New Orleans the best way to access America's western interior. The Civil War brought an abrupt end to New Orleans heyday and it never regained its position among the major ports.

Besides US ports, many immigrants arrived at **Canadian ports,** especially Quebec City and Halifax, and then crossed the border into the US.

War I). The database includes images of the passenger lists digitized from microfilm in partnership with the Hamburg State Archive.

The database also includes a partial index, covering the years 1850-1914 (complete for these years). The lists include about 5 million records of individuals, about 80% of whom (4 million) were destined for the US, 475k to South America, 214k to Canada, 100k to Africa, 54k to Australia, and 10k to Asian countries.

Ancestry also provides the *Swiss Overseas Emigration* database which contains registration cards of about 142k individuals who left Switzerland for overseas destinations from 1910-1953.

One Step Site - FREE

http://stevemorse.org/ellis/passengers.php?mode=hamb&firstkind=starts&FNM=&lastkind=starts&LNM=

This is using the Steve Morse site to search the Ancestry Hamburg outbound lists easier in one step. Free site; subscription links.

Ancestry.com - $
UK Departure Passenger Lists, 1890-1960

http://search.ancestry.com/search/db.aspx?dbid=2997

This database contains passenger lists recording the names of people leaving from UK ports for destinations outside of Europe. While outbound passenger lists before 1890 have not survived, this collection still covers decades of peak emigration. It includes not only British citizens but also others who traveled through the UK on their way to other destinations.

FindMyPast Outbound Lists - $

www.findmypast.co.uk/passengerListPersonSearchStart.action

These passenger lists include long-haul voyages to destinations outside Britain and Europe from all British (English, Welsh and Scottish) ports, all Irish ports before partition in 1921 and all Northern Irish ports after partition. In addition to searching for your ancestors in the passenger lists by their name it is also possible to browse by ship. This will allow you to view all of the voyages that a ship undertook from the UK, between 1890 and 1960.

CyndisList - Departures FREE

www.cyndislist.com/portsdepart.htm

Links to the major European ports of departure.

ProGenealogists Article - FREE

www.progenealogists.com/germany/articles/gdepart.htm

A valuable article on Passenger Departure Lists, 1709-1914.

You may want to know where your ancestors came from, when they arrived in North America, and when they became citizens. Naturalization and immigration records are the answer. Sometimes naturalization records for an ancestor is the only way to discover your family origins.

Border Crossings

Border crossing records can be rich sources of information on your immigrant ancestors. You can find details similar to those found on passenger arrival records. Immigrants traveling to North America typically found better rates on ships sailing to Canada, making it an appealing route to the United States. Until 1894, there were no U.S. immigration records created for immigrants coming to the U.S. through Canada.

In addition to the cheaper fares, many immigrants avoided U.S. immigration screening and hassles by choosing the Canadian route. In 1895 the U.S. government closed this loophole by requiring Canadian steamships and railroads to complete manifest forms and only provide transportation to U.S. destinations to immigrants that would have been allowed to enter the country via other U.S. ports.

Mexican border crossing records begin in

1903, and include aliens and some citizens crossing from Mexico into the U.S. through 1957. A variety of record types are included in this collection, with varying degrees of information. Separate cards or "card manifests" for each person were used at the ports of entry along the Mexican border. These cards contained the same information as was collected on traditional ship passenger arrival lists.

As would be expected, Mexican nationals comprised the vast majority of alien arrivals at the U.S./Mexico land border. However, Europeans also entered the U.S. through these ports, as well aliens from elsewhere in the world.

Here are links to databases for border crossings:

http://search.ancestry.com/search/category.aspx?cat=114

www.familysearch.org/search/collection/list

https://familysearch.org/learn/wiki/en/US_Immigration_Canadian_Border_Crossings

https://familysearch.org/learn/wiki/en/US_Immigration_Mexican_Border_Crossings

www.archives.gov/research/immigration/border-mexico.html

www.archives.gov/research/immigration

Suggested Activities

- Review the information you already have on your pedigree chart to help you decide what new information to look for.
- Use your computer to network with others who may be working on the same family line you're working on.
- Verify the information you find online because it may not always be correct.

Not all immigrants came to America through Ellis Island. It was the busiest port of entry, but there were many other entry points in the U.S., including Baltimore, Detroit, New Orleans, Philadelphia, San Francisco, etc.

Research Tip

Don't get discouraged if you don't find your ancestors in the Ellis Island database.

Finding Your Ancestors' Naturalization Records

US Naturalization and Citizenship

Naturalization is the process of granting citizenship privileges to foreign-born residents. Naturalization papers are an important source of information about an immigrant's origin, his foreign and "Americanized" names, residence, and date of arrival, but are often overlooked.

Before 1906 they are not likely to give town of origin or names of parents, but post-1906 records are more detailed and can help you find the date of immigration, ship's passenger list, spouse's name, port of arrival, and the place of birth for your ancestor. Some naturalization records include occupations, names and ages of minor children and more.

In 1862, the Homestead Act was passed that provided a special incentive for immigrants to become citizens. It specified that only US citizens, or immigrants who had filed a declaration of intention to become citizens, could own land.

Many immigrants who applied for citizenship did not complete the requirements. Evidence that an immigrant became a citizen can be found in censuses, court minutes, homestead records, passports, voting registers, and military papers. Even if an immigrant ancestor did not complete the process, he may have begun the process and filed a *declaration of intention* which contains valuable information.

> The typical naturalization process involved three steps.

U. S. Naturalization Process

1. Declaration. The immigrant filed a *declaration of intention* (first papers) to renounce allegiance to foreign governments and to later prove he or she had resided in the country long enough to apply for citizenship. Some were filed in a court at the port of arrival, some en route to a new home, and some in the immigrant's new home. The immigrant could use the court's record of his declaration to apply for homestead land, to enroll in the military, or to use as proof of residency if he went to another court to complete the naturalization process. The immigrant was also required to pledge his allegiance to the United States and sign a written oath which is often found with the petition, and generally gives his name, the date, and the country of origin.

2. Petition. After 2-7 years the immigrant filed a *petition for citizenship* (second or final papers). Most often the petition was filed in a court (any of 5,000 federal, state, or local courts) nearest to the town where the immigrant settled. After accepting the immigrant's petition and witnessing his oath, a court granted citizenship which was recorded in the court's official records. In some cases this is the only naturalization record that you will be able to find. Since 1929 most (but not all) naturalizations have been handled by federal circuit or district courts. You may need to search the records of each place where your immigrant ancestor lived.

3. Certificate. After all requirements were completed, the immigrant was sworn in as a citizen and issued a *certificate of citizenship* for his personal use. The certificates were printed in books with attached stubs.

Certificate of Citizenship

Finding Naturalization Records

Naturalization Records	What to Look For	Location
Colonial Records	**Ancestry.com** Free to search and preview. Must subscribe to Ancestry to view details. *FREE* *$*	www.ancestry.com > *Search* > *Card Catalog* *Passenger and Immigration Lists Index* * *Selected U.S. Naturalization Records 1790-1974* includes digitized naturalization records for some Federal courts in Calif., NY, and Penn. * *U.S. Naturalization Records Indexes, 1794-1995* includes indexes for some Federal courts in Alaska, Calif., Delaware, Wash. D.C., Maryland, Massachusetts, Michigan, New York, Ohio, Oregon, and Pennsylvania.
Before September 1906	**FamilySearch.org** *FREE* Look first for the petition (second papers) in courts of the county or city where your immigrant lived.	www.familysearch.org > *Library* > *Library Catalog* > *Place Search* [STATE], [COUNTY], [TOWN] - then look under "Naturalization and Citizenship".
	Courts	Contact the county clerk to determine where the records are presently located
	National Archives *FREE*	www.archives.gov/genealogy/naturalization - Introduction & web site links
After September 1906	**US Citizenship and Immigration Services (CIS).** *FREE* *$* The federal government standardized the naturalization process (including the paperwork) requiring specific forms. Since 1929, most new citizens naturalized at federal courts.	www.uscis.gov > *Topics* > *Genealogy* Records available thru the mail (fee required): Naturalization Certificate Files and Alien Registration Forms. You can also use the Freedom of Information Act (FOIA) to obtain copies of these records.
	Fold3.com *$* Contains over 5.2 million searchable naturalization records, plus over 405 million other records.	http://go.fold3.com/naturalizations/ 7-day free trial, $49.95/year.

Family Search - FREE
Naturalization Records

https://familysearch.org >>Search >Browse
All Published Collections (scroll down) >Type
'Naturalization' in the filter box

Their Historical Records Collection features dozens of naturalization records, and new databases are added monthly. Search by state. The FamilySearch Wiki provides detailed information on the Naturalization process with numerous links to valuable web pages.

Ancestry.com Naturalization - $

www.ancestry.com >Search >Card Catalog >Type
'naturalization' in keyword search box

Note that the search results include both naturalization and many other immigration records.

NaturalizationRecords.com - FREE

www.naturalizationrecords.com

An excellent website to search for your ancestors in free Naturalization Records in U.S.A. and Canada. Find

Declarations of Intent, First Papers, Alien Registrations, Passport Applications, Naturalization Petitions and Citizenship Certificates. Search substitute naturalization records - ships passenger lists, census records, oaths of allegiance, voters registration lists and more.

Naturalization Process - FREE

www.genealogybranches.com/naturalization.html

A nice guide with links to the naturalization process.

Joe Beine's Searchable
U.S. Naturalization Records – FREE

www.germanroots.com/naturalizationrecords.html

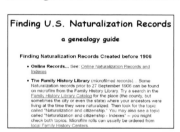

This website contains comprehensive links to naturalization indexes and records. It provides the statewide indexes and records first, then the nationwide indexes and records. This website is updated regularly and is a great source to begin searching for naturalization records on the Internet.

2 Make New Discoveries

Your Life is a Legacy

"There's a world of wisdom in our personal stories. Your life is a legacy, a gift that only you can give. Why waste something so precious?"

Dolly Berthelot

Dolly Berthelot, author, editor, professor

Honor Your Own Stories

"If you don't recount your family history, it will be lost. Honor your own stories and tell them too. The tales may not seem very important, but they

Madeleine L'Engle

are what binds families and makes each of us who we are."

Madeleine L'Engle (1918-2007), American author

Understand US Migration Trails

Oregon Trail by Albert Bierstadt (1830–1902

Understanding the transportation systems available to ancestors can help you determine their place of origin. Connect the place where an ancestor settled to the nearby canals, waterways, trails, roads, and railroads to look for connections to places they may have lived previously.

Mountains, forests, waterways, and the gaps between them channeled migration into predictable settlement patterns. Events like gold or land rushes, and Indian treaties also affected settlement.

Migration research may help you discover:

• A place of origin, previous hometown, or place where an ancestor settled

• Biographical details such as what they experienced, or with whom they traveled on their journey

• Clues for finding other records

Actual lists of travelers are unusual. A few passenger lists are available at the New York State Archives for the Erie Canal from 1827-1829. Lists of pioneers who settled an area are sometimes available on the Internet, or in the form of county or local histories. The diaries and journals of people on the move may help you learn who they had as companions on the journey, and what their trip was like.

Censuses, directories, land and property

records, plat maps, tax records, and voting registers can sometimes be used to learn where new arrivals settled. Starting in 1850 federal censuses show where a person was born, and starting in 1880 where the parents were born.

CyndisList Migration -
www.cyndislist.com/migration

Links to Internet genealogical resources about traces, trails, roads and related mailing lists, geography, settlers, and societies.

Family History Wiki - FREE
www.academic-genealogy.com
> *Emigration & Human Migration*
also > *Citizenship/Naturalization*

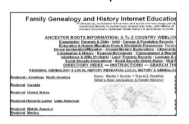

A large mega-portal directory of links to Immigration and naturalization databases.

Westward Expansion Trails - FREE
http://en.wikipedia.org/wiki/Westward_Expansion_Trails

Wikipedia article on trails of the West.

Other US Migration Routes -
https://familysearch.org/learn/wiki/en/Category:Migration_Routes

A FamilySearch Wiki portal to other US migration routes: Canals, Ports, Railroads, Rivers and Lakes.

Maps are keys to understanding the places where your ancestors lived.

Immigrant Ancestors Project - FREE
http://immigrants.byu.edu

Sponsored by the Center for Family History and Genealogy at BYU, it uses emigration registers to locate information about the birthplaces of immigrants in their native countries, which is not found in the port registers and naturalization documents in the destination countries.

Educational Articles and Links - FREE
www.genealogy.com/00000388.html

Helpful links and information about the immigrant experience and finding records related to immigration.

Mormon Migration - FREE
http://mormonmigration.lib.byu.edu

About 90,000 Latter-day Saint converts crossed the oceans beginning in 1840, followed by a continual flow of immigrants over the next decades. Discover stories, letters, journal entries, and other accounts of their voyage, including stories of their trek to the Western US.

Migration Maps

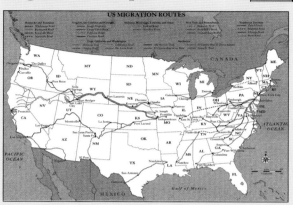

If you can find a map of a locality made about the time your ancestors lived there, the boundary and jurisdiction changes will help you understand the land records and movements of your ancestors more clearly than a more recent map. Your ancestors' childhood, education, occupations, and migration were affected by the topography of the land. If your ancestors lived in a farming area, a mining area, or a city, they would likely have followed occupations that were common to that location.

Maps are an important source of family and local information. Maps may be found individually as well as in atlases; gazetteers; town, county, regional, and state histories; and encyclopedias. Many are available on microfilm, microfiche, compact disc, or on the Internet. For more information about maps, see page 172.

2 Make New **Discoveries**

Wisdom of Former Generations

"But those who came before us will teach you. They will teach you from the wisdom of former generations."   Job 8:10

World Is Not Complete
"The history of the world is not complete until it includes yours."

LaRae Kerr, genealogist, author
http://alfreefamily.blogspot.com/

LaRae Kerr

Major Historic Migration Trails FREE

Name and Web Links	Date Opened / Length	Usual Origin	Usual Destination
Great Indian Warpath (Seneca Trail) https://familysearch.org/learn/wiki/en/Great_Indian_Warpath http://en.wikipedia.org/wiki/Great_Indian_Warpath	network of ancient Indian trails		Alabama, Virginia, Tennessee, Penn., New York, Great Lakes
King's Highway (Boston Post Road, Kennebunk Road, Potomoc Trail) https://familysearch.org/learn/wiki/en/King%27s_Highway	1650/1735 1300 miles	Boston, Massachusetts	Charleston, South Carolina
Albany Post Road (Queen's Road) https://familysearch.org/learn/wiki/en/Albany_Post_Road http://en.wikipedia.org/wiki/Albany_Post_Road	1669 150 miles	New York City, New York	Albany, New York
Mohawk or Iroquois Trail https://familysearch.org/learn/wiki/en/Mohawk_or_Iroquois_Trail	ancient Indian trail / 1722 190 miles	Albany, New York	Fort Oswego, New York Fort Niagara, New York
Great Valley Road (Great Wagon Road) https://familysearch.org/learn/wiki/en/Great_Valley_Road	prehistoric / 1744, 735 miles	Philadelphia, Pennsylvania	Virginia, Tennessee, N. Carolina, Georgia
Nemacolin's Trail (Cumberland Road) http://en.wikipedia.org/wiki/Nemacolin%27s_Trail	ancient Indian trail / 1750	Cumberland, Maryland	Brownsville, Pennsylvania
Fall Line Road (Southern Road) https://familysearch.org/learn/wiki/en/Fall_Line_Road http://en.wikipedia.org/wiki/Fall_line	1735 170 miles	Fredericksburg, Virginia	Augusta, Georgia
Natchez Trace (Chickasaw Trail) https://familysearch.org/learn/wiki/en/Natchez_Trace http://en.wikipedia.org/wiki/Natchez_Trace	before 1742 450 miles	Natchez, Mississippi	Nashville, Tennessee Maysville, Kentucky
Unicoi Trail https://familysearch.org/learn/wiki/en/Unicoi_Trail www.telliquah.com/unicoi.htm	pre-Colonial, setters 1795 68 miles	Charleston, South Carolina	Knoxville, Tennessee
Upper Road https://familysearch.org/learn/wiki/en/Upper_Road	1750s 585 miles	Fredericksburg, Virginia	Greenville, South Carolina

Major Historic Migration Trails FREE

Name and Web Links	Date Opened / Length	Usual Origin	Usual Destination
Forbes Road (Raystown Path) https://familysearch.org/learn/wiki/en/Forbes_Road http://en.wikipedia.org/wiki/Forbes_Road http://www.clpgh.org/exhibit/neighborhoods/point/point_n715.html	1759 320 miles	Philadelphia, Pennsylvania	Pittsburgh, Pennsylvania
Wilderness Road https://familysearch.org/learn/wiki/en/Wilderness_Road	1775	Virginia	Kentucky, Tennessee
Catawba Trail https://familysearch.org/learn/wiki/en/Catawba_Trail	before 1777	S. Carolina	Kentucky, Tennessee, N. Carolina
Avery's Trace (Nashville Road) https://familysearch.org/learn/wiki/en/Avery%27s_Trace http://en.wikipedia.org/wiki/Avery%27s_Trace	1787 300 miles	East Tennessee	Middle Tennessee
Zane's Trace http://en.wikipedia.org/wiki/Zane%27s_Trace www.fhwa.dot.gov/infrastructure/back0803.cfm	1796 30 miles	West Virginia	Maysville, Kentucky
Jackson's Military Road https://familysearch.org/learn/wiki/en/Jackson%27s_Military_Road	1814 516 miles	Nashville, Tennessee	New Orleans, Louisiana
National Road (Cumberland Road) https://familysearch.org/learn/wiki/en/National_Road http://en.wikipedia.org/wiki/National_Road	1818 620 miles	Baltimore, Maryland	Vandalia, Illinois
Camino Real de Tierra Adentro (Chihuahua Trail) https://familysearch.org/learn/wiki/en/Camino_Real_de_Tierra_Adentro www.caminorealcarta.org	1598-1884 1500+ miles	Mexico City, Mexico	Santa Fe, New Mexico
Camino Real de California (California Mission Trail) http://en.wikipedia.org/wiki/El_Camino_Real_%28California%29	1683 600 miles	San Bruno, Mexico	Sonoma, California

2 Make New Discoveries

Major Historic Migration Trails FREE

Name and Web Links	Date Opened / Length	Usual Origin	Usual Destination
Camino Real de los Tejas (Old San Antonio Road) http://en.wikipedia.org/wiki/El_Camino_Real_de_los_Tejas_National_Historic_Trail, www.elcaminorealdeloste-jas.org	1690s 2,500 miles	Guerrero, Mexico	Louisiana
Santa Fe Trail https://familysearch.org/learn/wiki/en/Santa_Fe_Trail http://en.wikipedia.org/wiki/Santa_Fe_Trail	1821	Franklin, Missouri	Santa Fe, New Mexico
Old Spanish Trail https://familysearch.org/learn/wiki/en/Old_Spanish_Trail http://en.wikipedia.org/wiki/Old_Spanish_Trail_%28trade_route%29	1830	Santa Fe, New Mexico	Los Angeles, California
Oregon Trail https://familysearch.org/learn/wiki/en/Oregon_Trail	1841 2,000 miles	Independence, Missouri	Oregon City, Oregon
California Trail https://familysearch.org/learn/wiki/en/California_Trail	1841 1,950 miles	Independence, Missouri	Sacramento, California
Mormon Trail https://familysearch.org/learn/wiki/en/Mormon_Trail	1846/1847 1,300 miles	Nauvoo, Illinois	Salt Lake City, Utah
Mormon Trail to Southern California https://familysearch.org/learn/wiki/en/Mormon_Trail_to_Southern_California	1848 706 miles	Salt Lake City, Utah	Los Angeles, California
Butterfield Overland Mail https://familysearch.org/learn/wiki/en/Butterfield_Overland_Mail	1857	Memphis, TN, St. Louis, MO	San Francisco, California
Central Overland Trail (Pony Express) https://familysearch.org/learn/wiki/en/Central_Overland_Trail	1859 650 miles	Salt Lake City, Utah	Carson City, Nevada
Bozeman Trail http://en.wikipedia.org/wiki/Bozeman_Trail	1863-1868	Fort Laramie, Wyoming	Virginia City, Montana

Search Military Records

Track Your Ancestors Footsteps Through History

Whether you are looking for military records for your family tree or simply want to learn more about the service of one of your family members, military records can offer the information you are looking for.

Throughout US history, more than 43 million courageous men and women have served and protected our country in times of conflict. Over 650,000 American lives have been lost and more than 1.4 million service members wounded in battle. Were your ancestors among them?

Some of the most interesting and helpful records available to assist you in tracing your family roots and stories are military records: service or pension records, draft registration cards, veterans' grave sites, soldier pension indexes, enlistment records, bounty land records, muster rolls, discharge lists, fatalities, prisoner of war records, and history of battles and wars.

Military records contain large amounts of biographical information, from the color of a person's eyes to the day-by-day muster rolls that track your ancestor's footsteps through history. There are numerous opportunities to learn the stories of your ancestor's courage and sacrifice with hundreds of military record databases.

Ancestry.com - $

www.ancestry.com >Search >Military

Discover the heroes in your family tree in their huge U.S. Military Collection covering more than three centuries of American wars and conflicts. With more than

Military Search Tips

Because military records often hold such rich and detailed information, you'll want to look for all family members who served—direct ancestors and collateral relatives as well. Look through your family tree for men who would have been of the right age to serve and search for all of them in records related to that conflict.

Some census records include information on military service. The 1840, 1910, 1930 and 1940 U.S. Censuses included questions about military service, and the 1890 Veterans' Schedule is available for states alphabetically beginning with Kentucky (partial) through Wyoming, and the District of Columbia. It lists the residence, unit, and years of service of Civil War soldiers or their surviving widows.

100 million names and 700 titles and databases in military records from all 50 U.S. states, there are countless opportunities to learn the stories of courage and sacrifice in your family tree. Contains records from most major American wars, including DAR Rolls of Honor, the Civil War Collection, and World War I Draft Registrations. Also includes selected Loyalist and Confederate sources. $19.95/month. Free at Family History Centers (Library edition).

Ancestry's NARA Collections $

http://search.ancestry.com/search/db.aspx?dbid=1572

Since 1998, Ancestry.com has digitized and indexed millions of NARA (National

(Continued on page 108)

2 Make New Discoveries

How to Find Your Ancestors in the Military

The first step in searching for the military records of your ancestors is to determine when and where they served in the armed forces, their military branch, and whether they were in the enlisted ranks or an officer. You can find the clues you need in your family stories, journals or diaries, old newspaper clippings, service medals and memorabilia, census records, correspondence, scrapbooks, death records and obituaries, grave markers, local histories and photographs.

Military records are wonderful sources that provide unique facts and insights into the lives of men and women who have served in the armed forces. They may include dates of birth and death, residence, names and addresses of family members, military rank and affiliation, among other details.

The types of records you'll find in this category include: service records, pension records, draft records, bounty land records, claim records, online histories of battles and battlefields, veteran's memorials, and many more.

Military service records - these records are primarily available through the National Archives and the National Personnel Records Center.

Compiled Military Service Record - a compilation of abstracts of a person's service records, such as: enlistment and discharge documents, muster rolls, rank rolls, payrolls, hospital records, and prison records. These compiled military service records are primarily available for veterans of the American Revolution, War of 1812, and the Civil War.

Pension records - the National Archives has pension applications and records of pension

payments for veterans, their widows, and other heirs. The pension records are based on service in the armed forces of the US between 1775 and 1916.

Draft registration records - There were 3 different drafts of World War I; 24 million men born between 1873-1900. There were 4 different draft registrations for WWII, but the majority of these records are still protected by privacy laws. The fourth registration (born between 1877-1897) is the only WWII registration currently available to the public.

The fourth registration WWII draft registration cards for most southern states (including Alabama, Florida, Georgia, Kentucky, Mississippi, North Carolina, South Carolina and Tennessee) were destroyed in error by NARA in the 1970s and were never microfilmed. The information on these cards has been lost for good. Other registrations for these states were not destroyed, but are also not yet available to the public.

Kimberly Powell provides good information on what you can learn from WWI and WWII draft records and how to search at:

WWI - http://genealogy.about.com/od/ records/p/w wi draft.htm

WWII - http://genealogy.about.com/od/ records/p/wwii draft.htm

Bounty land records - A land bounty is a grant of land from a government as a reward to citizens for the risks and hardships they endured in the service of their country, usually in a military related capacity. If your ancestor served in the Revolutionary War, War of 1812, early Indian Wars, or the Mexican War, a search of bounty land warrant application files may be worthwhile. Documents found in these records are similar to those in pension files. Federal bounty land warrants are kept at the National Archives in Washington D.C. and can be ordered online.

National Archives Military Records

www.archives.gov/research/military **FREE**

Your search for military records will begin at the U.S. National Archives and Records Administration (NARA). Most records regarding veterans of the U.S. Armed Forces (Air Force, Army, Navy, Coast Guard, Marine Corps, National Guard), can be found here, dating all the way back to the Revolutionary War. You may be able to find information such as service records, pension applications, and bounty land records through this one site.

You can often access these records with just the name of the person. But providing dates of service and military branch can make the search faster and more accurate. You can download these online public records for free, but if you want official copies they need to be ordered directly from the office where they are filed for a fee.

The National Archives holds Federal military service records in two repositories:

Revolutionary War - 1912 - The National Archives Building in Washington, D.C. www.archives.gov/research/military

Check the Microfilm Catalog, or contact the Regional Archives in your area, as the Regions may also have the military service records that you are looking for on microfilm. http://www.archives.gov/locations

You can find Information and online links to military reference material, military history and research, and to specific resources by branch of service or by military engagement at www.archives.gov/research/alic/reference/military/index.html.

WWI - present - National Military Personnel Records Center (NPRC), in St. Louis, Missouri www.archives.gov/st-louis/military-personnel.

The repository of millions of military personnel, health, and medical records of discharged and deceased veterans of all services during the 20th century.

NARA Online Catalog

www.archives.gov/research/arc/topics/genealogy

The Archival Research Catalog (ARC) is the online catalog of NARA's nationwide holdings in the Washington, DC, area; Regional Archives; and Presidential Libraries. It contains descriptions of records held by the National Archives where you can conduct keyword searches and filtered searches.

Access to Archival Databases (ADD)

http://aad.archives.gov/aad/

This is the online databases for NARA.

US National Archives YouTube Channel–

www.youtube.com/user/usnationalarchives

You can access hundreds of videos about the archives and their collections and services.

2 Make New Discoveries

(Continued from page 105)

Archive) records thus enabling access to more U.S. historical records online than ever before. This database is a catalog to NARA collections published on Ancestry.com, and allows you to easily find what NARA collections are available on Ancestry. It includes more than 750 million names and 80 million images in military, census, immigration, naturalization records, passenger arrivals, border crossings, and published passenger lists. It will be continuously updated as they add more NARA records online.

Fold3.com - $

www.fold3.com

A wonderful collection of over 420 million (and growing) original US military records, including the stories, photos, and personal documents of the men and women who served. Almost all the documents are found nowhere else on the web. It helps you discover and share stories about these everyday heroes, forgotten soldiers, and the families that supported them.

You can also combine records found on the site with what you have in your own albums and shoeboxes to create an online memorial *(Memorial Pages)* for someone who served.

They feature digitized and indexed National Archives documents, including: Revolutionary War and Civil War Service Records, Civil War Widows Pensions, Mormon Battalion Pension Files, Pension Index-Civil War to 1900, Revolutionary War Pensions, Southern Claims Commission, WWI and WWII records, draft registrations, etc. The internet's best Revolutionary War, Civil War, WWII and Vietnam War collections.

They also offer *free* military collections, including: US Milestone Documents, Constitutional Convention Records, War of 1812 Pension Files, a Civil War maps collection, Brady Civil War photos, an interactive USS Arizona Memorial, a Vietnam Service Awards collection, and an interactive Vietnam Veterans Memorial collection with over 58,000 images of soldier's names, and more. Generally, all their databases are free to search, but require a membership to view the records and images. 7-day free trial. $11.95/month, $79.95/year.

FamilySearch Wiki and Historical Records– (FREE)

https://familysearch.org/learn/wiki/en/Main_Page >Military

www.familysearch.org/search/collection/list#page=1&recordType=Military

FamilySearch has a huge collection of US historical military records which also includes some international military records. FamilySearch Wiki provides many links to databases, resources, as well as state military records, articles about military conflicts, and record types, e.g. prisoners of war, bounty land warrants awards, etc. Most of the wiki pages are very comprehensive and very worthwhile.

Also remember that the main Family History Library in Salt Lake City has many National Archives military, census, immigration, land, and naturalization records on microfilm. You can order copies of these microfilms for viewing and copying at your local Family History (FamilySearch) Center for free. There are over 4600 branches worldwide. Search the catalog at https://familysearch.org/catalog-search.

You can find a list of microfilms (and cross-reference numbers) at both NARA and the Family History Library at https://familysearch.org/learn/wiki/en/NARA_and_FHL_film_numbers.

RecordsBase.com –

www.recordsbase.com/resources/military-records

Find family members who served in the military, including military documents, information of US historic wars, veterans and military divisions. A comprehensive and trusted source of over 2 Billion military records, public records, vital records (marriage, death, birth, divorce records), census records, immigration lists, cemetery listings, obituaries, and passenger lists. $39.95/year

Civil War Soldiers and Sailors –

www.nps.gov/civilwar/soldiers-and-sailors-database.htm

This is the US National Park Service database containing information about the men who served in the Union and Confederate armies, including Colored Troops, during the Civil War. Other information on the site includes histories of Union and Confederate regiments, links to descriptions of significant battles, and selected lists of prisoner-of-war records and cemetery records.

US Army Heritage Center –

www.carlisle.army.mil/ahec

An extensive, digitized collection of 23,000 Civil War photographs. Also contains: personal papers, oral histories, letters and diaries of veterans, military units and associations, images of historical property, military publications, about 1.5 million photographs that represents the history of the US Army and covers all major conflicts from the Civil War,

the Spanish American War, Philippine Insurrection, both World Wars to the Korean War, the Vietnam War, the Cold War era, the Persian Gulf War to current operations in Iraq and Afghanistan.

HeritageQuestOnline –

www.HeritageQuestOnline.com

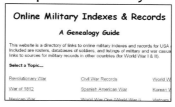

Search the Revolutionary War Pension and Bounty-Land Warrant Application files. You can log on yourself at home by using your local library card (if they subscribe). Check with your library.

MilitaryIndexes.com – (FREE)

www.militaryindexes.com

An updated directory of links to online military indexes and records (including links to state archives) including: rosters, databases of soldiers, and listings of military and war casualties. Also included are some links to sources for military records in other countries (for World War I & II).

Cyndi's List U.S. Military – (FREE)

www.cyndislist.com/us/military

Links to hundreds of web pages everything military.

OliveTree Military Links – (FREE)

www.olivetreegenealogy.com/mil/index.shtml

These military pages provide historical background for each conflict, chronological timelines, statistics, battles, famous Americans and Canadians, biographies of soldiers, heroes and their stories, contributions of women, muster rolls for conflicts before 1900, Letters Home (from soldiers at the front), music and poetry, guest authors' submissions, links to other online resources, and Research Libraries.

GenealogyBank Historical $ Documents –

www.genealogybank.com/gbnk/documents

Research your American military ancestry and family war history with thousands of U.S. government documents. Provides details that are difficult to find elsewhere. $9.95 30-Day trial, $69.95/year.

Mary's Genealogy Treasures – *FREE*

www.telusplanet.net/public/mtoll/usmil.htm

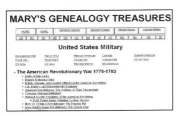

Numerous links to resources, photographs, articles, timelines, databases, records, cemeteries, and much more of US military conflicts, and each military service (Army, Navy, Air Force, Marines).

Veterans History Project – *FREE*

www.loc.gov/vets

The Library of Congress' Veterans History Project of the American Folklife Center collects, preserves, and makes accessible the personal accounts of

American war veterans so that future generations may hear directly from veterans and better understand the realities of war. They collect first-hand accounts of U.S. Veterans from all the conflicts since WWI.

Veterans Stories – *FREE*

http://veteranshistoryinstitute.org/index.htm

National Veterans History Archival Institute is working to preserve the historical heritage of U.S. veterans of all service branches (U.S. Army, U.S. Navy, U.S. Marine Corps, U.S. Coast Guard, U.S. Air Force and the Merchant Marines). They collect, arrange, and describe the oral histories as well as the military service records of all U.S. veterans.

Veterans Affairs Grave Locator – *FREE*

http://gravelocator.cem.va.gov

Search nationally for burial locations of veterans and their family members in VA National Cemeteries, state veterans cemeteries, various other military and Department of Interior cemeteries, and for veterans buried in private cemeteries when the grave is marked with a government grave marker. A map of the cemetery is also displayed, showing the section where the grave is located. VA operates 128 national cemeteries and 33 soldiers' lots and monument sites.

Thomas Jefferson by Rembrandt Peale

The Happiest Moments

"The happiest moments of my life have been the few which I have passed at home in the bosom of my family."

Thomas Jefferson (1743-1826), American Founding Father, 3rd President of the US

Heidi Swapp

Strength of Those Who Went Before

"Generations pass like leaves fall from our family tree. Each season new life blossoms and grows benefitting from the strength and experience of those who went before."

Heidi Swapp, artist, scrapbooker
www.heidiswapp.com/

U.S. Online Military Records Chart

War/ Casualties	Conflict Years	Approx. Birth Years	Location	Available Records / Documents
Colonial Wars King William's War (1689-97), Queen Anne's War (1702-13), King George's War (1744-48), French and Indian War (1754-63)	1607-1763	1557-1747	http://www.bio.umass.edu/biology/conn.river/philip.html _FREE_ www.olivetreegenealogy.com/mil/index.shtml	Links to information about the colonial wars
			www.let.rug.nl/usa/essays/before-1800/french-and-indian-wars _FREE_ http://en.wikipedia.org/wiki/French_and_Indian_War www.loc.gov/rr/program/bib/french indian	French-Indian Wars background
			www.ancestry.com* $ > Search > Military	Connecticut Soldiers, French and Indian War
Revolutionary War 250,000+ servicemen, 50,000+ casualties	1775-1783	1726-1767	www.familysearch.org/search/collection/list _FREE_	2m Compiled Service Records, 6.9m Pension Payment Ledgers, Pension and Bounty Land Warrant Applications, Muster Rolls
			www.HeritageQuestOnline.com * _FREE_	Muster Rolls, Pension Files, Bounty-land Warrants
			www.fold3.com * $	Muster Rolls, Pension Files, Service Records, Vouchers Index for Military Pensions
			www.Ancestry.com * $ > Search >Military	Compiled Service Records, 426k Muster Rolls, DAR Linage Books, SAR Membership apps, Bounty Land Warrants
			www.militaryindexes.com _FREE_	Links to records on assorted sites, including states.
			http://www.Dar.org www.dar.org/library/onlinlib.cfm#search _FREE_	DAR Online Library Catalog and the Genealogical Research System (GRS)
			www.RoyalProvincial.com _FREE_	Loyalist Records: Muster Roll Index, Regimental Documents, Land Petitions, Postwar Settlement Papers
			www.archives.gov/research/military/american-revolution _FREE_	Photos, documents, maps
War of 1812 530,000 servicemen, 2,000 casualties	1812-1815	1762-1799	www.Ancestry.com* $ > Search >Military	600k Service Records, Pension Application Index, Bounty-land Warrants, Prisoner of War Records
			www.fold3.com * $	Pension Files, Service Records, Milestone Docs

2 Make New Discoveries

U.S. Online Military Records Chart

War/ Casualties	Conflict Years	Approx. Birth Years	Location	Available Records / Documents
War of 1812 Continued			www.familysearch.org/search/collection/list **FREE**	91k US Index to Pension Application, US Index to Service Records, Louisiana Pension Lists
			www.militaryindexes.com **FREE**	Links to records on assorted sites, including states.
Mexican War 100,000 servicemen, 13,000 casualties	1846-1848	1796-1831	www.familysearch.org/search/collection/list **FREE**	Index and Service Records, 52k Pension Index, Mormon Battalion Pension Applications,
			www.militaryindexes.com **FREE**	Links to records on assorted sites.
			www.olivetreegenealogy.com >Military **FREE**	Links to records on assorted sites.
			www.archives.gov/research/military/index.html **FREE**	Historical information, Veterans Monuments
			www.fold3.com * **$**	Service records, Mormon Battalion Pension files, Ratified Indian Treaties, Cherokee Indian Agency
			www.ancestry.com * **$**	American Volunteer Soldiers
Civil War 2.8 million+ servicemen, 510,000+ casualties	1861-1865	1811-1848	Civil War Soldiers and Sailors System www.itd.nps.gov/cwss **FREE**	6.3m Service Records, Regimental Histories, Battle Descriptions, Prisoner Records
			www.Ancestry.com * **$** > Search >Military	4m+ Soldier Index, 2.5m Pension Index, Draft Registration (Union), US Army Enlistments (Union), Colored Troops Service Records, Veteran Headstones (Union), 1890 Veterans & Widows Census Schedules
			www.fold3.com * **$**	Confederate Service Records, Union Pension Index, "Widows' Pension" Files, Southern Claims
			www.familysearch.org/search/collection/list **FREE**	6.3m Soldiers Index, 3m Pension Index, 80k Confederate Applications for Pardons, 925k Confederate Soldiers Papers, 2.2m NARA Confederate Service Records, 900k US 1890 Census - Union Veterans and Widows, 2.3m Union Colored Troops, States Service Records

War/ Casualties	Conflict Years	Approx. Birth Years	Location	Available Records / Documents
Civil War Continued			www.CivilWarData.com $	Pension Indexes, Rolls of Honor, State Rosters
			www.archives.gov/research/military/ index.html > Civil War FREE	Union Pension Index links, Confederate Pension Records (by State Archive links)
Spanish-American War 280,564 servicemen, 2,061 casualties	1898	1848-1881	www.spanamwar.com FREE	Rosters, Historical info, Photos
			www.accessgenealogy.com FREE >Military records	How to obtain Spanish American War records.
			www.archives.gov/research/military/ index.html > Spanish American FREE	Service Records, Selected documents
			www.militaryindexes.com FREE	Links to records on assorted sites.
			www.ancestry.com * >Search >Card Catalog >Spanish American $	Spanish American War Volunteers 1898, Selected state records
Philippine Insurrection 125,000+ servicemen, 4,200 casualties	1899-1902	1849-1885	http://www.ancestry.comwww.cyndis list.com/us/philippine-american-war FREE	Links to selected records.
			www.archives.gov/research/military/ index.html > Philippine Insurrection FREE	Historical information
World War I 24 million+ registered for draft; 4.7 million+ served, 116,516+ casualties	1917-1918	1872-1900	www.ancestry.com * $ > Search > Military	24m Draft Registration Cards, 1.2m Civilian Draft Registrations Index, Soldiers Death Index
			www.fold3.com * $	AEF Air Service, Military Cablegrams, Expeditionary Forces, FBI Case Files
			www.familysearch.org/search/ collection/list FREE	24m Draft Registration Cards, Service Records, 18k Index to Naturalizations of WWI Soldiers, 6k Calif. Enemy Alien Registration Affidavits
			www.archives.gov/research/military/ index.html > World War I FREE	Selected Records Online, Draft Registration Cards, Disabled Veterans
			www.militaryindexes.com FREE	Links to records on assorted sites.
World War II 16.5 million+ servicemen, 405,399+ casualties.	1941-1945	1877-1925	www.ancestry.com * $ > Search > Military	Draft Registration Cards, Army Enlistment Records, POW Records, Dead Roster, 160k Veterans Buried Overseas, Muster Rolls

2 Make New Discoveries

U.S. Online Military Records Chart

War/ Casualties	Conflict Years	Approx. Birth Years	Location	Available Records / Documents
The majority of WWII, Korean and Vietnam War records are not publicly available yet.			www.fold3.com * $	"Old Man's Draft" Registration Cards, Holocaust Collection, Missing Air Crew Reports, Air Force Photos, Hero Pages, Pearl Harbor Muster Rolls
			www.familysearch.org/search/ collection/list $	24m Draft Registration Cards 9m Army Enlistment Records
			www.archives.gov/research/military/ index.html >World War II FREE	Selected Records, Casualty Lists, 9m Army Enlistment Records, Captured German Records, Japanese Interment Records
			www.militaryindexes.com FREE	Links to records on assorted sites.
Korean War 33,642 casualties	1950-1953	1900-1936	www.archives.gov/research/military/ index.html >Korean War FREE	Electronic records online, Casualties / MIA, Links
			www.militaryindexes.com FREE	Links to records on assorted sites.
			www.ancestry.com * $ >Search >Military	143K Casualty List, POWs, Veterans Interred Overseas, 14m Beneficiary Identification Records
Vietnam War 110,000+ casualties	1964-1972	1914-1955	www.archives.gov/research/military/ index.html >Vietnam War FREE	Casualty and POW/MIA Records
			www.fold3.com * $	Interactive Veterans Memorial database, Service Awards, Marine Corp Photos
			www.ancestry.com * $	100k+ Military Casualties List, Awards and Decorations of Honor, 14m Veterans Affairs BIRLS Death File, 1850-2010
			www.militaryindexes.com FREE	Links to records on assorted sites.
			www.dtic.mil/dpmo FREE http://lcweb2.loc.gov/pow/powhome .html	161k POW/MIA list

*Ancestry (Library Edition), Fold3 and HeritageQuestOnline are free at most local Family History Centers. HeritageQuestOnline is also searchable free through subscribing libraries; check your local library whether you can log on from home via the library's Web site using your library card.

Use Libraries, Archives and Societies

Rich Sources of Unique Information and Assistance

Even though the Internet contains a seemingly endless depth of information for tracing your own family roots and stories, sooner or later you will need to visit a library, archive, repository, court house, churches or cemetery to find records that you can't find as yet on the Internet.

It's difficult to physically visit the library in every town in which your ancestors may have lived, but most libraries around the world now have their library catalogs and collections online, so their information is becoming increasingly available to us. You can quickly know whether that library has the information or title you want, if it's available by interlibrary loan, or found in a nearby branch library. It's fast, convenient, and time-saving.

See more information–including county and state archives–beginning on page 185.

The Family History Library - FREE

www.familysearch.org

The library houses a collection of genealogical records that includes the names of more than 3 billion deceased people. It is the largest

collection of its kind in the world, including: vital records (birth, marriage, and death records from both government and church sources); census returns; court, property, and probate records; cemetery records; emigration and immigration lists; printed genealogies; and family and county histories.

National Archives - FREE

www.archives.gov

Your can search for military, immigration and other records at the archives of the US government. This site offers two digital databases into the archives' holdings. The ARC (Archival Research Catalog) indexes 6.4 million records and includes 153,000 digital records. The AAD (Access to Archival Databases) lets you search more than 85 million historical records, such as: photos, maps, immigration records, and over 9 million WWII enlistment files. Scroll down to *Online Databases* on the home page.

Library of Congress - FREE

www.loc.gov

The Library's mission is to make its resources available and useful to the American people and preserve a universal collection of knowledge and creativity for future generations. Since its founding in 1800, it has amassed more than 119 million items and become one of the world's leading cultural institutions. Just a few of the vast sections of the library include:

American Memory - FREE

http://memory.loc.gov

A gateway to rich primary source materials relating to the history and culture of the United States. The site offers

more than 7 million digital items from more than 100 historical collections.

America's Story - FREE

www.america'slibrary.com

Here you can discover what Abraham Lincoln had in his pockets on the night he was assassinated. Or you can read about Buffalo Bill Cody and his "Wild West" show; the heroism of Harriet Tubman, who helped many slaves escape bondage; the music of jazz great Duke Ellington; or the inventions of Thomas Edison. Click on *Jump Back in Time* and find the settlers who landed on Plymouth Rock. Or jump to a more recent age and read about be-bop, a type of music invented long before hip-hop. Do you know what happened on the day you were born? You can find out here.

Library of Congress Genealogy - FREE

www.loc.gov/rr/genealogy

Description with links to genealogy resources. The Library has more than 50,000 genealogies and 100,000 local histories. The collections are especially strong in North American, British Isles, and German sources. Their 'Vertical File' is an alphabetical index of materials on file but to view the items you must be at the library. It contains miscellaneous materials relating to specific family names, states, towns, and cities.

American Treasures - FREE

www.loc.gov/exhibits/treasures

An unprecedented permanent exhibition of the rarest, most interesting or significant items relating to America's past, drawn from every corner of the world's largest library.

The following web sites are directories of genealogy libraries and archives.

Library Directories

Cyndi's List - FREE

www.cyndislist.com/lib-b.htm

Links to libraries, archives and museums.

Directory of Genealogy Libraries - FREE

www.gwest.org/gen_libs.htm

Alphabetically listed by state and national.

Academic Genealogy - www.academic-genealogy.com/librariesmuseums.htm FREE

A comprehensive directory of links to genealogy libraries and museums.

WorldCat - www.oclc.org > *WorldCat* FREE

The window to the world's libraries. WorldCat is a global network of library content and services.

LibDex - www.libdex.com FREE

An easy-to-use index to 18,000 libraries worldwide, library home pages, Web-based library catalogs, Friends of the Library pages and library e-commerce affiliates.

World Wide Library Catalogues FREE

www.loc.gov/z3950

An online gateway from the Library of Congress with links to library catalogs.

European Library - FREE

www.theeuropeanlibrary.org/tel4

An online portal that offers quick and easy access to the collections of the 48 National Libraries of Europe and leading European Research Libraries.

Become familiar with local libraries, historical and genealogical societies, and Family History Centers in your area.

FREE

Major Family History Libraries

Family History Library, Salt Lake City, Utah - www.familysearch.org. The largest genealogical library in the world houses 2 million rolls of microfilm and more than 270,000 compiled family histories.

Library of Congress, Genealogical Room, Thomas Jefferson Annex, Washington, DC - http://lcweb.loc.gov/rr/genealogy/

U.S. National Archives and Records, Washington, DC - www.archives.gov/index.html

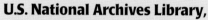

U.S. National Archives Library, College Park, Maryland - www.archives.gov/research_room/genealogy/index.html

National Genealogical Society Library, Arlington, Virginia - www.ngsgenealogy.org

New England Historic Genealogical Society Library, Boston, Massachusetts (Specializes in data about New England and NY, and the states to which they migrated.) - www.newenglandancestors.org

Daughters of the American Revolution Genealogical Library, Wash., D.C. - www.dar.org/library/library.html

Palatines to America National Library, Columbus, Ohio (ancestors from all German-speaking lands) - www.palam.org

New York Public Library, New York, New York - www.nypl.org

Newberry Library, Chicago, Illinois - www.newberry.org

Allen County Public Library, Ft Wayne, Indiana - www.acpl.lib.in.us

Use state and national resources after you have thoroughly explored what is available to you locally which will save you time and money.

Allen County Public Library - **FREE**
www.genealogycenter.org

A unique and valuable resource. They have one of the largest research collections available, incorporating records from around the world, including: compiled genealogies, printed volumes, US census records, city directories, passenger lists, military records, and many local records and special collections.

Making of America - **FREE**
http://moa.umdl.umich.edu and http://moa.cit.cornell.edu/moa

This is a joint project between the University of Michigan and Cornell University which provides free access to a large collection of 19th century books, journal articles, and imprints available on two websites. Two separate online archive sites put digitized books at your fingertips. The first collection contains some 10,000 books and 50,000 journal articles; the second site covers 267 monograph volumes and more than 100,000 journal articles.

Canadian Genealogy Centre - **FREE**
www.collectionscanada.gc.ca/genealogy

Library and Archives Canada collects and preserves Canada's documentary heritage including publications, archival records, sound and audio-visual materials, photographs, artworks, and electronic documents such as websites. It offers genealogical content, services, advice, research tools and searchable databases for vital, census, immigration and naturalization, military, land and people records, all in both official languages.

Family History Books –
www.lib.byu.edu/fhc

A collection of more than 100,000 published genealogy and family history books. The archive includes histories of families, county and local histories, how-to books on genealogy, genealogy magazines and periodicals, medieval books, and gazetteers. Combines family history books from the collections of the Family History Library, the Allen County Public Library, Houston's Clayton Library, the Mid-Continent Public Library Midwest Genealogy Center, the BYU Harold B. Lee Library, the BYU Hawaii Joseph F. Smith Library, and the LDS Church historical library.

DenverLibrary Western History –
http://history.denverlibrary.org

The collection includes 200,000 cataloged books, pamphlets, atlases, maps, microfilm titles, 600,000 photographs, 3,700 manuscript archives, and a remarkable collection of Western fine art and prints. You can order photo prints and digital photos on line for a fee.

New York Library Collections –
www.nypl.org/collections

Collections include more than 14 million books, 400 databases, 700,000 images digitized, 30,000 ebooks, music, and video items, and 66,000 linear feet of manuscripts. It covers American Indian portraits, African-American history and migration, historical photographs, surveyors of the American West, Holocaust memorial books and much more.

Online Archive of California –
www.oac.cdlib.org

Compilation of historical materials from museums, historical societies and archives. You'll find more than 170,000 images, 50,000 pages of documents, letters and oral histories, and 8,000 guides to collections.

WorldCat.org –
www.worldcat.org

Search the collections of libraries in your community and thousands more around the world; more than 10,000 libraries worldwide with more than 1 billion holdings. There's no better tool to identify obscure or out-of-print books to borrow on interlibrary loan.

DAR Library - www.dar.org/library

Daughters of the American Revolution library, one of the largest genealogical libraries in the world, is an essential destination when researching your family history. Since its founding in 1896, the library has grown into a specialized collection of American genealogical and historical manuscripts and publications.

Repositories of Primary Sources -
www.uidaho.edu/special-collections/other.repositories.html

A listing with Internet links of over 5300 websites describing holdings of manuscripts, archives, rare books, historical photographs, and other primary sources for the research scholar.

Genealogical and Historical Societies

Many genealogical and historical societies have re-invented themselves in recent years, embracing social media, virtual education, digital publishing, and other tools to reach a far-flung audience.

They are great for social interaction among like-minded colleagues. They may offer educational classes, workshops, and discounts on annual conferences. In addition, there is often a discount for online research subscriptions and society publications, as well as lookup or research services.

Genealogical and historical societies can help you find an ancestor's place of origin. You can also find living relatives, others researching the same family, and records or indexes revealing your ancestor's place of origin.

Subscribing to historical publications from your area of interest, and membership in genealogical societies, should be part of every family historian's working strategy. These periodicals should be studied closely for the information that they provide. Working in large library collections, or online indexes, can provide you with access to other titles which you otherwise would not have access to.

Below you can find online lists of societies of your interests for your consideration, but some of the key societies include:

National Genealogical Society -
www.ngsgenealogy.org

Founded in 1903 as a non-profit organization, the National Genealogical Society (NGS) is a dynamic and growing membership of individuals and other groups from all over the world that share a common love of genealogy. Whether you're a beginner, a professional or somewhere in between, NGS can assist you in your research into the past. The NGS is one of the important genealogical societies in the U.S., and is an excellent site for learning genealogy standards and methods.

NEHGS - New England Historic Genealogical Society -
www.americanancestors.org

They provide expertise and research in 17th-century colonial New England through twentieth-century immigration research. Their website offers more than 200 million searchable names covering New England, New York, and beyond. Their databases include Massachusetts Vital Records, Abstracts of Wills, Administrations and Guardianships in NY State, 1787-1835, and more.

Ohio Genealogical Society -
www.ogs.org

The largest state genealogical society in the US. Annual state conferences, summer workshops, boot camp for beginners — all offer assistance for beginners and even experienced family history researchers. Online databases and educational resources help members find ancestors in Ohio and beyond. Publications target Ohio research and history.

Utah Genealogical Association -
www.infouga.org

https://familysearch.org/learn/wiki/en/Utah_Genealogical_Association

Provides genealogical information, sources and education through personal instruction and published media on state, national and international family history topics. They sponsor week-long courses annually at the Salt Lake Institute of Genealogy. Pioneer certificates are issued to anyone proving pioneer heritage in Utah. http://www.ngsgenealogy.org

Indiana Genealogical Society -

www.indgensoc.org

They currently have 1,089 databases offering more than 500k records. Their databases include African-American records, church records, county records, and military records.

Illinois State Genealogical Society -

www.ilgensoc.org

They offer a great quarterly journal and free monthly webinars. They are very active in different projects, including the War of 1812 Pensions Project. Their free collections include: African-American, Ancestor Photos, Certified Prairie Pioneers, Family Bible Records Surname Index, Illinois Cemetery Locations, Evangelical Church records, and Military Certificates.

California Genealogical Society -

http://californiaancestors.org

They offer research services, online one-of-a-kind genealogical indexes and databases, and a research library housing over 38,000 reference materials from California, the US, and around the world. Their Library is rich in genealogy reference materials covering people and places in California and the rest of the country. They also offer a wide array of educational opportunities including workshops and classes.

Southern California Genealogical Society -

www.scgsgenealogy.com

You can list queries, survey indexes, join special interest groups and provide support for other members. They offer a research library with over 40,000

volumes including 6,000 family histories. Research resources also include manuscripts, microforms, maps, periodicals and electronic data resources. The annual Genealogy Jamboree is recognized as one of the premier education and exhibitor events in the United States. They also provide free webcasts with knowledgeable genealogists.

German Genealogy Group -

www.germangenealogygroup.com

Provides support to all those researching their Germanic ancestors, such as help sessions, finding aids, lectures, mentoring, a monthly newsletter, translation services, an extensive CD and book lending library and a forum to meet and discuss research problems and solutions. Their collections include: Church, naturalization, New York vital records, and German and immigrant databases.

Check out your local or national genealogical society for addition resources to help you.

Where to Locate a Genealogical Society

Ancestry Wiki List - (FREE)
www.ancestry.com/wiki/index.php?title=List_of_Genealogical_Societies

Cyndi's List - (FREE)
www.cyndislist.com/societies

FGS - Federation of Genealogical Societies - (FREE)
www.fgs.org
www.fgs.org/cstm_memberLocList.php

GeneaBloggers Blog List - (FREE)
http://geneabloggers.com/genealogy-blogs

Search Adoption Records

Know something about your birth family if appropriate

If you are adopted, it's only natural that you will have some curiosity about your birth family. After all, they are the people from whom you've inherited your DNA. The way you look, any genetic conditions you may have, and even some of your interests and talents may all be determined by your biological heredity.

> Trying to find family members that were lost years ago seems like a daunting task, especially when some State's have closed adoption records, but it is possible.

Research Tip

A positive outlook is key. Don't give up hope. They may be looking for you too. Start by researching the resources found here, plus visit your local library to read about how to search for adoption records. Google the first names and birth dates, and make a Facebook and MySpace page with the birth date information. *Check out the other social networking options on page 45.*

You and your birth parents and relatives who were separated by adoption may decide to search for each other at some point in your lives. But locating information about an adoption in your family usually takes time. When your search is successful, you may consider meeting your birth relatives.

Even if you don't want to contact your birth family, you may still want to know something about them in order to learn more about yourself. Access to one's own information is a vital part of life, including shaping a positive identity. No matter if you're a mother looking for your child or an adult child looking for your birth parents, here are some resources that will help you in your quest.

Sealed Adoption Records

At present, seven states offer open or semi-open adoption records: Alabama, Alaska, Delaware, Kansas, Maine, Oregon and Tennessee. In most States, adoption records are sealed after an adoption is finalized. The adopted person, birth parents, and adoptive parents must follow procedures established by the State to obtain identifying confidential information from the adoption records. But you may be able to obtain non-identifying information from the agency that arranged the adoption.

How Many are Adopted?

It is estimated that 2% of the U.S. population, or about 6-10 million Americans, are adoptees. Including biological parents, adoptive parents, and siblings, this means that 1 in 8 Americans are directly touched by adoption. Another source suggests that 6 in 10 people are touched by adoption (that is an estimated over 100 million people in the U.S.), over half are trans-racial or multicultural adoption experiences. Source: www.mixedrootsfoundation.org/about. **FREE**

There is NO single source for the total number of children adopted in the United States, and there is currently no straightforward way of determining the total number of adoptions, even when multiple data sources are used. No single agency is charged with compiling this information, and agencies that do collect adoption-related data do so for their

7 Tips: How to Locate Your Birth Parents

1. **Talk to your parents** who raised you about your desire to locate your birth parents. Visit with every family member and ask what they remember. They may be able to provide valuable clues that will help you trace your background.

2. If your parents are able to give you the name of your birth mother or birth father, plug those names and the town where you were born into **a search engine.** Even if the mother or father do not still live in the area, a search may turn up old newspaper articles or high school sports information.

3. Run the names through **social networking** and bookmarking sites if you know your birth parents' approximate ages when you were born. Married women often opt to include both their married and maiden names on social networks so old friends can find them. *See page 47.*

4. **Contact the records department at the hospital** where you were born. Explain that you are attempting to obtain information contained in your birth record. If you live close enough to the hospital, visit in person. Although your birth certificate was amended to list the names of your adoptive parents, your birth record, in most cases, will still contain the name of your birth mother. Hospital policies differ regarding the distribution of records.

5. **Call the local court** to ask for an adoption intermediary, an individual designated to attempt to initiate contact between biological parents and their birth children. The adoption intermediary will be allowed access to all of the original records from your birth and will then contact your biological parents on your behalf. However, the adoption intermediary is not permitted to pass any confidential information onto you unless your birth parents agree.

6. **Hire a private investigator** if you have some specific information on your birth parents.

7. **Register at an adoption registry,** such as www. registry.adoption.com. Adoption registries help connect biological parents with children through voluntary search profiles. Some adoption registries, such as www.adopteeconnect.com, also provide lists of state adoption and confidentiality laws that may affect your search.

own purposes and therefore count adoptions differently (e.g., by court cases filed, birth certificates modified, adoptions completed by public agencies), which makes aggregation difficult.

Here's a report that uses data from 2007 and 2008 – rather than more recent years – because of the length of time it takes States and secondary data sources to process the data and make them available. www.childwelfare.gov/pubs/adopted 0708.pdf

Learn More about Searching - FREE

www.childwelfare.gov/adoption/search

Start here to learn more about searching: Obtaining birth and/ or adoption records, Searching for birth relatives, Reuniting with birth relatives, Lifelong impact of adoption, When your child wants to search for birth relatives.

How to 'Open' Court Adoption Records

1. **Research the laws** regarding adoption records in your state.

2. **Find out what court** handled your adoption. Your adoptive parents are usually the best source for this information. If asking them is not possible, inquire at the court in the town where you were born (if you know what town it was) or where your adoptive parents were living at the time of your birth.

3. Go to the court that handled your adoption and **ask the clerk for a petition to open your records.** You'll usually be given this free of charge – no questions asked.

4. **Fill out the petition.** You'll be asked the reason you want your adoption records to be unsealed. Having a reason beyond simple curiosity increases your chances of success.

5. **Submit the petition to the court clerk.** You'll be given a hearing date. That is the date the judge will consider and rule on your petition.

6. **Show up in court** for the hearing. In most cases, your physical presence is not required, but it reflects favorably upon you and can improve the odds of the judge granting your request.

In your search, consider the following records, because they may contain information that can give you clues.

2 Make New Discoveries

Searching for Birth Relatives: Adoption General Information - FREE
www.childwelfare.gov/pubs/adoption_gip_three.cfm

This packet of four fact sheets from the federal government site is designed to help the adopted person, the birth family, and the adoptive family learn about the impact of adoption. Coping skills, support groups, resources for searching, and State laws regarding access to adoption records are discussed. An additional fact sheet addresses the topic of searching for birth relatives and is designed for both adopted persons and for birth family members.

Access to Adoption Records: Summary of State Laws - FREE
www.childwelfare.gov/systemwide/laws_policies/statutes/infoaccessapall.pdf

In nearly all States, adoption records are sealed and withheld from public inspection after an adoption is finalized. Most States have instituted procedures by which parties to an adoption may obtain both non-identifying and identifying information from an adoption record while still protecting the interests of all parties. This resource provides definitions of non-identifying and identifying information, an overview of who may access such information,

Research Tip

Local and county records such as court records and adoption proceedings.

https://familysearch.org/learn/wiki/en/United_States_Court_Records FREE.

Death certificates, obituaries, cemeteries, and funeral home records.

https://familysearch.org/learn/wiki/en/United_states_vital_records, and https://familysearch.org/learn/wiki/en/United_States_Obituaries.

Archived historical newspapers. *See Bring Your Ancestors to Life Using Newspapers on page.196.*

Hospital records

and information about access to original birth certificates. Summaries of laws for all States and U.S. territories are included.

Statutes for a Specific State - FREE
www.childwelfare.gov/systemwide/laws_policies/state/index.cfm?event=stateStatutes.processSearch

Search this site's database to access the statutes for a specific State.

Links to Adoption Records of Each State

https://familysearch.org/learn/wiki/en/United_States_Adoption_Research **FREE**

Provides detailed information and links to records (including adoption records) of each US state.

How to Access Adoption Records - **FREE**

www.ehow.com/how_5732881_access-adoption-records.html

The process of acquiring information about your adoption depends on the state where you were born and/or adopted. Each state has statutes that govern what kinds of information may be shared and with whom. Historically, adoptions have been kept secret with laws and policies governing adoption records designed to keep them closed. While many states governing adoption records have made strides in increasing access to this information – it is relatively easy to access unidentifying data such as physical appearance and medical history of birth parents – it is still difficult to find the names or whereabouts of birth parents or adopted children.

Searching for Birth Relatives - **FREE**

www.childwelfare.gov/pubs/f_search.cfm

This fact sheet provides guidance to adopted persons and birth families on the search process and information access, as well as resources for further help in conducting a successful search. This fact sheet is designed to address the concerns of both adopted persons who are searching for birth parents or other birth relatives, as well as birth parents (both mothers and fathers) who want to locate a child who was adopted. While not a complete "how to" guide to searching, this fact sheet provides information on the different types of searches, issues that might arise during searching, and additional resources.

How to Find Your Birth Family - **FREE**

http://genealogy.about.com/cs/adoption/a/adoption_search.htm

Steps for locating adoptees, birth parents, and adoption records by Kimberly Powell.

Adoption Resources - **FREE**

http://genealogy.about.com/od/adoption/Adoption_Resources_for_Your_Family_Tree.htm

You are definitely not alone in your search. Resources for tracking down adopted children or birth parents.

How to Handle 'Adoption' in your Family Tree - **FREE**

http://genealogy.about.com/od/adoption/a/family_tree.htm

Adoptees often face a bit of indecision when faced with a family tree chart? Should it include the adopted family, the birth family, or both? Should the adoption be noted in any special way? Learn how to address an adoption in your family tree and download family tree charts which include special options for adopted families.

All About Adoption Searching - **FREE**

http://adoption.about.com/od/searching/ss/adoptionsearch.htm

A good article by Carrie Craft about: How to Begin an Adoption Search, How to Find Family Through Various Web Searches, Why Use Adoption Registries in Your Adoption Search? Using an Adoption Search Angel, and DNA testing.

Write Everything You Know *FREE* to Find Birth Parents -

http://adoption.about.com/od/howtosearch/qt/write_to_find_birth_parents.htm

The first step in trying to find birth parents is to write everything you know about yourself and your adoption. Besides getting your non-identifying information, it may even be the most important step toward finding birth parents.

Cyndi's Resources - *FREE*

www.cyndislist.com/adoption

Provides dozens of web links to resources under the following categories: General Resources; Locality Specific; Mailing Lists, Newsgroups and Chat; Professionals, Volunteers and Other Research Services; Publications, Software and Supplies, and Societies and Groups.

Putting the Puzzle Together Using DNA - *FREE*

www.mixedrootsfoundation.org

A nonprofit organization to bring people and organizations together to make a difference and leave a legacy for the adoptee community and their families. Their new *Global Adoptee Genealogy Project* is creating a DNA database to help adoptees find relatives. They have partnered with two leading DNA testing companies, 23andMe and Family Tree DNA, and have established a fund to help adopted people and their families discover their biological and cultural roots through DNA testing. This project goes a long way toward giving adopted people the tools and knowledge to start putting together the pieces of their own puzzles.

10 Things Checklist: Help Find Family Separated by Adoption - *FREE*

http://adoption.about.com/od/howtosearch/tp/checklist_to_help_find_family.htm

A checklist to help find family members.

Unique Success Story *FREE* Using Facebook -

http://abcnews.go.com/blogs/technology/2013/01/utah-woman-finds-apparent-birth-mother-through-viral-facebook-post

A recent article about one woman's incredible story about finding her birth mother in 3 days using Facebook.

Ride Upon the Wings of Time

"Remember me in the family tree
My name, my days, my strife;
Then I'll ride upon the wings of time
And live an endless life."

Linda Goetsch

This poem is copyrighted and reproduced with kind permission from Linda Goetsch at www.grillyourgranny.com

You Will Find It

"The spirit and influence of your dead will guide those who are interested in finding those records. If there is anywhere on the earth anything concerning them, you will find it."

Melvin J. Ballard (1873-1939)

Melvin J. Ballard

Search Ethnic Records

African American Roots

The states and counties with the largest African American ancestry are indicated in purple, according to the US 2000 census.

www.census.gov/population/www/cen2000/census atlas/pdf/9_Ancestry.pdf

Many people have interesting challenges in doing ethnic research. This may be particularly true of African American research. However, many African Americans, believing they are descendants of slaves, falsely assume that records relating to the lives of their ancestors are non-existent. This is not necessarily the case today due to the availability of new information on the Internet and the compilation of records by thousands of people. For example, the 1870 Federal Census was the first to name all Blacks.

FreedmensBureau.com - FREE

www.freedmensbureau.com
www.africanaheritage.com/Freedmens_Bureau.asp
http://en.wikipedia.org/wiki/Freedmen%27s_Bureau

The Civil War had liberated nearly four million slaves and destroyed the region's cities, towns, and plantation-based economy. The Bureau was a government agency (est. 1865) that aided distressed freedmen (freed slaves) in 1865–1872. It issued food and clothing, operated hospitals

A Rosetta Stone

William Alexander Haley, chairman of the Alex Haley Center, said,

"The Freedman's Bank records may be more than just an historical record. They may be the Rosetta Stone – the piece that allows you to go in and make the connection."

It's difficult for us who are not the descendants of slaves to fully comprehend the sense of pain and loss of identity for African-Americans. We have never tried to piece together our ancestry from families who howled in pain as they were sold away from each other. Or who cannot find their grandparents in a census because they were considered only a possession. Or had no surname except for one they borrowed from a 'master' who claimed them as property.

and temporary camps, helped locate family members, promoted education, helped freedmen legalize marriages, provided employment, supervised labor contracts, provided legal representation, investigated racial confrontations, settled freedmen on abandoned or confiscated lands, and worked with African American soldiers and sailors and their heirs to secure back pay, bounty payments, and pensions.

The records not only contain the names of many thousands of freed slaves, but also provide details about the lives of freedpersons during the Reconstruction Period in America.

Freedman's Bank Index - FREE

www.familysearch.org
>Search >Browse All Published Collections

Freedman's Bank Records is a unique searchable database documenting several generations of African Americans immediately following the Civil War.

Congress chartered the Freedman's Savings and Trust Company in 1865 with the primary objective to assist former slaves and African-American soldiers with their new financial responsibilities. Ideally, this bank would be a permanent financial institution for savings deposits only and assist families with the challenges they faced in their transition from slavery to freedom. It was also designed to provide a place, safe from swindlers, to deposit money while individuals learned personal finance management skills. But mismanagement and outright fraud caused the bank to collapse in 1874, dashing the hopes and dreams of many African Americans. Bank deposits totaling more than $57 million were tragically lost.

Reginald Washington of the National Archives and Records Administration said, *"An idea that began as a well-meaning experiment in philanthropy had turned into an economic nightmare for tens of thousands of African Americans."*

A Silver Lining

Now, over 150 years later, there is a silver lining to the disaster. In an effort to establish bank patrons' identities, bank workers at the time recorded the names and family relationships of account holders, sometimes taking brief oral histories. Many of the records documented family relationships and relatives

Begin at home to find information about yourself and work back one generation at a time.

Research Tip

Interview relatives for family history stories. Enter the information that you have gathered on a pedigree chart, family group record and research log. Join an African American genealogical society. Learn about African American history and the records that are available to you.

who were sold into slavery to other locations. In the process, they created the largest single repository of lineage-linked African-American records known to exist.

It contains more than 480,000 names, documenting several generations of former slaves. Remarkably, the records of an institution that caused so much pain among African Americans following the Civil War now hold keys for their posterity to discover their roots. For the 8 to 10 million Americans who have ancestors whose names are recorded in the Freedman Bank Records, these records now cast a new light on their ancestry.

GenealogyBank.com - $

www.genealogybank.com/gbnk/ethnic/african_american

http://www.genealogybank.com/static/african-american-heritage.html

The leading provider of digitized historical and recent newspapers for family history research, including over 300 African-American newspapers from 1827-present. An especially rich resource for historical newspapers containing runaway slave ads, estate sale notices and Post-Emancipation obituaries; it offers fascinating insights into African American history, culture and daily life, and provides a vivid snapshot of virtually every aspect of the African American experience. You will find firsthand perspectives on notable Americans from Frederick Douglass to Martin Luther King, Jr., as well as obituaries, advertisements, editorials and illustrations. New content added daily. You can search for free, but you need to subscribe to view the details. $9.95/month, $69.95/year.

Afro-American Historical and $ Genealogical Society - www.aahgs.org

Strives to preserve African-ancestored family history, genealogy, and cultural diversity by teaching

African American research is no different from any other. Here's some tips to get started.

Research Tip

Getting Started with Your African American Research

First you start with what you know

Research all US census records back to 1870

1870 was the first census where everyone was listed by name

Before 1870 African Americans were listed only if free (FPOC - free person of color)

Before this time you have to search other resources

research techniques and disseminating information throughout the community. Their primary goals are to promote scholarly research, provide resources for historical and genealogical studies, create a network of persons with similar interests, and assist members in documenting their histories.

African-American Genealogy Group - $

www.aagg.org

A valuable resource for searching African-American roots. $25/membership dues.

Ancestry.com Articles and Webinars

Overview of African American Research - FREE

www.ancestry.com/wiki/index.php?title=Overview_of_African_American_Research

This article examines many of the records available, dealing both with slave and non-slave related records.

Expert Advice: FREE African American Family History-

www.ancestry.com/cs/Satellite?childpage-name=USLearningCenter%2FLearning_C%2FPageDefault&pagename=LearningWrapper&cid=1265125705236

African American family history has its challenges, but fortunately, those challenges don't become big hurdles until before 1870. And even then you may be able to discover more about your African American family line by getting creative with whom and how you research.

African American Family History - FREE

www.ancestry.com/cs/Satellite?childpage-name=USLearningCenter%2FLearning_C%2FPageDefault&pagename=LearningWrapper&cid=1265125698832

Juliana Smith gives good tips on doing African American research.

African American Research - FREE

www.ancestry.com/cs/Satellite?childpage-name=USLearningCenter%2FLearning_C%2FPageDefault&pagename=LearningWrapper&cid=1265125597281

Searching for African American families involves two distinct research approaches.

Making a Breakthrough in your African American Research - FREE

www.ancestry.com/cs/us/videos (Scroll down)

Avoid Traps in African American Genealogy - FREE

www.ancestry.com/cs/us/videos (Scroll down)

Cyndi's List.com - www.cyndislist.com FREE

A comprehensive, categorized and cross-referenced list of over 327k links in 199 categories that point you to genealogical research sites online. Contains hundreds of links for doing African American research. Each category in this section is helpful, but the "How To" category helps you find a place to get started. Each category is helpful, but the *"How To"* category helps you find a place to get started.

Fold3 African-American Collection -
http://go.fold3.com/blackhistory

View more than a million photos and documents from the National Archives found nowhere else on the internet. These newly digitized records provide a view into the lives of African Americans that few have seen before and cover subjects including slavery, military service, and issues facing African Americans dating back to the late 18th century. These records will help you to better understand the history and sacrifice that took

place in this country. 7-day Free trial, $11.95/month. Free at Family History Centers.

AfriGeneas.com - www.afrigeneas.com FREE

A searchable database of surnames for researching families of African ancestry. They offer a guide to family history resources around the world, and a mailing list of information about families of African ancestry. They also have impressive links to other websites to do research.

African American Cemeteries - FREE
http://africanamericancemeteries.com

Listing of African American cemeteries created by the Millenium Project Coalition.

Christine's Genealogy Website - FREE
www.ccharity.com

An excellent site about African-American history and genealogy.

Archives.com Articles

5 Sources for African-American Genealogy - FREE
www.archives.com/experts/berry-karin/hiding-in-plain-sight-5-sources-for-african-american-genealogy.html

You can find your relatives in common (and some not-so-common) records — you just need to know where and how to look.

Early African American and Anti-Slavery Newspapers - FREE
www.archives.com/experts/perez-marjory/early-african-american-and-anti-slavery-newspapers.html

These newspapers are valuable resources for African American genealogy research.

Researching African American Soldiers of the Civil War - FREE
www.archives.com/experts/hait-michael/researching-african-american-soldiers-of-the-civil-war.html

African Americans have a proud history of military service in the United States, including the Civil War.

FamilySearch Wiki Pages and Videos

African American Research - FREE

https://familysearch.org/learn/wiki/en/African_American_Research

A portal into many different topics and strategies for research, including: Keys to success in African American research, links to specific pages for different states, and numerous other key Internet links.

African American Introduction - FREE

https://familysearch.org/learn/wiki/en/African_American_Introduction

Specific strategies for tracing African-American roots prior to 1870.

Quick Guide to African American Records - FREE

https://familysearch.org/learn/wiki/en/Quick_Guide_to_African_American_Records

A comprehensive guide to strategies for discovering your African American ancestors in various periods of history, the most useful records and indexes to search, and specific information you need to trace your African American ancestors.

Free 25-Minute Video: African American Research - FREE

www.familysearch.org/learningcenter/lesson/ancestors-season-1-african-american-research/164

Learn ways to research African-American ancestry and manage the difficulties that arise in doing so. Learning the family stories is a very basic tool in beginning the research of your family.

Free 29-Minute Video: FREE Research at the Library of Congress -

https://familysearch.org/learningcenter/lesson/ancestors-season-1-african-american-research/164

https://familysearch.org/learningcenter/lesson/african-american-genealogical-research-at-the-library-of-congress/63

This presentation describes the African American collections found in the Library of Congress.

Free 59-Minute Video: Avoid Traps in African American Genealogy - FREE

www.familysearch.org/learningcenter/lesson/avoid-traps-in-african-american-genealogy/77

Tony Burroughs tells us how to avoid the "traps" in doing African American research.

Free 18-Minute Video: Finding the Slave Generation - FREE

www.familysearch.org/learningcenter/lesson/finding-the-slave-generation/37

This course will help you understand some basic research strategies to find your family who lived before the Civil War.

Free 73-Minute Video: National Underground Railroad - FREE

www.familysearch.org/learningcenter/lesson/national-underground-railroad-activities-and-accomplishments/147

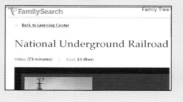

This lesson focuses on African-American history; the legacy of Afro-American roots.

Free 48-Minute Video: Research in Black Culture - *FREE*

www.familysearch.org/learningcenter/lesson/howard-dodson-chief-of-the-schomburg-center-for-research-in-black-culture-of-new-york-public-library/153

Howard Dodson lectures on the legacy of African-American history and the genealogical value of the book, "Roots" by Alex Haley. This is a very informative lecture.

Free 60-Minute Video: African-Native Americans - *FREE*

www.familysearch.org/learningcenter/lesson/researching-african-native-american-ancestors-of-indian-territory/148

Angela Walton-Raji lectures on researching African-Native American history. She stresses using standard genealogical methodology.

http://www.familysearch.org/learningcenter/lesson/making-a-breakthrough-in-your-african-american-research/86

Free 35-Minute Video: Roots West - *FREE*

www.familysearch.org/learningcenter/lesson/roots-west-african-american-history-in-the-trans-mississippi-west/150

Dr. Quintard Taylor discusses the nature of African-American history in the western United States, as it relates to genealogical research.

Free 35-Minute Video: *FREE* Tracing Slaveholdings and Slavery -

www.familysearch.org/learningcenter/lesson/tracing-slaveholdings-and-slavery-in-the-family/336

You will learn how tracing slaveholdings challenges you to explore the personal relationship and history in instituting slavery on the family.

Free 46-Minute Video: Trails Back - *FREE*

www.familysearch.org/learningcenter/lesson/trails-back-tracing-ancestors-in-slavery-through-census-probate-and-land/151

Beth Wilson focuses on tracing your Afro-American ancestors through census, probate and land records starting with the 1930 U.S. census and going back in time.

Free 60-Minute Video: Finding Records 1870-Present - *FREE*

www.familysearch.org/learningcenter/lesson/finding-records-of-your-ancestors-1870-present/155

Mary Hill instructs you how to find records of your Afro-American ancestors, starting with you and your family, and going back to the 1870's.

Guide to Black History - **FREE**

www.britannica.com/blackhistory

Encyclopedia Britannica's *Guide to Black History* features a timeline, Eras in Black History; a numerous collection of articles; related Internet links to history, culture, literature and music; and a study guide.

National Archive Resources - **FREE**

www.archives.gov/research/alic/reference/ethnic-heritage.html

Directory of web links to African-American resources.

African American Genealogical Society of Northern California - **$**

www.aagsnc.org

A non-profit organization dedicated in its commitment to national and international African-ancestry family history research. $30 membership.

Suggested Activities

■ Regardless of your ethnic background, historical events affected the lives of your ancestors, and learning about those events can help you in your family history search. Using the dates and places on your pedigree chart, create a simple time line that shows some of the historical events that your ancestors may have experienced, such as the Civil War, or the Great Depression.

■ Locate history books about those events that will help you better understand the lives and experiences of your ancestors. For African American research, three main historical eras influenced African American records:

- Civil War and Reconstruction (1861-1877)
- Segregation (1896-1954), and
- Civil Rights Movement (1954-1970).

You may want to join the FamilySearch-sponsored Genealogy Research Community on Facebook for free research help for your African American ancestors. Ask questions, find answers, teach others what you know.

Research Tip

FamilySearch / Facebook Free **FREE** African American Research Help

www.facebook.com/AfricanAmericanGenealogy

You can participate simply by...

Asking your research questions,

Collaborating on your own research,

Sharing knowledge you have gained as you've done your own research in a specific area, and

Clicking on the LIKE button and participating in the discussions on the page.

Ancestry's African-American Records -

www.ancestry.com/africanamerican **$**

Colored Volunteer Army Soldiers 1864

Colored Troop Deaths - Civil War 1862–1865

Slave Records, 1672–1917

Negro Newspapers, 1829–1947

Free Colored Censuses, 1815–1832

Buffalo Soldiers 1866–1916

California, African American Who's Who, 1948

Interviews with Former Slaves, 1936–1938

Colored Troops Military Service Records, 1861–1865

Freedmen's Bureau Records, 1865–1878

Louisiana Slave Manifests, 1807–1860

Slave Ads and Abstracts, 1823–1849

Slave Owner Petitions, 1862–1863

Slave Emancipation Records, 1851–1863

U.S. Southern Claims Commission, 1871–1880

U.S. Federal Census - Slave Schedules, 1860

Slave Ads and Abstracts, 1823–1849

Slave Owner Petitions, 1862–1863

Slave Emancipation Records, 1851–1863

Slave Narratives - (FREE)

http://docsouth.unc.edu/neh

The University of North Carolina collects books and articles that document the individual and collective story of African Americans' struggle for freedom and human rights in the 18th, 19th, and 20th centuries.

Using Census Indexes to Find a Slaveholder – (FREE)

www.africanaheritage.com/Federal_Census_Indexes.asp

Tom Blake has written a valuable article about Using Federal Census Indexes to Find an 1860 Slaveholder.

U.S. Federal Slave Schedules – (FREE)

www.genealogyinc.com/census-records/slave-schedule

This database details those persons enumerated in the Slave Schedules of the 1850 and 1860 U.S. Federal Census and are linked to the actual images of the Census.

Slave Voyages.org - (FREE)

www.slavevoyages.org

The Trans-Atlantic Slave Trade Database has information on almost 35,000 slaving voyages that forcibly embarked over 10 million Africans for transport to the Americas between the sixteenth and nineteenth centuries. It offers a chance to rediscover the reality of one of the largest forced movements of peoples in world history. It documents the slave trade from Africa to the New World from the 1500s to the 1800s. The names of 70,000 human cargo are also documented (slaves' African names).

MySlaveAncestors.com - (FREE)

www.myslaveancestors.com

A small resource center by professional genealogists who understand the needs of beginning researchers. They offer a sound strategy for tracing your African-American roots, plus some professional help if you desire.

Lowcountry Africana.net - (FREE)

http://lowcountryafricana.net

This free site focuses on records that document the family and cultural heritage of African Americans in the historic rice-growing areas of South Carolina, Georgia and extreme northeastern Florida, home to the rich Gullah/Geechee culture. It will be a treasure trove of primary documents, book excerpts and multimedia for exploring and documenting the dynamic cultural and family heritage of the Lowcountry Southeast.

Afro-Louisiana History and Genealogy - (FREE)

www.ibiblio.org/laslave

A free site providing information on 100,000 Louisiana slaves 1719-1820 compiled by Gwendolyn Midlo Hall, Ph.D.

Documenting the American South - (FREE)

http://docsouth.unc.edu

This rich site from the University of North Carolina is especially strong on the African-American experience, including such collections as The Church in the Southern Black Community, Colonial and State Records of North Carolina, and North American Slave Narratives. It provides access to texts, images, and audio files related to southern history, literature, and culture. It currently includes twelve thematic collections of books, diaries, posters, artifacts, letters, oral history interviews, and songs.

Hispanic / Latino American Roots

Caribbean, Central and South America, Mexico and Spain

There are lots of great resources for tracing your Spanish language family roots and stories especially in Spain and Latin American countries. There are great articles, aids and tips about how-to begin, and the process for researching your Hispanic ancestors. The records of Hispanic countries are unmatched anywhere in their quality, quantity, and availability. In most cultures, church records are the beginning point of research, but this is especially true of the Hispanic culture, for the parish records of Spain, Mexico, and Peru are the oldest and most complete of any in the world.

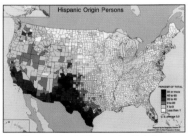

Percent of Hispanic Origin
www.census.gov/population/
www/cen2000/censusatlas/p
df/9_Ancestry.pdf

From the southwestern US to the tip of South America, and from the Philippines to Spain, Hispanics are a diverse population. From the small country of Spain, tens of millions of Spaniards emigrated to Mexico, Puerto Rico, Central and South America, Latin America, North America and Australia. Spaniards settled the Caribbean islands and Mexico more than a century before the English settled Jamestown and Plymouth in 1607 and 1620. The earliest Hispanic settlers in the United States settled Saint Augustine, Florida, in 1565 and New Mexico in 1598.

The greatest challenge is often identifying the place of origin in the mother country. Fortunately, there are many good records available that can help you find this information. Nothing is more exciting than to discover that your ancestry leads back to Mexico or bridges the ocean back to Spain. Whether the mother country is Argentina, Cuba, Mexico, Spain, or another Latin American or European country, the types of records to be searched and the process of searching those records remain basically the same.

Find Your Family's Place of Origin

In order to discover your Hispanic roots and stories, you need to use the records of your Mother country to trace your family back to the country of origin. You'll need to search through public records of the place where your ancestors lived to do that.

FamilySearch: Mexico - FREE

https://familysearch.org/learn/wiki/en/Mexico
https://familysearch.org/mexico-genealogy

In FamilySearch Wiki you can learn how to find, use, and analyze Mexican records featuring links to Mexican states. FamilySearch's vast historical record collections, includes:

- Mexico, Baptisms, 1560-1950 - 43 million records
- Mexico, Deaths, 1680-1940 - 362k
- Mexico, Hidalgo, Catholic Church Records, 1546-1971 - 1.5 million
- Mexico, Marriages, 1570-1950 - 6.2 million
- Mexico, National Census, 1930 - 3.1 million

Click here www.familysearch.org *>Search >Browse* All Published Collections to access the historical record collections directly.

FamilySearch Wiki: Mexico Land and Property - FREE

https://familysearch.org/learn/wiki/en/Mexico_Land_and_Property

Land records are primarily used to learn where an individual lived and when he or she lived there. They often reveal other information, such as the name

Slave Narratives - (FREE)

http://docsouth.unc.edu/neh

The University of North Carolina collects books and articles that document the individual and collective story of African Americans' struggle for freedom and human rights in the 18th, 19th, and 20th centuries.

Using Census Indexes to Find a Slaveholder – (FREE)

www.africanaheritage.com/Federal_Census_Indexes.asp

Tom Blake has written a valuable article about Using Federal Census Indexes to Find an 1860 Slaveholder.

U.S. Federal Slave Schedules – (FREE)

www.genealogyinc.com/census-records/slave-schedule

This database details those persons enumerated in the Slave Schedules of the 1850 and 1860 U.S. Federal Census and are linked to the actual images of the Census.

Slave Voyages.org - (FREE)

www.slavevoyages.org

The Trans-Atlantic Slave Trade Database has information on almost 35,000 slaving voyages that forcibly embarked over 10 million Africans for transport to the Americas between the sixteenth and nineteenth centuries. It offers a chance to rediscover the reality of one of the largest forced movements of peoples in world history. It documents the slave trade from Africa to the New World from the 1500s to the 1800s. The names of 70,000 human cargo are also documented (slaves' African names).

MySlaveAncestors.com - (FREE)

www.myslaveancestors.com

A small resource center by professional genealogists who understand the needs of beginning researchers. They offer a sound strategy for tracing your African-American roots, plus some professional help if you desire.

Lowcountry Africana.net - (FREE)

http://lowcountryafricana.net

This free site focuses on records that document the family and cultural heritage of African Americans in the historic rice-growing areas of South Carolina, Georgia and extreme northeastern Florida, home to the rich Gullah/Geechee culture. It will be a treasure trove of primary documents, book excerpts and multimedia for exploring and documenting the dynamic cultural and family heritage of the Lowcountry Southeast.

Afro-Louisiana History and Genealogy - (FREE)

www.ibiblio.org/laslave

A free site providing information on 100,000 Louisiana slaves 1719-1820 compiled by Gwendolyn Midlo Hall, Ph.D.

Documenting the American South - (FREE)

http://docsouth.unc.edu

This rich site from the University of North Carolina is especially strong on the African-American experience, including such collections as The Church in the Southern Black Community, Colonial and State Records of North Carolina, and North American Slave Narratives. It provides access to texts, images, and audio files related to southern history, literature, and culture. It currently includes twelve thematic collections of books, diaries, posters, artifacts, letters, oral history interviews, and songs.

Hispanic / Latino American Roots

Caribbean, Central and South America, Mexico and Spain

There are lots of great resources for tracing your Spanish language family roots and stories especially in Spain and Latin American countries. There are great articles, aids and tips about how-to begin, and the process for researching your Hispanic ancestors. The records of Hispanic countries are unmatched anywhere in their quality, quantity, and availability. In most cultures, church records are the beginning point of research, but this is especially true of the Hispanic culture, for the parish records of Spain, Mexico, and Peru are the oldest and most complete of any in the world.

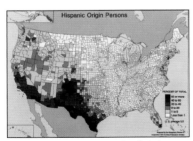

Percent of Hispanic Origin
www.census.gov/population/
www/cen2000/censusatlas/p
df/9_Ancestry.pdf

From the southwestern US to the tip of South America, and from the Philippines to Spain, Hispanics are a diverse population. From the small country of Spain, tens of millions of Spaniards emigrated to Mexico, Puerto Rico, Central and South America, Latin America, North America and Australia. Spaniards settled the Caribbean islands and Mexico more than a century before the English settled Jamestown and Plymouth in 1607 and 1620. The earliest Hispanic settlers in the United States settled Saint Augustine, Florida, in 1565 and New Mexico in 1598.

The greatest challenge is often identifying the place of origin in the mother country. Fortunately, there are many good records available that can help you find this information. Nothing is more exciting than to discover that your ancestry leads back to Mexico or bridges the ocean back to Spain. Whether the mother country is Argentina, Cuba, Mexico, Spain, or another Latin American or European country, the types of records to be searched and the process of searching those records remain basically the same.

Find Your Family's Place of Origin

In order to discover your Hispanic roots and stories, you need to use the records of your Mother country to trace your family back to the country of origin. You'll need to search through public records of the place where your ancestors lived to do that.

FamilySearch: Mexico - FREE

https://familysearch.org/learn/wiki/en/Mexico
https://familysearch.org/mexico-genealogy

In FamilySearch Wiki you can learn how to find, use, and analyze Mexican records featuring links to Mexican states. FamilySearch's vast historical record collections, includes:

- Mexico, Baptisms, 1560-1950 - 43 million records
- Mexico, Deaths, 1680-1940 - 362k
- Mexico, Hidalgo, Catholic Church Records, 1546-1971 - 1.5 million
- Mexico, Marriages, 1570-1950 - 6.2 million
- Mexico, National Census, 1930 - 3.1 million

Click here www.familysearch.org >Search >Browse All Published Collections to access the historical record collections directly.

FamilySearch Wiki: Mexico Land and Property - FREE

https://familysearch.org/learn/wiki/en/Mexico_Land_and_Property

Land records are primarily used to learn where an individual lived and when he or she lived there. They often reveal other information, such as the name

of a spouse, heir, other relatives, or neighbors. You may learn where a person lived previously, his or her occupation, and other clues for further research.

Mexico Free Research Guide - *FREE*

https://familysearch.org/learn/wiki/en/images/7/7f/Mexico_Research_Outline.pdf

An older but still valuable 68-page Research Outline from FamilySearch about Mexican family history records to search.

FamilySearch Free Videos - Mexico - *FREE*

https://familysearch.org/learningcenter/results.html?q=mexico

Crossing the Frontier - How to search for your ancestor if they crossed the U.S. border from Mexico between 1895 and 1957.

U.S. Hispanic Immigrants: Finding their Place of Origin - Ideas of different record types you can use to help identify the country of origin for your Hispanic ancestor.

Mexican Border Crossings - *FREE*

www.archives.gov/research/immigration/border-mexico.html

This article gives background information about the records, and describes available NARA microfilm publications containing these records. The National Archives and Records Administration (NARA) is currently processing microfilmed immigration records of persons crossing the U.S.-Mexican land border ca. 1903-1955.

KindredTrails.com Mexico - *FREE*

www.kindredtrails.com/mexico.html

Links to Mexican genealogy, including: Census, cemeteries, immigration, military records, maps, city directories, history, etc.

Genealogy of Mexico - *FREE*

http://garyfelix.tripod.com/~GaryFelix/index1.htm

Gary Felix's website about the early settlers and history of Mexico.

Mexico Genealogy Forum - *FREE*

http://genforum.genealogy.com/mexico

An active forum to post inquiries about Mexican genealogy and/or search for ancestors.

Getting Started with Spain Research -

https://familysearch.org/learn/wiki/en/Spain *FREE*

You can learn how to find, use, and analyze Spanish records with links to the 50 Spanish provinces and numerous wiki articles about Spanish records.

Spain Civil Registration Vital Records - *FREE*

https://familysearch.org/learn/wiki/en/Spain_Civil_Registration_-_Vital_Records

Provides links to numerous FamilySearch Wiki articles describing online collections which may contain pre-1870 civil registration records. Spanish civil registration records (births, marriages, and deaths) began in 1871. Spain does have a national index or central repository for civil registration. Spanish civil registration birth records are among the richest genealogical records in the world.

PARES – Portal de Archivos Españoles - *FREE*

http://pares.mcu.es

Search for ancestors in various archives of Spain – Spanish only.

GenWeb Spain Project - FREE

www.genealogia-es.com

Provides links, resources, databases and discussions related to genealogy research in Spain – Spanish only.

Ancestry Article:
Overview of Hispanic Research - FREE

www.ancestry.com/wiki/index.php?title=Overview _of_Hispanic_Research

A good article by George Ryskamp covering keys to success, basic research concepts, and where to search.

Hispanic Family History - FREE

www.ancestry.com/learn/learningcenters/default. aspx?section=lib_HistoriaFamiliar

A must-read article by George Ryskamp about Hispanic research. The records of Hispanic countries are unmatched anywhere in their quality, quantity, and availability.

Spanish Emigration Records - FREE

www.ancestry.com/wiki/index.php?title=Spanish_ Emigration_Records_in_Hispanic_Research

Detailed Ancestry article on finding passenger lists for emigration from Spain.

Church Records in Hispanic Research -

www.ancestry.com/wiki/index.php?title=Church_ Records_in_Hispanic_Research FREE

The records of the Roman Catholic Church represent the single best Spanish-language source for finding the family's place of origin. An article by George Ryskamp on this subject.

You may want to join the FamilySearch-sponsored Genealogy Research Community on Facebook for free research help for your Hispanic ancestors. Ask questions, find answers, teach others what you know.

FamilySearch / Facebook
Free Hispanic Research Help

FREE

www.facebook.com/HispanicGenealogy (English)
www.facebook.com/familysearch.argentina
www.facebook.com/GenealogicaBrasil
www.facebook.com/ChileGenealogy
www.facebook.com/ColombiaGenealogy
www.facebook.com/EcuadorGenealogy
www.facebook.com/GuatemalaGenealogy
www.facebook.com/HondurasGenealogy
www.facebook.com/MexicoGenealogyResearch
www.facebook.com/PanamaGenealogy
www.facebook.com/ParaguayGenealogy
www.facebook.com/PeruGenealogy
www.facebook.com/PuertoRicoGenealogy
www.facebook.com/Genealogica.en.Venezuela
www.facebook.com/VenezuelaGenealogy (English)

You can participate simply by...

• Asking your research questions,

• Collaborating on your own research,

• Sharing knowledge you have gained as you've done your own research in a specific area, and

• Clicking on the LIKE button and participating in the discussions on the page.

Archives.com Article:
Spanish Genealogy FREE

www.archives.com/genealogy/family-heritage-spanish.html

Explains the process to find your Spanish ancestors. The key to finding your Spanish roots lies in going from the known to the unknown. Once you have positively identified your immigrant ancestor in census or other records here in the United States, look for records that list a place of origin in the old country. Finding a parish of origin is absolutely critical to your search.

Spanish Genealogy & Family History -

http://genealogy.about.com/od/spain/Spanish_Geneal
ogy_Family_History.htm *FREE*

Explore genealogy and family tree records and tutorials for Spain with information on tracing your Spanish ancestors, locating Basque records, message and query boards, genealogy research sites and databases, archives, libraries, maps and history.

Introduction to Hispanic Genealogy -

http://genealogy.about.com/cs/hispanic/a/
ancestry.htm *FREE*

Kimberly Powell offers excellent tips and links to websites on researching your Hispanic heritage.

Researching Basque Country - *FREE*

www.buber.net/Basque/Diaspora/search.html

Tips for doing genealogical research of the Basque Country – the country that spans the border between France and Spain on the Atlantic coast.

National Hispanic Cultural Center - *FREE*

www.nhccnm.org

Their mission is to document and preserve Hispanic history, culture and literature. The permanent collections encompasses over 14,000 books, full text electronic databases, 2,000 rolls of microfilm, hundreds of video and audiotapes, as well as photo archives, maps; articles, e-books, books, journals, and more.

Catholic Church parish registers are the most reliable sources of information for Hispanic family history research in Latin America.

137

Catholic Church Parish Registers

Parish registers pre-date civil registration records, and they act as a supplement to them after civil registration began. Authorized parish priests created parish registers to record church sacraments. The most commonly used sacramental records (parish registers) are: baptisms, marriages, and burials.

CyndisList.com Hispanic *FREE*

www.cyndislist.com/mexico
www.cyndislist.com/central-and-south-america
www.cyndislist.com/caribbean
www.cyndislist.com/spain
www.cyndislist.com/portugal

A comprehensive, categorized and cross-referenced list of over 327k links in 199 categories that point you to genealogical research sites online. Contains hundreds of links for doing Hispanic research.

Hispangen - $

www.hispagen.es

A Spanish Association of Hispanic Genealogy to help you with your family history of Spain and the Hispanic world – in Spanish and English. € 36.00 ($47)/year.

Hispanic Genealogical Research Center - $

www.hgrc-nm.org

A non-profit society for encouraging and nurturing the pursuit of Hispanic ancestors and history. They feature genealogical collections, Church and government records, and a genealogy database of the Hispanic ancestors of New Mexico and their descendants called the Great New Mexico Pedigree Database. They publish monthly and quarterly newsletters. $22 membership/year.

Library of Congress: Hispanic - *FREE*

www.loc.gov/rr/genealogy/bib_guid/hispanic/mexico.html

Selected titles of Hispanic local history and genealogy in the US.

Hispanic Genealogy Blog - *FREE*

http://hispanicgenealogy.blogspot.com

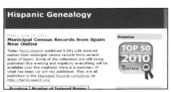

This blog by Lynn Turner provides research tips, latest news, and links related to Hispanic genealogy. Website is in English and Spanish.

Mexican Genealogy Blog - *FREE*

http://mexicangenealogy.info

A blog by Moises to educate and provide resources to locate your Mexican ancestors. Click on his Get Started Page.

Hispanic Genealogical Resources - *FREE*

www.genealogiahispana.com

A Directory of Hispanic web links in Spanish and English.

http://mexicangenealogy.info/8-websites-where-you-can-find-your-mexican-ancestors

SomosPrimos.com - *FREE*

www.somosprimos.com

This site is dedicated to Hispanic heritage and features a database of over 200k records of individuals, connected through pedigree and family group lines. Some lines have been traced back 40 generations. They have a monthly online newsletter.

Latin American and Spanish Videos - *FREE*

http://libguides.library.albany.edu/content.php?pid=570045&sid=428746

This is the most comprehensive Hispanic digital library by the University of Albany, New York. Its goal is to preserve and make accessible the Hispanic cultural heritage available in various formats (mainly texts, images and videos).

Historical Map Collection - *FREE*

www.davidrumsey.com

The David Rumsey Historical Map Collection has over 41k maps online. The collection focuses on 18th and 19th century North and South American cartographic materials. It includes atlases, globes, school geographies, maritime charts, and a variety of separate maps including pocket, wall, children's and manuscript maps.

Map of Mexico - *FREE*

http://geology.com/world/mexico-satellite-image.shtml

Atlas of Mexico - *FREE*

www.atlasdemexico.gob.mx

Hispanic Genealogical Societies

Non-profit public service and educational organizations.

New York - www.hispanicgenealogy.com

New Mexico - www.hgrc-nm.org

South Texas, Northern Mexico, New Mexico & California - www.hispanicgs.com

Texas Rio Grande Valley - www.rgvhispanicgenealogicalsociety.com

Colorado - www.hispanicgen.org

Houston - www.hispanicgs.org/societies.html

San Antonio - www.losbexarenos.org

California - http://shhar.net

Cuba - www.cubagenweb.org/refs/index.htm

Native American Roots

The history and heritage of the Native Americans who inhabited the American continent is a significant part of the American story. Searching for American Indian ancestors, although difficult, has become much easier today.

There are some facts you need to know in researching your Indian Ancestry. First, you need to know the name of the ancestor. Many Indian ancestors had only one name. Their surname may have been given to them by agents of the US Government or chosen from a list. Next, you need to know approximately when the person lived, and what state or territory they lived in. Then determine the federally-recognized or state-recognized 'tribal' affiliation of your ancestor. It is important to determine the tribal affiliation because most of the records are associated with the tribe. Do some basic homework on tribal history. Then, check out the 'how-to' resources and search for your ancestor in the records listed here.

Free 26-minute Video:
Native American Genealogy - *FREE*
www.byutv.org/watch/0d291ddf-7a46-4c37-9ee1-c81c39e28e71/questions-and-ancestors-native-american-genealogy

A good BYU Broadcasting introductory video featuring Jimmy Parker, a Native American Specialist, about tracing your Native American genealogy. It's a questions and answers format that introduces sources, tips and techniques on how to get-started.

FamilySearch Wiki:
Indians of the United States *FREE*
https://familysearch.org/learn/wiki/en/Indians_of_the_United_States_and_Their_Records

The native people who lived on the North American continent at the time of the first contact with European explorers and settlers were called Indians by the Europeans. They lived in families which often grouped themselves together in larger bodies, often given the name of tribes by the newcomers. For the purpose of studying the native population, they can be divided into classifications of different-sized groups. All of these groups are represented in this wiki article. It covers chronological history, historical background, records, and links to Tribal lists.

US Federal Census Records *FREE*

Until 1900 the Federal Census Records will be of little value for Indian families. The first federal decennial census that clearly identifies any Native Americans is the 1860 census. Although the 1870 census schedule is the first to list "Indian" as a choice in the column heading for "Color," Native Americans were enumerated earlier. Even though the 1860 census schedule does not include "Indian" as a choice in the column heading for "Color," enumerators nevertheless followed the instructions cited in the previous paragraph and recorded more than 40,000 Indians.

Testing for Indian DNA helps to determine whether or not individuals are in fact from a real Native American heritage or not. However, your linage must be proven by genealogy, regardless of DNA testing. Tribal membership will not be granted by DNA results alone. You have the opportunity to gain benefits if you are of Native American ancestry, but more importantly, you will be able to discover the knowledge of your family and a heritage that you can be proud of. Look at this site explaining DNA: **Proving Native American Ancestry Using DNA** http://dna-explained.com/2012/12/18/proving-native-american-ancestry-using-dna

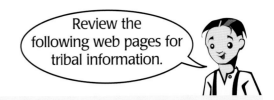

Review the following web pages for tribal information.

FamilySearch Catalog: Indians of North America - *FREE*

FREEhttps://familysearch.org/search/catalog/results#count=20&query=%2Bsubject_id%3A316050

Searching American Indians (subject No. 316050) in the catalog shows 234 results for books, microfilm and links to web pages for American Indians. You can order microfilms through your nearest family history center.

Allotment Records - *FREE*

https://familysearch.org/learn/wiki/en/American_Indian_Allotment_Records

Individual American Indians were given a prescribed amount of land on a reservation based upon what land was available and the number of tribal members living on that reservation. Not all tribes and reservations were allotted. On allotted reservations, each person was recorded in an allotment register, which included that person's name, the location of the allotment, the number of acres, an allotment number, age of the allottee, and his or her relationship to other individuals on the reservation.

American Indian Removal Records - *FREE*

https://familysearch.org/learn/wiki/en/American_Indian_Removal_Records

Several tribes were forcibly uprooted from their homelands in Georgia, Alabama, Mississippi and Florida. They were taken west of the Mississippi River in what is now Oklahoma. There are records of these removals, mostly buried within the set of records known as the General Correspondence Files of the Bureau of Indian Affairs. The collection has been microfilmed by the federal government and is available at the Family History Library at these sites:

National Archives microfilm publications

https://familysearch.org/search/catalog/822938?availability=Family%20History%20Library

https://familysearch.org/search/catalog/403528?availability=Family%20History%20Library

http://www.familysearch.orgAmerican Indian

Tribal Information

North American Indian Tribes - *FREE*

www.accessgenealogy.com/native/indianlocation.htm

www.accessgenealogy.com/native/index.htm

Offers over 250k pages of records, rolls, and information mostly on Native American research, including where to start.

Indian Tribes of the US - *FREE*

https://familysearch.org/learn/wiki/en/Indian_Tribes_of_the_United_States

American Indians have long been identified by "tribal" names. In the United States, there are hundreds of names by which these tribes are known.

Tribe index - *FREE*

www.dickshovel.com/trbindex.html.

Alphabetical Index of federally recognized tribes in US and Canada.

Carve Your Name on Hearts

"A good character is the best tombstone. Those who loved you, and were helped by you, will remember you when forget-me-nots are withered. Carve your name on hearts, and not on marble."

Charles Spurgeon

Charles Spurgeon (1834-1892), British Baptist preacher

Indian Census Records

American Indian Census Rolls - FREE

https://familysearch.org/learn/wiki/en/American_Indian_Census_Rolls

FamilySearch's wiki page on Indian census records. There are over 424k records in Indian Census Records which are available on the National Archives site below for free, and on Ancestry.com and Fold3.com (subscription sites).

Indian Census - 1885-1940 - FREE

http://archive.org/details/indian_census

The Internet Archive database contains an index to the Indian census rolls from 1885-1940. The data on the rolls varies to some extent. For certain years – including 1935, 1936, 1938, and 1939 – only supplemental rolls of additions and deletions were compiled. There is not a census for every reservation or group of Indians for every year. Only persons who maintained a formal affiliation with a tribe under federal supervision are listed on these census rolls.

Indian Census Records - FREE

www.accessgenealogy.com/native/census/index.htm

AccessGenealogy provides numerous links to

census records by tribe, links and information to other records such as rolls and cemeteries, tribal histories, and the process to discover your American Indian heritage. Check out their pages Proving Your Indian Heritage and DNA - Native American.

National Archives Publication - FREE

www.archives.gov/research/microfilm/m595.pdf

A PDF file of information from the National Archives about the Indian Census Records, including lists of tribes and jurisdictions and contents of microfilm rolls.

Dawes Rolls - Five Tribes - FREE

http://www.archives.gov/genealogy/tutorial/dawes

www.archives.gov/research/native-americans/dawes/intro.html

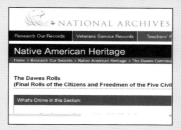

The Dawes Rolls are very important for Native American Research for anyone who has native American ancestors who were from the Five Civilized Tribes (Cherokee, Choctaw, Chickasaw, Creek and Seminole). It lists the individuals who were accepted for tribal membership, and contain more than 101,000 names from 1898-1914 (primarily from 1899-1906). They can be searched to discover the enrollee's name, sex, blood degree, and census card number.

Native American Census Rolls - FREE

www.us-census.org/native/m595

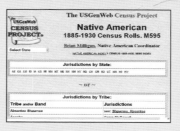

US GenWeb's chart of Indian census microfilm records 1885-1930 categorized by state and tribe.

American Indian Church Records - FREE

https://familysearch.org/learn/wiki/en/American_Indian_Church_Records

A number of denominations proselyted among the American Indians. The records created varied among the denominations.

American Indian Treaties - FREE

https://familysearch.org/learn/wiki/en/American_Indian_Treaties_with_the_United_States

Representatives of the federal government and of the particular tribes signed treaties, so at least some of the tribal members are listed on the treaty.

Annuity Rolls - FREE

https://familysearch.org/learn/wiki/en/American_Indian_Annuity_Rolls

One of the most common stipulations of a treaty with a tribe of American Indians was the provision of an annual payment to be made to that tribe.

When payments began to be made to heads of families, annuity payment rolls (which contain the names of those family heads) were kept. The National Archives has a very large collection of these annuity rolls (at least 959 volumes), which have not been microfilmed or otherwise made available outside of the National Archives Building in Washington D.C.

School Records - FREE

https://familysearch.org/learn/wiki/en/American_Indian_School_Records

This was an effort to educate the younger American Indians in agriculture, domestic skills, mechanical training, and the basic subjects of reading, writing, and arithmetic. A number of boarding

schools were established, all of which required the young person to leave their family, their reservation, and their culture to live at the school and be taught. School census records included names of school-age children, their age, place of birth, and, in some cases, the name of their parent or guardian.

Health Records - FREE

https://familysearch.org/learn/wiki/en/American_Indian_Health_Records

Indian Register of Vital Statistics - FREE

https://familysearch.org/learn/wiki/en/American_Indian_Register_of_Vital_Statistics

Fold3 Native American Records - $

http://go.fold3.com/results.php?category=native-american

Offers over 1.8m assorted records on Native Americans. 7-day free trial, $11.95/month.

Overview of Indian Research - FREE

www.ancestry.com/wiki/index.php?title=Overview_of_Native_American_Research

A short article about researching your ancestry. In beginning Native American genealogical research, it is important to employ a fundamentally sound research methodology.

Cyndi's List - Native America - (FREE)

www.cyndislist.com/native-american

Lists of resources, message boards, family trees and rolls. Information by tribe, surname, or state.

How to Search for Native American Ancestors - (FREE)

www.rootsweb.ancestry.com/~nvsgs/INDIAN.ARTICLE.htm

An article about fundamental steps to finding an Indian ancestor.

Native American Genealogy - (FREE)

www.archives.com/genealogy/family-heritage-native-american.html

A short article about the process to trace your Native American ancestry from Archives.com.

Native Heritage Project Blog - (FREE)

http://nativeheritageproject.com

An ongoing effort to document the Native American people as they obtained surnames and entered recorded history in the continental United States. Offers linked resources, and a fundamental core list of books and resources absolutely essential to understanding the native heritage.

Guide to Tracing Your American Indian Ancestry - (FREE)

www.bia.gov/idc/groups/public/documents/text/idc002656.pdf

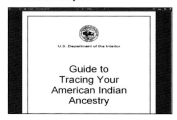

A small 10-page PDF guide about: Enrollment in a Federally Recognized Tribe, where to search for your Indian

ancestry, and a Brief Overview of Cherokee History.

American Indian Heritage Foundation - (FREE)

www.indians.org

They offer a Tribal Directory, articles that tell about the cultures of various tribes, and a collection of writings celebrating the rich and diverse cultures of Indigenous Peoples.

American Indian Oral Histories - (FREE)

https://familysearch.org/learn/wiki/en/American_Indian_Oral_Histories

Seven universities participated in the American Indian Oral History Project. Over 5000 oral histories were collected under this project. Most of the interviews have been transcribed. Some of the universities made copies of their transcripts available online.

a3Genealogy Blog - (FREE)

http://blog.a3genealogy.com/search/label/Native%20American

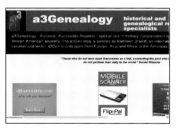

Specializes in military, naturalization records, Native American and African American ancestry; penned by Kathleen Brandt, an international genealogy consultant, speaker and writer.

Facebook Native American Page - (FREE)

www.facebook.com/NativePrideAndSpirituality

Share the cultures, history, wisdom and spirituality of the Nation's 1st People.

Jewish Resources

Jewish records (including synagogue records) contain information specifically about Jews. These include vital records (births, marriages, divorces, and deaths) prepared by or for Jewish communities, registers of name changes, account books of congregations, circumcision records, and burial records. In most countries Jews are recorded in the civil registration or vital records along with people of other religions. After 1826–1835, many European countries required separate registers to be kept of Jews. Some of the most valuable sources for Jewish family history research are local histories.

Many records of Jews – especially for cities of Europe that had significant Jewish populations – have been microfilmed, and many of those records and documents are available on the Internet.

FamilySearch Wiki - *FREE*

https://familysearch.org/learn/wiki/en/Jewish_History

https://familysearch.org/learn/wiki/en/Jewish_Vital_Records

https://familysearch.org/learn/wiki/en/Jewish_Archives_and_Libraries

https://familysearch.org/learn/wiki/en/Jewish_Genealogy_Research

https://familysearch.org/learn/wiki/en/Jewish_Holocaust

https://familysearch.org/learn/wiki/en/Jewish_Societies

Here are links to FamilySearch Wiki sites that

describe and link to valuable resources under many different categories, such as: Jewish history, Jewish archives, libraries and repositories housing records used for Jewish historical and genealogical research, vital records, immigration, key Internet links, helpful guides, Jewish societies, holocaust, concentration camps, cemeteries, maps, military records, probate records, and much more.

Effective research requires understanding historical events that affected your family and the records about them. Your ancestors will become more interesting to you if you also use histories to learn about the events that were of interest to them or that they may have been involved in.

Historical societies can be valuable sources of

The Second Jewish Temple
This image is licensed under the Creative Commons license.

information. They generally collect information about Jewish history in particular areas. Some may have information about specific individuals. Many societies have books and manuscripts about Jews that may be difficult to find in libraries and archives. Most publish historical periodicals. You may be interested in the services, activities, and collections of these groups.

Because many Jews had similar names, make sure you have enough information to identify your ancestor. If you do not find your ancestor, look for variations of the name or spellings that may have changed in America.

Free FamilySearch PDF Guide: Tracing Your Jewish Ancestors -

http://feefhs.org/guides/Finding_Jewish.pdf *FREE*

Follow the steps in this excellent guide to identify your ancestor's birthplace or place of origin. These instructions tell you which records to search first, what to look for, and what research tools to use. The first part of the guide explains the process for finding the information you need. It includes examples to show how others have found information. The second part of the guide gives detailed information to help you use the records and tools.

FamilySearch Knowles Collection -

http://histfam.familysearch.org *FREE*

https://familysearch.org/learn/wiki/en/The_Knowles_Collection

Six databases that include records of the Jewish people from: The British Isles, North America, Europe, South America and The Caribbean, Africa and the Orient, and South Pacific all linked together into family groups. A total of 615,000 individuals with genealogical details and family connections. New information is added regularly. All of the records from the Mordy Collection containing pedigree information and indexes that deal with the Jews of the British Isles are now part of this collection.

Ancestry.com Jewish Records - *FREE*

www.ancestry.com/jewishgen-all

Ancestry.com partnered with JewishGen, the American Jewish Joint Distribution Committee, the American Jewish Historical Society and The Miriam Weiner Routes to Roots Foundation to create a large online collection of Jewish historical records. They offer both free and subscription database collections. Clicking on the above link and then the link to 'See all Jewish Collections' at the bottom of the screen, allows you to browse which ones are free to search. Access Ancestry Jewish Message Boards here http://boards.ancestry.com/topics.religious.jewish.jewish-roots/mb.ashx.

New York Public Library - *FREE*

www.nypl.org

www.nypl.org/locations/schwarzman/jewish-division

https://familysearch.org/learn/wiki/en/New_York_Public_Library

The New York Public Library is an excellent place for research because most Jewish immigrants to the United States lived in New York for a time. The library has borough directories, census records for the greater metropolitan area, back issues of The New York Times, maps, atlases, gazetteers, community histories, yizkor books, indexes to some of the U.S. federal census returns, vital records for New York City, and ship passenger lists.

The library's Jewish Division has one of the most significant collections of Judaica in the world, including bibliographies, reference works, periodicals, and newspapers. The collection is only available in the Jewish Division's reading room. About 40 percent of the Division's holdings are in Hebrew; the remainder are in other languages, primarily English, German, Russian, and French.

Primary source materials are especially rich in the following areas: Jews in the United States,

2 Add New Branches

especially in New York in the age of immigration; Yiddish theater; Jews in the land of Israel, through 1948; Jews in early modern Europe, especially Jewish-Gentile relations; Christian Hebraism; antisemitism; and world Jewish newspapers and periodicals of the nineteenth and twentieth centuries.

New England Historic Genealogical Society -

www.americanancestors.org

https://familysearch.org/learn/wiki/en/New_England_Historic_Genealogical_Society

Over 100 million name database of vital records, compiled genealogies, journals, over 200,000 books, 100,000 microfilms, and over 20 million manuscripts with emphasis on New England and New York since the 1600s. The Great Migration Study Project seeks to identify every European settler in Massachusetts from 1620 to 1640. $79.95/year.

Center for Jewish History -

www.cjh.org

Home to five partner organizations: American Jewish Historical Society, American Sephardi Federation, Leo Baeck Institute, Yeshiva University Museum and YIVO Institute for Jewish Research. The partners' archival collections span more than 700 years of history and total over 500,000 volumes and 100 million documents (in 23 languages and 52 alphabet systems). The collections also include thousands of artworks, textiles, ritual objects, recordings, films and photographs.

YIVO Institute - FREE

www.yivoinstitute.org

Their mission is to preserve, study and teach the cultural history of Jewish life throughout Eastern Europe, Germany and Russia. YIVO's archival collections and library constitute the single greatest resource for such study in the world, including approximately 24 million letters, manuscripts, photographs, films, sound recordings, art works, and artifacts; as well as the largest collection of Yiddish-language materials in the world.

Leo Baeck Institute - FREE

www.lbi.org

A New York City-based research library devoted to the study of the history and culture of German-speaking Jews. It documents and engages this legacy through its library and archival collections, exhibitions, events and lectures.

Yad Vashem - Holocaust Memorial Museum - FREE

www.yadvashem.org

As the Jewish people's living memorial to the Holocaust, Yad Vashem safeguards the memory of the past and imparts its meaning for future generations. Established in 1953, as the world center for documentation, research, education and commemoration of the Holocaust, it is a dynamic and vital place of intergenerational and international encounter. Contains 68 million pages of documents, nearly 300,000 photographs along with thousands of films and videotaped testimonies of survivors, and 112,000 titles in many languages, and thousands of periodicals.

USC Shoah Foundation - (FREE)

http://college.usc.edu/vhi

Dedicated to making audio-visual interviews with survivors and witnesses of the Holocaust and other genocides a compelling voice for education and action. An archive of nearly 52,000 videotaped testimonies from Holocaust survivors and other witnesses videotaped in 56 countries and in 32 languages.

American Jewish Archives - (FREE)

http://americanjewisharchives.org

Offers organizational records, family and personal papers, and synagogue records (many of which have been filmed by FamilySearch).

US Holocaust Memorial Museum -

www.ushmm.org (FREE)

Provides access to archived material relating to the Holocaust. It's Survivors Registry and other resources such as transport lists, death lists, yizkor books, personal papers, and oral histories can be used to determine the fate of Holocaust victims and survivors. Most materials are in English, German, Polish, Russian, Yiddish, or Hebrew. It's collections include: 84,608 books and other publications, 63,493 oral history testimonies, 3,567 oral history testimonies, 28,946 names source records, 27,553 photographs, 8,601 document collections, and 4,612 historical film records in 834 collections.

JewishGen - (FREE)

www.jewishgen.org
http://jri-poland.org
www.jewishgen.org/databases
www.jewishgen.blogspot.com

This is the central Internet site for worldwide databases of Jewish lineages which hosts more than 20 million records. It features thousands of databases, research tools, and other

resources to help those with Jewish ancestry research and find family members.

You can search many name indexes to the records of Central and Eastern Europe.

The Family Finder database with over 500k entries features surnames and ancestral towns being researched by 99,000 Jewish genealogists worldwide. The Family Tree of the Jewish People contains data on more than 5.5 million people from family trees worldwide. The Holocaust Database contains more than 2 million entries regarding Holocaust victims and survivors.

Routes to Roots Foundation - (FREE)

www.rtrfoundation.org

Focuses on tracing Jewish Roots in Poland, Ukraine, Moldova, Lithuania, and Belarus. You can find articles, essays, maps, and a searchable database of vital records available in these countries, and additional information about the Jewish communities that once existed there.

American Jewish Historical Society -

www.ajhs.org (FREE)

Provides access to more than 25 million documents and 50k books, photographs, art and artifacts that reflect the history of the Jewish presence in the United States from 1654 to the present.

International Association of Jewish Genealogical Societies - (FREE)

http://iajgs.org

A non-profit umbrella organization coordinating the activities and annual conference of more than 70 national and local Jewish genealogical societies around the world.

Make New Discoveries 2

Holocaust Pictures - *FREE*

http://history1900s.about.com/od/holocaust/tp/
holocaustpictures.htm

A collection of pictures of the Holocaust, including pictures of the con-centration camps, death camps, prisoners, children, ghettos, displaced persons, Einsatzgruppen (mobile killing squads), Hitler, and other Nazi officials.

Sephardim.com - *FREE*

http://sephardim.com

This site is a research tool for Sephardic and Jewish genealogy. They cover many facets of Sephardic culture and add new information regularly.

Synagogue Scribes - *FREE*

http://synagoguescribes.com/blog

This site offers a unique and fully searchable database of London Ashkenazi Synagogue records, with the emphasis on UK pre-civil registration, which began on 1st July 1837. The bulk of the records contained in this database date between 1791-1860, with some either side of those dates and with few beyond 1865. More recently they have added several hundred burial records dating from 1776. The Synagogue Records database contains births, circumcisions, marriages, deaths and burials, as documented by the Synagogues Secretaries, Mohels (persons performing circumci-sions) or other Community Officials. The Secular Records database contains data abstracted from civil sources, such as tax records, wills, settlements, subscriptions etc.

EuropeGenWeb - *FREE*

www.rootsweb.ancestry.com/~easeurgw
www.rootsweb.ancestry.com/~ceneurgw

An on-line data repository for queries, family histories, and source records as well as

being resource center to identify other on-line databases and resources to assist researchers.

GenealogyLinks - *FREE*

www.genealogylinks.net/europe

This is a portal to 50,000 European countries sites that deal with many Jewish topics.

East European Societies - *FREE*

http://feefhs.org

The Federation of East European Family History Societies is a resource to help you get started. It's an umbrella organiza-tion that promotes family research in eastern and central Europe without any ethnic, religious, or social distinctions. It provides a forum for individuals and organizations focused on a single country or group of people to exchange information and be updated on developments in the field. It provides links to many Jewish Genealogy Resources

CyndisList.com - *FREE*

www.cyndislist.com/jewish

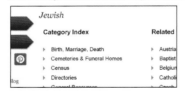

Hundreds of links to Jewish records, documents and histories, categorized and cross-referenced, in many categories.

CemeteryScribes - *FREE*

www.cemeteryscribes.com

Find headstone inscriptions, including Hebrew transliterations (where possible) and mini family trees for each individual. Also included are records from various sources such as census returns, wills, birth and marriage registers, and many more, to help you complete your genealogy and understand your ancestry.

LDS Records
The Best LDS Web Sites

Background

Mormon Temple, Salt Lake City, Utah

Millions of people who are interested in genealogy and family history around the world owe a great deal to The Church of Jesus Christ of Latter-day Saints (casually known as the LDS or Mormon Church). This is due to their unique collection of billions of records worldwide spanning more than a century. Their searchable collections currently total over 3.6 billion, but they are on-their-way to over 20 billion records from their vast archives as they digitize and index the records that are securely stored in their vaults.

Granite Mountain Records Vault

And then they make the records available to everyone for *free*, regardless of religious affiliation.

Unique Beliefs Drive Them

Latter-day Saints are actively involved in family history for unique reasons. So it's interesting to understand what drives them to do this.

The Church emphasizes the importance of the family, the value of learning about one's heritage and honoring one's ancestors. They believe that family and marital bonds can last forever. And that extended families can be together forever in the afterlife. So the primary purpose of their temples is to "seal" or unite families together forever – so their many ancestors who have died can also be sealed and united with their spouse and loved ones forever. It's a life-long, compassionate labor of love for their forbears.

Thus, LDS members feel strongly motivated to seek information about their deceased ancestors. These unique believes drive their heartfelt ambition to search for their ancestors.

Collecting Billions of Records Worldwide

To help members in tracing and documenting their family tree, the LDS Church has microfilmed (now digitally photographs) vital records throughout the world and has done so for over a century. And they continue to collect additional billions of records worldwide. They are currently digitizing and indexing these records for searchable, free, easy access by everyone. They provide access to these records through the Family History Library in Salt Lake City and in over 4,800 local FamilySearch Centers (Family History Centers) worldwide which are also free and without obligation to everyone. And through large databases of historical records which are available online at http://www.FamilySearch.org.

Fortunately for us, the LDS Church makes the records they collect worldwide for their members available to everyone for free – which is to our great benefit.

2 Make New **Discoveries**

An Interesting Glimpse Inside the LDS Approach to Family History

Family History Is for Everyone: *FREE* 9 Fun Ways to Participate -

www.lds.org/topics/family-history/family-history-is-for-everyone

Family history is much more than dates, records, and research. Learn below how new online resources make it easier than ever for anyone—young or old—to be blessed by participating in family history.

Youth: 6 Fun Ways to Do Family History - *FREE*

www.lds.org/youth/article/6-fun-ways-to-do-family-history

There's been a lot of talk lately about young people getting involved in family history. Your tech-savvy generation is made for this work and participating in family history brings blessings. But how exactly can you get involved? Learn more about how you can participate in family history.

Connect with your Family - *FREE*

www.lds.org/topics/family-history

Discover the joy of eternal connections across generations. **Step 1:** Share Your Stories and Photos. **Step 2**: View Yourself in the Family Tree. **Step 3:** Find An Ancestor.

The following collection of the best LDS Web sites for research is not meant to be a comprehensive listing, but is a selection of pre-screened, key web sites for your benefit and convenience.

Why is the LDS Church so Dominant over Genealogy? - *FREE*

www.geneamusings.com/2013/03/dear-randy-why-does-lds-church-exert-so.html

Read Randy Seaver's take on this – as a leading genealogy blogger and non-Mormon.

Tracing LDS Ancestors - *FREE*

https://familysearch.org/learn/wiki/en/Tracing_LDS_Ancestors

A valuable FamilySearch Wiki page with links to some useful websites to get started in searching for information about your LDS ancestors. If your LDS ancestors have been researched before, are they well-documented? Do your family group records show one or more sources of information for each event? Don't just settle for copying someone else's research, cite the evidence that proves it.

FamilySearch Database: Early Utah Families - *FREE*

http://histfam.familysearch.org >Advanced Search

The Community Trees searchable database is assorted genealogies from specific periods and localities around the world that have been linked according to family lineages, currently totaling over 9 million people. Many of the trees include associated documents and images. Check out the Early Utah Families tree that allows views of individuals, families, ancestors, and descendants and gives various options for printing.

FamilySearch Historical Records With Accompanying Wiki Pages

Utah Births and Christenings 1892-1941 - FREE

https://familysearch.org/learn/wiki/en/Utah_Births_and_Christenings_%28FamilySearch_Historical_Records%29

This 1892 to 1941 index is not necessarily intended to index any specific set of records. Nor is it complete for any particular place or region.

Utah Marriages 1887-1966 - FREE

https://familysearch.org/learn/wiki/en/Utah_Marriages_%28FamilySearch_Historical_Records%29

This index is not complete for any particular place or region. This collection (currently 309k) may include information previously published in the International Genealogical Index or Vital Records Index collections.

Utah, Indian War Service Affidavits - FREE

https://familysearch.org/learn/wiki/en/Utah,_Indian_War_Service_Affidavits_%28FamilySearch_Historical_Records%29

This collection consists of images of service affidavits of veterans who served in the militia during the Indian Wars.

Utah Veterans Burial Records - FREE

https://familysearch.org/learn/wiki/en/Utah_Veterans_Burial_Records_%28FamilySearch_Historical_Records%29

This collection includes records from 1847 to 1966 and consists of a card file arranged by county, then by city, and then by the

veteran's name. Only in Salt Lake City were the records filed by cemetery and then by veteran's name.

Utah Land and Property - FREE

https://familysearch.org/learn/wiki/en/Utah_Land_and_Property

Land records are primarily used to learn when and where an individual lived. They often reveal other family information, such as the name of a spouse, heir, other relatives, or neighbors. Also, you may learn where a person lived previously, his or her occupation, if he or she was a naturalized citizen, and other clues for further research.

Handcart Pioneers - FREE

https://familysearch.org/learn/wiki/en/Handcart_Pioneers

This is a FamilySearch Wiki page with links that details the 10 Pioneer handcart companies. Between 1856 and 1860 nearly 3,000 emigrants joined ten handcart companies – about 650 handcarts total – and walked to Utah from Iowa City, Iowa, (a distance of 1,300 miles) or from Florence, Nebraska (1,030 miles).

Pioneers and Prominent Men of Utah - FREE

https://familysearch.org/learn/wiki/en/Utah,_Pioneers_and_Prominent_Men_of_Utah_%28FamilySearch_Historical_Records%29

This collection includes records, genealogies, biographies, images and index from 1847-1868 of the Pioneers and Prominent Men of Utah.

Ancestry.com LDS Records - 💲

http://search.ancestry.com/search/db.aspx?dbid=5144

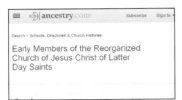

They have a number of databases about LDS records, including:

Early members of the Reorganized Church

LDS Biographical Encyclopedia

LDS Member Name Index, 1830-45

Encyclopedic History of the LDS Church

LDS Pioneer and Handcart Companies, 1847-1856

Seventy Quorum Membership, 1835–1846

A membership is required to view the records. 14-day free trial, $19.95/month.

Guide to Mormon Diaries and Autobiographies - FREE

https://byustudies.byu.edu/showtitle.aspx?title=8139

www.dialoguejournal.com/wp-content/uploads/sbi/articles/Dialogue_V11N02_65.pdf

http://uda-db.orbiscascade.org/findaid/ark:/80444/xv27203

https://familysearch.org/search/catalog/2605?availability=Family%20History%20Library

This collection contains: first and second person accounts (diaries, journals, autobiographies, biographies, life sketches, and local histories); and

transcripts of interviews with pioneer Utahns. Includes material dealing with early Mormon history; Mormon migration west; the march of the Mormon Battalion and its activities; missionary activities; the Civil War; and Indians and Indian welfare. The contents of these diaries provides valuable information on Mormon pioneer life.

You can browse the contents with an alpha list of names of people. Available to purchase from Amazon, and on microfilm from the Family History Library. You can order microfilms through your nearest family history center.

LDS Missionary Diaries - FREE

www.lib.byu.edu/dlib/mmd

A superb collection of over 575 volumes, and 101,000 missionary diary pages including some individuals fairly prominent in the LDS Church. It provides an opportunity to read and understand the missionary experiences, the joys, the sorrows, the struggles that can change lives. The earliest missionary diary in the collection is a diary penned in 1832 by Hyrum Smith.

Trails of Hope: Overland Diaries and Letters - FREE

http://overlandtrails.lib.byu.edu

A collection of the original writings of 49 voyagers on the Mormon, California, Oregon, and Montana pioneer trails who wrote while traveling on the trail; includes maps, trail guides, photographs, watercolors and art sketches between 1846-1869.

Pioneer Histories - >Histories >Pioneer Index

www.dupinternational.org FREE

The Daughters of Utah Pioneers collects and preserves the histories of pioneer ancestors with over 100,000 pioneer histories currently on file. Copies of these histories are available to direct descendants and/or DUP members. Check out the History Index online; click on "Go to History Card Index".

Nauvoo Community Project - FREE

http://nauvoo.byu.edu

An ongoing project to identify the residents of Nauvoo, Illinois, from 1839 to 1846. Wherever possible, each resident is

Utah State Historical Collections

Utah History Publications & Photos -

http://heritage.utah.gov/history/publications
http://heritage.utah.gov/history/digital-photos

FREE Discover how Utah's history is your history. All of Utah State History's publications are now easy to access, search, and read online, including periodicals, books and selected literature. To see all available online publications, leave the search box blank. The valuable periodicals include, among others:

Antiquities Selected Papers - a monograph series designed to examine and interpret the prehistoric cultures of Utah.

Utah Historical Quarterly has published the best of scholarly Utah history since 1928. The journal is filled with articles, memoirs, primary sources, book reviews, and photos. Utah State Historical Society members receive the Quarterly as a benefit of membership.
http://heritage.utah.gov/history/quarterly

Beehive History - published annually from 1974 to 2002, contains short, interesting stories and photos about Utah's past.

History Blazer - published monthly from 1995-1996, news of Utah's past from the Utah State Historical Society.
http://heritage.utah.gov/history/digital-photos

The photos are a great way to add life to history. They have more than one million photographs in their collection, and over 70k are now digital. The digital photographs span a multitude of subjects including how people lived their lives in Utah. To browse all available photos online, leave the search box blank.

Utah Death Certificate Index, **FREE** 1904-1961 -

http://archives.utah.gov/research/indexes/208
42.htm

Each death certificate includes the decedent's full name, date of death, county where death occurred, decedent's race and gender, place and date of birth, marital status, occupation, permanent residence, place and date of burial, time of death, chief cause and contributory factors of death, and if applicable, where illness was contracted and duration of illness. Death certificates also include the names and birthplaces of parents.

Utah Burial Database - **FREE**

http://cemeteries.utah.gov/burials/execute/
searchburials

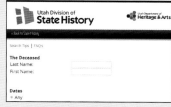

The database contains cemetery records for about 600,000 people buried in Utah, but they continue to add Utah cemeteries and burials to the database.

Utah Digital Newspapers - **FREE**

http://digitalnewspapers.org

The collection holds over 1,000,000 pages of historic Utah newspapers and it grows monthly. Its newspapers can be browsed by issue or searched by keywords, article titles, weddings, deaths, and births.

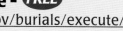

2 Make New Discoveries

documented from birth to death in the records of the time. This data is available to all who are interested in the history of the community, as well as descendants seeking information about their families. The documented information may include marriages, residences, death and burial records, census records, and migration records with links to original documents. A great resource.

Mormon Pioneer Overland Travel -
http://history.lds.org/overlandtravels *(FREE)*

Between 1847-1868, Mormon emigrants traveling in more than 300 companies departed from various places and

LDS Church History Websites -
http://history.lds.org

A portal to valuable information, documents, databases and links.

(FREE)

Church History Library - collects materials by or about LDS Church and its members. These materials come from a wide spectrum of sources and represent numerous points of view.
http://churchhistorylibrary.lds.org

Church History Catalog - digital assets and references to materials contained in the following libraries: Church History Library, digitized family history books, BYU digital collections, and Internet Archives.
http://churchhistorycatalog.lds.org

Church History Museum - learn about the history of the Church and what's happening at the museum.
http://history.lds.orghttp://history.lds.org/place/church-history-museum

Journal History - A day by day history of the Church from 1830–present taken mostly from

newspapers, but also from some minutes and diary entries. It is arranged by date, with the page numbers restarting with each date.
http://history.lds.org/article/chl-journal-history

Manuscript Collections - Many pages of manuscripts from the Church Archives. Included are about 4,000 pages from the papers of Joseph Smith; 34,000 pages of letters and typescripts of Brigham Young correspondence; as well as thousands of pages from other selected items in the Church archives.
http://history.lds.org/article/digital-manuscripts

Digital Photograph Collections - Selections of frequently accessed photographic collections from the Church History Library available in the Church Media Library. An LDS Account is required to view the Church Media Library.
http://history.lds.org/article/digital-photographs

Joseph Smith Papers - updates on the Joseph Smith Papers Project.
http://josephsmithpapers.org
http://josephsmith.net

Patriarchal Blessings Request - to obtain copies of patriarchal blessings for yourself or a deceased direct-line ancestor.
http://history.lds.org/article/chl-pb

headed for the Salt Lake Valley. More than 60,000 LDS Church members traveled in these companies – some traveling by foot, some in wagons, and some pulling handcarts.

This database is a compilation of names obtained from rosters and other reliable sources of individuals who immigrated to Utah during this two-decade period. Each company is listed under its captain's name, and basic information is provided, including a photographs. Many companies include a list of diaries, journals, letters, and reminiscences written by company members, as well as contemporary reports about the company. The content of several thousand of those narratives has been transcribed and is included in the database.

Winter Quarters Project -

http://winterquarters.byu.edu

An ongoing effort to gather information about members of the LDS Church who lived in the Winter Quarters area between the years of 1846-1853. They are also researching the settlements created by the pioneers and the causes of death among the Saints at that time.

Article: Some Must Push and Some Must Pull -

www.lds.org/ensign/2006/07/some-must-push-and-some-must-pull

Imagine what it was like to travel with one of the 10 handcart companies from 1856 through 1860 as you read the journal entries of those who did. This article is a sampling of events involving the handcart companies as they traveled to the Salt Lake Valley.

Article: They Came by Handcart -

www.lds.org/ensign/1997/08/they-came-by-handcart

An excellent educational article about those that came by handcart to the West.

Mormon Battalion Pension Files -

www.familysearch.org/search/collection/1852758

https://familysearch.org/learn/wiki/en/United_States,_Mormon_Battalion_Pension_Applications_%28FamilySearch_Historical_Records%29

Mexican War pension files for the 500 members of the Mormon Battalion. The files are arranged in alphabetical order by name of veteran.

Mormon Battalion - FREE

www.mormonbattalion.com

Contains a brief history of the U.S. Mormon Battalion along with a documented, researched roster, photographs, and maps. Established to shares the stories and history, and honor the memory of the original men and women who served in the Mormon Battalion which was part of the Army of the West during the Mexican-American war of 1846.

Book: A Guide to Mormon Family History Sources -

www.kipsperry.com

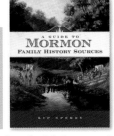

A comprehensive list of LDS family history websites, databases, and much more in one book by Kip Sperry, an author, lecturer, and Professor of family history at BYU. Available to purchase online from www.amazon.com/books/dp/1593313012. $16.95

Early Latter-day Saints - FREE

www.earlylds.com

This site provides information about the lives and families of pioneer Latter-day Saints (over 61,000 names) who lived in the more than 90 settlements of Latter-day Saints in the Missouri Valley, across the state of Iowa, and Winter Quarters in Nebraska from 1830–1868. It also links to maps, settlements, place lists, etc.

Their Crossroads to the West shares the story of the early Latter-day Saints on the Mormon Trail at Winter Quarters. Now available on the web and as a free iPhone and Android app. Visit the app store, search for Map-n-Tour.

Early Church Membership Records - FREE

https://familysearch.org/learn/wiki/en/Early_Church _Membership_Records_by_Susan_Easton_Black

A 50-volume set (and database) of information on early members of the church (about 113,000 names) from 1830-1848 and who lived in the United States, Canada or Great Britain. It was compiled by Susan Easton Black using more than 300 primary and secondary sources on early Latter-day Saints, but it does not necessarily include every member of the Church who lived during the time period.

It is a good beginning point to identify available information and sources for an early LDS ancestor. It is available in hard copy for free in the Family History Library and Brigham Young University collections and available on microfiche - FHL US/CAN Fiche 6031596. The database is available at World Vital Records, a subscription-based website at www.worldvital-records.com/indexinfo.aspx?ix=usa_il_nauvoo_early _lds_members. 3-day free trial, $16.25/month, $89.99/year.

LDS Membership Records - FREE

https://familysearch.org/learn/wiki/en/LDS_Mem bership_Records

The Church has only a few scattered membership records before 1847. Most membership records began in 1877. Membership records usually include information about births, marriages, deaths, and Church ordinances. This article offers background information on membership records and shows where and offers links to find membership records, including:

Early Church Information File - www.family-search.org >Search >Browse All Published Collections. It contains about 1,500,000 entries from over 1,200 sources about Latter-day Saints and their neighbors. The index is international in scope and should be among the first sources checked when searching for Latter-day Saint ancestors or persons living in areas heavily populated by Latter-day Saints. It mainly covers sources from 1830 to the mid- 1900s; includes LDS Church records, LDS immigration records, cemetery records, biographies, journals, and some published books.

Membership Card Index (or Minnie Margett's Card Index) - an index of most early English branch records for the years of 1839-1913. Also see http://user.xmission.com/~nelsonb/minnie

Scandinavian LDS Mission Index

Samoan Individual Membership Certificates

Patriarchal Blessing Index (1830's–1963)

Missionary Record Index (1830–1971)

Church Census Records (1914–1960)

Deceased Members File (1941–present) and more.

Nauvoo Marriages Online - FREE

www.cyberdriveillinois.com/departments/archives /databases/marriage.html

Search online for marriages in the Nauvoo area at the Illinois Statewide Marriage Index, 1763–1900.

Nauvoo Family Land and Records Center - FREE

http://byustudies.byu.edu/PDFLibrary/36.1BlackF amily-5cca0eb1-c1d1-438e-a512-4e4a4b2e9507.pdf

A PDF short article about the center in Nauvoo.

LDS Church Census - FREE

https://familysearch.org/learn/wiki/en/LDS_Census

This is a Wiki article with links about census

records. A well-indexed census is one of the easiest ways to locate where ancestors lived and to identify the dates when they lived there so that you can search other records. The Church took censuses to track members and Church growth throughout the world. In the winter of 1852–1853 the bishops of Utah took a census. They recorded the name of the head of each family in their ward or branch.

The first Church wide census was taken in 1914. Beginning in 1920, the Church took a census every five years until 1960, except 1945. Information in Church censuses consists of a card with information about each family in a ward or branch. Each person in the household is listed on the family card with their gender, age, priesthood office, and marital status.

To search the LDS Census records on microfilm, go to the Family History Library Catalog https://familysearch.org/search/catalog/126146? availability=Family%20History%20Library.

Tracing Mormon Pioneers - FREE

www.xmission.com/~nelsonb/pioneer

Tips for tracing Mormon Pioneer ancestry from Europe, Scandinavia, Australia, and South Africa to Salt Lake City, Utah. Includes an index of thousands of references of those who migrated to Utah during 1847-1868, plus an index search tool for Utah Census Records.

Mormon Immigration Index - FREE

https://familysearch.org/learn/wiki/en/Mormon_ Immigration_Index
http://mormonmigration.lib.byu.edu

This Index documents the journeys of over 94,000 LDS Church converts who crossed the Atlantic or Pacific oceans to gather in Nauvoo, Illinois, or other frontier outposts, between 1840 and 1890. Includes the name, age, and country of origin of each passenger, ports of departure and arrival, approximate number of passengers on each ship, the assigned company leaders, often a brief history of the voyage, plus autobiographies, journals, diaries and letters of approximately 1,000 immigrant converts.

These immigrant accounts are linked to over 500 known LDS companies and provide a composite account of those who crossed the Atlantic and Pacific oceans to gather in Zion. When you do a search at http://mormonmigration.lib.byu.edu/, you are also searching the Mormon Immigration Index. The Index is also available at the Family History Library in Salt Lake City and most family history centers.

Mormon Migration - FREE

http://mormonmigration.lib.byu.edu

This website offers inspiring first person accounts of international converts who turned their faces toward Zion from 1840-1932. The autobiographies, journals, diaries, reminiscences, and letters link to hundreds of known LDS immigrant voyages and they provide a composite history of those who crossed the Atlantic and Pacific, traveling by land and water to gather to Zion. It describes not only their experiences crossing the oceans, but also their trek to frontier outfitting posts, and entry into the Salt Lake Valley.

The journey to Zion often began with an ocean voyage. Crossing the ocean in the 19th century was difficult, expensive, and often dangerous. It also marked a dramatic turning point in the lives of early Latter-day saint converts who left their homelands and sailed for America. Discover stories, letters, journal entries, and other accounts of their voyage. It searches several databases, including the Mormon Immigration Index

Cyndi's List - LDS Records - *FREE*

www.cyndislist.com/lds

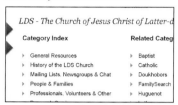

A comprehensive list of LDS related websites organized by various topics.

Cyndi's List - Utah - *FREE*

www.cyndislist.com/us/ut

Another good directory of over 1,600 web links.

Linkpendium - Utah -

www.linkpendium.com

Utah Genealogy (listed under Localities: USA). A good statewide directory of over 6,300 family history web links.

Utah Death and Marriage Notices - *FREE*

www.rootsweb.ancestry.com/~utsaltla/archive/obit_DeseretNews_1850s.html

http://www.rootsweb.ancestry.com/~utsaltla/obit_DeseretNews_1850s.html

Abstracts of Deaths and Marriages Notices in the Deseret News Weekly of Salt Lake City, Utah (1865-1900) made available by UtahGenWeb.

Western States Marriage Index - *FREE*

http://abish.byui.edu/specialCollections/westernStates/search.cfm

A current ongoing project that contains over 911k marriage records to date from counties in the western part of the United States. Very early marriages (1700's) in New Mexico are new. Most of the pre-1900 marriages are included in the index for Arizona, Idaho and Nevada. Many counties for those same states have been extracted into the 1930's and some, much later. At this time, the index is not comprehensive for the time period and/or localities described. However, the goal for this index is to have marriages from all 12 western states at the fingertips of family researchers.

Mountain West Digital Library - *FREE*

http://mwdl.org

A central search portal to enormous and valuable digital collections about the Mountain West region. They provide free access to over 700,000 resources from universities, colleges, public libraries, museums, historical societies, and government agencies, counties, and municipalities in Utah, Nevada, and other parts of the U.S. West. See the "Collections" list of the hundreds of digital collections that are available. There are extensive LDS-related records, photographs, and historical information.

Washington County Utah Pioneer Index - *FREE*

www.rootsweb.ancestry.com/~utwashin/pioneers/index.html

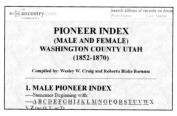

An index of the names and vital information of Utah Pioneers who entered Washington

County, Utah 1852-1870. The resources include: U.S. 1860 and 1870 Census, early LDS Ward membership records, cemetery records, local histories, family group sheets, and indexes of land deeds.

AccessGenealogy - Utah - FREE

www.accessgenealogy.com/utah

 Numerous free, categorized Utah genealogy data and links.

Utah GenWeb - FREE

www.rootsweb.ancestry.com/~utgenweb/index. html

 Links to Utah's counties, towns, searchable data-bases, maps, research aids, web resources, and much more.

Utah State Archives and Records - FREE

http://archives.utah.gov/research/indexes

 Most records held by the Utah State Archives are not indexed. Of those that are indexed – about 500 identified in paper or on microfilm in finding aids – only a few are digital.

Daughters of Utah Pioneers - FREE

www.dupinternational.org

www.dupinternational.org/forms/Pathways-con-solidated-index.pdf

 This is a society whose membership is based upon being able to trace an ancestor who arrived in Utah before the completion of the Transcontinental Railroad on 10 May 1869 which linked the United States for the first time by rail. They have

collected thousands of biographies of early pioneers (1847-1869). Their Index to Pioneer Pathways lists the name of the pioneer, maiden name, birth and death date, and means the DUP Library has information on that person.

Mormon Trail Map - FREE

http://overlandtrails.lib.byu.edu/trailmap.php

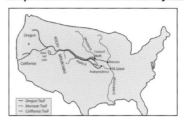

Digital Family History Books - FREE

https://books.familysearch.org

 A collection of more than 100,000 digitized genealogy and family history publications from the archives of some of the most important family history libraries in the world. The collection includes family histories, county and local histories, genealogy magazines and how-to books, gazetteers, and medieval histories and pedigrees. Using Advanced Search allow you to search using keywords, subject and author.

BYU Digital Collections - FREE

www.lib.byu.edu/digital/all.php

 A portal to all digital collections on file at BYU, including, among others: Over 30,000 historic photographic collec-tions, Historical Clothing Collection, The Evening and the Morning Star, Encyclopedia of Mormonism, Mormon Missionary Diaries, Latter-Day Saint Biographical Encyclopedia (over 5000 biographi-cal entries), Mormons and Their Neighbors (over 100,000 biographical sketches), etc.

Early Church Historical Documents -

https://byustudies.byu.edu >*Study Resources* >*Early Church Historical Documents*

A list of download-able documents that relate to events in the early history of the Church (to about 1850) as well as general characterizations of prominent early Church members. For example...

Joseph Smith's Own Story of a Serious Childhood Illness

The Wentworth Letter

History and handwriting analysis of the original Book of Mormon manuscript

A Letter Regarding the Acquisition of the Book of Abraham

Oliver Cowdery's Kirtland, Ohio, 'Sketch Book.'

John Moon's Account of the First Emigrant Company of British Saints

Eliza R. Snow's Nauvoo Journal

The King Follett Discourse

Thomas L. Barnes: Coroner of Carthage

Free 58-Minute Video:
Touching Your Posterity
from Beyond the Grave

http://history.lds.org/event/posterity

An interesting video about writing your life story and journal that in some way can allow you to touch the lives of your posterity from beyond the grave.

Welsh Mormon History -

http://welshmormon.byu.edu

Contains a list of immigrants, ship voyages infor-mation, journal excerpts, vital information, biographies, and photos. This site seeks to preserve and share information about the early converts to Mormonism in Wales, and is the product of Dr. Ronald Dennis' research.

FarWest History -

www.farwesthistory.com

Interactive map, history, and some scholarly resources of Far West, Missouri.

AncestorsWaiting.com -

www.ancestorswaiting.com

A website that focuses on finding your next ancestor ready to take to the temple. It automates the long manual steps on FamilySearch to find missing ordinances. First, it searches all your direct ancestors to the end of each ancestral line or to the year 1500. It then searches the spouses, children, siblings and parents and shows all the ordinances that need to be done in your tree. Sign in using your FamilySearch sign-in credentials. It searches your family tree for missing ordinances, reserves the ordinance for you, and generates your Family Ordinance Request. Certified by FamilySearch. $24.95/year.

Miscellaneous Historical Records - FREE

www.sidneyrigdon.com/dbroadhu/index.htm

Dale Broadhurst has created a number of linked websites with interesting LDS information.

The Oliver Cowdery Memorial Home Page - Oliver's Bookshelf

Joseph Smith's History Vault

Crisis at Kirtland

The Sidney Rigdon Memorial Home Page

Mormon Classics E-Texts Library

Readings in Early Mormon History

Spalding On-Line Documents Library

CHAPTER 3

3-Easy Steps
Follow These 3-Easy Steps to Build Your Family Tree

STEP 3 –
Connect With Your Family

Discover Your Family Stories, Photos, and Ancestral Village

3 Connect with Ancestors

Suggested Activities

1. Consider ways your family can best honor and pay tribute to your ancestors and inspire your children to know them.

2. Establish a new tradition in your family for honoring your ancestors which can be perpetuated from generation-to-generation.

3. Create a timeline of one or more of your ancestors lives combined with historical events to get to know the times in which they lived.

4. Visit the cemetery and gravesite of an ancestor(s) to better connect with them.

Family history is more than just names and dates. You should learn more about who your ancestors really were, where they lived, and what they did. You should try to gain information and an understanding of each of your ancestors if possible. Finding your roots and stories helps you gain a sense of belonging, and an understanding of who you are and where you come from.

The Internet is the perfect tool for opening a window to the past and connecting with the lives and stories of your ancestors. Discover more than you ever imagined about the lives of your ancestors that made you who you are today.

Family History Insights - 3

3 Connect with Ancestors

Alex Haley

Knowing Who You Are

"Knowing who you are and what responsibility you have towards your family forces your behavior to be consistent with your family values. It passes right down across the generations." Alex Haley, press conference, Freedman's Bank CD, 2001

Daniel Webster

Connecting the Past with the Future

"Those who do not look upon themselves as links connecting the past with the future do not perform their duty to the world." Daniel Webster (1782-1852), statesman

Helen Keller

A King Among Your Ancestors

"There is no king who has not had a slave among his ancestors, and no slave who has not had a king among his." Helen Keller (1880-1968), American author, political activist and lecturer

Boyd K. Packer
© by Intellectual Reserve, Inc.

Finding the Time to Connect to Your Ancestors

"There somehow seems to be the feeling that genealogical work is an all-or-nothing [ambition]. That is not so. Genealogical work is another responsibility for every [one]. And we may do it successfully along with all the other responsibilities that rest upon us. ... You can fulfill your [ambition to trace] your kindred dead... without forsaking your other responsibilities. ... You can do it without becoming a so-called 'expert' in it.

There is an old Chinese proverb which states: 'Man who sits with legs crossed and mouth open, waiting for roast duck to fly in, have long hunger.'

Once we started, we found the time. Somehow we were able to carry on all of the other responsibilities. There seemed to be an increased inspiration in our lives because of this work. But the decision, the action, must begin with [you]. ...

The process of searching...[is] worth all the effort you could invest. The reason: You cannot find names without knowing that they represent people. You begin to find out things about people. When we research our own lines we become interested in more than just names. ... Our interest turns our hearts to our fathers—we seek to find and to know and to serve them." Boyd Packer, Bookcraft, 1980, pp. 223-30, 239-40

George H. W. Bush

Living Link to the past

"You are our living link to the past. Tell your grandchildren the story of the struggles waged, at home and abroad. Of sacrifices made for freedom's sake. And tell them your own story as well – because [everybody] has a story to tell."
George H. W. Bush (1924-   ),
41st U.S. president,
State of the Union Address, 1990

Barack Obama, President

Our Journey Continued

"... greatness is never a given. It must be earned. Our journey has never been one of short-cuts or settling for less.... Rather, it has been...men and women... who have carried us up the long, rugged path towards prosperity and freedom. For us, they packed up their few worldly possessions and traveled across oceans in search of a new life. For us, they toiled in sweatshops and settled the West; endured the lash of the whip and plowed the hard earth. For us, they fought and died.... Time and again these men and women struggled and sacrificed and worked till their hands were raw so that we might live a better life. ... This is the journey we continue today." Barack Obama, Presidential Inaugural Address, Jan. 20, 2009

Connect With the Lives of Your Ancestors

Timelines of your ancestor's lives in context with historical events and photographs of the times in which your ancestors lived can provide an interesting perspective and add life to your story. You can discover stories about your ancestor's life from historic newspapers and by gaining a historical perspective about your ancestors. They also provide unique insight and a rare opportunity to understand the culture and customs of how your ancestors lived.

Online gazetteers and place databases help you discover the geographic location of the place your ancestors called home – their village or town and cemetery. Using precious photos will help you connect to your ancestors and preserve the past for future generations.

Finding your family roots – and the stories, values and traditions about your ancestor's lives – can help you better understand them. But it

Benefits of Connecting With the Lives and Stories of Your Ancestors

- **Knowledge** of your forebears will increase
- **Better Understand** your ancestors and yourself; the opportunity to learn more about your kindred dead will bless lives
- Gain a **Greater Appreciation** of your heritage, the sacrifices your ancestors made for you, and a better understanding of what their life was like
- **Gain Strength** from learning about how your ancestors met challenges in life
- Unite, weld, and **Strengthen Bonds** between family members forever; your family will grow closer
- Promote a **Sense of Belonging** that ties generations together, and foreshadows your belonging in the eternal family of God; your desire and willingness to honor your beloved ancestors prepares you to belong to Him who is our Father
- **Discover** within yourself a reservoir of patience, endurance, and love that you will never find without the deep commitment that grows from a sense of real belonging
- Gain a **Sense of Identity and Purpose in Life**
- Draw yourself and your family **Closer to God**
- Your ties with the eternal world suddenly become very real, **Sharpening Your Life's Focus** and lifting your expectations
- Exerting such immovable loyalty to your forebears **Teaches You More About How to Love Others.**

also helps you better understand yourself, and gives you a greater appreciation of your heritage and the sacrifices they made for you. Many of your ambitions and challenges in life are the same as theirs. You gain strength from learning about how your ancestors met life's troubling challenges.

> Doing family history work helps unite your family, and strengthens bonds between your family members.

Knowledge of your forebears will increase, your family will grow closer, families will be strengthened, and the opportunity to learn more about your kindred dead will bless lives. As you learn more about your ancestors, you weld eternal family links, and draw yourself and your family closer to God. It's a wonderful opportunity to find your family identity. And help promote that identity in your children and grand children.

Appreciating Your Heritage

Reflecting on the Past

Who were your ancestors? Each of us has hundreds of thousands of ancestors as part of our unique heritage. And each and every one of your ancestors had to exist in order for you to exist. Each one of them and everything they were have contributed to your being. Their genes are in you; their blood runs in your veins. You not only inherited their genes, but many of their physical traits, values and attitudes have been passed down to you from one generation to another showing up in the way you look, think, and act. The choices made by your ancestors over the generations have influenced the way you live and think. In many ways, your ancestors

have affected your life and molded your destiny. They are a part of who you are today. It took thousands of years of people having children with the right person at the right time to get to your existence.

Your ancestors are more than just a bunch of lifeless names and dates on a chart. They made a huge difference in who you are. And still do! The Best way to know who you are is to know where you came from. But it is strange how little most of us know about them or the times in which they lived. Most certainly, many of your ancestors lived a life of deprivation and hardship. Most of them sacrificed much for their posterity. Many left behind beloved family members, plush homelands, and previous possessions to come to often a barren, undeveloped strange land so that their descendants could have a better life. By tracing your own family roots and stories, you can come to appreciate your heritage more and more, and know and honor your fore-fathers as you discover what their lives were like.

Some people find great joy in discovering an ancestor's diary, journal or letter to help find their roots and collect their family traditions and stories. But usually it's the small bits of information from many different sources that help bring your ancestors to life. Everyone has his own unique history and family stories. And finding your family roots and treasured stories is one of the most meaningful ways you can honor your ancestors. You can honor those who have gone before by learning more about them and following in their footsteps. And you should be grateful for the rich abundance you enjoy today because of their great sacrifices and efforts. They helped forge a life that is so much better for you than anything they might have even dared dream about for themselves.

Your ancestors labored long and hard, built their own home with their own bare hands, and raised a family and created their own livelihood. They became pilgrims and pioneers and cowboys who etched out a new life for themselves. They had great dreams and aspirations which wielded a profound influence on the future, just like you. You should honor your

> Your ancestors deserve your recognition and honor for the determination and fortitude they portrayed in leaving the comfort of their home and emigrating to the New World to forge a new life.

forbears for who they were, what they accomplished, and even the mistakes they made. One of the great lessons—maybe the principal lesson—of doing family history is learning from the mistakes of your ancestors. Tracing your family roots and connecting to your ancestors can be one of the most intellectually stimulating, absorbing, and fulfilling ways you will ever find to spend your valuable time.

Honoring Your Ancestors

Every human being alive has ancestors: parents, grandparents, great-grandparents, and so forth. Knowing who your Ancestors are is fundamental to knowing who *you* are. Your ancestors DNA runs in your blood. All of your Ancestors are inside of you – whether you know them or not – so honoring them is honoring yourself.

How to Honor Your Ancestors

Once you get to know your ancestors, you invariably develop a sense of belonging to them. So it's natural and right to want to pay tribute to and honor them. You may write a family history or plan a family reunion which helps you reach out to others and ensure that the memory of your ancestors will survive. But there are countless ways you can pay tribute to the valuable insight and wisdom of those who have gone before you.

Learn About Them and Share

Learn about your ancestors: trace your family roots back a few generations. Make a family tree with your children. Collect interesting family stories about each person and write them down with a photo and some details. Visit their hometowns or

What Does it Mean to Honor Ancestors?

According to the dictionary, to *honor* means to regard with great respect, to have an attitude of admiration or esteem, to revere, and to manifest the highest veneration in words and actions.

Revering ancestors can support you in your life's journey because your ancestors are a source of wisdom. When you seek to connect with your ancestors, you connect with forbears who love you and are interested in you. Ancestors help you to know who you are. To know who you are and where you're going, you need to start at the beginning. Connecting with your ancestors is a way to trace your identify back through time. Knowing your past empowers you to make wise choices about your future.

Ancestors unite us with all of humanity. Virtually all of the human family are, on some level, our "cousins", no matter how near or distant. Recognizing this common connection with all

segments of the human family is a powerful doorway into universal brotherhood and peace. When we acknowledge our relatedness to the entire human family it helps us to treat others as our kindred.

We honor our ancestors for many reasons but also because they were brave, courageous men and women who fought stalwartly for our future destiny. For example, during the American Revolutionary War they were outnumbered, outgunned, and ill-equipped, yet they successfully defeated the greatest military and naval power of the 18th century. Our forefathers believed that *"all men are created equal, that they were endowed by their Creator with certain unalienable rights, that among these are life, liberty and the pursuit of happiness."*

They believed in consent of the governed, the right to bear arms and self-defense, and in limited interference by government. They were good people who believed in the sovereignty and guardianship of Almighty God. Their motto became *"In God We Trust"* which was later declared on all of our national coins.

homelands. Study the language or culture of your ethnic roots. Share what you learn with your children. You might even assign a report on an ancestor to each child.

Keep a Memento

One idea for celebrating mothers and grand-mothers on Mother's Day – and honor the special women in your family – is to create an online photo gallery. Your ancestors will be pleased to know that their smile can be viewed by family members everywhere. Gather family members together while visiting graves. Keep a memento, such as: Your grandfather's cufflinks, your grandmother's silk handkerchief or precious china keepsakes.

Have an Ancestor Feast

One way to honor your departed ancestor on the anniversary of their birth or death is to have an ancestor feast. Set an extra plate at the table, lit by a candle, and surrounded by a photo of your ancestor. Serve that person's favorite dishes, their signature recipes, or foods that reflect their cultural heritage. What were some of the special dishes they made that left a lasting impression on you? Have your children help in selecting and preparing foods for this commemoration. The flavors and aromas associated with a relative's favorite foods are a concrete way to keep memories alive. And if not an entire meal, baking or cooking something just like mom, dad, or grandma did can be just as effective a way to pass something of that person along to your own children.

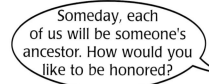

Someday, each of us will be someone's ancestor. How would you like to be honored?

Plant a Garden

Here's a lovely and lasting tribute. Plant a small garden in honor of an ancestor. Consider having a small tree, such as a Japanese maple or weeping cherry as the centerpiece. Designate an annual tradition of adding something to the garden in the late spring or early summer of each year. If space allows, place a bench near this garden for sitting, meditating, and remembering.

How Would You Like to Be Honored?

Is it enough to just keep up the gravestones and monuments to our ancestors? That must undoubtedly be done, but it's only a part of the honor that we owe to our gallant ancestors. What would honor them the most of all?

John Weaver wrote: *"The greatest honor that we could bestow upon our ancestors is to follow them in their faith, maintaining their cause, and fighting for the same truths and principles they tenaciously held. The greatest honor my grandchildren and great grandchildren can bestow upon me is to follow in the faith, principles, and truth that I communicate and teach."* (Pastor John Weaver, Freedom Baptist and Dominion Ministry.)

Live a Honorable Life

One of the best ways to honor your ancestors is by loving and caring for yourself, and living a respectable, honorable life since you are the carrier of their genes. Take care of yourself. Stay healthy, keep your body whole and hearty. After all, it is a gift from them. Ancestors gen-erally wish the best for you and your family. They take pride in your accomplishments, just as they did when they were living.

We honor best those who have gone before when we serve well in the cause of right, good-ness and truth. We should walk as they walked and embrace the goodness they embraced. It is not enough to just care for their grave sites and monuments. We should emulate their lives, their goodness, and their faith.

Shouldn't we honor the ancestors who touched our lives and pay tribute to the loving people who came before us? And shouldn't we help inspire our children to honor our ancestors so that they can also gain strength from the past?

Discover Your Ancestral Village

Our ancestors immigrated to America to find better lives for their families. They emigrated together by villages, families, occupations, and religious groups. They traveled by ships to various American and Canadian ports.

They often lived near each other, worshiped together, witnessed each other's documents, and were buried in the same cemetery. Often their spouses came from neighboring families or were the siblings of our friends or acquaintances. They were known in their communities and got their names in the local newspapers.

It's exciting to discover where your ancestors originated from. Many different records tell the story of your ancestor making that life-changing decision to immigrate and become an American citizen. In order to find out where your ancestors lived (your ancestral villages) and connect with

> If you have an ancestor who came from Europe...

...You need to identify their birthplace before you can add new branches to your family tree. It is virtually impossible to find your ancestors in Europe unless you know their ancestral village.

them, you need at least two key pieces of information: your ancestor's original name and the name of their place of origin (birthplace or ancestral village).

However, many records only list the country or state, but not the name of the actual town or parish. And even when a place is listed, it may only be the nearby better known town or city because that was a more recognizable point of reference for people not familiar with the region. If possible, check multiple sources that list birthplace for verification, including records for collateral relatives who also immigrated.

Also, keep in mind that It's possible your ancestor may have shortened or changed their name upon arrival in America, i.e. 'Americanized' their name, or there could have been spelling or transcription errors in official records, indexes, and online databases. This can be frustrating, but name issues can often be handled by trying alternate spellings or search combinations.

> Expect inconsistencies in information about your ancestral village.

For example, constantly shifting political and geographical boundaries in parts of Europe due to wars may have led to various countries being recorded as the birthplace of your ancestor.

Essentially, all record sources in foreign countries were kept at the local level, by the village or parish. Hence, it is essential to learn the name of the birthplace or place of origin in order to connect with your ancestors. To locate your ancestor's town or village of origin you may have to gather clues from numerous sources. Some of the key tools for locating your ancestral village are online records, social networking tools, maps, gazetteers, atlases, Google Earth, and published family histories.

Once you have identified your ancestral village, you have opened a huge door to the world of records in Europe. So here are some steps on how to find your ancestral village...and add new branches to your family tree.

7 Steps to Find Your Ancestral Village

1. Start With Your Family

The first place to check for information on your ancestral village is with your family. Ask all of your cousins, aunts, and uncles for copies of documents that have been passed down, such as: letters and envelopes, photographs, bible, baptismal certificate, passport, naturalization papers, etc. which are potential sources for listing the place of origin.

Learn everything you can about your immigrant ancestor from your home and your family so that you will be able to identify them in relevant records, and distinguish them from others of the same name. Pay attention to any other specific information that may help identify your ancestor, such as: religion, occupation, friends, neighbors, etc. As you find the place of origin of one ancestor, you may also find information about other members of the family. Be sure to copy all the information you find about the family onto your research log.

2. Look at Others Research

You're probably not the only one – nor the first one – searching for your ancestral village. Other unknown cousins may have already found where your ancestor came from. Look for published family histories, biographies, town histories, databases of compiled records, and indexes and genealogies.

You can save yourself a great deal of effort by hooking into work other researchers have done before you. However, treat every piece of information with a healthy dose of scepticism – check out their sources and verify every link.

3. Then Dig Deeper

Look for clues in assorted **US records,** such as: Census records, birth, marriage, and death records, ship passenger lists, newspapers, obituaries, cemetery records, funeral-home records, naturalization petitions, court records, land and property records, probate records, and military records. Usually, obituaries published in ethnic newspapers contain specific information about birthplace.

Many immigrants settled in areas and attended church with others of their same ethnic and geographic background. Check **both civil**

and church sources for their marriage record, children's births, children's baptismal records, and burial records. Death Certificates usually give place of birth (often just the country, but sometimes the town is given).

Census records usually provide the country, and perhaps the year of Immigration or whether a person was naturalized. Passenger arrival records, naturalization records, and passenger departure lists for a European port may contain the name of the town or village.

The 1900-1940 censuses each indicate the person's year of immigration and naturalization status ("Al" for alien, "Pa" for "first papers," and "Na" for naturalized). The 1850-1940 censuses indicate the person's state or country of birth, and the 1880-1940 censuses also indicate the parents' birthplaces.

With the information you glean from census records you can begin a search for your immigrant ancestor in **passenger lists** and naturalization records. "Last residence" (name of town) for each passenger is usually given on U.S. passenger arrival records starting about 1893 (this varies by port). All New York passenger arrival records starting with June 1897 and later should have this information for each passenger. Earlier passenger records (beginning with 1820) sometimes list the town of residence for the passengers, but most do not. Passenger lists can contain extremely creative spelling.

Naturalization records after1906 very likely contain their ancestral village, but pre-1906 generally only provide the country of birth.

Social Security Applications almost always give place of birth and names of parents. First, search the Social Security Death Index – https://familysearch.org/search/collection/1202 535. Then, with the information from the index you can order a copy of the application they filled out when they applied for a social security card. There is a fee (digital $16, photocopy $27) and here are the links: http://genealogy.about.com/od/online_records/ a/ss5_request.htm and https://secure.ssa. gov/apps9/eFOIA-FEWeb/internet/main.jsp.

WWI Draft Registration cards may also state their village – nearly 11 million (men born about June 1886 to June 1897) of the 24 million total draft cards asked for location of birth (town, state, nation).

Also search for these same records in each place where the immigrant lived. And be sure to investigate available records in the town, parish, county, state, as well as national.

> See Chapter Two for numerous links to census, Immigration, naturalization, and military records.

Convenient Directories

These websites www.researchguides.net and http://genrootsblog.blogspot.com /2009/02/german-immigrant-ancestor- hometown.html provide basic links to research guides and online records as convenient directories, but the key websites are detailed in Chapter Two.

FREE

4. Check the Neighborhood

Immigrants often traveled together and put down roots among their friends, relatives, and neighbors. Or they may have emigrated to join a relative or friend who had previously emigrated. So if you've located your family in the Census, pay attention to the neighborhood. Who lived close to them?

Search the records of identified family members to see if you can find the village associated with them. Search for records of friends who may have associated with your ancestor at church, or in a social organization. Perhaps these records list key details about place of origin not noted in official records.

5. Do a Google Search

When your online searching turns up a potential village, or a general location, do a Google search. Search the name by itself, as well as your ancestor's name plus the locality. Most cities, and even smaller towns or villages, have their own web sites. You can use advanced search to be more or less specific as needed.

Click on the 'Images' tab on the top of the main Google page to check out any possible photographs. And search for historical books at http://books.google.com which you can preview or read for free.

6. Utilize Social Networking

It's easier than ever to connect with family, discover long-lost relatives, and network with other researchers who may be searching the same information. Learn about and use message boards, queries, blogs, family tree sites, and other social networking sites, such as: Facebook, Twitter, Google Plus, and Instagram. Search for family trees, scour message boards, and consider posting queries with surnames and ancestral villages.

> Cast as wide a net as possible by networking with others.

Networking with Others

For more detailed information on networking, check out the links to social networking sites beginning on page 47, for links to existing family trees page 74, and for key blogs page 20 . Check blogs for specific surnames, an ethnic group, or country.

7. Look for Your Village in Gazetteers and Atlases

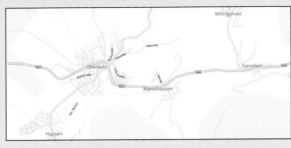

We know that one's surroundings can have a profound effect in shaping our lives. The information gleaned from gazetteers, maps and atlases can help you breath life into your family history and help you envision what it might have been like living there at that time. They can help you become familiar with the places where your ancestors lived, learn more about the environment they lived in, and what civil jurisdiction may hold the records they left behind.

A gazetteer is a geographical dictionary that can help you locate your ancestral village, and provide the correct spelling and alternative spellings. It may also indicate the nearby villages that your ancestors may have come from or moved to. It lists and describes all the towns and villages in a particular country that will help you identify the jurisdiction (provinces, counties, districts) that may have kept the records when your ancestor was there.

Your ancestors who lived in a small village may have traveled several miles to a parish church for the christenings of children, marriages or burials. Their village may have had no church of its own, but was within the jurisdiction of a parish in a neighboring town. Learn the names of seats of jurisdictions that included the ancestral home town or village. Determine if archives or libraries in jurisdictional seats or state capitols have records that name persons who lived where your ancestors did.

A gazetteer tells you the pronunciation of the name, the local history of the village, sizes of population, how many residents practiced various religions, where the inhabitants went to church, and geographical features (such as elevation and size, rivers and mountains). It usually includes only the names of places that existed at the time the gazetteer was published, generally listed in alphabetical order.

When gazetteers are used in conjunction with maps and atlases, they are very powerful tools. Atlases help you understand your ancestral terrain. Maps show the range and township numbers printed on maps of US public domain states, generally east of the Mississippi. Knowledge of the range and township numbers will help you track down lands purchased from the federal government or homesteaded under the Homestead Act of 1862. Atlases published in other countries

near the times forebears lived there will also show state and national boundaries.

Remember that place-names and jurisdictions change. If possible, use a gazetteer that was published near the time when your ancestor was born. Old gazetteers are often called "historical" gazetteers. A historical gazetteer may also help you identify the church records for your ancestor's birthplace. Knowing the church may be useful because births, marriages, and deaths were usually recorded in the Catholic registers, especially before the 1850s.

You will need to know how boundary changes might have affected your family's migration, as well as any name changes for the town or village so that you know where to look for records.

FamilySearch Gazetteers - FREE

https://familysearch.org/learn/wiki/en/Category:Gazetteers

 This is an index with links to FamilySearch Wiki sites featuring Gazetteers for the U.S., England, Wales, Europe, Australia, Mexico China, etc. The Family History Library has an extensive collection of gazetteers in print and on microfilm.

Wikipedia Gazetteer - FREE

http://en.wikipedia.org/wiki/Gazetteer

 Provides a history and a listing with links to gazetteers worldwide.

FuzzyGazetteer - FREE

http://isodp.hof-university.de/fuzzyg/query/

 Allows you to search for 7 million place names worldwide.

Duke University Libraries - FREE

http://library.duke.edu/research/subject/guides/maps/gazetteers.html

 The libraries listing of gazetteer directories in the US and worldwide.

Alexandria Digital Library Project - FREE

www.alexandria.ucsb.edu/

 The University of California, Santa Barbara links to online gazetteer and related sites.

US HomeTownLocator - FREE

www.hometownlocator.com

 Links to US cities and state gazetteers; profiles for 179,000 cities, towns, neighborhoods and subdivisions.

Map Your Ancestors

Discover and Map the Place Your Ancestors Called Home; Best Map Sites

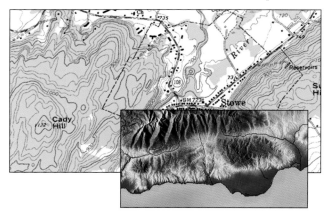

Maps are one of the resources you need in order to get a complete picture of your ancestors. They provide clues to where your ancestors may have lived, and where to look for written records about them. Old and new maps can help you track down facts about your family tree. In fact, the key to finding the records you need is to map your ancestors.

FamilySearch Wiki: US Maps - *FREE*

https://familysearch.org/learn/wiki/en/United_States_Maps

Maps can be used to locate the places where your ancestors lived. They identify political boundaries, names of places, geographical features, cemeteries, churches, and migration routes. Historical maps are especially useful for finding communities and political boundaries that no longer exist. This site outlines valuable information about the different kinds of genealogical information in various types of maps, and provides links to Atlases and broad collections, state maps, country boundary maps, township and city maps, land ownership (plat) maps, military maps, slavery maps, topography maps, and recommended books and research helps.

Putting Your Ancestors on the Map - *FREE*

https://familysearch.org/techtips/2011/10/putting-ancestors-map

Most of the so-called brick wall problems can be solved by focusing first on the geography rather than blindly searching records. It helps to know where the records might be kept, so before searching randomly, you should always know where your ancestors lived. The key to finding the records is putting your ancestors on the map, literally. A worthwhile article by James Tanner who explains how to find your ancestor's land patent.

5 Maps Sites Everyone Should Know -

www.archives.com/experts/ortega-gena/genealogy-maps.html *FREE*

Gena P. Ortega's article about using maps when you research your ancestors. Maps are an essential part of your genealogical research for a variety of reasons. Maps can show you where and when boundaries changed. Some maps provide you a bird's eye view of the city your ancestor lived in. They can help you recreate your ancestor's community leading you to additional resources. Maps can show the migration route your ancestor took.

Using Historical Maps to Pinpoint Big City Ancestors - *FREE*

http://genealogy.about.com/od/historical_maps/a/city-maps.htm?nl=1

Kimberly Powell's worthwhile article about pinpointing your research in large cities. Research in heavily populated areas requires you to localize your research, using map and ward boundaries to identify exactly where your ancestors lived to determine what

records are available for that locality. A variety of historical maps can help you pinpoint your ancestors exact location, along with nearby churches, schools, and other important community resources.

CyndisList Maps & Geography - FREE
www.cyndislist.com/maps

Links to numerous websites featuring maps, atlases and gazetteers.

US Geological Survey Maps - FREE
www.usgs.gov >Maps, Imagery
http://nationalmap.gov

The National Atlas offers a wide variety of maps that you can browse or print for free at home. You can find maps of the US, as well as ones for your own state with county lines, cities, lakes, and rivers.

Download or buy current maps, historic topographic maps from1882, and aerial and satellite images. You can also use the Map Maker to make your own, custom, interactive map of the US.

USGS PDF GUIDE
Using Maps in Genealogy - FREE
http://pubs.usgs.gov/fs/2002/0099/report.pdf

A PDF guide from the U.S. Geological Survey (Dept.

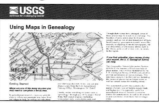

of the Interior) about using maps to provide clues to where your ancestors may have lived and where to look for written records about them.

Comparison of Web Map Services - FREE
http://en.wikipedia.org/wiki/Comparison_of_web_map_services

A comprehensive Wikipedia chart comparing 7 web map services.

Popular Web Map Services

Name and Address	Description
Google Maps https://maps.google.com	Interactive maps. Clicking anywhere will focus the map on that location and show you helpful things, like related places and the best ways to get there.
Apple Maps www.apple.com/ios/maps	Gives you turn-by-turn spoken directions, interactive 3D views, a Flyover feature, and a beautiful interface that scales and zooms with ease.
OpenStreetMap www.openstreetmap.org	A free wiki map of the world. The data is free to download and use under its open license.
Microsoft Research Maps http://msrmaps.com	Free public access to a vast data store of maps, satellite imagery and aerial photographs of the United States.
MapQuest www.mapquest.com	For driving directions and maps. See local traffic and road conditions, find nearby businesses and restaurants, plus explore street maps and satellite maps.
Pictometry www.pictometry.com	A birds eye imagery provider showing the fronts and sides of buildings and locations on the ground which can be integrated into all mapping programs.
Yahoo! Maps http://maps.yahoo.com	Driving Directions, Satellite View and Traffic. Rated the best online mapping experience.
Bing Maps www.microsoft.com/maps	Maps for business users

David Rumsey Maps - *FREE*
www.davidrumsey.com

Focuses on rare 18th and 19th century North American and South American maps and other cartographic materials.

Historic maps of the World, Europe, Asia, and Africa are also represented. Popular collection categories include antique atlas, globe, school geography, maritime chart, state, county, city, pocket, wall and case, children's, and manuscript maps. If you're using Google Earth, you can view maps in the Rumsey Historical Map layer, available in the Gallery layer.

Perry-Castaneda Library Maps - *FREE*
www.lib.utexas.edu/maps

Includes more than 250,000 maps, but less than 20% of the collection is currently online. How about a map of the British Isles 1603-1688, or Central Europe 980-1871, or England and France 1455-1494, or North America 1797, or Boston 1842? Essentially all of the maps courtesy of the University of Texas Libraries are in the public domain, and you may download them and use them as you wish.

Historic Map Works - *FREE* *$*
www.historicmapworks.com/Articles/genealogy_maps.php

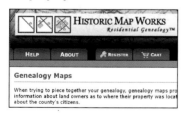

A historic digital map database of North America and the world, with over 1,662,956 individual images. Their collection includes: US Property Atlases, Antiquarian Maps (antiques), Nautical Charts, Birdseye Views, Special Collections (Celestial Maps, Portraits, and other historical images), and Directories and other text documents. Currently, 54% of their collection can be viewed in Historic Earth, their geographic time machine viewer. The basic version is free; the premium version requires a monthly or yearly subscription. The rest of the collection can be accessed through Browse and Search for free (points of interest, location, keyword, modern address, etc.), but a prominent watermark is shown over each map preventing you from printing the image. $0.99/print, $4.99/download, or $29.99/month.

Google Maps - *FREE*
www.maps.google.com

Google Maps is a web mapping service that powers many map-based services, and is valuable in your family history research. You can look up addresses and view images taken of that address in the present day. It offers street maps, a route planner for traveling by foot, car, bike, or with public transportation, and a locator for urban businesses in numerous countries around the world. Google Maps satellite images are not updated in real time, but are somewhat older.

Using a Google Account sign-in you can unlock a feature called My Maps that allows you to pinpoint locations on maps and then share those maps publicly or with chosen family members and friends. It's a way to help you track a family through time, marking every place they lived, or a migration trail they followed, or Civil War battlefields that your ancestor fought at.

Using Google Maps To Recreate Your Ancestor's Neighborhood - *FREE*
www.archives.com/experts/kramer-heather/ancestral-archaeology-google-maps.html

A worthwhile article by Heather Kramer about how to use Google Maps. Google Maps allows you to highlight areas of interest by dropping pins on specific locations. Information, notes, or pictures may be attached to these pins. This is especially helpful if you are trying to create a timeline for an ancestor or an ancestor's family. By dropping pins at various geographic points, you can recreate a migration pattern and recreate the neighborhood that an ancestor lived in.

An ancestor lived, communicated with, and interacted with people who lived around them. Census records, deeds, church lists, probate records and other records all list names of people that came into contact with an ancestor. By geotagging known facts about an ancestor's and their neighbor's activities, you can begin to recreate an ancestor's neighborhood which can add historical and geographical context to a family's heritage while leading to other discoveries.

LOC Maps - *FREE*

http://memory.loc.gov/ammem/gmdhtml/gmdho me.html

The Library of Congress map division provides the largest and most comprehensive cartographic collection in the world with collections numbering over 5.5 million maps, 80,000 atlases, 6,000 reference works, over 500 globes and globe gores, 3,000 raised relief models, and a large number of cartographic materials in other formats, including over 38,000 CDs/DVDs. The online Map Collections represents only a small fraction of what has been digitized. The Memory Collection Map Collections is organized into seven major categories: cities and towns, conservation and environment, cultural landscapes, discovery and exploration, general maps, military battles and campaigns, and transportation and communication.

Boston Library Maps - *FREE*

http://maps.bpl.org

The Norman B Leventhal Map Center at the Boston Public Library is in the process of digitizing a significant portion of its 200,000 historic maps and 5,000 atlases. The collection's scope is the World, Europe, and Amer-

ica, with particular attention to New England, Massachusetts, and Boston from the 15th century to the present day. They have a particular interest in developing innovative uses of maps and geographic materials to engage young people's curiosity about the world, thereby enhancing their understanding of geography, history, world cultures, and citizenship.

New York Library Maps - *FREE*

www.nypl.org/locations/schwarzman/map-division

One of the world's premier map collections in terms of size, scope, unique holdings, diversity and intensity of use.

Holdings include more than 433,000 sheet maps and 20,000 books and atlases published between the 15th and 21st centuries. The collections range from the global to the local scale and support the learning and research needs of a wide variety of users.

Ancestry.com Maps, Atlases & Gazetteers - $

http://search.ancestry.com/search/category.aspx?cat=44

Beyond knowing the name of the city or township where your ancestor lived, a good working knowledge of each location can be critical when it comes to knowing

> Often you will find multiple places on a map with the same name.

Or you may find that the town or village has changed jurisdictions or even disappeared. It is very important to correlate with historical maps and other sources of information to be sure that you have identified the correct town.

what records are available, where you can find them, why your ancestors made the choices they did. $19.99/month

Featured collections include:

U.S. Indexed County Land Ownership Maps
http://search.ancestry.com/search/db.aspx?dbid=1127

Land ownership maps are portrayals of land purchased, granted, or inherited. Contains approximately 1,200 U.S. county land ownership atlases from the Library of Congress' Geography and Maps division, covering the years 1860-1918

Historic Land Ownership and Reference Atlases
http://search.ancestry.com/search/db.aspx?dbid=1205

A collection of maps and atlases 1507-2000 detailing land areas that comprise the present-day US and Canada, as well as various other parts of the world. It contains a variety of maps and atlases, including land ownership atlases and bird's-eye view maps. Land ownership atlases usually show the names of contemporary owners or occupants of land and structures.

FREE 18-MINUTE VIDEO
Maps: A Path to Your Ancestors - FREE
www.youtube.com/watch?v=ySksjOLsDJk

Learn about how to use maps in your family history, and what maps are available on Ancestry.com. Juliana will share with you how to find them and how they can help you learn more about your ancestors.

Color Landform Atlas - FREE
http://fermi.jhuapl.edu/states/states.html

You can view new maps and imagery that have never before been posted to the internet. You will see 3-D maps, high resolution maps, registered maps, as well as maps of Mars, Europe, Asia, all of the continents, and more.

Newberry Historical County FREE
Boundaries -
http://publications.newberry.org/ahcbp

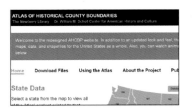

A free interactive atlas from Newberry Library of historical county boundaries, showing changing boundaries for each state. You can also download a boundary timeline for every US County.

US Census Bureau - State & FREE
County Boundaries -
www2.census.gov/geo/maps/general_ref/us_base/stco2003/stco2003.pdf

This map shows the entire US broken down into counties.

State and County Boundary Maps - FREE
www.genealogyinc.com/maps

This is a simplified map collection that allows you to choose a state which contains rotating animated maps showing all the county bounty changes. It also allows you to see a map of the state for specific census years.

USGenWeb Maps - FREE
www.usgenweb.org

A great resource for maps, including State and County Maps, the US Digital Map Library and 67 maps from Indian Land Cessions in the United States.

Family Tree Mapping
Family history software programs and utility apps for mapping your ancestors

Name and Address	Description	Cost	Windows/ MAC/Web
Ahnenblatt www.ahnenblatt.com	Uses the supplied Google-Earth Plug-In	FREE	Windows
Ancestral Quest www.ancquest.com	Links to Ancestry.com and FamilySearch.org	Basic version is FREE, $29.95	Windows
AniMap http://goldbug.com/animap	Contains historical maps that show the changing county boundaries for US	$79.95	Windows
Centennia Historical Atlas www.historicalatlas.com	Map-based guide to history of Europe and Middle East from 11th century to the present, including over 9,000 border changes.	FREE download from 1789-1819, Full ver. $59.00	Windows / Macintosh OSX
Family Atlas www.rootsmagic.com/ Family-Atlas	Imports data from genealogy software for mapping with its own internal maps	$29.95	Windows
Family Historian www.family-historian.co.uk	Free plugin for mapping, timelines and more	Free 30-day trial, $46.50	Windows
Family Tree Maker www.familytreemaker.com	Virtually visit maps of ancestral events without leaving your tree	Windows $39.99, Mac $69.99 (requires Ancestry.com membership)	Windows/Mac
GEDitCOM II www.geditcom.com	Links to maps displaying the place, its neighbors, points of genealogical interest	$64.99	Binary (OSX 10.4)
GenoPro www.genopro.com	Ability to convert geographical locations and export them in Google Maps	FREE 14-day trial, $49.00	Windows
GRAMPS http://gramps-project.org	An interactive map views highlighted places	Contributions accepted	Linux, Windows, Mac OS X
Legacy FamilyTree www.legacyfamilytree.com	Automatically pinpoints and plots important locations in ancestors' lives; See 3D, satellite and bird's eye images	FREE Essentials version, Deluxe $29.95	Windows
MacFamilyTree www.syniumsoftware.com /macfamilytree	Uses Apple maps from OS X Mavericks	$49.99	Mac OS X
Map My Family Tree http://progenygenealo-gy.com/products/family-maps.aspx	Imports data from Genealogy programs; uses an internal viewer but individual placemarks can be viewed using Google Earth, Google Maps, TerraServer-USA or MapQuest	$34.95	Windows

3 Connect with Ancestors

Red Book: American State, County, and Town Sources - (FREE)

www.ancestry.com/wiki/index.php?title=Red_Book : American_State,_County,_and_Town_Sources

Red Book helps you learn where to find information about your ancestors by focusing on localities. It is an expansive guide to the most useful resources. Organized by state, the content directs you to information-rich resources in all states. Some of the best resources are the county maps as they are today. To personalize any map, open it in Microsoft Paint (a free accessory program that comes with any Microsoft Office package), and mark up the map. You can highlight counties, draw migration routes, color-code families and their locations.

Sanborn Maps Online - (FREE)

http://en.wikipedia.org/wiki/Sanborn_Mapshttp://sanborn.umi.com/splash.html
www.loc.gov/collections/sanborn-maps/about-this-collection
http://genealogy.about.com/od/historical_maps/tp/Sanborn-Fire-Insurance-Maps-Online.htm?nl=1

From 1867 to 1977, the Sanborn Map Company produced large-scale color maps of over 13,000 towns and cities across the US. The Library of Congress web site refers to these color-coded maps as "probably the single most important record of urban growth and development in the United States during the past one hundred years." These sites provide links to free online collections of Sanborn Fire Insurance Maps for select states, cities, and towns.

eHistory Maps - (FREE)

http://ehistory.osu.edu >Maps & Images

This Ohio State University site contains hundreds of fully searchable historical maps and photos from the Civil War, WWII, and Vietnam.

Europe Aerial Photography - (FREE)

http://aerial.rcahms.gov.uk

The Aerial Reconnaissance Archives contains more than ten million declassified aerial reconnaissance images taken by Allied forces during the war which offers a fascinating way to view your ancestor's homes and landscapes. Aerial photographs circa 1940s are currently available for many European countries. You can also access the extensive Scotland collection from this website. The site offers aerial images overlaid with modern satellite images. This is a very useful tool to help you locate your ancestor's home. Access to most low-resolution images is free; high-resolution photographs require a subscription. £15/year (about $24)

East European Map Library - (FREE)

www.feefhs.org/maplibrary.html

The Federation of East European Family History Societies Map Library offers links to maps from the Austro-Hungarian Empire, German Empire, Russian Empire, and Balkans.

The Best Day

"Write it on your heart that every day is the best day in the year." Ralph Waldo Emerson (1803-1882), Philosopher and poet

Ralph Waldo Emerson

Good in Every Heart

"God has put something noble and good into every heart His hand created." Mark Twain (Samuel Clemens) (1835-1910), Author and humorist

Mark Twain

How can Google Earth Help me Find My Ancestral Home?

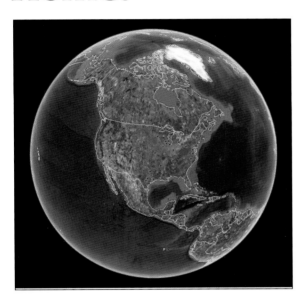

FREE WEBINAR
How to Use Google Earth for Genealogy - *FREE*

http://lisalouisecooke.com/free-google-earth-for-genealogy-video-class-by-lisa-louise-cooke

Watch this free video of Google Earth for Genealogy by Lisa Louise Cooke of Genealogy Gems.

Overview of Google Earth - *FREE*

http://geography.about.com/od/geographicproducts/gr/googleearth.htm

An article by Matt Rosenberg offering a review of Google Earth with pros and cons.

ONLINE COURSE
Google Earth for Genealogists: $ Plot Your Ancestors' Lives -

www.familytreeuniversity.com/google-earth-for-genealogists-plot-your-ancestors-lives

A four-week online course sponsored by FamilyTree University. $99.99

Bureau of Land Management General Land Office Records - *FREE*

http://www.glorecords.blm.govwww.glorecords.blm.gov/search/default.aspx?searchTabIndex=0&searchByTypeIndex=0

Federal land title records issued since 1820 and the present, including images plus survey plats and field notes, dating back to 1810.

Flying to the Past With Google Earth - *FREE*

www.archives.com/experts/hendrickson-nancy/flying-to-the-past-with-google-earth.html

An informative article by Nancy Hendrickson. If you've used Google Earth to view your house from satellite imagery, you're going to love flying to places your ancestors lived, worked, or farmed. The uses are many, but three favorites are: using the program in conjunction with historical census addresses, cemetery locations and Bureau of Land Management data.

Knowing Our Ancestors

Marcus Cicero

"To be ignorant of what occurred before you were born is to remain always a child. For what is the worth of human life, unless it is woven into the life of our ancestors by the records of history?" Marcus Cicero (106-43 BC), Roman philosopher, stateman

Google Earth *FREE*

www.google.com/earth

Most of us never get to travel to all the places our ancestors lived, but you can easily follow in their footsteps. Now you can take a virtual journey of your ancestral village, or any location in the world. With Google Earth, a free software program, your computer becomes a window to anywhere on the planet, allowing you to view high-resolution aerial and satellite imagery, maps, elevation terrain, road and street labels, the ocean and even galaxies in outer space. Discover hundreds of maps covering all corners of the globe, from historical imagery to the latest high-resolution underwater terrain. You can explore rich geographical content, save your toured places, and share with others.

You can locate your ancestral home, view your ancestor's home with street view, plot their homestead, and create a virtual "family history tour" to share with others. Google Earth lets you experience faraway locations from the comfort of your own home. You can tap into the program's robust features to bring depth and a new perspective to your family history research.

Find Your Ancestors Land Records Using Google Earth

FREE 4-MINUTE VIDEO - *FREE*
www.youtube.com/watch?v=h_uUkgH-Z1M

Watch this short video which demonstrates how to find land patent records at the BLM website and view the patent description in Google Earth. The patents are given in township and range which can be viewed easily in Google Earth.

Finding Historical U.S. County Boundaries Using Google Earth - *FREE*
www.archives.com/experts/hendrickson-nancy/county-boundaries-using-google-earth.html

The magic of Google Earth lies in the ability to find things like the site of an old family cemetery, a Civil War battlefield, track historical county boundaries, or even the remnants of an original family homestead.

Google Earth Help Center - *FREE*
https://support.google.com/earth

The help center features many aids, such as: Getting started and basics, user guide, video tutorials, overview, new features in Google Earth 6 (ground-level navigation, 3D, measuring tools), advanced features, FAQ, other ways to use.

EarthPoint - www.earthpoint.us

Tools for Google Earth; a web site that offers a variety of mapping services, all of which display map coordinates on Google Earth. You can display townships and ranges, and convert Township, Range, and Section into latitude and longitude, or convert latitude and longitude into Township and Section. It offers some features free but requires payment for more sophisticated features.

Joined for Life

Mary Anne Evans by François D'Albert Durade

"What greater thing is there for human souls than to feel that they are joined for life — to be with each other in silent unspeakable memories."

Mary Anne Evans (1819-1880), (known by her pen name George Eliot) English novelist, journalist

Create Timelines of Your Ancestors

An Important Research Tool

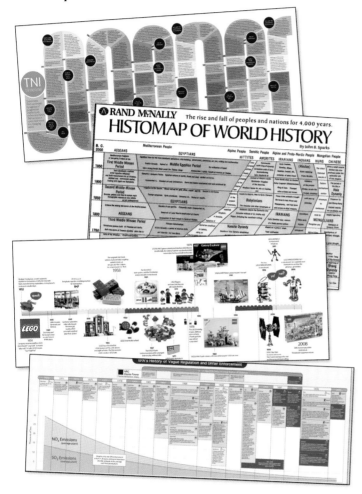

Check out these exciting tools to help you create and customize historical timelines of your ancestors.

A Timeline is an important research tool that provides a quick view of history to put your ancestor's lives into perspective, a sort of "history in a nutshell". Wars, politics, disasters, epidemics and such had a huge impact on their lives. Other events closer to home – including births, marriages, deaths, etc. – also affected them greatly.

Timelines are chronological listings of historical events. Historical events help you place your ancestor's lives in context with history so you can get to know the times in which they lived. They take you beyond names, dates and locations so you can see the big picture – events, situations and surroundings which had some sort of impact on your ancestors. But they can also help you identify gaps where you may need more infor-

mation about your ancestor's life.

Major historical events like wars, gold rushes, plagues, etc. may have caused your ancestors to move, or may explain the disappearance of a particular ancestor. Boundary changes may explain why you can't find your ancestor in the records of a particular area at a particular time. Social timelines, such as timelines of clothing or hairstyles, can provide details on how your ancestor's lived.

And it's interesting to realize what events were happening simultaneously. For example, In 1778 George Washington defeated the British at Monmouth, NJ, while Beethoven was being presented as an infant prodigy, and James Cook was discovering Hawaii.

When writing a timeline, organize your ancestor's life in chronological order but also insert historical events that occurred during your ancestor's lifetime,

Why use Timelines?

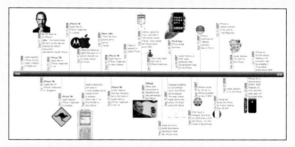

- Summarize a person's life
- Focus on further research needed
- Demonstrate problems, e.g. a 5-year old giving birth
- Aid in evaluating another persons research
- Divide an ancestor's life into workable parts, e.g. childhood, marriage, old age
- Demonstrate how lives interconnect
- Discover discrepancies and inconsistencies
- Eliminate possibilities of individuals of same name, same area, same time
- Suggest cause and effect when compared to historical data
- Ease in writing biography, memoir, or obituary

Jacobson, Judy. *History for Genealogists: Using Chronological Timelines to Find and Understand Your Ancestors.* Baltimore, MD. Clearfield Publishing, 2009.

How to Build a Timeline

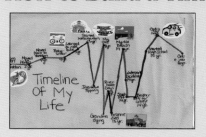

- Identify objective
- Review records and decide which events to include: organize your ancestor's life in chronological order but also historical events that occurred during your ancestor's lifetime, including world events, events within the country, district and town and within their own family.
- Decide on units of time
- List events in chronological order
- Label dates
- Use historical resources to find out what's happening in the community, state, national, world

including world events, events within the country, district and town and even within their own family. This can often provide explanations as to an ancestor's motivation or and reason for their life choices, perhaps demonstrating a cause and effect.

Begin the timeline with your ancestor's birth and end with their death. Between, write everything you know about him/her, including their marriage date and children's birth dates and places. Add events, such as immigrations, naturalizations, migrations, etc. as you uncover them.

Most family history software programs can automatically insert events to create an individual timeline. Some even allow you to include the addition of sound, images and movies. You will be amazed at the excitement this can add to your family stories.

OurTimeLines - FREE

www.ourtimelines.com

This site helps you create free, personalized timelines for your ancestors that show how their life fits into history. You can

generate as many timelines as you like, and if you're into creating your own family web site, you can insert the timelines into your own pages.

WhoWhatWhen Timelines - FREE

www.sbrowning.com/whowhatwhen

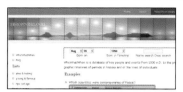

A database of key people and events from 1000 A.D. to the present which allows you to create graphic timelines of periods in history and of the lives of individuals for free.

Twentieth Century Timeline - FREE

http://history1900s.about.com/library/weekly/aa1 10900a.htm

A free decade-by-decade timeline of the entire U.S. 20th century.

Timeline Template - FREE

www.vertex42.com/ExcelArticles/create-a-timeline.html

A template that creates a free timeline using Microsoft's Excel, along with instructions on how to create a timeline.

Genelines - $

www.progenygenealogy.com/genelines.html

A powerful research and storytelling tool, lets you SEE your ancestor's lives in time. By bringing together elements of time, history and family relationships on visual timeline charts, Genelines can bring your family history to life, and even help you find new directions for your family. Different versions of the software let you use the visual timeline charts with various popular genealogy software programs, including Legacy, Ancestral Quest, Family Tree Maker, Personal Ancestral File and GEDCOM. $29.95

Timeline Maker Professional - 💲
www.timelinemaker.com

A robust software application to build quality timeline charts instantly. Features include: Unlimited chart themes/styles, seamless integration with Microsoft PowerPoint, exclusive sharing capabilities, and output to a range of graphic files, PDF and HTML. Not specifically designed for genealogy, though many do use it for that. $195.95 download. 7-Day Free Trial.

Easy Timeline Creator - 💲
www.timelinecreator.com

See history unfold with this easy-to-use software that enables you to easily and efficiently create historic timelines. You add you own events, choose fonts and icons, and add clipart images if you wish. $29.95

> By attaining a historical perspective of your ancestors, you also gain a greater perspective about your own life, and help link the past with the present.

Winston Churchill

"The farther backward you can look, the farther forward you are likely to see."
– Winston Churchill, Prime Minister of UK, 1874-1965

"It is useful...to look at the past to gain a perspective on the present."
– Fabian Linden, economist, 1916-1995.

George Santayana

"Those who cannot remember the past are condemned to repeat it."
– George Santayana, philosopher, poet, novelist,1863-1952

D. Joshua Taylor

"Exploring connections between history and genealogy offers a unique and fulfilling experience, as we uncover the roles our ancestors played in the past. Our ancestors were not just farmers or merchants – they were fathers, sisters, associates, and friends. ... The study of family history goes far beyond names and dates, and focuses on the desire to understand our own past within a larger context."
– D. Joshua Taylor, genealogist, speaker, author, www.djoshuataylor.com

Lloyd D. Newell

"All history is really family history, one generation after another. With each find comes a sense of belonging to something much bigger than this day, this time, this place. Indeed, with family history we find ourselves in what might just be called good company."
– Lloyd D. Newell, TV journalist, announcer, author
http://fans.musicandthespokenword.org/2010/07/25/to-know-our-heritage

"History is not just a collection of documents—and all records are not created equal. To analyze and decide what to believe, we also need certain facts about the records themselves."
– Elizabeth Shown Mills

http://historicpathways. com/howtocite.html# Evidence

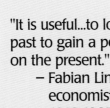

3 Connect with Ancestors

Time Capsule - FREE
www.dmarie.com/timecap

What was it like back then? Go to this website and learn what happened on any date. They currently have data online for the years 1800 through 2002, although data for the years 1800 - 1875 may be spotty. You can select specific headlines, birthdays, songs, TV shows, toys, and books for the selected date.

US History Timelines - FREE
www.datesandevents.org/american-timelines/index.htm

Provides a view of American key dates, events, people and places which were important to American History. Details of the first explorers and important Presidents and Politicians are all featured, as well as state timelines.

Simple Ancestor Timeline - FREE
www.genealogydecoded.com/genealogy_resources.html

A Microsoft Excel spreadsheet that provides the framework for building a timeline or chronology for an individual. Number each source in the Source List and cross reference them in the timeline.

Family Group Timeline - FREE
www.geneosity.com/genealogy-timeline-chart

A free 3-generation family group worksheet where you can identify family events over a 100-year span.

Tools to Help Reflect on the Past

Here are some good tools that may help bring your ancestors to life. They can help you gain an insight into understanding their heritage, lifestyle, traditions, and what it was like "way back when".

Making of America - FREE
http://moa.umdl.umich.edu and http://moa.cit.cornell.edu/moa

This is a joint project between the University of Michigan and Cornell University which provides free access to a large collection of 19th century books, journal articles, and imprints available on two websites. Two separate online archive sites put digitized books at your fingertips. The first collection contains some 10,000 books and 50,000 journal articles; the second site covers 267 monograph volumes and more than 100,000 journal articles.

Library of Congress - FREE
www.americaslibrary.org

The Library of Congress in Washington, DC is the largest library in the world and has millions of amazing things that will surprise you. This is a site that teaches American history in a manner that is appealing to both adults and older children. Their **"America's Story"** section contains many documents, letters, diaries, records, tapes, films, sheet music, maps, prints, photographs, digital files, and other materials from the past, and wants you to have fun with history while learning at the same time. They want to show you some things that you've never heard or seen before. You can look at pictures of American inventors, listen to Thomas Edison's voice extracted from an early recording, watch vaudeville acts filmed about

100 years ago, and even watch a film clip of Buffalo Bill Cody's Wild West show made in 1902. Their **American Memory Collection** at http://memory.loc.gov/ammem offers more than seven million digital items from more than one hundred historical collections.

You can download a PDF form with pre-filled date ranges from 1850-1950, or a Microsoft Word version which can be edited to suit your needs.

Family Census Timeline - *FREE*

http://shoestringgenealogy.com/form/FamilyCensus TimeLine.pdf

A free timeline worksheet for recording family census records from 1790-1910. There are other free Genealogy charts and forms in PDF format at http://ShoeStringGenealogy.com http://shoestringgenealogy.com/form.html including an individual timeline worksheet.

Cyndi'sList Timeline Links and Printable Charts & Forms - *FREE*

www.cyndislist.com/timelines www.cyndislist.com/free-stuff/printable-charts-and-forms

A timelines index to numerous links and free printable worksheets and forms.

Paint a Picture of Your Ancestors Lives

Add Life to Your Family Story and Link the Past, Present and Future with a Historical Perspective of Your Ancestor

Gain Historical Perspective

For us, our ancestors packed up a few worldly possessions and traveled across oceans in search of a new life. They built their own home and painstakingly raised their own food. They traveled on foot, by horse and wagon, sailing and steamer ship, handcart, and train. They had nothing more than quills and ink to write with. They struggled and sacrificed and worked till their hands were raw. It's hard to imagine what that must have been like.

What historical, financial, and military events, inventions, and advances in communication, medicine, and transportation took place and affected your ancestor's lives? Were they involved in any wars or conflicts? What influence did the arrival of motor cars or the railways have on their life? When did your forbears have indoor plumbing or even toilet paper on a roll as basic conveniences? Were their any epidemics such as the Spanish influenza of the 1920's or Cholera or TB?

Understanding the historical context in which your ancestors lived can be immensely valuable to you.

When you see the lives of your ancestors in perspective, you learn how to overcome trials and difficult circumstances in your own life by learning from the example of your ancestors. By learning about your ancestry, their experiences, and the way they handled them, you can overcome the challenges of your own life. You need to understand the events and context of your forbears in order to bring your ancestors to life. Being familiar with their corner of the world is an important part of your family story. It can help you fill-in your family story, and even lead to more records. What story would be complete without descriptions of your ancestors?

One way to add details to your family story is to paint a picture of the environment in which they lived. Your ancestors may have lived in dramatic and historic places and times, and placing them into a global or national context is essential to discovering and understanding their stories. It's essential to build a historical and social context for your ancestors.

Check out these great historical resources to unravel mysteries and discover your family stories.

Best of History Websites - FREE

www.besthistorysites.net

This website aims to provide quick, convenient, and reliable access to the best history-oriented resources online. Ranked #1 by Google for history web sites. It provides links to over 1200 history-related web sites that have been reviewed for quality, accuracy, and usefulness. Categorized by: Prehistory, Ancient/Biblical History, Medieval History, American History, Early Modern Europe, Modern History, World War II, Military History, History Today, Art History, Oral History, General History, Resources, Social Sciences, Geography, and maps.

Sites with engaging educational content and stimulating and useful multimedia technologies are most likely to be included. However, useful general resources and research-oriented sites have been included as well. It has won many awards and recognition. It also includes K-12 history lesson plans, teacher guides, activities, games, quizzes, and more.

Mayflower History.com - FREE

www.mayflowerhistory.com

A worthwhile website by author and historian Caleb Johnson dealing with the Mayflower passengers and the history of the Pilgrims and early Plymouth Colony. He has been researching and studying the Mayflower passengers for twenty years, and has authored and edited a number of books. Contains important primary source documents related to the ship's voyage, a history of the Mayflower, representations of the ship, and more.

Finding Mayflower Families - FREE

www.genealogymagazine.com/finmayfam.html

An excellent magazine article on how to do research on your pilgrim ancestors. Several good books are mentioned, to help further your study.

Book: Plymouth Colony - FREE

http://books.google.com/books/about/Plymouth_Colony.html?id=17zCU76ZtH0C

This is the first truly complete treatment of the history and genealogy of Plymouth Colony. It includes a concise history of the colony, both chronologically and topically, and more than 300 biographical sketches of its inhabitants. Richly documented and illustrated with maps and photographs. $5.67 (used) to $19.95

Plymouth Colony Archive - $

www.histarch.illinois.edu/plymouth/index.html

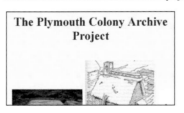

This site focuses on Plymouth from 1620-1691 and has been selected as one of the best humanities sites on the web by the National Endowment for the Humanities. Includes fully searchable texts of early laws, court records, wills, and probates; analyses of the colony legal structure, domestic relations, early settlement, criminal records, and interactions of the Wampanoag people and the colonists; biographical and social network profiles of members of the colony; a study of social and legal relationships between indentured servants and masters; and archaeological analyses of house plans and material culture.

Pilgrims and Plymouth Colony - FREE

www.rootsweb.ancestry.com/~mosmd/index.htm#part1

This is a detailed study guide of the Pilgrims and Plymouth Colony. You can use the "Search this Site" field that will look for any topic or click on the "Site Map" to produce an interactive map that allows for selection of any of the individual web pages. Duane Cline, the creator of the site, has written two books: *Navigation in the Age of Discovery,* and *Centennial History: General Society of Mayflower Descendants.*

Archiving Early America - FREE

www.earlyamerica.com

A worthwhile commercial site for links to historical documents, biographies, and even on-line books, on 18th century America. These archival materials are displayed in their original formats so they can be read and examined close-up and in detail. Of special interest is the Maryland Gazette containing

Library of Congress - FREE

www.loc.gov

The Library of Congress is the nation's oldest federal cultural institution, and serves as the research arm of Congress. It is also the largest library in the world, with more than 119 million items on approximately 530 miles of bookshelves. The collections include more than 18 million books, 2.5 million recordings, 12 million photographs, 4.5 million maps, and 60 million manuscripts. The Library's mission is to make its resources available and useful to the Congress and the American people and to sustain and preserve a universal collection of knowledge and creativity for future generations.

George Washington's Journal of his historic trip to the Ohio Valley. It is the only original copy privately held. Materials are free for personal use.

Early America's Digital Archives - FREE

http://mith.umd.edu//eada

The Maryland Institute for Technology in the Humanities has produced a searchable collection of electronic texts written in or about the Americas from 1492 to approximately 1820. The Archive also features a collection of links to early American texts on the Internet.

American Colonist's Library - FREE

www.freerepublic.com/focus/f-news/1294965/posts

A massive collection of historical works which contributed to the formation of American politics, culture, and ideals. Arranged in chronological sequence (500 B.C.-1800 A.D.). A very helpful scholarly resource.

eHistory.com - FREE

www.ehistory.com

Serves up more than 130,000 pages of historical content, 5,300 timeline events, 800 battle outlines, 350 biographies and thousands of images and maps. A favorite resource here for Civil War buffs is, incredibly, the searchable 128 volumes of *The War of the Rebellion: A Compilation of the Official Records of the Union and Confederate Armies.* This series is the authoritative reference to army operations during the Civil War.

US History.org - FREE

www.ushistory.org

The Independence Hall Association in Philadelphia has produced this fun and engaging site

3 Connect with Ancestors

U.S. National Archives FREE

www.archives.gov

The National Archives is America's national record keeper. It provides ready access to essential records of what the Federal Government does – why, how, and with what consequences. Those valuable records are preserved and are available to you, whether you want to see if they contain clues about your family's history, need to prove a veteran's military service, or are researching an historical topic that interests you.

It holds the original copies of the three main formative documents of the United States and its government: the Declaration of Independence, the Constitution, and the Bill of Rights. NARA also maintains the Presidential Library system, a nationwide network of libraries for preserving and making available the documents of U.S. presidents since Herbert Hoover.

Online Public Access (OPA) - FREE

www.archives.gov/research/search

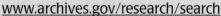

Search the online catalog and other National Archives resources at once for information about their records. This is the online public portal to the records and information about the National Archive records. The catalog consists of about 10 billion data records describing 527 thousand artifacts. There are also 922 thousand digital copies of already digitized materials.

OPA replaces the Archival Research Catalog (ARC), and also provides access to the Electronic Records Archives (ERA). OPA searches all web pages on Archives.gov, and presents those pages in the search results along with any catalog records, biographies and histories from the Archival Research Catalog. You no longer need to perform separate searches for finding aids or other information related to the records on Archives.gov.

You can search military, census, immigration, and land records, maps, cities and states, America's founding documents, events, and much more. There are also other valuable resources for genealogists, such as numerous blank family history forms to record your research results at www.archives. gov/research/genealogy/charts-forms.

Partnerships

In an effort to make its holdings more widely available and more easily accessible, the National Archives has entered into public-private partnerships with Google (YouTube), Fold3, Internet Archive, Flickr, and others.

There is a **YouTube** channel to show-case popular FREE archived films, and bring National Archives exhibits to the people. www.youtube.com/user/usnation-alarchives

There is also a **Flickr** photostream to share portions of its photographic holdings with the general public. FREE

www.flickr.com/commons

Fold3 provides $ access to premier collections of original military records. www. fold3.com

Wikimedia Commons is a media file repository making available public domain and freely-licensed educational media content (images, sound and video clips) to everyone, in their own language. You can find collections of similar files grouped by topic or by almost any other characteristic you can think of. Contains over 15 million files as of publication date. http://commons.wikimedia.org FREE

Wikisource - the free library that anyone can **FREE** improve. http://en.wikisource.org

The Internet Archive is a non-profit digital library with the stated mission of universal access to all knowledge. It provides

permanent storage of and free public access to collections of digitized materials, including websites, music, moving images, and nearly three million public-domain books. http://archive.org

where you can enjoy a virtual tour of Philadelphia and visit Betsy Ross' House. You can also learn why Pennsylvania is misspelled on the Liberty Bell and the story of its crack. The Electric Franklin provides resources for you to explore the diversity of Benjamin Franklin's pursuits, and there are several sections that deal with the revolutionary war.

World History.com - $

www.worldhistory.com

A large online historical newspaper database that contains tens of millions of newspaper pages from 1753 to present. Every newspaper in the archive is fully searchable by keyword and date, making it easy for you to quickly explore historical content. $9.95/month

European History - FREE

http://eudocs.lib.byu.edu/index.php/Main_Page

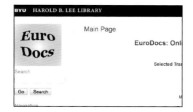

BYU library provides us with European primary historical documents – ancient, medieval, renaissance, and modern times – that shed light on key historical happenings within the respective countries and within the broadest sense of political, economic, social and cultural history.

America's Story - FREE

www.americaslibrary.gov

This site was designed especially with young people in mind, but there are

great stories for people of all ages. The Web site contains many documents, letters, diaries, records, tapes, films, sheet music, maps, prints, photographs, digital files, and other materials from the past, and wants you to have fun with history while learning at the same time. They want to show you some things that you've never heard or seen before. You can look at pictures of American inventors, listen to Thomas Edison's voice extracted from an early recording, watch vaudeville acts filmed about 100 years ago, and even watch a film clip of Buffalo Bill Cody's Wild West show made in 1902.

American Memory - FREE

http://memory.loc.gov

Perhaps you're curious to look at the world through your ancestor's eyes. Thanks to the American Memory Collection of the Library of Congress, now you can. This site offers more than seven million digital items from more than one hundred historical collections.

Library of Congress Catalogs - FREE

www.loc.gov/library

The Online Catalog contains 15 million records for books, serials, manuscripts, maps, music, recordings, images, and electronic resources. The Prints and Photographs Catalog allows you to search digital images. There is also a valuable gateway for access to hundreds of other universities and colleges across America.

Search Local, County, and State Histories

USGenWeb - CanadaGenWeb - FREE

http://usgenweb.org
www.canadagenweb.org
www.worldgenweb.org

Provides resources and queries for every state and country in the US. Clicking on a state link takes you to the state's website and a listing of directories for each county. Canada GenWeb provides links to every province.

State and Local Government Internet Directory - FREE

www.statelocalgov.net

Provides convenient one-stop access to the websites of thousands of state agencies and city and county governments.

Library of Congress: Resources for Local History and Genealogy by State - FREE

www.loc.gov/rr/genealogy/bib_guid/states/states_intro.html

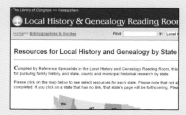

This site identifies key resources for pursuing family history, and state, county and municipal historical research by state. Click on the map to see select resources for each state.

FamilySearch Histories - FREE

https://familysearch.org/search/collection/list

Vast collections of local, county and state records.

Ancestry.com Stories, Memories & Histories - FREE

http://search.ancestry.com/search/category.aspx?cat=33

This category includes thousands of rich collections of published resources that can add depth to your family history. In addition to actual family histories in biographies, there are several indexes to genealogical and biographical materials. 14-Day Free Trial, $19.99/month.

Allen County Public Library - FREE

www.genealogycenter.org

A unique and valuable resource. They have one of the largest research collections available, incorporating records from around the world, including many local records and special collections.

The Newberry Library - FREE

www.newberry.org/genealogy-and-local-history

Explore the Newberry's rich collection of local histories. The collection includes county, city, town, church, and other local histories from all regions of the United States, as well as from Canada and the British Isles. It holds a comprehensive collection of New England town histories, as well as a strong collection of county histories from the Midwest and Mid-Atlantic states. The collection of local histories from the British Isles is also noteworthy.

FamilySearch Digital Books - FREE

www.familysearch.org >Search >Books

A collection of more than 100,000 digitized genealogy and family history publications from the archives of some of the most important family history libraries in the world. The collection includes family histories, county and local histories, genealogy magazines and how-to books, gazetteers, and medieval histories and pedigrees.

HeritageQuest Online - FREE

www.heritagequestonline.com

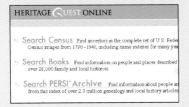

This site is not available to individual users. Instead, check with your local library to see if they subscribe. Most often, you can use the collection from home by logging in through your library's web site. It features genealogy and local history books that deliver more than 7 million digitized page images from over 28,000 family histories, local histories, and other books. Also, the Periodical Source Index (PERSI) is a comprehen-

sive index of genealogy and local history periodicals. It contains more than 2 million records covering titles published around the world since 1800.

National Archives - FREE

http://archive.org/details/genealoghttp://archive.org/details/genealogy

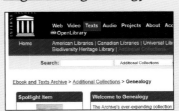

Resources include among many things books on surname origins, vital statistics, parish records, census records, passenger lists of vessels, and other historical and biographical documents.

Cyndi's List - FREE

www.cyndislist.com/us/state-level-records-repositories
www.cyndislist.com/lib-b.htm

Extensive links to state libraries, archives, genealogical and historical societies.

Strategies for Specific States - FREE

www.archives.com/experts/learn/states

Learn from numerous experts about doing research with links for a specific state (or any state), sponsored by Archives.com.

3 Connect with Ancestors

LOC Online Exhibitions - FREE

http://lcweb.loc.gov/exhibits

Here you can visit the Library online and experience the world's largest collection of culture and creativity like never before. It features exhibitions and installations that bring the Library's unparalleled collections to life. Let the Library of Congress take

you on a unique and personal journey through history and culture. Millions of items are waiting for you – explore, discover, and be inspired.

Manuscript Collections - FREE

www.loc.gov/rr/mss

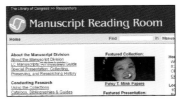

The Manuscript Division's holdings, approximately sixty million items in eleven thousand separate collections, include some of the greatest manuscript treasures of American history and culture and support scholarly research in many aspects of political, cultural, and scientific history. Among these are Jefferson's rough draft of the Declaration of Independence, James Madison's notes on the Federal Convention, George Washington's first inaugural address, the paper tape of the first telegraphic message, Abraham Lincoln's Gettysburg Address and second inaugural address, and Alexander Graham Bell's first drawing of the telephone.

Daughters of the American Revolution (DAR) Library - **FREE**

www.dar.org

https://familysearch.org/learn/wiki/en/Daughters_of_the_American_Revolution_%28DAR%29_Library

 The DAR Library houses one of the largest genealogical collections in the US. Its book collection includes more than 150,000 volumes concerning people and places throughout the nation. The collection focuses primarily on the generation of the American Revolution, but also includes substantial resources for studying people from the colonial period and the nineteenth century. Assess the online catalog at www.dar.org/library/onlinlib.cfm, and the Genealogical Research System (GRS), the master search engine for databases and indexes resource to aid general genealogical research at http://services.dar.org/_public/dar_research/search/?tab_id=0.

Smithsonian Libraries - **FREE**

www.sil.si.edu

 A comprehensive museum library system that unites 20 libraries into one system supported by an online catalog. They also maintain publication exchanges with more than 4,000 institutions worldwide. It offers its treasures to the nation through book exhibitions, lectures, special tours, and an extensive public website. Collections include: 1.5 million printed books, of which 40,000 are rare books (with electronic versions), 2,000 manuscripts, 180,000

microfilm and microfiche, and 300,000 commercial trade catalogs.

Ancestry.com Stories & Histories - **$**

http://search.ancestry.com/search/category.aspx?cat=33

 You can search their vast Stories & Histories category which includes thousands of rich collections of published resources that can add depth to your family history. Published family histories may link to your family lines and can include the names, birth, marriage, and death dates, relationships, as well as stories about that family. The biographical sketches and oral histories of other people may give insights into what life was like for your ancestor. You'll also find a record of events that had a profound impact locally.

Founders Documents - **FREE**

http://rotunda.upress.virginia.edu/founders/FOEA.html

www.upress.virginia.edu/rotunda

 The National Historical Publications and Records Commission and the University of Virginia have put online 5,000 previously unpublished documents from the founders of America. Included are letters, papers, and diaries of George Washington, Benjamin Franklin, Alexander Hamilton, James Madison, John Adams, and Thomas Jefferson, amongst others. Also contains The Documentary History of the Ratification of the Constitution.

DoHistory - **FREE**

http://dohistory.org

 This site invites you to explore the process of piecing together the lives of ordinary people in the past. It is an experimental, interactive case study based on the research that went into the book and film A Midwife's Tale, which were both based upon the remarkable 200 year old diary of midwife/healer

Martha Ballard. Although it is centered on her life, you can learn basic skills and techniques for interpreting fragments that survive from any period in history. They hope that you will be inspired by this story to do original research on your "ordinary" people from the past.

Measuring Worth.com - *FREE*

www.measuringworth.com/calculators/ppowerus

Purchasing power of money in the United States from 1774 to present. A calculator compares the relative value of a past amount of dollars to a present amount.

Also see "Published Family Histories" on page 77, and "Genealogical and Historical Societies" on page 119 to help you paint a picture of your ancestors.

Discover Your Family Stories

Telling Family Stories Brings You Strength

Have you ever told your children about where their grandparents grew up? Or how Mom and Dad fell in love? Or why Aunt Sadie has 10

Collecting and sharing family stories is an important part of family history...

...Not just because it preserves the information across generations, but also because learning your family stories can strengthen you in difficult times.

cats? If so, then you and your children may be better equipped to weather the inevitable challenges of everyday modern life, according to research conducted by psychologists Robyn Fivush, Jennifer G. Bohanek, and Marshall Duke of Emory University. (www.marial.emory.edu/faculty/profiles/duke.html)

"Family stories help you by evoking pride, personal history, a sense of connectedness and feelings of being special, even in the most ordinary family", Duke said. "Ordinary families can be special because they each have a history no other family has. ... You need to make [children] feel special. You need to tell them stories. They need to know who they are, where they come from. They need to know what happened to Grandma and Grandpa. They need to know where you were when you were kids. They need to have a connection and continuity," Duke said.

You can discover and record stories about your ancestors – and yourself – and share them with your children and grandchildren. The more that you share the stories of your ancestors' struggles and triumphs, the more all of your family members can learn from their lives. No matter how you tell your stories – through your family history, at your child's bedside, on your blog, or from a stage – your stories matter.

Dennis C. Brimhall,
CEO for
FamilySearch

"Every person who has ever lived has a right to be remembered and is a story waiting to be told. ... Every family is a story in progress."

– Dennis C. Brimhall,
CEO for FamilySearch

Learn Your Stories

Names, dates, and places can be boring without personalities and stories to bring them to life. Use what you know to learn more. Read old letters or stories carefully: what do they tell you about a relative's personality or attitudes? Take a fact and run with it. For example, if great grandpa was a carpenter who immigrated from a small village in Denmark, do some research online to see what else you can learn about his home town.

When personal accounts of ancestors don't exist, study the culture, town, or era in which they lived. Visit a historic site to get a general sense of their lives. Quote the stories of people like them. Find books or documentaries on everyday life during that time or the experiences of particular ethnic or laborers' groups. If you are tracing many generations, look at where they lived over a long period of time. See if their migrations match a larger national, regional, or cultural pattern.

Your Own Story Is Family History

Keep a record of your family starting now. Your stories are often the most interesting information available, because they not only tell you the who's and when's of your lives, but they also give you insight to what your lives are really like. Sharing your family's stories will give your descendants a glimpse into what your life and your family are like.

See "Leave a Meaningful, Lasting Legacy" in Chapter Four about writing your own story.

Ponder this insightful statement.

"Create your history as you live in the present, discover the past by learning of the stories of your ancestors, and shape the future by sharing your stories."

– Allan F. Packer, businessman, religious leader (1948-)

Allan F. Packer

FREE 2-MINUTE VIDEO
Discover Your Story - FREE

https://familysearch.org/learningcenter/lesson/step-1-discover-your-story/737

A FamilySearch short video about how to get started with family history and discover your story. The first step in discovering your story is reaching out to parents, grandparents— any relative that can share stories, photos, or other information with you. Using the FamilySearch Photos and Stories, you can capture, preserve, and share what you find. As you do, you will find yourself on the path to discovering your own story.

Breathe Life Into Your Ancestor's Story - FREE

www.archives.com/experts/malesky-betty/ancestral-stories.html

A valuable article by Betty Malesky about writing your ancestor's story – a story interesting and compelling enough that your descendants will be eager to read it. She offers suggestions for finding details and filling in the blanks about your ancestor's unique story.

4YourFamilyStory - *FREE*

www.4yourfamilystory.com
www.4yourfamilystory.com/blog.html

 Caroline is a coach to help you learn how to use technology to find your ancestors and get your family trees in shape, how to use technology to find your family story, how to use more than just Ancestry.com to find your ancestors, and of how to use online and offline resources effectively.

Caroline Pointer's family stories boards on Pinterest http://pinterest.com/familystories http://pinterest.com/familystories feature tons of

 pins for research, photo and video tips, genealogy and social media apps, family reunion ideas, blogging, technology, recipes, and much more. Learn more about bringing technology and genealogy together at her website and blog.

Tips to Telling Your Story So People Will Listen - *FREE*

http://familycherished.blogspot.com/2011/11/family-history-story-disfunction-tips-to.html

 If your family isn't interested in their family history - you aren't telling the right story or telling the story right. Being a good storyteller is a skill and one that can be learned! Here are some tips from Valerie Elkins to give your storytelling ability a boost.

A Tradition of Storytelling - *FREE*

https://familysearch.org/node/1505

 Sharing your stories is easy; much easier than most people think. So how can you create a tradition of story-

telling? Shantel Park shares some tips on how to do this. Growing up, I loved listening to my Mom and Dad tell me their stories. I didn't realize it at the time, but the desire to know who I was, where I came from, and where I belonged, was fulfilled whenever I heard my parents' stories. With each story, my feelings of contentment and assurance grew stronger…not because these were fairy tales, but because these stories were real.

DIGITAL Storytelling - *FREE*

http://moultriecreek.us/gazette
http://moultriecreek.us/gazette/digital-publishing
http://paper.li/moultriecreek/1354711892
http://moultriecreek.us/gazette/digital-storytelling-delayed

 This is a weekly news magazine by Denise Barrett Olson focused on the creative side of family history. Here you'll find inspiration, ideas and resources to help you tell the stories of both your ancestors and your current family.

Topics range from writing and publishing to video production and even scrapbooking. It's a way to share the stories of your families – both yesterdays and todays. It's like a technically-advanced version of the journals, diaries and photo albums of your ancestors. And, thanks to technology, you can share your projects online to reach a world-wide audience. As many of you have already discovered, this has helped discover and meet distant relatives who also share your interest in family history.

Denise writes about research technology and personal publishing at her Moultrie Creek Gazette blog. Moultrie Creek Gazette is a blog magazine covering genealogy and family history topics. It specializes in technology tools for research and digital publishing and offers many family history project ideas. She is also the proprietor of Moultrie Creek Books, an online book store specializing in genealogy

3 Connect with Ancestors

and family history publications. It offers a central location to spotlight self-published family histories.

Treelines.com -
www.treelines.com *FREE*

Treelines are storylines for your family tree. It's an online gathering place for families to collaboratively record and share the best stories, pictures, memories, and memorabilia from your family trees. It allows you and your relatives to work together on your family history in a way that is meaningful and satisfying for all. Winner of the 2013 RootsTech Developer Challenge.

It's a tool focused entirely on the stories that your discoveries reveal. The stories are told along a corresponding timeline, displaying the stories of how you did the research while sharing what you learned. You can write a story about a person, or groups of people, upload your favorite family photographs and records, design your story pages, and tag the people, places, dates and sources on the page.

Don't miss a worthwhile article by Tammy Hepps about turning family trees into stories at

http://b.treelines.com/treelines-featured-by-new-york-genealogical-biographical-society. It's about finding ways to reveal the vibrant people behind the dry records they leave behind. It's about putting yourself in the shoes of your ancestor to imagine their world and how they experienced the important events of their lives.

"It's just cool to know your story – not your own, but your family's."
– Kelly Clarkson, singer, songwriter, actress (1982-   )

Kelly Clarkson

Using Newspapers to Glimpse into the Lives of Your Ancestors

Archived newspapers give you the remarkable ability to see history through eyewitness accounts. They are the day-to-day diaries of community events and allow you to glimpse into the lives of your ancestors and gain detailed information about them and their stories.

Sometimes newspapers may be the only surviving information about the daily lives of your ancestors.

Newspapers covered the news, reported on events, and recorded the births, marriages and deaths of the people in their community and beyond. Sometimes newspapers fill in gaps in family stories. And sometimes they provide vital records where no other proof of birth, marriage, or death exists.

So newspapers can serve as a partial substitute for non-existent vital and civil records helping fill the void where records have been destroyed or before official records were kept.

For example, obituaries often fill the gap when a death record cannot be found. Newspapers often contain far more information than an official vital record because reporters and editors were usually scrambling for information.

The Power of the Internet

Discovering the date and place of an event through a newspaper can open doors to additional research sources and documentation.

Not long ago (in pre-digital days), finding your family history treasure in newspapers was incredibly laborious at best. It meant spending many days muddling through dusty stacks in the library, scrolling through rolls of microfilm, scanning endless headlines, articles and photo captions, and usually turning up…not very much.

However, thanks to the power of the Internet and the digital revolution, it is easier than ever to access millions of articles from any number of newspapers across the country – and even across the world.

In fact, it is quite possible to access over three-centuries of US historical newspaper articles in a matter of seconds through the use of keyword search tools. Although some key newspaper archive websites charge a subscription fee, there are just as many excellent websites that are free of charge.

You can trace your ancestors military career, research your Revolutionary War patriot, experience the birth of freedom in America, find your ancestors who fought in the Civil War, pull up vintage photos on your grandfather's grocery store, find your great grandparents' marriage record, find your ancestors original name if it was changed, follow the fortunes of an old family business, or find dramatic stories of your ancestors crossing the plains in a covered wagon.

The information you glean from historical newspapers can also be used to track down other data such as birth records, or baptismal entries in parish registers. For example, sometimes a baptism would be announced in the local paper giving the names of the parents and godparents.

Historical newspapers offer you a treasure chest. There are literally billions of newspaper articles throughout history just waiting for you to explore.

The stories you may discover by looking through newspaper archives can be downright fascinating, and it can do much to provide small and large details to those life stories you're searching for.

NewspaperArchive.com - $

www.newspaperarchive.com

One of the largest historical newspaper databases online 5,000+ titles and counting. Currently contains over 120 million newspaper pages from 1753 to present for the US, Canada, UK, Ireland, Denmark, Germany, So. Africa, Jamaica, and Japan.

Every newspaper is fully searchable by keyword and date, making it easy for you to quickly explore historical content. They are adding newspaper pages at explore millions of free articles collected by surname, category, and event. You can read million about 2.5 million pages per month. They offer free newspaper archive collections where you can search articles covering over 400 years of history, every state, and more than 10 countries. Explore free newspaper archives about everything from your favorite actor to interesting articles on politics and science. $29.97/3 months, $47.94/6 months, $71.88/year. Available for free at FamilySearch Centers.

Bring Your Ancestors to Life Using Newspapers

Powerful Family History 'How-To' eBook

You can get to know your ancestors' stories and how they met life's challenges using free archived newspapers.

DAILY NEWS
BRING YOUR ANCESTORS TO LIFE USING NEWSPAPERS

Best Free Archived Newspapers

Paul Larsen

Find Family Stories Using Free Newspapers

Now for the first time ever, you can get to know your ancestors' stories – the lives they lived, their hardships, their triumphs, and how they met life's challenges – in record-breaking time. Archived newspapers allow you to tap into a reliable source of hundreds of years of history, and give you the remarkable ability to see it through eyewitness accounts. You can easily explore your family tree and bring your family history to life for free using historical newspapers... if you know where to look.

eBOOK (download or CD): $

www.easyfamilyhistory.com
>Store >eBooks

An illustrated eBook by Paul Larsen that will undoubtedly help you greatly in adding richness to your family story. It's a PDF e-book (regular book format) for your computer, iPad, eReader or smartphone. It contains "live" (hyperlinked) websites, linked *YouTube* tutorial videos, and many valuable resources with descriptions in a user-friendly format.

LEARN ABOUT...

✔ How to glimpse into the lives of your ancestors

✔ How to gain detailed information about them and their stories

✔ Best Free online newspaper repositories

✔ How to access millions of articles from thousands of newspapers

✔ How to search over 300 years of historical newspapers in seconds

✔ How to find vintage photos of your ancestors life

✔ How to trace your ancestors that fought in the Civil War

✔ How to tap into historic secrets of the past without the hassle of manually sorting through mounds of newspapers

✔ Tips for searching newspapers

ORDER TODAY

Order your eBook by phone or online! And immediately begin to bring your ancestors to life using newspapers. 801-358-6692
www.easyfamilyhistory.com/store?page=shop.product_details&flypage=flypage.tpl&product_id=20&category_id=3 $14.95

GenealogyBank - $

www.genealogybank.com

One of the largest and fastest growing newspaper archives for family history research. Featuring over 6,400 news-papers (all 50 states, small and big cities), a powerful search engine, over 1 billion articles, currently has 215 million newspaper obituaries and death records covering over 320 years from newspapers (1690-current). New obituary records are added daily. Also contains Historical Documents (1789-1984): military records, Revolutionary and Civil War Pension requests, land grants and many more government records. $9.95/30-Day Trial, $69.95/year.

FREE 60-MINUTE WEBINAR
How to Find Family History Stories in Old Newspapers Using GenealogyBank - FREE

www.youtube.com/watch?v=Ceh53tOZxd0

www.dailymotion.com/video/xy0fkz_how-to-find-your-family-history-stories-in-old-newspapers_lifestyle

In this video, expert Tom Kemp shows you how to search newspapers at GenealogyBank.com to find your family history stories. Find out where you can uncover key genealogical information in newspapers that will help you trace your family tree and discover your family's past.

Ancestry.com Newspapers -

www.ancestry.com >Search >Card Catalog $ >Newspapers

www.newspapers.com

Ancestry.com has over 1000 searchable news-papers, and their subsidiary Newspapers.com has over 1700 different searchable newspapers across the US,

U.K. and Canada dating back to the 1700's with millions of additional pages added every month.

Ancestry.com

$19.99/month

Newspapers.com 7-day free trial. $19.95/month, $39.95/year for Ancestry or Fold3 members, .

FREE 3-MINUTE ANCESTRY VIDEO
Use Newspapers To Find Articles On Your Family - FREE

www.youtube.com/watch?v=vilk_CbmptA

Fold3.com -

www.fold3.com $

Millions of historical newspapers from small towns and big cities across the United States are available as part of a paid subscription. 7-day free trial. $11.95/month, $79.95/year. *Free at FamilySearch Centers.*

WorldVitalRecords -

www.worldvitalrecords.com $
>Search >Newspapers

Provides access to more than 4.2 billion names in family history record collections worldwide. Includes: Over 100 million pages of newspapers, 1739 to present, over 158 million digitized images, including US and UK Censuses, over 300 million names from birth, marriage and death records, over 75 million names from military records, one of world's largest historical map collections with 1.5 million maps, more than 8,000 high school, college and military yearbooks, more than 30 million tombstone photos. 3-day Free trial. $16.25/month, $89.99/year. *Free at FamilySearch Centers.*

Godfrey Memorial Library - $

www.godfrey.org

Offers access to many historic newspapers, including the London Times, 19th century US newspapers, and early American newspapers. $10/day, $45/year (without newspapers), $80/year with newspapers).

Chronicling America - FREE

http://chroniclingamerica.loc.gov

This is produced by the Library of Congress making historic American newspapers freely available to Internet users everywhere. You can search and view historic newspaper pages from 1836-1922 or use the U.S. Newspaper Directory *(top right-hand corner button)* to find information about American newspapers published between 1690-present. Provides access to information about historic newspapers and select digitized newspaper pages.

Library of Congress Reading Room -

www.loc.gov/rr/news   FREE

In addition, the LOC maintains one of the most extensive newspaper collections in the world in their *'Reading Room'*.

It is exceptionally strong in US newspapers, with 9,000 titles covering the past three centuries on *microfilm* and *bound volumes.* With over 25,000 *non-US titles,* it is the largest collection of overseas newspapers in the world.

Plus, it also offers a multitude of additional resources for finding and searching historic newspapers, including the American Memory project which has newspaper clippings, photos,

scattered articles, and limited series of newspapers at http://memory.loc.gov/ammem/index.html.

FREE ONLINE WEBINAR
Marriages and Anniversaries: FREE Mining Newspapers -

www.millenniacorp.com/_videos/webinars/2012-06-20-news/2012-06-20-news.html

Newspapers are packed with information celebrating engagements, marriages and anniversaries. They also reported on the heartbreak of those marriages that ended in divorce. Learn what you can discover about your family in this free webinar (web-based seminar) by Tom Kemp. Being able to search specifically for marriages, or engagement records, or divorce records is a great new search tool on GenealogyBank.com. Hosted by Geoff Rasmussen, Legacy Family Tree.

FREE ONLINE WEBINAR
Newspapers: Critical Resource to FREE Complete Your Family Tree -

www.millenniacorp.com/_videos/webinars/2011-02-02-newspapers/2011-02-02-newspapers.html

Learn how to document the daily life of your ancestors in over 300 years of fragile, rare newspapers, books and documents. See how you can click and read articles about your ancestors, obituaries and marriage notices, military reports and even the sermons preached at their funerals! History comes alive as you climb beyond the names and dates on your family tree to the recorded details of their lives.

Join librarian, lecturer, newspaper expert, and GenealogyBank.com's Thomas Jay Kemp for this free webinar on U.S. newspaper research, including a demonstration of the historical newspapers, books, and documents available at GenealogyBank.com. Hosted by Geoff Rasmussen, Legacy Family Tree.

Newspapers for Genealogists -
Using GenealogyBank.com to document every day of your ancestors' lives.

www.millenniacorp.com/_videos/webinars/2011-08-17-newspapers/2011-08-17-newspapers.html

Learn about the genealogical value of newspapers with tips/techniques for finding family history details: engagements, marriages, births, obituaries, advertising, legal notices, military records and much more. Join librarian, lecturer, newspaper expert, and GenealogyBank.com's Thomas Jay Kemp for this one-hour webinar on U.S. newspaper research, including a demonstration of the historical newspapers, books, and documents available at GenealogyBank.com. Hosted by Geoff Rasmussen, Legacy Family Tree.

Use Photographs to Connect to Your Ancestors

PhotoTree.com -
www.phototree.com

The proprietor of this site, my friend Gary Clark, is committed to collecting, documenting, and preserving 19th century photographs. He is primarily driven by genealogical research and the love of photography. He is also dedicated to passing on the vast amount of knowledge and information he has collected, organized, and studied. You can learn the fundamentals of dating vintage photographs for your genealogy studies, family history, or collectible antique photo research. Of particular worthwhile is a brief history of 19th century photographs from the view of five distinct photographic technologies and their eras.

PhotoTree.com can help you fix old photos or restore antique photos for you. You can also find the books, archival materials, and other resources to help you solve your photograph challenges. They also offer a fun set of boards on Pinterest with great images covering genealogy, 19th century photos, 20th century photos, restoration, and many other categories at http://pinterest.com/phototree.

A Photo Detective -
www.maureentaylor.com

Do you have family photograph you wish you knew more about? Maureen Taylor is an internationally recognized expert on photograph identification and genealogy, bringing together her knowledge and skills in history and research into family stories while giving insight into the invention and development of photography itself. Through private consults and group seminars, Maureen helps people solve a range of photo-related mysteries, from dating a Civil War era daguerreotype to organizing gigabytes of family photos from a digital camera. Maureen finds clues in photographs as if she were a private detective out to solve a case. She discovers stories behind family pictures by sometimes following the most mundane clue: a hat, the shape of a woman's sleeve, or a sign in the background.

Hidden Secrets in Your Old Photos -

www.archives.com/experts/haas-david/old-photos.html `FREE`

A worthwhile article by David Haas. Our goal is to understand the individuals in old photos and their stories. So what more can be derived from a single photo or a group of photos than just the face of a family member? In this article he explores a few ways to read between the pixels to learn more about the people and places in your old photos.

Facial Features Analysis - `FREE`

www.photorestorics.com/article-312.html

To learn more about analyzing faces in photographs. Bones do not lie, neither do ears, nor facial features nor clothing styles nor the types of photographic processes used at any given point in time. In addition to authentication of identifies of people, they also do digital photo restoration and retouching for a fee.

How to Identify a Photograph - `FREE`

www.archives.com/experts/fitzpatrick-colleen/how-to-identify-a-photograph-without-looking-at-the-picture.html

Colleen Fitzpatrick offers more tips and clues to dating a photograph.

Locating Images of Ancestors - `FREE`

www.archives.com/experts/likins-andy/ancestor-images.html

It's great fun to look back at photos and see how traits had been passed along. There are few thrills in genealogy like finding the image of an ancestor. Not only can family resemblances be observed, but there is

also great satisfaction in putting a face with a name that you've been researching for years. A worthwhile article by Andy Likins offers some tips on how to find photos of your ancestors.

BOOK
How to Date Your Family Photos -

www.outofstylethebook.com

www.familyrootspublishing.com/store/product_view.php?id=2554

Out-Of-Style: A Modern Perspective of How, Why and When Vintage Fashions Evolved by Betty Kreisel Shubert, fashion historian, author, illustrator. This is an amazing and worthwhile reference book to help you date old family photos. It offers beautifully drawn illustrations by the author combined with descriptions about how small differences in the shape of a dress sleeve or length of a hem can pinpoint a photograph to within a year or two. It begins in the 1830s and continues into the 1960s, and beyond.

It also contains men's and children's clothes styles. Even accessories, shoes, hats, bonnets and hairstyles are included in the commentary. Both the index and table of contents make it easy to find a particular period or fashion component when looking for elements from a photograph you're researching. List price $34.

Learning About Clothing Styles - `FREE`

www.archives.com/experts/piecznski-jeanette/genealogy-clothing.html

Jeannette Piecznski's article talks about learning the history of clothing styles to help you date photographs. When looking at the styles of clothing and the purposes for them, be it a fancy gown worn at a wedding or a day dress, there are a few places to look that can help you gain an approximate era for the clothing. Once you know the styles worn during each historical era, you can identify the time period of the photograph, portrait, or actual garment of your ancestor.

Nothing like Family Photos

Nothing tells the story of your family history like family photos. They capture the essence of people, places, and things and are among the most precious of our family treasures. They help you illustrate and understand your family history. They are personal reminders of loved ones and days gone by. They help link generations together, and add life to your family tree.

Collecting photos and stories of your ancestors lets you preserve and share your precious family memories. Technological advances have enabled you to retrieve photos with digital cameras and scanners and easily add them to your family tree. Photos that were taken 10-minutes-ago or a century ago are all within your reach with today's technology and online collections.

Learn from Your Photos

There is much to learn about your ancestors from old photographs. They are a window to the past that allows you to witness a still glimpse of a moment in time. Can you identify the age of a vintage photo by the type of photo or photographic processes used? Once you're able to determine a general time period of a photo, you can then estimate the birth year of the individual.

Look closely at the images and get an idea of how people looked, their physical features, their clothing and how they arranged their hair. Where did they live, what animals did they keep and what transport did they have? How tall was an ancestor in a photo? Does the home of an ancestor still exist? Your old photos could provide enough information to verify whether it does or not.

Time Honored Principles

Dennis C. Brimhall, CEO for FamilySearch

"A family photo and story preserved and shared in the context of one's family tree, in an instant, can personally touch us and teach us time-honored principles by those who have gone on before us, like the value of hard work, dealing with life's ups and downs, and the impact of choices."
– Dennis C. Brimhall, CEO for FamilySearch

The Past, Present and Future

Gail Lumet Buckley

"Family faces are magic mirrors. Looking at people who belong to us, we see the past, present, and future.
– Gail Lumet Buckley (1937-   ), Author, daughter of Lena Horne, actress

Write a paragraph describing what you see and what you have learned. For example describe the appearance of the person or people in the photograph; are they big or small, happy or sad? are their clothes well tailored and clean - suggesting their affluence and the formality of the photograph. Can you draw any other assumptions from the photo about the stage they were in their life?

3 Connect with **Ancestors**

FamilySearch Photos -

https://familysearch.org/photos

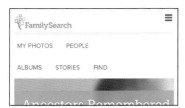

Provides simple tools to preserve, identify, and share your priceless family treasures. Create and share ancestor photos, and connect to ancestors in your family tree at FamilySearch. You can also create online albums of ancestors.

Ancestry.com Photos

http://search.ancestry.com/search/category.aspx?cat=43

Ancestry has a vast collection of photos images in various collections, such as: Public Member Photos & Scanned Documents, Passenger Ships and Images, Library of Congress Photo Collection, 1840-

2000, U.S., Historical Postcards Free Index, U.S. Civil War Photos, 1860-1865, and African American Photo Collection, 1850-2000. Millions of photographs have been added to Ancestry family trees by users who have indicated that their tree can be viewed by Ancestry members. Free trial, $19.99/month.

Treasure Family Photos - *FREE*

www.myheritage.com/old-family-photos?s=214653371

This is a free service from MyHeritage.com that allows you to save, digitize and back-up irreplace-able family photos and precious memories for future generations. Scan and upload photos onto an online shoe-box for your family. Tag them, add details and share them with family members....it's private, easy and free.

Flickr: Historical Photo Collections

www.flickr.com/commons

Hidden treasures from the world's public photo archives. An online photo management and sharing application, Flickr hosts a wide variety of historic photo collections contributed by library, archive and historical society collections. Click on *"Participating Institutions"* to view a list of the libraries and archives available. Most of them are continually adding new collections. You can also search for groups using an event or locality name as a search term to find groups. A requirement for participation in the program is that they may rightly claim "no known copyright restrictions" on the content.

Some of the key archive collections include:

Library of Congress

US National Archives

National Archives UK

Smithsonian Institution

New York Public Library

10 Don't Miss Photo Collections on Flickr

http://genealogy.about.com/od/historic_photos/tp/historic-photo-collections-flickr.htm

Kimberly Powell from About.com shares her take on 10 photo collections on Flickr you need to see.

Western History Photography Collection - *FREE*

www.photoswest.org

This searchable selection of over 120,000 images from the collections of the Denver Public Library and the Colorado Historical Society documents the history of the American West. Bring your Old West family history to life with scenes of American Indians, pioneers, railroads, mining, frontier towns, ranch life, scenery, news events and more.

Library of Congress Photos - *FREE*

www.loc.gov/pictures
http://www.loc.gov/index.html

The LOC is chock full of pictures, alphabetically categorized by collections with descriptions. Unfortunately, only a small percentage of their vast collections are online, but growing every day. The LOC also has a Flickr Photostream at http://www.flickr.com/photos/library_of_congress/. It's made for browsing, but you'll still either need to order prints or go to the LOC website to download image files.

National Archives Photos - *FREE*

http://aad.archives.gov/aad/series-list.jsp?cat=IT40www.flickr.com/photos/usnation-alarchives

The best way to view the photos in the National Archives is through their Flickr Photo-stream at the above link. All of the Flickr photos from the National Archives can be reproduced without permission.

Wikipedia Photos - *FREE*

http://en.wikipedia.org

The huge online encyclopedia, Wikipedia, also includes useable images on their pages.

Photos for Free... Or Nearly Free - *FREE*

www.archives.com/experts/taylor-maureen/free-genealogy-photos.html

Maureen A. Taylor says that there are ways to find photos for no or little cost. It's all about where you look and about knowing the rules. She offers some key websites that feature photos you might be able to reproduce − after checking the rights and permissions of each picture.

Ancestry's U.S. School Yearbooks - *$*

http://search.ancestry.com/search/db.aspx?dbid=1265

This is an indexed collection of 35,000 yearbooks and 7 million images from 1884 to 2009 from middle school, junior high, high school, and college yearbooks.

Dead Fred Photos - *FREE*

www.deadfred.com

A genealogy photo archive of over 111k images.

Heritage Collector Suite

www.heritagecollector.com (FREE) $

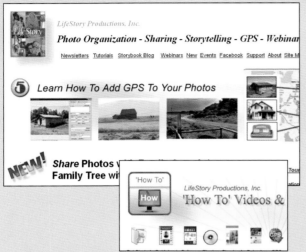

My friend, Marlo Schuldt, has created an amazing program that helps you organize, preserve and share your photos and stories. You can personalize and create interactive storybooks, talking calendars, slide shows and multimedia collections. You can increase interest with photo labels, oral narrative and GPS maps. You can also share your photos and stories via cloud, or on self-running CD/DVDs, or printing.

The Suite software comes with different add-on modules for free:

Storybook. Use your photos to create personalized pages. Make fun and fast beautiful scrapbook pages with add-on templates and 'QuickPages'.

• Calendar. Create, print and share family calendars.
• GPS Tags. Add captions and tags to photos.
• Photo Enhancement.
• Find any photo or file in seconds.

• Share by creating self-running CD/DVDs or use a free Internet Cloud.
• Create simple slide shows.

You get more than software... You get access to their knowledge and experience, development team, and become part of their family of users. You get: Free monthly Webinars for ideas, tips, and suggestions; 'How To' video tutorials; step-by-step documentation; a free 200-page digital family history guidebook; and online support. Standard version: Free (without add-on modules), Suite $79.95 ($125 value).

FREE TUTORIAL (FREE)
How to Create and Share Family History Storybooks / Scrapbooks -

http://heritagecollector.com/Steps/TutorStorybook. htm

You can create elegant digital scrapbooks and storybooks using Heritage Collector software which you can print at your favorite printer if you wish. Scrapbooks make memorable gifts and help create bonds between family members.

Marlo's GPS Tutorials - (FREE)

http://heritagecollector.com/Steps/TutorGPS.htm #Fun_Ways_to_Use_GPS

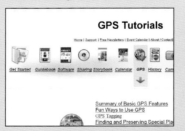

GPS is not just for computer geeks and gurus. Learn about GPS and how you can benefit from this new technology. Best of all, you don't need a GPS device to use GPS Map Module in Heritage Collector to get a coordinate. Learn how to use the GPS navigator in your car to get GPS coordinates. Create, print and share a GPS cemetery map in seconds!

http://heritagecollector.com/Steps/Recipes/Get_GPS_Coord.pdf

AncientFaces - FREE

www.ancientfaces.com

Share photos and memories of the people and places from your past. Look through millions of vintage photos shared by the community.

Family Old Photos - FREE

www3.familyoldphotos.com

A free site displaying over 26,000 vintage photographs, tintypes, illustrations and antique images of ancestors, relatives, kinfolks, family and some other folks and the places they lived. Find people and the places were they lived. Search for your surnames.

Ancestor Archive - FREE

www.ancestorarchive.com

A free genealogy database of family photos containing online vintage photographs.

Google's Photo Organizer - FREE

http://picasa.google.com

Find, organize and share your photos. Picasa is a free software download from Google that helps you: Locate and organize all the photos on your computer, edit and add effects to your photos with a few simple clicks, find, organize and share your photos.

Photo-Related iPad Apps - FREE

www.4yourfamilystory.com/blog.html

Here are Caroline Pointer's 20 photo-related iPad apps (see the 08/07/2013 blog entry), categorized by: Heavier Duty Photo Editing, Light and Fluffy Photo Editing, Text on Images, Photo Scanning, and Miscellaneous.

Best Photo Sharing Option - FREE

www.4yourfamilystory.com/1/post/2013/06/the-best-family-photo-sharing-option.html

Caroline Pointer did some comparison shopping on photo sharing sites and decided on Flickr as the best option, and explains why.

FlickStackr App - $

http://ipont.ca/ip/flickstackr

https://itunes.apple.com/us/app/flickstackr-for-flickr/id364895358?mt=8

An app that brings Flickr photo sharing to the iPad and iPhone. It allows you to easily browse photos in the Flickr universe, upload photos, edit your photos, and share photos via email, Facebook, Twitter and Tumblr. $1.99

LOC: Care for Your Photographs - FREE

www.loc.gov/preservation/care/photo.html

Care, Handling, and Storage of Photographs by the Library of Congress, featuring General Guidelines for the Proper Storage, and Dealing with Condition Problems.

Family Photoloom - $
www.photoloom.com

A web application that connects your photos, genealogy, stories, and documents to create truly seamless family history. You can organize your pictures around your family history (and into albums), index family relationships, and tag faces and resource documents. You can literally browse your pictures by simply clicking on an individual and every picture of him/her will appear in the portrait window. Plus it helps protect your family photos and documents from loss or damage by storing them on secure servers to give you security and peace of mind. Private, safe and secure. Unlimited image uploads and invited guests. 5GB storage space. Free trial. $39/year. *FamilySearch certified.*

3 Connect with Ancestors

FREE WEBINAR
Scanning for Better Results - FREE
http://heritagecollector.com/Webinar/Scan/Scanning.html

A worthwhile video by Marlo Schuldt on everything about scanning photos.

Civil War Photographs - FREE
www.archives.com/experts/hendrickson-nancy/civil-war-photographs.html

A worthwhile article by Nancy Hendrickson provides information and links to the best resources for copyright-free Civil War images online.

Search Cemeteries, Obituaries and Death Records

Best Online Cemetery/Gravesite Articles and Databases

FamilySearch Wiki: Cemeteries - FREE
https://familysearch.org/learn/wiki/en/United_States_Cemeteries

Provides links to online cemetery websites, cemetery resources by State, as well as different types of cemetery records to look for.

Digging Into Cemetery Research - FREE
www.archives.com/experts/likins-andy/digging-into-cemetery-research.html

Cemeteries are such a tangible link to our ancestors, and essential to helping us establish relationships and dates. They can even give us insights into the personalities of our ancestors. Where do you start looking? And what are they trying to tell you? Excellent article by Andy Likins.

Cemeteries Help You Connect to Your Ancestors

For centuries, people worldwide have made pilgrimages to the burial sites of religious icons and leaders. During the 19th century, garden cemeteries began to appear that encouraged a visitor to stay and visit in the cemetery.

Visiting cemeteries is a very rewarding part of connecting with the lives of your family and ancestors. Your ancestor's tombstone is one of the few remaining physical evidences of the life they lived. There is something special about being able to stand in the one place on earth which contains their mortal remains, and to touch their gravestone inscription. For many people, cemeteries are the one place where you can be the closest to your ancestors, both physically and spiritually. You can connect to your ancestor with this perhaps once-in-a-lifetime, inspiring experience.

Cemetery records have also been a way of verifying genealogical data. Making gravestone rubbings was in practice for centuries as a way of providing this documentation and appreciating the carvings on the tombstones. Scouring cemeteries looking for the graves of ancestors is a common and longstanding practice with individuals often relying on limited and outdated information to find burial sites.

The appreciation of cemeteries has evolved along with science and technology. Now, the Internet allows you to visit cemeteries and the grave sites of your ancestors anywhere in the world in the comfort of your home. The hunting of graves has become digital with the use of GPS systems to locate the area where a graveyard containing a grave is reputed to be. However, you need to know that not every burial has been recorded, and that only a fraction of the available tombstone or burial records are online.

Check out these outstanding 'how-to' articles, cemetery, obituary and death record resources. I hope they are beneficial to you.

3 Connect with Ancestors

Locating Cemeteries And Identifying People - FREE
www.archives.com/experts/pollock-michael/locating-cemetery-records.html

Visiting cemeteries can be a means to acquire information about an ancestor that may be available nowhere else, says Michael Pollock. Even when one knows where a cemetery is located, it can be problematic identifying who may be buried there. He provides examples of how he was able to locate and identify buried people.

FREE 24-MINUTE VIDEO Cemetery Records - FREE
www.byutv.org/watch/22b00352-865e-4dd6-ab58-3004c33eece6

Cemetery records are a favorite resource and for good reason. This is the original broadcast on PBS TV using an example of tracking down an ancestor's tombstone.

Find A Grave - FREE
www.findagrave.com

A free resource for finding (and adding) the final resting places of your family members and friends. With millions of grave records (currently over 103 million), it's an invaluable tool for finding the graves and cemeteries of your ancestors. It contains listings of cemeteries and graves from all around the world. American cemeteries are organized by state and county, and many cemetery records contain Google Maps (with GPS coordinates supplied by contributors) and photographs of the cemeteries. You can also create virtual memorials, add 'virtual flowers' and a note to a loved one's grave, etc.

Billion Graves - FREE
www.billiongraves.com

A free website to look up headstone photos from around the world. Their goal is to photograph all the headstones in each cemetery, and then transcribe the headstone images, and thus, build a database so anyone, anywhere, can find ancestors' graves with just a few clicks of the mouse. As a volunteer, you can use your iPhone, iPad or Android Smartphone to take GPS tagged photos of headstones and upload to the website using their app.

You can also quickly and easily locate your ancestor's gravesite while at the actual cemetery site using the free Billion Graves mobile app. Access the free video to show you how at www.billiongraves.com/contribute.php. The records index is also accessible at FamilySearch.org at https://familysearch.org/search/collection/2026973.

The free app is available to download at...
https://itunes.apple.com/us/app/billiongraves-camera-app/id602792141?

https://play.google.com/store/apps/details?id=com.apptime.BillionGraves.

Interment.net - FREE
www.interment.net

Provides free access to thousands of cemetery records, tombstone inscriptions and veteran burials, from cemeteries in the USA, Canada, England, Ireland, Australia, New Zealand, and other countries. There are currently 3.9 million cemetery records across 8,375 cemeteries available for searching on this site.

Veterans Gravesite Locator - FREE
http://gravelocator.cem.va.gov

Search for burial locations of veterans and their family members in VA National Cemeteries, state veterans cemeteries, various other military and Department of Interior cemeteries, and for veterans buried in private cemeteries when the grave is marked with a government grave marker. It has over 6.5 million burials in over 320 national and state military and veterans' cemeteries.

Canadian Headstones - FREE
www.canadianheadstones.com

You can browse over 690,000 gravestone photo records from across Canada. While there were a number of websites storing photos of gravestones, none also included the inscriptions on the gravestones. As decades pass, it is becoming harder – if not impossible – to read the inscriptions these stones originally contained. By archiving the images and transcriptions, these important records are saved.

WeRelate Cemetery Portal - FREE
www.werelate.org/wiki/Portal:Cemetery

WeRelate is a free public-service genealogy wiki sponsored by the Foundation for On-Line Genealogy in partnership with the Allen

County Public Library, and currently contains pages for over 2,400,000 people and growing.

Among other things, it contains a large number of pages representing cemeteries. Each cemetery has a wiki page, where you can find out and contribute information about that cemetery. The page also contains preferred and alternate names, latitude and longitude (for displaying on maps), a map of the area, historical information and research tips. It has at least one cemetery Place page for each state in the US and the District of Columbia. Currently, there are over 3,800 cemetery placename pages.

Graveyard Rabbit Association - *FREE*

www.thegraveyardrabbit.com

This blog is the headquarters for a network of "graveyard rabbits" (and their own associated blogs) dedicated to transcribing tombstones and documenting local cemeteries in words and pictures (names and dates, historic statuary, and spots to contemplate the lives of ancestors committed to the earth long ago). As such, it gives digital ink to a variety of interesting voices while offering insight into broad trends in cemeteries of yesterday and today, as well as fascinating facts about cemeteries around the world. You even may be tempted to

become a "graveyard rabbit" yourself. Scroll down the right-hand column for links to other Graveyard Rabbits blogs.

Their online journal is located at http://oj-graveyardrabbit.blogspot.com. Check out these posts by Denise Olson about the 1.2 million cemetery photos on Flickr at http://oj-graveyardrabbit.blogspot.com/2009/10/tech-tip-october-22-2009.html, and about the WeRelate Cemetery Portal at http://oj-graveyardrabbit.blogspot.com/2009/07/tech-tip-july-2-2009.html.

Cyndi's List Cemeteries - *FREE*

www.cyndislist.com/cemeteries
www.cyndislist.com/death
www.cyndislist.com/obituaries

Numerous links to cemeteries, funeral homes, death records, obituaries, and more.

Access Genealogy Cemeteries - *FREE*

www.accessgenealogy.com/cemetery

US cemetery transcription listings listed by state, and a Historical Cemetery Records database.

Tombstone Transcription Project - *FREE*

http://usgwtombstones.org/photo.html

Volunteers from across the U.S. have uploaded tombstone transcriptions and photos from thousands of cemeteries, hosted by US GenWeb. Records are organized by States and Counties.

Rootsweb Cemetery Records - *FREE*

http://userdb.rootsweb.ancestry.com/cemeteries

Offers over 1 million records with over 84k distinct surnames. Use the Search box on the page.

JewishGen Burial Registry - *FREE*

www.jewishgen.org/databases/cemetery

A database of more than two million names and other identifying information from cemeteries and burial records worldwide, from the earliest records to the present.

Best Online Obituary and Death Record Articles and Databases -
Search also Newspaper Obituaries.

Death Indexes - FREE

www.deathindexes.com

A valuable directory of links to websites with online death indexes, listed by state and county. Included are death records, death certificate indexes, death notices and registers, obituaries, probate indexes, and cemetery and burial records. Some of the state records are free and some require a fee.

Death Records Search - $

www.deathrecordsobituarysearch.com

Complete and accurate official U.S. death records and obituary records; more than 300 million records.

14-day membership $8.40

National Archives Vital Records - FREE

www.archives.gov/research/alic/reference/vital-records.html

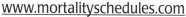

Hot links to vital records collections at the National Archives.

Mortality Schedules - FREE

www.mortalityschedules.com

If your ancestor died within the 12 months preceding the 1850, 1860, 1870 or 1880 census enumeration, you won't find them in the regular census, but you will find them in lists know as Mortality Schedules available on this site.

FamilySearch Wiki Pages US Death and Cemetery Records - FREE

https://familysearch.org/learn/wiki/en/United_States_Death_Records

https://familysearch.org/learn/wiki/en/Summary_of_Death_Records_in_the_United_States_by_State

https://familysearch.org/learn/wiki/en/United_States_Cemeteries

https://familysearch.org/learn/wiki/en/United_States_Military_Records

Death records are especially helpful because they may provide important information on a person's birth, spouse, and parents. Some researchers look first for death records because there are often death records for persons who have no birth or marriage records.

Anatomy of a Death Certificate - FREE

www.archives.com/experts/ortega-gena/anatomy-of-a-death-certificate.html

A worthwhile article by Gena Ortega. Death certificates give us so many more clues that just the date of a person's death. Family relations, years at a residence, occupation, military service, and family health history are just a few of the details you may find. Depending on when your ancestor died, death certificates are one of the first sources you should seek to learn more about your ancestor. They can lead you to other documents such as cemetery records, newspapers, city directories and more.

Dissecting Obituaries - FREE

www.archives.com/experts/alzo-lisa/researching-obituaries.html

Article by Lisa Alzo about obituaries are useful resources. They often provide a wealth of information about an ancestor's life tucked into what's into a relatively small column of space. If you spend some time dissecting obituaries, you may find they provide some nice family history nuggets, not to mention some potential surprises. A thorough dissection of the parts can often provide you with a clearer picture of the whole when it comes to fleshing out the details of an ancestor's life.

FREE ONLINE WEBINAR
Obituaries: Clues to Look For 🔵 FREE

www.millenniacorp.com/_videos/webinars/2012-03-28-obit/2012-03-28-obit.html

Free tips by Thomas Kemp (Genealogy Bank.com guru) for making sure you get the full benefit from an obituary notice. Newspapers have been publishing obituaries for over 300 years. Dig in and identify every clue as you learn how newspaper editors have changed their syntax, style and scope of obituaries over the years. Obituaries are critical for building an American family history. Hosted by Geoff Rasmussen, Legacy Family Tree.

Clues in Death Records - 🔵 FREE

www.ancestry.com/cs/Satellite?childpagename=US LearningCenter%2FLearning_C%2FPageDefault&pagename=LearningWrapper&cid=1265125303539

A worthwhile article by Juliana Smith. In addition to providing names and death information, death records include clues, and in some cases stories that can enrich your family history.

Alternative Sources for Death Records - 🔵 FREE

www.ancestry.com/cs/Satellite?childpagename=US LearningCenter%2FLearning_C%2FPageDefault&pagename=LearningWrapper&cid=1265125842778

Death certificates aren't the only place to find details about an ancestor's death. Ancestry.com's sources can provide dates, places, and even causes of death, as well as important clues leading to new sources of information, such as: Mortality Schedules, Coroner's Records, City Directories, Heirlooms, Court Records, Cemetery Records, Passenger Lists, etc.

Search Court, Land, Property & Financial Records

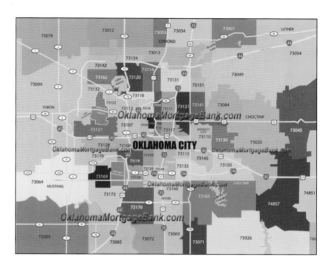

Best Articles Online

Superheroes of Genealogy - 🔵 FREE

www.archives.com/experts/henderson-harold/property-records.html

The property deeds, mortgages, and other legal instruments filed in county courthouses are the superheroes of genealogy. They may appear to be mild-mannered, but once unleashed they can demolish brick walls. They can tell you where people lived, the neighbors (who may also be relatives), name a wife or other relative, indicate whether an individual was able to sign his or her name, approximate a death date, locate someone who never owned property, confirm whether two people with the same name are the same person, and substitute for a non-existent will or probate. An excellent article by Harold Henderson.

Land & Property Records - FREE

http://genealogy.about.com/od/land_records

Learn how to research your ancestors using deeds and other land records, including how to decipher old deeds and draw a plat map. Plus, how and where to access land records on the Internet. This is a very worthwhile directory to numerous articles on the About.com and other sites about land and property records.

US Land and Property - FREE

https://familysearch.org/learn/wiki/en/United_States_Land_and_Property

A worthwhile FamilySearch Wiki article about an introduction to acquiring land from the government or from an individual. It offers links to articles and records for federal land states and state land states.

County and Town Records - FREE

https://familysearch.org/learn/wiki/en/County_and_Town_Records

When an individual received the patent or title to his land, he went to a local government office to have his ownership recorded and to obtain a deed. These land records and all subsequent exchanges of land through sales, foreclosure, divorce, or inheritance were usually recorded by a county clerk, county recorder, or county register of deeds. These officials also kept records of mortgages and leases. This FamilySearch Wiki article shows you where to find the deed books and indexes (and sometimes the mortgage and lease records) of more than 1,500 county and town courthouses.

Property and Court Records

Land, property, court and financial records reveal an enormous amount of information about your ancestors. They can be incredibly rich in detail due to the fact that family details and witnesses were often used to identify people.

The right to own land was a great incentive for many of our ancestors to immigrate to the United States, and encouraged westward expansion. Land records are primarily the records kept by town, county, and state officials regarding property owned, sold, or bequeathed to others. In the days before civil registration, the record of their acquisition of property in some cases can help link generations, as that property passed from one generation to the next. Land records provide two types of important evidence for you. First, they often state kinships, and second, they place individuals in a specific time and place, allowing you to sort people and families into neighborhoods. Deeds, land grants, and land tax lists help distinguish one person from another.

Court records can include wills, which include the names and addresses of family members, and details about your ancestor's estate. Tax records will typically include information on taxable items your ancestor owned, as well as his or her income and address.

Financial and insurance records can be particularly helpful because they frequently contain personal details used to identify the person in question – details that presumably only that person or family members would know.

While bureaucracy may not be popular with the people who had to navigate their way through it to buy land, probate an estate, pay taxes, manage finances, serve a sentence, or otherwise deal with red tape, the paper trails left behind can be incredible resources for family historians.

Finding Land and Court Records - *FREE*

http://rwguide.rootsweb.ancestry.com/lesson29.htm

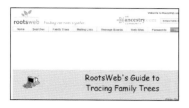

Two valuable articles on RootsWeb's Guide to Tracing Family Trees series. Land records are valuable for gene-alogical research. They provide evidence of places where our ancestor lived and for how long, when he moved into or out of a locality, at least the given name of his wife and sometimes a surprising amount of detailed information about him. Court records are located at http://rwguide.rootsweb.ancestry.com/lesson30.htm.

Tracing the Trails of Your Ancestors Using Deed Records - *FREE*

www.genealogyblog.com/?p=23386
www.genealogyblog.com/?p=23758

William Dollarhide demonstrates the power of deeds in retracing the trail of an ancestor by presenting a case study of one of his own ancestors. This is a real example of the use of deeds to solve a difficult genealogical problem. Let's see if he can solve a "needle in the haystack" search for an ancestor when all he knew is that he was born in Virginia in about 1788.

The second link above is a follow up article. He elaborates on the facts and how they were obtained. A very valuable research example.

What to Expect from a Deed - *FREE*

www.ancestry.com/cs/Satellite?c=Learning_C&chil
dpagename=USLearningCenter%2FLearning_C%2
FPageDefault&pagename=LearningWrapper&cid=
1265125549808

A worthwhile article by Michael John Neill. Land records are a great source. Two of the main reasons land

records can be useful are: 1) For a significant part of American history, a relatively high proportion of the population owned at least some property, and 2) U.S. Land records are frequently kept from the earliest days of settlement in an area.

Homestead Records: A Glimpse Into Your Ancestor's Past - *FREE*

www.archives.com/experts/king-roberta/homestead-records-a-glimpse-into-your-ancestors-past.html

The Homestead Act of 1862, considered one of the most significant pieces of legislation in American history, persuaded our ancestors to embrace the notion of founding a home somewhere out there. This article by Roberta King gives an historical over-view, explanation of the depth and importance of the records, and links to location of the records.

Probate Records and Wills - *FREE*

www.archives.com/experts/henderson-harold/probate-records-for-genealogy.html

Harold Henderson talks about probates and wills. Like all sources, wills need to be analyzed and carefully compared with other evidence. These records can often lead you to other records.

Where There's a Will There's a Deed - *FREE*

www.archives.com/experts/henderson-harold/wills-and-deeds.html

An interesting article by Harold Henderson about wills and deeds.

Probate Records:
An Underutilized Source - *FREE*

www.ancestry.com/cs/Satellite?c=Learning_C&chil
dpagename=USLearningCenter%2FLearning_C%2
FPageDefault&pagename=LearningWrapper&cid=
1265125550206

A valuable article by Donn Devine. When a person dies, every state has laws that provide for public supervision over the estate that is left, whether or not there is a will. The term "probate records" broadly covers all the records produced by these laws, although, strictly speaking, "probate" applies only when there is a will. Sometimes an earlier look at probate records would greatly shorten your search.

Finding And Using Tax Records - *FREE*

www.archives.com/experts/jackman-susan/tax-
records-in-genealogical-research.html

A worthwhile article by Susan Jackman. Tax records are the best kept secret when it comes to solving a multitude of genea-logical problems – especially pre-1850 census. You can discover the birth, marriage or death year of your early ancestor when no other record may have survived. You may not only find your ances-tor's residence but his year of birth, year of marr-iage, parentage, occupation, status in the commu-nity, migration patterns and finally his year of death.

Best Indexes and Databases Online

National Archives: Land Records - *FREE*

www.archives.gov/research/land

The land records that are generally of most interest to genealogists are the land entry case files. These are records that document the transfer of public lands from the U.S. Government to private ownership. There are over 10m such individual land trans-

actions in the custody of the National Archives. These case files cover land entries in all 30 public land states.

Land Patent Records - *FREE*

www.glorecords.blm.gov

The Bureau of Land Management site provides access to Federal land convey-ance records for the Public Land States, including image access to more than five million Federal land title records issued between 1820 and the present, indexing the initial transfer of land titles from the Federal government to indi-viduals. They also have images related to survey plats and field notes, dating back to 1810.

Bureau of Land Management Tract Books - *FREE*

https://familysearch.org/learn/wiki/en/United_States
,_Bureau_of_Land_Management_Tract_Books_%28
FamilySearch_Historical_Records%29

https://familysearch.org/search/collection/2074276

The first link is a FamilySearch Wiki article about using the records, and the second link is the actual historical records. It features 3,907 tract books containing official records (942,374 images) of the land status and transactions involving surveyed public lands arranged by state and then by township and range. These books indicate who obtained the land, and include a

physical description of the tract and where the land is located.

Read Kimberly Powell's short explanation of how to use this resource at http://genealogy.about.com/b/2013/07/30/searching
-blm-tract-books-on-familysearch.htm.

Ancestry's General Land Office Records -

http://content.ancestry.com/iexec/?htx=List&dbid=1246

 This database contains approximately 2.2 million land patents, primarily cash and homestead, land patents from 1796-1907 for 13 U.S. states. Information recorded in land patents includes: name of patentee, issue date, state of patent, acres of land, legal land description, authority under which the land was acquired, and other details relating to the land given.

Ancestry's Tax, Land, Wills and Criminal Records -

http://search.ancestry.com/search/category.aspx?cat=36

 In this category, you'll find indexes as well as some collections of actual records: Land Records; Tax Lists; Court, Governmental and Criminal Records; Wills; Estates and Guardian Records; and Bank and Insurance Records.

Cyndi'sList Links - FREE

Land Records - www.cyndislist.com/land.htm

Taxes - www.cyndislist.com/taxes

Wills & Probate - www.cyndislist.com/wills

 Links to various online resources for land records, deeds, homesteads, how-to, locality specific sites, tax records, and wills and probate records.

Public Records Online - $

www.netronline.com

 Links to available state and county Tax Assessors' and Recorders' offices. Online public records may include copies of deeds, parcel maps, GIS maps, tax data, ownership information and indexes. Some Recorders' offices have marriage and birth records available online. $2.95/3 days, $29.95/year.

Revolutionary War Bounty Land Warrants - FREE

https://familysearch.org/learn/wiki/en/Revolutionary_War_Pension_Records_and_Bounty_Land_Warrants

 Revolutionary War Pension and Bounty Land Warrant Application Files (NARA M804) cover about 80,000 pension and bounty land warrant application files. Most are dated between 1800 and 1900. This FamilySearch Wiki article provides explanations and links to the records.

Canada Land Records - FREE

https://familysearch.org/learn/wiki/en/Canada_Land_Records

 A FamilySearch Wiki article with links to the historical records. Many immigrants came to North America because they saw an opportunity to own land. Many settlers came from the US into the Canadian homestead areas to take advantage of the available land.

Ontario Land Records - FREE

www.olivetreegenealogy.com/can/ont/land.shtml

 Land records are very useful. Originally all land in Ontario belonged to the Crown. Although there were small areas of settlement in 1763 after the British took over, major settlement of Upper Canada began in 1783 and utilized Crown Grants. Many early settlers, both military and civilian, submitted land petitions to the Governor in order to obtain Crown land. Provides links to county and township records.

Family History Insights - 3

The Seeds of Our Heritage

Rex D. Pinegar
© by Intellectual Reserve, Inc.

Etched in stone at the National Archives building in Washington, D.C., is this meaningful truth: *"The heritage of the past is the seed that brings forth the harvest of the future."* Two hundred years ago the seeds of our heritage were being planted by men and women of great spiritual drive and steadfastness of purpose. Seeds of devotion and willing sacrifice for a just cause, seeds of courage and loyalty, seeds of faith in God were all planted in the soil of freedom that a mightier work might come forth. In Richard Wheeler's *Voices of 1776* we read firsthand accounts of some of those who were engaged in this "planting" process. Their expressions stir our souls to a greater appreciation of the heritage we enjoy and upon which we must build. A young doctor of Barnstable, Massachusetts, recorded in his journal on the 21st of April, 1775, the following: *"This event seems to have electrified all classes of people … inspiriting and rousing the people to arms! to arms! … Never was a cause more just, more sacred, than ours. We are commanded to defend the rich inheritance bequeathed to us by our virtuous ancestors; it is our bounden duty to transmit it uncontaminated to our posterity. We must fight valiantly."* (Richard Wheeler, *Voices of 1776*, New York: Thomas Y. Crowell Co., 1972, pp. 33-34.) Rex D. Pinegar

Unlock the Knowledge of Who You Really Are

James E. Faust
© by Intellectual Reserve, Inc.

"I encourage you...to begin to unlock the knowledge of who you really are by learning more about your forebears. ... Without this enriching knowledge, there is a hollow yearning. No matter what our attainments in life, there is still a vacuum, an emptiness, and the most disquieting loneliness. We can have exciting experiences as we learn about our vibrant, dynamic ancestors. They were very real, living people with problems, hopes, and dreams like we have today. In many ways each of us is the sum total of what our ancestors were.

The virtues they had may be our virtues, their strengths our strengths, and in a way their challenges could be our challenges. Some of their traits may be our traits. ... It is a joy to become acquainted with our forebears who died long ago. Each of us has a fascinating family history. Finding your ancestors can be one of the most interesting puzzles you...can work on. James E. Faust

Just by Chance?

"Having been brought up in an orphanage, I knew very little about my family... [but] I wanted to...learn about my ancestors. One day, as I was preparing to go on a business trip to Canton, Ohio, I...called an older half-sister and asked her if she knew our grandparents' names and where they had been buried. She gave me their names and told me that when she was a child she would visit them in a town in Ohio called Osnaburg.... I was amazed because this was only a few miles from where I would be going. I was very excited...I said a prayer that I would be guided if there was anything for me to find. I found myself in front of a small cemetery.... I saw an elderly man coming toward me on the sidewalk. I walked up to him and told him about my search for the grandparents of Fanny and John Robert Gier. He directed me to a house in town. When I went there, I found a woman in her 80s, Gurtie Baker.... When I said my maiden name was Irene Gier, she began to cry. She said she knew Uncle Bobby had remarried and had other children but that she never expected to see any of them. It turned out her mother and my father were brother and sister. I left the home with pictures... of my father, all his siblings and his mother and father. She also gave me all their birth and death dates and told me where my grandparents were buried. Throughout the visit, she said several times, 'This didn't just happen by chance.' I agree." Irene Durham

CHAPTER 4

Leave a Meaningful, Lasting Legacy

Suggested Activities

1. Conduct an oral interview with a parent, grandparent, aunt, etc.

2. Make a commitment to start keeping your personal history. Record your thoughts and feelings as well as the events of your day-to-day life.

3. Begin to write your own life story. Schedule a regular time for working on it. If writing it down seems difficult, talk into a tape recorder or video camera and then find someone who can transcribe it for you.

4 Leaving a Legacy

Everyone has a Story to Tell

Some people may mistakenly believe they have nothing of importance to pass on to others...no legacy they can leave. You don't have to be wealthy, famous, or talented to leave a meaningful legacy for your descendants. Some of the most inspirational, enduring legacies are from people outside of history books and newspaper headlines. Everyday, plain ordinary people are creating and passing down inspirational, lasting legacies. And you can be one of them.

The Gift of a Lasting Legacy

"What do you want to be known for? Love? Hard work? Patriotism? Faith? It's never too late to start developing such traits. It's simply a matter of the small choices we make every day. Each choice demonstrates to others — and, more importantly, to ourselves — what we consider important.

Lloyd D. Newell   Then, perhaps one day, your loved ones will [have] a gift that reminds them of you — the gift of a meaningful, lasting legacy that they pass down to the generations that follow." http://fans.musicandthespoken-word.org/2013/08/18/a-meaningful-lasting-legacy

— Lloyd D. Newell, TV journalist, Announcer, Author

Family History Insights - 4

Ellen Goodman

Our Most Valued Legacy

"What the next generations will value most is not what we owned, but the evidence of who we were and the tales of how we loved. In the end, it's the family stories that are worth the storage." Ellen Goodman, Pulitzer Prize winning syndicated columnist, www.BostonGlobe.com.

Dennis B. Neuenschwander
© by Intellectual Reserve, Inc.

Gathering and Sharing Family Keepsakes

"Every family has...keepsakes. ... These include genealogies, family stories, historical accounts, and traditions. These eternal keepsakes... form a bridge between past and future and bind generations together in ways that no other keepsake can. ... Bridges between generations are not built by accident. Each [individual] has the personal responsibility to be an eternal architect of this bridge for his or her own family. ...

If I want my children and grandchildren to know those who still live in my memory, then I must build the bridge between them. I alone am the link to the generations that stand on either side of them. It is my responsibility to knit their hearts together through love and respect, even though they may never have known each other personally. My grandchildren will have no knowledge of their family's history if I do nothing to preserve it for them. That which I do not in some way record will be lost at my death, and that which I do not pass on to my posterity, they will never have. The work of gathering and sharing eternal family keepsakes is a personal responsibility. It cannot be passed off or given to another.

A life that is not documented is a life that within a generation or two will largely be lost to memory. What a tragedy this can be in the history of a family. Knowledge of our ancestors shapes us and instills within us values that give direction and meaning to our lives." Dennis B. Neuenschwander

Spencer Kimball
© by Intellectual Reserve, Inc.

Your True Self

"Begin today to write and keep records of all the important things in [your] own lives and also the lives of [your] antecedents. ... Your own private journal should record the way you face up to challenges that beset you. Do not suppose life changes so much that your experiences will not be interesting to your posterity. Experiences of work, relations with people, and an awareness of the rightness and wrongness of actions will always be relevant. ...

No one is commonplace. ...Your own journal, like most others, will tell of problems as old as the world and how you dealt with them. Your journal should contain your true self rather than a picture of you when you are 'made up' for a public performance. There is a temptation to paint one's virtues in rich color and whitewash the vices, but there is also the opposite pitfall of accentuating the negative. ... The truth should be told, but we should not emphasize the negative. ...

Your journal is your autobiography, so it should be kept carefully. You are unique, and there may be incidents in your experience that are more noble and praiseworthy in their way than those recorded in any other life... Your story should be written now while it is fresh and while the true details are available...What could you do better for your children and your children's children than to record the story of your life, your triumphs over adversity, your recovery after a fall, your progress when all seemed black, your rejoicing when you had finally achieved? Some of what you write may be humdrum dates and places, but there will also be rich passages that will be quoted by your posterity.

Get a notebook...a journal that will last through all time, and maybe the angels may quote from it for eternity. Begin today and write in it your goings and comings, your deepest thoughts, your achievements and your failures, your associations and your triumphs, your impressions and your testimonies." Spencer W. Kimball

Your Own Story Is Family History

> When we say 'Legacy', we mean...

Your story, a gift that you bequeath to your descendants, or a gift that you receive from an ancestor.

photo, what happened when each child was born, etc.

Other ways to gather family stories include starting a blog where family members can record personal memories, or e-mailing family members one question a week. This allows for their answers to be compiled in one place.

Getting Started

Writing our personal and family histories may sometimes seem daunting. We may not know where to begin, or what to say or how to organize our thoughts. Here are some ideas and excellent resources to help you get started and organize your work.

Keeping a journal is not necessarily difficult. But does take some discipline. Here are some suggestions:

Keep a record of your family starting now. Your stories are often the most interesting information available, because they not only tell you the who's and when's of your lives, but they also give you insight to what your lives are really like. Sharing your family's stories will give your descendants a glimpse into what your life and your family are like.

There are various ways for you to record your family stories. Of course you can always write them down, but you can also record someone telling the stories on a video or audio recording, and include photographs in the record.

Some ideas for family stories you can record, include: An incident that made you laugh, how you met and fell in love, a memorable evening together, a difficult time that strengthened your family, your earliest memories, the story behind a

Choose a Convenient Method

Select either a book to handwrite your journal or a computer. By choosing a method that is convenient, you will be more likely to follow through. Specialized computer software is available, or you can use just your word-processing software if you choose. You could consider turning the writing into a ritual.

Choose the *right* book to write in, and with a pen that feels good to you and looks good on the page.

Establish a Schedule

Like any new habit, keeping a journal is something that you must work at, especially at first. You will discover more about what you are experiencing if you write in your journal at the same time in the same place every day or every time. Decide how often you will make entries: daily, weekly, monthly, etc.

When will you make the entries – early in the morning, at bedtime, on Sundays?

With today's busy schedules, we often find ourselves rushing from one task to the next. By scheduling a little time to record your personal history, you are allowing time for yourself to reflect on the day and on your life as a whole. This may be very therapeutic for you. When you have decided, stay with it.

Decide What to Record

A journal is a record of your day-to-day life, but it is more than just a diary. It deals with your experiences and how you handled them. It deals with the

One Hundred Years from Now, Will Anyone Know Who You Are?

an enduring, meaningful legacy to your kin. The whole world is in your hands – the legacy of your life (or the life of a family member) may be determined by what you do today. Are you up to the challenge?

Whether you realize it or not, you have profited in your lifetime by the experiences, achievements and heritage of your parents and forefathers. Likewise, your acquired knowledge, values, achievements and life challenges that you have overcome will become of great benefit to your descendants.

What Legacy Will You Bequeath to Your Heirs?

A life that is not documented will largely be lost to memory within a generation or two. If you do not record your life, the memory of your life will soon be largely lost.

You have a wonderful opportunity to leave

If you do this, one hundred or two hundred years from now, your descendants can know who you are. And they may find *their* lives forever changed for the better because of the legacy of uplifting, faith-promoting strength you left them.

Consider recording your life history and experiences for your children and grandchildren, and beyond. In this way, they can benefit and learn from your life. Even if they have never met you, they can come to love you and turn their hearts to you.

Through keeping journals and writing or recording personal and family histories, you can build the bridge between your past and future generations.

values and principles you have learned and how you applied them in your life.

It should also record events in your life, such as education, employment, marriage, and children. It should be something you can reflect back on...and learn from. Allow your mind to roam freely through the present, the distant past, and the shifting future. Don't deny whatever comes up as you are writing, no matter how silly it seems. You remembered it for some reason.

Take It Easy

Writing or recording your personal history may seem overwhelming at first, but if you do it a little at a time, it's much less intimidating. If you focus on short periods of your life, it will seem much more manageable. And you don't have to write in chronological order. You can write about any event or period of your life as your memories are stirred.

Bringing Back Memories

Include news events that were happening at that time in your life which not only help set it against the circumstances of the times, but also make your story more interesting. You may also find that by remembering historical events, you will be stimulating more of your personal memories. Memorabilia can also help bring back memories, such as: music, photos, letters, talking with family or friends, even familiar smells and sounds.

Be Personable

Record your triumphs over adversity, your recovery after a fall, your progress when all seemed black, your rejoicing when you had finally achieved. Share your thoughts and feelings; give your descendants a glimpse into the real you.

Be inspired by others. Check out your local library for other people's family histories. Reading the works of others may inspire you in your own writing.

John H. Groberg

Benefits of Preserving Our Heritage

"So often we think of our responsibility to do something for those who have gone before. We need to understand that probably one of the most important benefits of preserving our heritage is what it does for us today. If we want our problems to be solved, one of the surest ways of doing that is to search for our past, for therein we receive strength, guidance, and understanding.

We are giving an added eternal dimension to our lives as we learn and study the past. We can receive strength and help from those who have gone on before. To raise our families today, we need to do family research and genealogy."

– John H. Groberg, Chairman of the Olympic Events Executive Committee, Press Conference 2002

Theodore M. Burton

Uplifting, Faith-Promoting Strength

"We ought to write of our own lives and our own experiences to form a sacred record for our descendants. We must provide for them the same uplifting, faith-promoting strength that the ancient scriptures now give us."

– Theodore M. Burton

4 Leaving a Legacy

Our Posterity is Interested in All We Do and Say

Spencer W. Kimball

"We may think there is little of interest or importance in what we personally say or do — but it is remarkable how many of our families, as we pass on down the line, are interested in all that we do and all that we say. Each of us is important to those who are near and dear to us — and as our posterity read of our life's experiences, they, too, will come to know and love us. And in that glorious day when our families are together in the eternities, we will already be acquainted."

– Spencer W. Kimball

Your Journals Will be a Source of Inspiration

"Any...family that has searched genealogical and historical records has fervently wished their ancestors had kept better and more complete records. On the other hand, some families possess some spiritual treasures because ancestors have recorded the events surrounding their [life] and other happenings of interest. ...

People often use the excuse that their lives are uneventful and nobody would be interested in what they have done. But I promise you that if you will keep your journals and records they will indeed be a source of great inspiration to your families, to your children, your grandchildren, and others, on through the generations."

– Spencer W. Kimball

Enjoy

Have fun creating your memoirs and most likely others will enjoy reading it. You can include interesting things like photos, maps, news articles, receipts, favorite quotations and jokes, cards, etc.

Capturing Your Family Stories FREE

https://familysearch.org/learn/wiki/en/Creating_Oral_Histories

A FamilySearch Wiki article about how to capture memories before they are lost. Oral interviews are one of the best ways to preserve a wealth of stories, testimonies, thoughts, and feelings. Is any relative's memory or health fading? Capture endangered memories first. This article offers before, during, and after the interview of family members or relatives, including a list of open-ended questions, and the pros and cons of various recording equipment.

7 Tips to Easily Write Your Story FREE

http://familycherished.blogspot.com/2011/09/easiest-way-to-write-family-history.html

Taken from Eleanor C. Jensen's writing class at UGA Family History Conference.

Writing The Story Of Stories FREE

www.archives.com/experts/liberty-lou/family-history-stories.html

Lou Liberty – a historian, author and storyteller – writes a worthwhile article about some basic principles that can guide you to successfully presenting your discoveries.

Hidden Benefits of Keeping A History

Gawain & Gayle Wells

Gawain and Gayle J. Wells provide us with excellent insight on the many hidden benefits that come from: 1) gathering and reading histories of our progenitors, 2) writing our own personal history, and 3) keeping a journal. Here are some excerpts from a wonderful magazine article they wrote:

"Many unanticipated joys and blessings come from keeping a history. The blessings come not only from *completing* the records, but also from the process of *writing* them. What are some of these unexpected blessings?"

Journaling Helps Us Get Past Difficult Times

"...important in journal writing is the recording of both our failures and successes. If we can look back and see where we failed in the past and why, we are better able to chart a course for success in the future. Likewise, recounting triumphs and accomplishments can be a great source of strength in periods of discouragement and frustration and can help us get past other difficult times."

Gawain and Gayle J. Wells

We Are Strengthened

"It can be a great thrill to discover a diary or journal written by a grandparent or loved one. For example, the record of a great-grandmother's experiences as a bride and young mother can touch the heart of a granddaughter and cause deep love, even though the two are generations apart. ...We

greatly benefit from the testimonies of our own ancestors as they recount for us their trials and sacrifices. But many of our parents and grandparents left no written account of their lives for us to read. Even so, it is possible – and important – to obtain a record about them. ... Discovering our family and our heritage can help us discover ourselves."

Reliving Each Experience

"As I began recording my earliest recollections for chapter one of my personal history," Gayle recalls. "I found myself reliving each experience. Details and images came into my mind that I hadn't remembered before. I became so absorbed that I found myself weeping—and laughing—as I recorded certain incidents. It was as if I were actually stepping back in time. ... I was experiencing my own past, but observing it now with the advantage of maturity and perspective. ... We can also gain a greater appreciation for our parents as we write about them in our personal histories. Recalling our lives' formative events from an adult point of view helps us recognize how often we depended upon our parents for emotional support as well as physical help."

Touching the Lives of Others

"Writing in a journal is the best way to keep our personal history current. But a journal can best play its important role in our lives if we use it consistently. We might consider our journal as a map of our past, present, and future. We can look back to see where we have been, and then, with greater understanding and perspective, go forward, strengthened by our own experiences. ... We are and must continue to be a history-keeping people. As we are blessed in reading records kept by ancient prophets as well as our own ancestors, we...may touch the lives of those who follow us. And...we will experience greater joy and meaning in our lives." Hidden Benefits of Keeping a History, Gawain and Gayle J. Wells

Leaving a
4 Legacy

FREE ON-DEMAND WEBINAR
Start Writing Your Life Stories
www.familytreeuniversity.com/free-webinar-write-life-stories

Everyone has a story to tell, but recording those stories for future generations can be a daunting task. What should you share? How much should you write? How can you clear the fog from memories made long ago? View this webinar where Sunny Jane Morton, author of *My Life & Times: A Guided Journal For Collecting Your Stories*, shares tips and ideas for capturing the stories of a lifetime—whether they're your own or those of a loved one. (Note: By signing up to download this webinar, you will automatically be signed up to receive Family Tree Magazine's free email newsletters.)

Personal Historian Software 💲
www.personalhistorian.com

Software which assists you in writing personal histories about yourself and other individuals. It breaks this seemingly monumental task into small, manageable pieces and then reconstructs it into a complete, publishable document. It includes an extensive library of timelines, historical facts, cultural trivia, and memory triggers which give color and context to the history. You can publish your completed history to your printer, word processor or PDF file. $29.95

SOFTWARE
Write Your Life Story! 💲
http://home.netcom.com/~genealogy/life_story.htm

This is a software program that was created after talking to a group of writers. When asked "how do you even begin…" they all replied, "Make an outline of each year of your

life." With this program you are guided through creating your basic outline right through to the finished manuscript. It can be difficult to organize the various data you have collected and generate a life story. The software can help you organize the details of an ancestor's life or your own. $19.95

Genwriters FREE
www.genwriters.com

An online source to add life to your family history. It points you to resources, both online and in print, that will add variety and substance to your research.

 "Telling your stories is like collecting little gems to give to the next generation."
– Leah Abrahams

Cyndi's List: Writing FREE
www.cyndislist.com/writing.htm

Provides numerous links about writing your family's history.

Writing & Publishing FREE
Your Family History
http://genealogy.about.com/od/writing_family_his tory/Writing_Publishing_Your_Family_History.htm

Steps, tips, and guides for writing, editing, and publishing your family history, including family history books, genealogy websites, and family history newsletters from About.com. Plus, details on copyright laws and source documentation as they apply to genealogy and family history.

Tell your own story using your pictures.

Collecting Your Family Stories

Every person has a story to tell. Family stories are tales about people, places, and events related to your family and your ancestors. The memorable stories of our lives and of others in our family take on special importance, even if everyone tells different versions of the same event. These tales are family heirlooms held close to the heart. They are a gift to each generation that preserves them by remembering them and passing them on to future generations, and will become some of the most valuable and exciting information you can document about your family history. We call these family stories *oral history,* which is history the way our parents and grandparents remember it.

There is some urgency in collecting these precious family stories because older people will obviously not be around forever. Often, a parent, grandparent or great aunt is the last living person who knows these stories, and if they pass on before their story is recorded, it is lost forever and may never be known. By gathering your family stories, and learning more about the personalities and heritage of your ancestors, they become more than just

names and dates. They become real people with real struggles and dreams and triumphs in their lives just like you.

It doesn't matter if your family was famous or just regular people like most of us, there is great value in getting to know them. Start with older people who you believe might not be able to wait for you to get around to gathering their story. Decide what you would like to learn about from each family member, and don't delay in interviewing them. And don't limit yourself to one person, collect several perspectives on the same subject by getting lots of stories from different family members. One thing you can count on, your family stories are guaranteed to become absolutely priceless possessions in your family for many generations to come.

Use Social Networking to Collect Your Family Stories

https://familysearch.org/techtips/2012/01/social-networking-genealogy

James Tanner has a worthwhile article about using social networking to communicate with relatives. Not many years ago, the only way to talk to people was either in person, by telephone, by the occasional telegram or through letters. Pre-computer and pre-Internet genealogists were usually prolific letter writers. Today, that has all changed. Personal contact is still nice, but telephones to some extent and personal letters are mostly a thing of the past. It is now much easier to identify and communicate with distant relatives.

See the Social Networking pages beginning on page 47.

Book / eBook $
Producing a Quality Family History

www.amazon.com/s/ref=nb_sb_noss?url=search-alias%3Daps&field-keywords=Producing+a+Quality+Family+History

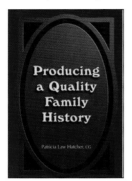

A well-written guide book for anyone looking to create a useful, lasting history of their family. Patricia Law Hatcher guides you through the steps required to create an attractive, functional family history report, and have made understanding the organization and creative process simple. It covers every aspect for the beginner and focuses the attention of even the advanced family historian and experienced writer on what is needed to generate a high quality publication. List $19.95

BOOK
You Can Write Your Family History $

www.amazon.com/You-Write-Your-Family-History/dp/0806317833/ref=sr_1_2?ie=UTF8&qid=1377543621&sr=8-2&keywords=Producing+a+Quality+Family+History

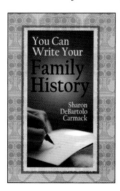

Sharon DeBartolo Carmack shows genealogists, history buffs, and writers at all levels exactly how to record the fascinating tales of their ancestors. Based on her own extensive experience writing family histories, the author shares her best methods. List $22.00

Conducting an Oral Interview

Whether your interview is in person, by phone, or by mail, there are some important steps which will encourage a more open and thorough interview.

Older relatives can be very helpful in piecing together your family's history. Often there is at

least one person in a family who has assumed the role of family historian – *the keeper of the flame* – and may already have accumulated and organized a great deal of genealogical information. Get reacquainted with family members through family history interviews.

Some of the things you will need to conduct an interview are: digital recorder or video camera, and a list of questions to help you remember what things you want to know about this person. You can *listen* better if you don't have to be thinking about your next question.

Usually, the *less talking* you do, the better the interview. So don't interrupt when they're telling their story. And usually limit your interview to 1½ hours so they don't get worn out. Store your recording in a safe place and make a transcription as soon as convenient.

Oral History in the Digital Age FREE
www.oralhistory.org/oral-history-in-the-digital-age

Connects you to the latest information on digital technologies pertaining to all phases of the oral history process. Contains 14 articles that cover issues of collecting, curating, and disseminating oral history as well as a number of case studies. Of the 14 articles, 6 are free to access online. Check out the article Choosing a Digital Audio Recorder. Also there is a wiki that provides 153 articles on oral history at http://wiki.ohda.matrix.msu.edu/index.php/Main_Page.

Baylor University Oral History Workshop *FREE*

www.baylor.edu/oral_history/index.php?id=61236
www.baylor.edu/oralhistory/index.php?id=23560

A good digital oral history workshop with Internet resources, equipment, transcribing, and editing recommendations. Guides you in tooling or retooling for the digital age, including topics on digital audio and video recording, digitization, and archiving digital oral history, with links to exemplary online projects, centers, and resources, as well as a glossary of terms on digital oral history.

Cyndi'sList Oral History & Interviews

www.cyndislist.com/oral

FREE

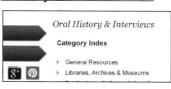

Provides numerous links to resources for collecting your family stories.

Making Sense of Oral History *FREE*

www.historymatters.gmu.edu/mse/oral

A guide by Linda Shopes, historian at the Pennsylvania Historical and

> Here's a list of possible questions for your interview, but don't feel bound by them. Write down other ideas and questions you can ask at an appropriate time.

Interview Questions

FamilySearch Wiki: Interviews *FREE*

https://familysearch.org/sites/all/themes/frankie/documents/Step-1-Conducting-interviews.pdf

https://familysearch.org/learn/wiki/en/Creating_Oral_Histories

Refer to the suggested interview questions for ideas on what to ask.

FamilyTree Magazine *FREE*

www.familytreemagazine.com/article/20-questions

20 Questions for interviewing relatives to use as a springboard for planning your oral history interviews.

JewishGen Questions *FREE*

www.jewishgen.org/InfoFiles/Quest.html

A list of questions and topics that may be used when interviewing family members.

Genealogy.com List *FREE*

www.genealogy.com/00000030.html?cj=1&o_xid=0001029688&o_lid=0001029688&o_xt=1029688

Suggested topics and questions for oral histories.

About.com 50 Questions *FREE*

http://genealogy.about.com/cs/oralhistory/a/interview.htm

Fifty questions for family history interviews. What to ask the relatives.

4 Leaving a Legacy

Museum Commission, offers tips to finding and using oral history online and what questions to ask.

Publish Your Family History Without Being Overwhelmed (FREE)

www.archives.com/experts/morton-sunny-mcclellan/publish-your-family-history-without-being-overwhelmed.html

Sunny McClellan Morton looks at some painless ways to publish your work. You have a lot of choices for publishing and distributing your written family history, whether you've got one page of material or one hundred. Start writing and sharing now and your research efforts will be preserved and magnified for present and future generations to enjoy.

Do Worthy Things

"If you would not be forgotten, as soon as you are dead and rotten, either write things worthy of reading, or do things worthy of writing."

Benjamin Franklin

Benjamin Franklin (1706-1790), Founding Father, author, printer, politician, scientist, musician, inventor, diplomat

God's Gift to You

"You don't choose your family. They are God's gift to you, as you are to them."

Desmond Tutu

Desmond Tutu (1931-   ), South African social rights activist, Anglican bishop

An interview is a great way to capture stories, testimonies, thoughts, and memories before they are lost. Here are seven tips for you.

7 Tips for Conducting Family Interviews

1. Decide whom to interview. Don't limit yourself to individuals close by. Use technology to talk with individuals living anywhere around the world.

2. Schedule an appointment when possible, but be prepared at family parties or reunions when an opportunity may arise. Choose a time and place to meet that is quiet so you don't have background noise in your recording. While face-to-face interviews are the most effective, telephone or online video interviews are alternatives.

3. Prepare a list of questions. Create a mix of open-ended and direct questions. Open-ended questions help the interviewee talk about what is most important to him or her, for example, "What is your earliest memory?" or "What was your hometown like?" Direct questions help you get specific information, such as "What year were you born?" or "What are your parent's names?" Find ideas on family history interview questions.

4. Be sure to pack: extra batteries for your recording equipment, paper and a pen or pencil to take notes, your list of questions, and other references, such as family pedigree charts or photos.

5. Look for signs of fatigue. Take time to rest or drink water to refresh.

6. Don't interview for more than an hour. While the subject is speaking, make a note of anything you don't understand, then spend a few minutes after to ask clarifying questions and how to spell the names of people and places mentioned in the interview. If you have a lot to talk about, consider scheduling follow up interviews.

7. Immediately after the interview, label your recording with your name, the name of the person you interviewed, and the date and place of the interview.

CHAPTER 5

Best of the Internet

Key Family History Web Sites

The internet contains a wealth of information and makes it easy to contact and stay in touch with others who might be working on their family roots. Whether you are experienced or a novice in tracing your family roots using the Internet, these personally-reviewed and singled-out-for-excellence web sites will empower you in your search for your treasured family heritage.

A virtual *treasure trove* of empowering, irreplaceable knowledge and information–much of which had been essentially "lost" to mankind in dusty archives around the world–is now instantly available to you at your fingertips at any time.

Web sites come in all degrees of value, efficiency, and friendliness. And since everyone has different needs, not all are equally useful for every family historian, but each may have something of immense value to offer you and perhaps add an important piece to your family history puzzle.

This collection of key web sites is not meant to be a comprehensive listing of family history web sites available, as there are well-known web directories, such as *Cyndi's List,* that do this very well. Searching the various online genealogy databases can be time-consuming and even difficult. Rather, this is a valuable, easy-to-use selection of personally pre-screened, key web sites to save you valuable time, help you get started and get organized, and help you add new branches to your family tree, thus empowering you with the *Best of the Internet.* These sites and resources are **(FREE)** unless marked with an **($)** to signify that access to some or all of the content requires a fee.

Opportunity in Difficulties

"A pessimist sees the difficulty in every opportunity; an optimist sees the opportunity in every difficulty." – Winston Churchill (1874-1965)

Winston Churchill

Family History Insights - 5

Help From the Other Side

Spencer W. Kimball
© by Intellectual Reserve, Inc.

"...my grandfather...searched all his life to get together his genealogical records; and when he died... he had been unsuccessful in establishing his line back more than the second generation beyond him. I am sure that most of my family members feel the same as I do—that there was a thin veil between him and the earth, after he had gone to the other side, and that which he was unable to do as a mortal he perhaps was able to do after he had gone into eternity. After he passed away, the spirit of research took hold of...two distant relatives. ... The family feels definitely that...our grandfather had been able to inspire men on this side to search out these records; and as a result, two large volumes are in our possession with about seventeen thousand names." Spencer W. Kimball

The Miracle of the Chinese Bamboo Tree

After the seed for this amazing tree is planted, watered, and fertilized regularly every year you see NOTHING for four years except for a tiny shoot coming out of a bulb. During those four years, all the growth is underground in a massive, fibrous root structure that spreads deep and wide in the earth. But sometime during the fifth year the Chinese Bamboo tree grows to EIGHTY FEET IN SIX WEEKS! Family history is much akin to the growing process of the Chinese bamboo tree. It is often discouraging. We seemingly do things right, and nothing happens. But for those who do things right and are not discouraged and are persistent things will happen. Through patience, persever-ance, diligence, work and nurturing, that "fifth year" will come, and all will be astonished at the growth and change which takes place. Finally we begin to receive the rewards. To paraphrase Winston Churchill, we must "never, never, NEVER give up!"

Where Are You Headed?

Oliver Wendell Holmes

"The greatest thing in this world is not so much where we are, but in what direction we are moving." Oliver Wendell Holmes (1809-1894), Physician & professor

What Are You Doing?

Henry David Thoreau

"It is not enough to be busy; so are the ants. The question is: What are we busy about?" Henry David Thoreau (1817-1862), Author, poet & naturalist

Close to Success

Thomas A. Edison

"Many of life's failures are people who did not realize how close they were to success when they gave up." Thomas A. Edison (1847-1931), Inventor & businessman

Know Where You're Going

Maya Angelou

"No man can know where he is going unless he knows exactly where he has been and exactly how he arrived at his present place." Maya Angelou (1928-) Poet, civil rights activist, actress

Promptings that Help

David E. Rencher

"In this day and age of computer technology and computer wizardry there are things which do and do not work. We cannot overcome the promptings [we feel] and expect to find our ancestors. If we ignore that, above all else, we will not have the experiences which we continue to have if we listen to the promptings and go when and where we are told to go." David E. Rencher, AG, FUGA, Chief Genealogist FamilySearch

Deserve to be Remembered

Pliny the Younger

"It is a noble employment to rescue from oblivion those who deserve to be remembered." Pliny the Younger (AD 61-112), Author and philosopher

Best Web Sites to Search for Your Ancestors

These *Best of the Internet* web sites can help you trace your family roots, connect to your ancestor's lives, and locate information about your ancestor's culture, traditions, homeland, and history.

There are literally thousands of Web sites available on the Internet to help you trace your family roots and stories which can become overwhelming if you don't know where to start. But some sites really stand out at providing the best information and records to get you headed in the right direction. Here's my list of the top sites.

Web sites can be categorized into different types. Explore all kinds of Web sites and bookmark the ones that seem the most helpful and interesting for you.

Web Site Categories

Huge Web portals or gateways - provide numerous links to collections of Web sites

Major collections of records - big Web sites, libraries, archives, public records, etc. that have parish records, censuses, wills, military and immigration records, maps, etc.

Support Web sites - local sites, how-to sites, blogs, podcasts, databases, maps, etc. that provide valuable information, keep you up-to-date, and help you collaborate with others who share your family tree.

Top 11 Genealogy Websites

(based strictly on Alexa rankings at print time)

Rank Global	Rank USA	Website	Category	Free / $
1	1	Ancestry www.ancestry.com	records	$
2	2	FamilySearch www.familysearch.org	records	FREE
3	3	Find A Grave (Ancestry subsidiary) www.findagrave.com	cemetery	FREE
4	5	MyHeritage www.myheritage.com	records	$
5	8	Geni (MyHeritage subsidiary) www.geni.com	family tree	$
6		Ancestry UK (Ancestry subsidiary) www.ancestry.co.uk	records	$
7	4	Archives (Ancestry subsidiary) www.archives.com	records	$
8		GeneaNet www.geneanet.org	forum	FREE
9	6	GenealogyBank www.genealogybank.com	newspapers	$
10	7	Genealogy (Ancestry subsidiary) http://genealogy.com	records	$
11	9	Eastman Genealogy Newsletter www.eogn.com	blog, forum	FREE

Top 10 FREE Genealogy Websites

www.genealogyintime.com/articles/top%20100%20genealogy%20websites%202013%20page4.html

(based strictly on Alexa rankings at print time)

Rank	Website	Category
1	FamilySearch www.familysearch.org	records, family trees
2	Find A Grave (Ancestry subsidiary) www.findagrave.com	cemetery records
3	GeneaNet (French site in English) www.geneanet.org	forum, family trees
4	Eastman's Genealogy Newsletter www.eogn.com	blog, news, reviews
5	Arkivverket Digitalarkivet http://arkivverket.no/eng/content/view/full/629 (Norwegian Archive in English)	records, information, forum
6	Ancient Faces www.ancientfaces.com	forum, vintage photos
7	GenealogyInTime Magazine www.genealogyintime.com	magazine, help site
8	USGenweb Archives http://usgwarchives.net	genealogy records
9	Deutschen Genealogieserver (in German) http://compgen.de	forum, news, information
10	Genealogy.About.com http://genealogy.about.com	'How-to' articles

Edmund Burke

Reflecting on Ancestors

"People will not look forward to posterity, who never look backward to their ancestors."
Edmund Burke (1729-1797), Irish statesman & author

Top 100 Genealogy Websites Worldwide

www.genealogyintime.com/articles/top%20100%20genealogy%20websites%202013%20page2.html

Rank	Website	Category	Country	Free Pay	2012 Rank	Address
1	Ancestry.com	records	USA	pay	1	http://www.ancestry.com/
2	MyHeritage.com	family tree	USA	pay	2	http://www.myheritage.com/
3	Find A Grave	cemetery	USA	free	4	http://www.findagrave.com/
4	FamilySearch	records	USA	free	3	https://www.familysearch.org/
5	Geni.com	family tree	USA	pay	5	http://www.geni.com/
6	Ancestry.co.uk	records	UK	pay	8	http://www.ancestry.co.uk/

GenealogyInTime Magazine has an annual review and ranking of the top 100 genealogy websites from around the world. They spent countless hours compiling an extensive collection of genealogy websites from various countries. Many old favorites made the current list, as well as some interesting new ones. Find out what is hot and what is not.

There are three main services that provide internet traffic rankings: Alexa, Compete and Quantcast; these last two measure primarily US internet traffic. Alexa measures global traffic. Their list is based strictly on Alexa rankings. The global traffic rank is a measure of how a website is doing relative to all other sites on the web over the past 3 months. The rank is calculated using a combination of the estimated average daily unique visitors to the site and the estimated number of page-views on the site. The site with the highest combination is ranked #1.

The top 100 list serves as a useful guide for both beginning and advanced genealogy users. It is always helpful to know what websites other people find useful and relevant. The list also provides some interesting insight into how the field of genealogy has evolved over the past year. The most popular websites for genealogists are those that provide ancestral records. Family history is becoming dominated by four entities: Ancestry, MyHeritage, FamilySearch and DC Thompson (brightsolid).

101 Best Web Sites by Family Tree Magazine

2009 Best Web Sites
www.familytreemagazine.com/article/101best2009

2010 Best Web Sites
www.familytreemagazine.com/article/101-Best-Websites-2010

2011 Best Web Sites
www.familytreemagazine.com/article/101-best-websites-2011

2012 Best Web Sites
www.familytreemagazine.com/article/101-best-websites-2012

2013 Best Web Sites
http://familytreemagazine.com/article/101-Best-Websites-2013

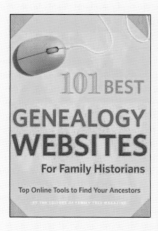

Includes: Mega web sites, US resources, state libraries and archives, local and regional resource sites, ethnic sites, map tools, sharing and storing data online, Canadian resources, death records and DNA, and immigration sites. Also includes: Best state web sites, top genealogy blogs, and sites for 'news'.

Top Genealogy Blogs

	Website and Host
1	**Eastman's Online Genealogy** Newsletterwww.eogn.com by Dick Eastman
2	**Genea-Musings** www.geneamusings.com by Randy Seaver
3	**GeneaBloggers** www.geneabloggers.com by Thomas MacEntee
4	**Genealogy Blog** www.genealogyblog.com by Leland and Patty Meitzler
5	**Canada's Anglo-Celtic Connections** http://anglo-celtic-connections.blogspot.com by John D Reid
6	**DearMyrtle** http://blog.dearmyrtle.com by Pat Richley-Erikson
7	**Olive Tree Genealogy** http://olivetreegenealogy.blogspot.com by Lorine McGinnis Schulze
8	**British Genes** http://britishgenes.blogspot.com by Chris Paton
9	**Irish Genealogy News** http://irish-genealogy-news.blogspot.com by Claire Santry
10	**The Armchair Genealogist** www.thearmchairgenealogist.com by Lynn Palermo
11	**Ancestry Insider** http://ancestryinsider.blogspot.com by anonymous
12	**Ancestry.com Blog** http://blogs.ancestry.com/ancestry
13	**Genealogy's Star** http://genealogysstar.blogspot.com by James Tanner
14	**Moultrie Creek** http://moultriecreek.us by Denise Barrett Olson
15	**Climbing My Family Tree** www.climbingmyfamilytree.com by Jennifer
16	**4YourFamilyStory** www.4yourfamilystory.com/blog.html by Caroline Pointer
17	**GenealogyWise** www.genealogywise.com/profiles/blog/list

Ancestry.com

*The World's Largest Online
Resource for Family History*

www.ancestry.com

Ancestry is a fast-paced, high-tech company guided by a very human mission: to help every person discover, preserve and share their family history. They have a family of brands that work together across the globe to provide something truly priceless: authentic family stories.

With more than 12 billion historical records, Ancestry.com is the world's largest online collection of family history records, including the complete US Federal Censuses (1790–1940), US immigration records, vast military records, immeasurable passenger arrivals records at major U.S. ports, city directories, vital records, and many exciting collections from around the world.

Ancestry users have created more than 50 million family trees containing over 5 billion profiles. More than 175 million photographs, scanned documents and written stories have been uploaded. They have approximately 2.7 million worldwide subscribers across their family history sites.

They have been helping people discover, preserve, and share their family history for 30 years since their founding in 1983. And as an internet company, they've been a leader in online family history ever since they launched their Ancestry.com website 17 years ago.

They have made family history easier, more accessible, and more fun for millions of people around the world. People join Ancestry.com for many reasons – to explore roots, discover their ethnicity, and to seek community with distant, perhaps unknown, relatives. Their members have made more than six billion connections with other members who potentially share a common ancestor since adding their family tree feature to the site in 2008.

They have digitized billions of family history records of all descriptions from 40 countries reaching back to the late 1300s, enabling their members to create millions of family trees. Their servers handle 40 million searches daily and they have expanded the Ancestry.com experience to reach mobile and social media worlds. US$19.99/month, $99/6-months

Here are the other Ancestry brands, businesses and products that help Ancestry.com connect families across distance and time.

Ancestry.com DNA -

http://dna.ancestry.com

It's amazing what your DNA can reveal about your past. Just provide a simple saliva sample and mail it in. Using some of the latest DNA technology, AncestryDNA will tell you all about where your family is from and maybe match you with distant cousins you never knew you had. $99.

Archives.com - www.archives.com

Archives.com makes it easy for anyone to begin to discover their heritage. With its clean and powerful design, no-fuss tree wizard, and other innovative features, Archives represents an affordable and powerful solution to any family history researcher, from beginner to expert.

It hosts more than 2 billion records – from U.S. vital records and newspaper clippings to obituaries and other assorted documents – and is equipped with a variety of notable features capable of shedding a little light on your family's past. Aside from the standard ability to build a family tree, the site also features Facebook integration and a laudable search engine that fishes around for any relevant information or potential matches.

Archives offers a vast collection of databases for researching all of the important events of your ancestors' lives – 269 searchable databases with 1.6 billion unique records. Archives can help you access 300 million U.S. vital records. Among them you will find a full collection of the U.S. Census – from 1790 to 1940 – which is one of the best documents for genealogy research. In some cases you can even see a scanned copy of the original document. The Archives search feature gives higher weight to documents with accompanying images, so they are listed first in search results, and a graphic indicates which information comes with each document.

The digital newspapers collection on this site is noteworthy, offering 120 million scanned newspaper images. It can be very exciting to find a relative's name in a paper from another era. Newspaper accounts offer so much more than just names and dates. They offer information about your ancestor's time and culture. 7-day free trial, $7.95/ month or $39.95/year.

Fold3.com - www.fold3.com

The web's premier collection of original military records. Wars have created genealogy gold mines about our ancestors. Registration records. Service records. Pensions. Photos. And More. There is no end to what you might find about your ancestors. Not only are there the usual family history facts such as who was related to who,

when they were born and died, and where they lived, but you can also learn how their lives were impacted by the wars.

This site provides convenient access to US military records, including the stories, photos, and personal documents of the men and women who served. The Fold3 name comes from a traditional flag folding ceremony in which the third fold is made in honor and remembrance of veterans who served in defense of their country and to maintain peace throughout the world.

Original records at Fold3 help you discover and share stories about these everyday heroes, forgotten soldiers, and the families that supported them. On Fold3, you can combine records found on the site with what you have in your own albums and shoeboxes to create an online memorial for someone who served. 7-Day free trial, $11.95/month or $79.95/year. Ancestry subscribers get half off.

Find a Grave - www.findagrave.com

This site contains listings of cemeteries and graves from around the world. As of print date, the site contains over 107 million burial records worldwide. American cemeteries are organized by state and county, and many cemetery records contain Google Maps (with GPS coordinates supplied by contributors) and photographs of the cemeteries.

Individual grave records contain some or all of the following data fields: dates and places of birth and death, biographical information, cemetery and plot information, photographs (grave marker, the individual, etc.), and contributor information. A registered user may create memorials without any fact checking or review. Although an active user forum exists, it is still possible that memorials are duplicated, incomplete or incorrect.

Contributors must register as members to submit listings (called memorials on the website). Upon submitting a listing, that member becomes the manager of the listing, but may transfer management. Only the current manager of a listing may edit the listing. Members and non-members may send correction requests regarding listings. Members and non-members can submit notations, which consist of images or pictures or flowers, flags, religious symbols, etc., which are posted on the individual listings, usually including a message of sympathy or condolence. Managers of listings may connect them via hyperlink to listings of deceased spouses and parents for genealogical purposes. Members may also request photos of graves which other members may then fulfill.

It also maintains links to memorials of famous persons such as Medal of Honor recipients, religious figures, educators and miscellaneous other celebrities. Ancestry.com acquired Find a Grave in September 2013.

Newspapers.com - $

www.newspapers.com

A powerful and affordable website designed to offer a historically rich collection of U.S. newspapers dating from the late 1700s into the early 2000s. The search and other site features are optimized for newspapers and allow easy access to the growing collection of newspaper images with millions more added each month.

It hosts 52+ million pages of historical newspapers from 1900 newspapers from around the United States and beyond. Newspapers provide a unique view of the past and can help us understand and connect with the people, events and attitudes of an earlier time. $19.95/month or $79.95/year.

FamilyTree Maker - $

www.familytreemaker.com

For 20 years, Family Tree Maker has been a best-selling family history software program. And now it's easier than ever to create beautiful family trees and charts, integrate maps and timelines,

and update your tree from anywhere using the new TreeSync feature that connects your desktop with Ancestry.com. $29.99 PC, $34.99 Mac, Complete Collection (includes companion guide and photo album software) $59.99.

ProGenealogists - $

www.progenealogists.com

The official research firm of Ancestry.com. With hundreds of years of cumulative research experience, researchers are highly skilled and well-trained, serving thousands of professional, government, media, and individual clients worldwide. ProGenealogists provides you and your family or associates with accurate historical and genealogical research — a wide range of research services from single item document retrieval services to highly specialized genealogical problem solving and family history book and Internet publishing. Genealogists's rates range from $65 to $135 per hour depending on the nature and difficulty of the research.

Check out their 'Free Stuff' page at http://www.progenealogists.com/freegenealogy.htm which provides links to free tools, forms, and software.

Also check out their U.S. and International Genealogy Sleuth pages at http://www.progenealogists.com/linkslibrary.htm which provides numerous links to key websites in many different categories.

Shoebox App - FREE

http://shoebox.ancestry.com

http://blog.1000memories.com

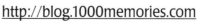

Provides a compelling way to share family history discoveries with friends and family as well as scan and add old photos to your family tree. With more than 500,000 downloads since its launch, the ShoeBox app for iPhone, iPad, and Android has become a popular way for people to get their old photos out of their shoeboxes and into the cloud.

If you've enabled Shoebox in your phone's privacy settings, each scan will be added to your camera roll. In addition, your scans will be added to the media gallery in your account on Ancestry.com (accessible with the same username and password you used for Shoebox).

MyCanvas - www.mycanvas.com

MyCanvas.com gives you amazing creative flexibility that lets you express yourself, share photos and preserve memories in custom, heirloom-quality books, posters and calendars. Start with helpful templates or use their online tools to create a project from scratch.

MyFamily.com - www.myfamily.com

MyFamily.com makes it easy to stay in touch with friends and family at any distance. Create your own family web site and use it to share photos, news, recipes, calendars and much more.

RootsWeb - http://rootsweb.ancestry.com

Roots Web is one of the oldest and most useful free genealogy sites on the Web. Not only does it help you connect and collaborate on projects online, but it also serves as one of the most extensive learning communities dedicated to genealogy, complete with a family tree builder and a robust forum selection. The search utility isn't the most inclusive or thorough when it comes to filtering through public records, but it does a decent job finding some of the most basic types of records, including births and deaths. The forums and help guides are where the heart of the site thrives. You'll find millions of

members communicating on thousands of message boards in this expansive environment for learning, collaborating and sharing with others.

Mundia - www.mundia.com/us

Mundia enables people around the world to create their family tree and connect with living relatives. Mundia is available in 16 languages within 113 countries.

Ancestry.com's Roots Reach Around the World

They also have web sites directed at seven countries, including: U.K., Canada, Germany, Italy, France, Sweden, and Australia. 14-Day Free trial. U.S. Membership - $19.99/month, $99 for 6 months. World Membership - $34.99/month, $149 for 6 months.

UK Ancestry - www.ancestry.co.uk

The UK's favorite family history website, offering you access to 1 billion searchable UK family history records. Launched in 2002, this extensive collection enables you to explore your family history using censuses, the fully indexed birth, marriage and death records, passenger lists, the British phone books, military and parish records. You can also explore names in other family trees and upload photographs of your own, and in doing so connect to millions of other members making their own discoveries.

The most comprehensive online collection of England, Wales and Scotland Censuses from 1841 to 1901,the fully indexed England and Wales Birth, Marriage and Death records from 1837 to 2005, the British phone books from

Best of the
5 Internet

1880 to 1984, UK Incoming Passenger Lists from 1878 to 1960, the London Historical records, 1500s to 1900s, and other records dating back before the 1300s.

Canada Ancestry - www.ancestry.ca

Offers you access to 129 million searchable Canadian family history records. Launched in 2006, this historical record collection reflects Canada's multicultural heritage and enables you to explore their family's history using Canadian and international records including the Canadian censuses, passenger lists, English, Welsh and Scottish censuses, birth, marriage and death records as well as user-contributed family trees, and by connecting to millions of other members making their own discoveries.

Key Canadian collections exclusive online access to the complete and fully indexed Censuses of Canada from 1851 to 1916, The Drouin Collection – the complete set of French-Canadian vital records from 1621 to 1947, Ontario and British Columbia vital records from as early as 1813 and U.S./Canada Border Crossings from 1895 to 1956

Germany Ancestry - www.ancestry.de

Hosts a significant collection of German family history records, currently more than 50 million, including the Hamburg Passenger Lists, both the German Phone and City Directories, plus international censuses, military and parish records with German relevance in German.

Australia Ancestry - www.ancestry.com.au

Offers members access to one billion searchable Australian, New Zealand and UK family history

records. Record collections including the Australian Birth, Marriage and Death Indexes, 1788-1985, Convict Lists from 1788 to 1868 and Free Settler Lists from 1826 to 1922, Australian and New Zealand electoral rolls and military records, the most comprehensive online collection of England, Wales and Scotland Censuses from 1841 to 1901, England and Wales Birth, Marriage and Death records from 1837 to 2005 and other records dating back before the 1300s.

Italy Ancestry - www.ancestry.it

Hosts more than 14 million Italian family history records including civil registration records of births, marriage banns, marriages and deaths assembled from provinces across Italy, plus international immigration and census records with Italian relevance, in Italian.

France Ancestry - www.ancestry.fr

Hosts more than 42 million French family history records including Paris vital records of births, deaths and marriages from as early as 1700s and other civil registration records from a variety of French provinces, plus international immigration and census records with French relevance, in French.

Sweden Ancestry - www.ancestry.se $

Hosts more than 47 million Swedish family history records including immigration records from as far back as the early 19th century, Varmland church records from the 1600s, plus international censuses and vital records with Swedish relevance, in Swedish.

FamilySearch

The World's Largest Collection of Free Family History Records and Resources

www.familysearch.org **FREE**

FamilySearch™ is one of the comprehensive, preeminent family history Web sites on the Internet. Each month over 3 million people use FamilySearch records, resources and services to learn more about their family history. It is the largest collection of *free* family history, family tree, genealogy records and resources in the world. It's an excellent site with huge database resources for researching names and extensive information, including articles, research guidance, the Research Wiki, forums, and online

classes. All of these tools are available to help you with your research.

Since 1894, FamilySearch has been actively gathering, preserving and sharing genealogical records worldwide. You can access their services and resources for free online, or through more than 4,800 FamilySearch Centers (or

Family History Centers) in 70 countries, including the world-famous, main Family History Library in Salt Lake City, Utah.

For over a century, FamilySearch has served as a collaborative partner to records custodians around the world. It has worked with more than 10,000 archives in over 100 countries throughout the world. It partners with archives to broaden your access to valuable historical records. It has been a catalyst in the development of industry standards for gathering, imaging, indexing, and preserving records. It has also developed tools that utilize a core of more than 200,000 volunteers.

You can do significant research online and discover what records you need to search to find your ancestors in record-breaking time. It provides easy access for the gathering, collaborating and sharing of family history information in ten languages.

FamilySearch contains billions of records about individuals and readily helps you see what information their database already has about you and your ancestors. In addition to names, dates, places, and relationships, you can see comprehensive source citations, including links to source images, photos, stories, and 'proof' documents, such as birth, marriage, and death certificates. You can add new information and make corrections and work with other relatives on shared family lines.

Using FamilySearch for research is nice because the underlying philosophy is different than other genealogy search sites. It has nothing to

do with making money. Their commitment to helping people connect with their ancestors is rooted in the belief that families are meant to be a central part of life and that family relationships are intended to continue beyond this life, which is why they have been gathering, preserving, and sharing family records for over 100 years. They offer what they find for free to the public. FamilySearch is a nonprofit organization supported by The Church of Jesus Christ of Latter-day Saints (casually known as the LDS or Mormon Church).

Search Billions of Records Instantly

Discover your family history at FamilySearch. Explore the world's largest collection of free

family trees, genealogy records and resources. You can access this wealth of records and document images online through their free *Historical Records Collection,* which includes more than 3.5 billion names in 1,400+ collections from countries all over the world.

FamilySearch has 6.875 billion historic records on microfilm that have been gathered and preserved for over a century that are currently being digitized and indexed. These records contain an estimated 20.6 billion names. Each year, over 200 million new indexed names are added for free viewing on FamilySearch through their indexing project by volunteers.

In addition, FamilySearch also has over 200 digital record preservation camera teams in 45 countries who produce more than 100 million new digital images for free online publication each year.

Create a Free, Colorful Family History Fan Chart

https://createfan.com   FREE

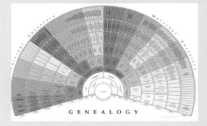

See your family tree like never before. This site allows you to create a 9-generation colorful fan chart for free using your family tree information as found in FamilySearch FamilyTree. You log into FamilySearch from this site, and it extracts your family tree automatically and creates a PDF fan chart of your tree. [Note: Be patient while it gathers all your information. It may take awhile.]

You can easily print an 8 ½ x 11" chart on your home printer, but if you want to print a beautiful wall chart, simply email the PDF file to www.generationmaps.com/family-chartist or www.genealogywallcharts.com. You may want to merge possible duplicates of your ancestors and check for accuracy in FamilySearch before you print it. It's nice to have a working chart to review your information, or a large beautiful wall chart for your family to enjoy.

Search for Your Ancestors Using the Family History Library Catalog

Family History Library Catalog
Search the catalog of materials (including microfilm, microfiche, and

The Family History Library online catalog describes the books, microfilms, and microfiche in the Family History Library in Salt Lake City, Utah. The library houses a collection of genealogical records that includes the names of more than 3.5 billion deceased people. It is the largest collection of its

FamilySearch branches out with some exciting new features.

FamilySearch Branches Out

FamilySearch added significant new enhancements and features, an updated look, and easier site navigation that allow beginners and experts to discover what others have found about their ancestors, collaboratively build their family tree online, share precious family photos and stories, and add life to their family tree.

The enhancements include **FamilyTree**, an online application where you begin by adding information about yourself and then add information about your ancestors to collaboratively build, manage, and share your family history. The tree is already populated with over a billion records contributed by patrons. And there are billions of historic records that can be searched for free to help further expand your family tree.

The **Photos and Stories** feature lets you preserve favorite family photos and stories of ancestors and easily share them with others. You can tag people in a photo to identify who they are and connect them to respective ancestor profiles in the FamilyTree. You can upload as many as 5,000 ancestral photos (15mb limit per image), and each story can be up to 100 pages long. Photos and stories can also be seamlessly shared via Facebook, Twitter, Google+, Pinterest and email. These personal reminders of loved ones and days-gone-by add life to your family tree and help connect generations together.

Dennis Brimhall, CEO FamilySearch

According to FamilySearch's Dennis Brimhall, photos and stories matter because they "personally teach us time-honored principles from those who have gone on before us, like the value of hard work, dealing with life's ups and downs and the impact of choices."

The **interactive Fan Chart** feature is a tool to create a wheel of your ancestry with you at the center. It's great for showing family members what you have done, and for seeing what is left to discover. Each layer of the wheel represents a different generation, and the wheel extends out to as many as 6-generations. You can print a fan chart for each child, with the child's name at the center so they can see themselves in the context of a larger family that extends out for generations.

Paul Nauta, FamilySearch Public Affairs Manager

"Seeing yourself in a fan chart changes you," Paul Nauta says. "You see yourself standing on the shoulders of all these people who have gone before you. You realize you're not alone, and it adds meaning and perspective to your life."

And **Live Help** is a global online community that provides free product help and personal research assistance by phone and web chat 24 hours a day/7 days a week. The help website and services are available in 10 languages, including Spanish, French, German, Italian, Portuguese, Russian, Chinese, Japanese and Korean.

These new enhancements have made it easier to connect with generations past, and preserve your legacy for the future – all intended to help record and share the "family" part of family history. And help move family history beyond just 'research' to appeal to a larger audience of people who are very interested in their family stories...but who don't consider themselves genealogists or researchers.

When you create a new free account at FamilySearch, a world of family history possibilities comes to life.

Track Changes to Your Family Tree

When you register for free then sign-in each time at FamilySearch, your name will appear in the upper right-hand corner of the home page. You should set your desired *Profile Settings*. To do this, hover your cursor over your name. A drop-down menu box will appear. Click on *Settings*.

This will give you the opportunity to change your username and/or password if you want, indicate which contact information you want to make public (viewable by other FamilyTree users when you add or change data in FamilyTree), and select which notifications you want to receive. You should at least check the first notifications box, so you will receive notifications of changes which are made by other patrons to the ancestral records you are *'Watching'*. FamilySearch allows you the ability to track any changes made to your ancestor's records at any time.

Here's a short but valuable free video about searching records in FamilySearch.

FREE 2-MINUTE VIDEO
How to Search FamilySearch -

http://link.brightcove.com/services/player/bc
pid1995251660001?bckey=AQ~~,AAAAsMO
7iuE~,0a6boL_aMzSw_yxPb4s-
860v3o94zt2u&bctid=2270136557001

Searching for an ancestor in millions of records can be challenging, but there are ways you can increase your success. Here are some tips from the experts.

kind in the world, including: vital records (birth, marriage, and death records from both government and church sources); census returns; court, property, and probate records; cemetery records; emigration and immigration lists; printed genealogies; and family and county histories.

The library holds genealogical records for over 110 countries, territories, and possessions, including over 2.4 million rolls of microfilmed genealogical records; 742,000 microfiche; 310,000 books, serials, and other formats; and 4,500 periodicals. The microfilm and microfiche can be ordered and viewed at over 4,800 library branches (called FamilySearch or Family History Centers) worldwide.

To locate the nearest FamilySearch Center, simply click on *"Live Help"* on the home page, then search for a *FamilySearch Center*. Or click on *"Get Help"* in the upper right hand corner. Or you may call 1-866-406-1830 in the United States and Canada.

Before you use the Catalog, choose a person about whom you want to find more information, and decide what you want to learn about him or her. For example, you may want to find your great-grandmother's death date and place. To do this, you need to decide what types of records are likely to contain that information.

To use the Family History Library catalog, search for your surname and various places that your ancestors lived, looking for information that might be relevant to your research.

Using the Library Catalog

The type of search you should do is determined by the kind of catalog entries or records you want to find. Choose from the following search options.

Place names: used to locate records for a certain place such as city, county, state, etc. Each jurisdiction has different records available, so it is important to search all jurisdictions for your area (i.e. both the city and county records).

Last names: Find family histories (and more) by a particular family name.

Title: Find a record by its title.

Author: used to search for a record by author.

Subjects: used to search for a certain topic (based on Library of Congress subject headings).

Keywords: To find entries that contain a certain word or combination of words.

Call Number: See catalog entries by finding their book, compact disc, or pedigree call number.

Before concluding the record is not in the Family History Library Catalog try the following strategies.

If It's Not in the Catalog

Look again in Surname Search for variations of the family name. Change the jurisdiction in Place Search. For example, if it is not at the county level, try again under the town, state, or national levels, or in neighboring counties and towns.

Try a variety of searches. Use a Keyword Search, Subject Search, Author Search, or Title Search.

Try again later. The Library is constantly acquiring new materials.

What is FamilySearch
FamilyTree?

A Family Tree for Everyone

www.familysearch.org/tree FREE

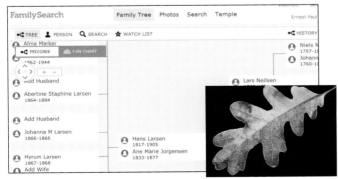

FamilySearch FamilyTree is a new application for organizing, preserving, and sharing your genealogy online (development of this application is ongoing so you can expect frequent updates). It is a free, universal family tree that all of us share and work on in common – *a family tree for everyone.*

> This is a great 10-minute video and handout that provides information about using alternative *search techniques* in FamilySearch.

FREE 10-MINUTE VIDEO AND HANDOUT

Advanced Search Tips to Find Your Ancestor - FREE

www.familysearch.org/learningcenter/lesson/familysearch-tips/360

A basic search in FamilySearch involves inputting a name in the search fields and clicking *Search.* However, this may not yield the information you want. This short video shows 5 simple but excellent strategies for finding your ancestors in FamilySearch, and is one of the best instructional videos I've seen. The video is also available as a power-point type PDF and as a printable 3-page handout. Try this link for the video or just click the above link and follow the prompts: http://broadcast.lds.org/elearning/FHD/Community/en/FamilySearch/FamilySearch_Tips/Player.html.

It focuses on:
Narrow your search with filters
Use wild cards
Add a relationship
Add an event
Browse images

FREE 11-MINUTE VIDEO
Overview of Family History FREE Library Catalog -

https://fch.ldschurch.org/WWSupport/Courses/LibraryCatalogOverview/Catalog%20Overview/player.html It

5 Best of the Internet

Here's a 'quick start' video to FamilySearch FamilyTree.

FREE 4-MINUTE VIDEO
Using FamilyTree - FREE

http://link.brightcove.com/services/player/bc
pid1995251660001?bckey=AQ~~,AAAAsMO
7iuE~,0a6boL_aMzSw_yxPb4s-
860v3o94zt2u&bctid=2270136551001

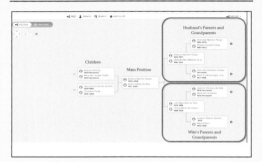

How do I move around FamilyTree, add people, or correct information? And how do I display my pedigree on a fan chart? Are people missing from your tree? See how simple it is to move around FamilyTree, add people, correct information, and attach a photo, 'proof' document or story to your ancestor's record.

- **Connect and collaborate** with others on shared family lines
- **Edit and delete incorrect data,** including relationships
- **Provide sources and links** to online information that shows where you found family information
- **Preserve family tree information** for future generations
- **Use FamilyTree on behalf of someone else** (as a 'helper')
- **Preserve and share precious family photos and stories**
- **Easier navigation –** drag, zoom, easily move between tree and other views. The click-and-drag feature allows you to seamlessly move up and down, side to side, and zoom in and out on your pedigree chart.
- **Ability to see more** than four generations in the tree
- **Optimized for tablets;** no 'Flash' requirements.

In FamilyTree you can make your email address public so other people will be able to network or collaborate with you.

merges the best features and data from previous versions of FamilySearch and adds powerful new tools for data accuracy, usability, and collaboration.

You begin by adding information about yourself and then add information about your ancestors to collaboratively build, manage, and share your family history. The tree is already populated with over a billion records contributed by patrons organized in family lineages. And there are billions of historic records that can be searched for free to help further expand your family tree. Or you can simply key-in your ancestor(s).

You can get free personalized help to find your ancestors. You can directly edit and delete incorrect data, including relationships. And importantly, you can connect and collaborate with others on shared family lines.

FamilyTree has many exciting new features and benefits.

FamilyTree Features and Benefits

Network with Others on Your Family Tree

FamilyTree is all about collaboration – sharing information and working together. In the past, there was no good way to effectively network with others who have the same interests in family history. But one of the benefits of FamilyTree is the ability to work together with close or distant relatives to make the information about your shared history as complete and accurate as possible.

You can identify descendants of your common ancestors and hopefully communicate easily with

> You may want to send emails to other contributors of FamilyTree to collaborate on the most accurate data, and share family photos and stories.

> Here are a few benefits of networking with others.

Communicate with Others

You can share your information and sources with them with the idea that your communication will result in your ancestors' records being more accurate.

Email is a safe and effective way to communicate. If you have any reservations, you can always create a separate email address solely for family history networking. Or you can use any anonymous name you wish. It is absolutely essential to provide your email address for collaboration purposes if you contribute information to FamilyTree so other people can communicate with you.

> You can easily create email addresses for *free* at many websites, including www.gmail.com, www.yahoo.com, www.hotmail.com and www.aol.com.

Some Benefits of Collaboration

- Prominence of sources and citations help the discussion to be focused on the evidence and drive toward a single conclusion
- Ability to monitor changes to FamilyTree
- Ability to conduct discussions with other interested users

Protecting Privacy Rights

To protect the privacy rights of *living people*, FamilyTree limits the amount of information that you can see about individuals who may still be living. If you contribute an individual who might be living, only you can see him or her. Other users cannot, even close relatives and the individuals themselves. FamilySearch considers that an individual may be living if *both* of the following situations apply:

1. He or she was born at least 110 years, or married at least 100 years ago.

2. The record contains no death information.

In FamilyTree, you can easily identify individuals who may be living. The word "Living" appears next to the individual's name.

each other. Obviously, the objective is that descendants of common ancestors will communicate with each other via email, share your information and your sources, jointly analyze the data and come to the most accurate information concerning your ancestors. Networking allows you to build your family tree easier, faster, and more accurately.

To be able to work with others, you need to provide a valid e-mail address in your user profile where you can be contacted. Also make sure that your profile settings are set to allow contact by e-mail. You can work with others in these ways:

- You can contact the user who contributed information about a person or family.
- You can participate in "discussions" about what is the most accurate information.

- You can "watch" people in the tree. The system sends you a weekly e-mail to notify you if changes occurred.

As you look at your family tree, you will find places where an ancestor is missing or has incomplete information. Before you add a new individual or family, search FamilyTree to see if someone else has already added that information. If you find it, you can just connect it to your family line. There is no need to enter it again.

Together, you can discuss your findings and insights to improve the accuracy of your information. The capability for everyone to add and edit data on a shared family tree enables continual improvement. This *teamwork* will help create a more complete and correct world family tree for everyone.

Other people who are doing research on lines that connect with yours can contact you and share information they have gathered. You can also use this to get in touch with others who might be related to you. FamilyTree automatically displays your contact name with every piece of information that you contribute, if you so choose.

Another way to see if someone else has already entered information about an individual is to see if FamilyTree can find *any possible duplicates.* If it finds a possible duplicate, you decide if the information is about the same individual. If so, you can merge records for your ancestor.

Everyone interested in an individual can more easily evaluate the accuracy of the information and make corrections if needed, and add notes and sources. After all of an individual's information has been combined, it is time to start adding new information and make corrections. FamilyTree simplifies the process of building a family tree, and helps eliminate duplication of the information.

FamilyTree Training Resources

Check them out at https://familysearch.org/tree-training. FREE

How Do I Find and add a Name to FamilyTree?
How Do I Find a Name that is Ready for Ordinances Now?
My Family Tree is Empty – What Should I do?

Guides and Manuals
FamilyTree Quick Start Guide
FamilyTree Reference Manual

Lessons and Activities
FamilyTree
Introduction to the FamilyTree

Handouts on Advanced Topics
The Case for Moving to "Our Tree"
Managing Ordinances
Moving Information from new FamilySearch to FamilyTree
Dealing with Duplicate Records
Adding Sources
Release Notes
This Doesn't Look like my Ancestor

Online Courses
Introduction to the FamilyTree
FamilyTree Overview
Policies for Submitting Names to the Temple

How-To Videos
Switching to FamilyTree
Adding Information
Correcting Family Relationships
Correcting Information about a Person
Adding Sources
Reserving Ordinances in FamilyTree
Assigning Names to the Temple in FamilyTree

Webinar Classes
Introduction to the FamilyTree
FamilyTree Advanced Topics: Editing Relationships
FamilyTree Advanced Topics: Sourcing
FamilyTree Advanced Topics: Merging

How to Use FamilyTree

A Family Tree for Everyone

www.familysearch.org/tree **FREE**

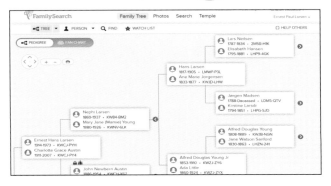

There are a number of valuable resources to help you get started, and learn how to use FamilyTree. Get started by simply registering on FamilySearch to open a free account.

FamilySearch training resources include: online courses, 'how-to' videos, guides and manuals, lessons and activities, handouts, and webinars.

FamilyTree Free User Guide - **FREE**

http://broadcast.lds.org/eLearning/fhd/Community/en/FamilySearch/FamilyTree/pdf/familyTreeUserGuide.pdf.

FamilySearch maintains a 165 page online 'how-to' reference guide.

It currently includes the following chapters:

1. Getting to FamilyTree
2. Navigating the Tree
3. Seeing Details about People
4. Adding and Correcting Information about People and Relationships
5. Searching for Deceased People
6. Printing Information
7. Attaching Sources to People and Relationships
8. Merging Duplicate Records
9. Working with Other Users
10. Signing into FamilyTree for Someone Else

- Quick Reference: What You Can Do on the Tree
- Quick Reference: What You Can Do on a Person's Detail Page
- Comparison of Features in FamilyTree and new.FamilySearch.org
- Where the Information in FamilyTree Came From

Step-by-Step Guide To Using FamilyTree Wisely -

www.usingfamilysearch.com **FREE**

A 100-page step-by-step online manual to help you clean up your family tree, written by George Scott, an experienced FamilySearch instructor, is available in PDF format for everyone to use for free. He updates it online whenever there is a significant revision in the FamilyTree program. The changes are identified and dated so you won't have to review or reprint the entire guide.

Since FamilyTree is still in the advanced developmental stage, the program and the manual may be updated frequently. Therefore, George uses an alphabetized (but cumbersome) system for the 12 chapters, and the page numbering system is by chapter to facilitate adding or deleting pages, rather than a running number system. He suggests working in logical order step-by-step through FamilyTree, as well as running several different programs simultaneously so you can toggle easily between the programs, e.g. FamilyTree, your family history computer program, and any database that may contain additional information about your family tree. The purpose of this is to simply verify information from a variety of sources for greater accuracy. See more on page 251.

Track Changes to Your Ancestor's Records

The FamilyTree Watch feature (an automatic notification system) is an important tool to help you maintain a vigil over

5 Best of the **Internet**

Consider getting involved in the following ongoing family history activities throughout the remainder of your life.

Family History Activities

Collaborate: Network with others to divide your family tree so each person works on a distinct niche, and then shares all his research with the other researchers.

Watch: Watch the records in the portion of your FamilyTree which you have researched (your research niche), through the Watch feature (automatic notification system).

Index: Serve at least one hour a week as an Indexer or Arbitrator in the FamilySearch Indexing program. *See page 261 for more information.*

your ancestor's records. You can watch sources and records. To add your ancestor to your 'watch' list, simply click the Watch button in the upper right-hand corner of your ancestor's Details Page. You will receive a weekly email notifying you of changes which have been made to the records you are watching. You can also "un-watch" any person at anytime.

The 'Discussions' feature is a great and easy way to coordinate your family history with other FamilyTree users.

Use 'Discussions' Feature

It works like social networking sites that you may already use. In a discussion board, you can:

Work out issues that require interaction with other interested researchers.

Post questions requesting more or better information about a person.

Coordinate additional research with other interested users.

Procedure

1. Open the *details page* of a person whose discussions you want to see.

2. Scroll down to the Discussions section.

3. Read through the discussions.

4. To add a comment to an existing discussion, click the *Add Comment* link of the discussion. In the field that appears, enter your comment and click Save. To start a discussion about a new topic, click *Add a New Discussion.*

Note: The system does not allow a discussion board for people who are living, or who have restricted records.

Link 'Sources' and Proof Documents to Your Ancestors

FamilyTree provides a multi-language, internet-based environment for everyone to collaborate as partners, and includes capabilities to link sources and scanned images of proof documents with each of your ancestors records. The links to images of documents is a key component to compiling very accurate lineages. This ability to combine your genealogy data with online proof documents is actually revolutionizing family history research collaboration and is a boon to tracing and sharing your family roots and stories.

You can link source records from any website. You should especially link the appropriate records in FamilySearch's database collections into your ancestors' FamilyTree records, but other appropriate records from any website as well. Simply use the search feature, or you can access the FamilySearch record collections directly from the home page: click on Search, scroll down and click on *Browse All Published Collections* or *Browse by Location.*

Each individual can have up to 1,000 sources

attached to his FamilyTree record. When you attach a source, you attach it to an ancestor's record, then you can create a Tag which attaches the source directly to a person's name, gender, birth, christening, death, or burial data to help prove their vital information. Thereafter, everyone will be able to readily access that source record and all other source records you link into your ancestor's FamilyTree record, just by clicking the logo in front of the source.

You can save yourself lots of time (and frustration) in cleaning up your family tree by following the 18 steps George Scott prescribes below.

Continued from page 249.

Chapter Headings and Step-by-Step Guide ⬭FREE⬭

Best Way to Attach a Web Source or Image to Your Family Tree

http://recordseek.com

RecordSeek.com has a great feature to save any webpage or any image on any website as a source on FamilySearch FamilyTree. It's called *TreeConnect*. And it's *free*. There's no need to even visit FamilySearch to add the link,

Attaching a Subscription Website to Your Family Tree

Citing a *subscription* website as a source may be a problem because people without a subscription to that particular web service won't be able to view the information. However, if you are at the Family History Library, or a large FamilySearch Center, or a participating library, it may be possible to view an Ancestry.com source without a subscription.

When you are viewing the details page for an ancestor in FamilyTree, and are looking at the listed sources, if you find a source for Ancestry you have the option of tweaking the source information to enable you to view the information without a subscription. For an Ancestry.com source, look near the beginning of the address, the part just before the *.com*. Change it as follows to indicate where you are trying to view the record:

ancestry.com – for viewing if you have a subscription

ancestryinstitution.com – for viewing at the Family History Library or a FamilySearch Center

ancestrylibrary.com – for viewing at a participating library or institution.

[source: *The Ancestry Insider* - http://ancestryinsider.blogspot.com/2013/03/capturing-ancestrycom-sources-in.html]

TreeConnect does it for you.

First, go to http://recordseek.com and download the green *TreeConnect* button to your Bookmark (or Favorites) Bar on your computer.

When you find a source of data or an image you want to attach to a Family Tree record from any website, highlight the data or image.

Then click the *Tree Connect* bookmarklet in your Bookmark Bar (while still viewing the data or image).

FamilySearch's sign-in screen will appear. Sign in.

FamilySearch's *'Create a Source'* screen will appear with the information generated by TreeConnect.

In the *Describe the Record* (Notes) box, you can describe the information.

Click *Save* and the source is now saved in your FamilyTree Source Box.

Lastly, go to your ancestor's individual family tree record in FamilySearch. Scroll down to Sources and click *Go To Source Box*. The newly-added source should be the first source listed. Click *Attach,* and the source is attached to your ancestor's FamilyTree record.

Attach Photos and Stories to Your Ancestors Record

https://familysearch.org/photos

The Photos and Stories feature lets you preserve favorite family photos and stories of ancestors and easily share them with others. You can tag people in a photo to identify who they are and connect them to your ancestor profiles in FamilyTree. You can upload as many as 5,000 ancestral photos (15mb limit per image only in JPG or PNG formats), and each story can be up to 100 pages long. Photos and stories can also be seamlessly shared via Facebook, Twitter, Google+, Pinterest and email. These personal reminders of loved ones and days-gone-by add life to your family tree and help connect generations together.

You can upload and attach to your ancestor any photo available on your computer. Photographs of living individuals, except your own minor children, should not be posted without their consent. You need to identify the people in the photo by tagging them, then link them to your tree. You can also upload PDF files to FamilyTree. This is in addition to the .jpg and .png files that you have been able to upload in the past.

All added photos are public. All information that you post will be displayed and is available for others to search, view or hear. Do not contribute data which you do not want to be accessed by others.

You view the photos on your ancestor's Details Page by simply clicking the *Photos* button. The faces on each photo are extracted out of the photo and listed on the right. You can also share the photos, albums, and photo person pages with others using email, Facebook, Twitter, Pinterest, etc. You can also upload photos to your family tree using FamilySearch affiliates such as http://recordseek.com and http://ilived.com.

Stories have a unique ability to draw you closer to your ancestors and help you understand more about who you are.

Add Your Family Story

https://familysearch.org/photos/storynewhttps://familysearch.org/photos/stories

"Every person who has ever lived has a right to be remembered

Dennis Brimhall, CEO FamilySearch

and is a story waiting to be told," said Dennis C. Brimhall, CEO for FamilySearch. "Every family is a story in progress...We all treasure memorable family photos and ancestral stories that inspire, amuse, or connect us. Families can now share and preserve for posterity those social heirlooms that help vitalize their family history.

> Here's a valuable free video about using photos and stories in FamilySearch.

FREE 4-MINUTE VIDEO
About Photos and Stories - FREE
http://link.brightcove.com/services/player/bcpid1995251660001?bckey=AQ~~,AAAAsMO7iuE~,0a6boL_aMzSw_yxPb4s-860v3o94zt2u&bctid=2270136549001

Follow these simple steps to link photos and stories to your ancestor's records in FamilyTree.

http://link.brightcove.com/services/player/bcpid1995251660001?bckey=AQ~~,AAAAsMO7iuE~,0a6boL_aMzSw_yxPb4s-860v3o94zt2u&bctid=22

When a parent or grandparent takes the time to tell you a story, there's a bonding that occurs there. Likewise, a family photo and story preserved and shared in the context of one's family tree, in an instant, can personally touch us and teach us time-honored principles by those who have gone on before us, like the value of hard work, dealing with life's ups and downs, and the impact of choices."

There are great helps within the FamilySearch websites. Simply click the *Get Help* button on the top-right corner of any screen.

Get Help

When you click the *Get Help* button on any screen, it gives you lots of options:

Call Us - lists worldwide toll-free phone numbers. Their call center is always open. Call day or night with any problems or questions that arise. In the USA and Canada call toll-free (866) 406-1830 .

Live Chat - lets you have a live conversation with a support person right on your computer

In-Person Help - visit the main Family History Library in Salt Lake City, or you can search for a FamilySearch Center near you; there are 4,800 local branches worldwide. There are local Family History Consultants for your area that will be happy to assist you for free if you can't find your answer in the Help Center.

Send a Message - lets you submit your problem or question to FamilySearch and they'll get back to you as soon as possible

Help Center - In the Help Center you can choose the kind of help you need: Product Support, Research Assistance, Getting Started, the Learning Center, or FamilySearch Blog.

Product Support - You can get help with any of the family history tools provided by FamilySearch by browsing a topic, searching all product support articles, or looking for your question among the *Frequently Asked Questions (FAQs)*.

Research Assistance - This is a community of researchers that are ready to assist you with your questions. You can ask a specialist about general research help on a number of pre-determined topics, or you can visit the excellent Research Wiki which currently contains over 75,000 articles on many subjects. *See Research Assistance on page 255 for more information about getting community assistance.*

FamilySearch Blog - FREE

https://familysearch.org/blog

The FamilySearch blog provides the latest information about FamilySearch. You can search by key words and browse the blog archives for help.

Learning Center - FREE

https://familysearch.org/learningcenter

In the Learning Center, you can browse hundreds of free online courses and short how-to videos to help you discover your family history. The major resources available include: Research Wiki, Research Courses, and a new Research Assistant.

Research Wiki - FREE

www.familysearch.org/learn/wiki

Research Wiki is a free collection of family history articles provided by family history enthusiasts from around the world. You can find tens of thousands of articles and 'how-to' instructions about doing family history. Get research advice, or learn where to find record collections. It assists you in finding your ancestors, and offers information on how to find, use, and analyze records for beginners, intermediate and expert researchers.

You can search by place or topic. Start with broad localities, e.g. England, then click through to smaller ones. Use keywords, not phrases, e.g. *Hispanic Resources.*

James L. Tanner
A leading
genealogical
expert and blogger

James L. Tanner, a leading genealogical expert and blogger, calls the FamilySearch Wiki "easily the most valuable genealogical resource on the Internet...a hidden wonder...a solidly useful reference for teaching and instructing anyone with the good sense to use its resources."

—The Guide to FamilySearch Online http://genealogysstar.blogspot.com/p/guide-to-familysearch.html

FREE 6-MINUTE VIDEO
Using FamilySearch Wiki - (FREE)

http://hiddenancestors.com/FStour.html

You can watch short tutorial videos (2-3 minutes), read step-by-step guides, and connect to other beginners. It guides you through these 3 steps.

Research Courses -

https://familysearch.org/learningcenter

FamilySearch offers a variety of free research classes online and in person to help you discover your family tree. Whether you are just beginning your family history research or are an experienced genealogist, you can learn something new. These classes are taught by genealogy research consultants at the Family History Library in Salt Lake City, Utah, as well as experts from around the world.

Browse hundreds of online genealogy courses to help you discover your family history by place (geographic location), skill level, subject, format (audio, video, video with slides), or language (currently 14 different languages).
You can also choose from beginner, new or most popular courses.

Research Assistance - (FREE)

www.facebook.com/familysearch

FamilySearch sponsors various Facebook pages to provide personal assistance to you.

FamilySearch Research Communities (Facebook) - (FREE)

https://familysearch.org/learn/wiki/en/Research_Communities_on_Facebook

These are area-specific research help pages which are monitored and responded to daily by FamilySearch

Getting Started

Step 1. Discover Your Story. The first step in discovering your story is reaching out to parents, grandparents—any relative that can share stories, photos, or other information with you. Using the FamilySearch Photos and Stories, you can capture, preserve, and share what you find. As you do, you will find yourself on the path to discovering your own story.

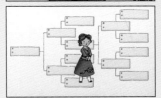

Step 2. Explore Your Family Tree. Family Tree is where your family history comes together. The second step to getting started is to explore your family tree. Since researchers and volunteers from around the world are adding to Family Tree daily, some work may have already been done for you. Add missing names, dates, and relationships, collaborate with other family members, and watch your family tree grow.

Step 3. Find Your Ancestors. Step three is to grow your family tree by searching historical records on FamilySearch.org. Your ancestors' everyday milestones and experiences – like birth, marriage, and death – often created historical records that have been indexed and made searchable online. Use Search to find more details about the people in your family story.

Find an Ancestor Using FamilySearch Wiki

https://familysearch.org/learn/wiki/en/Help:Tour

FamilySearch Wiki is a tool you can use to learn how to find your ancestors. It offers information on how to find, use and analyze records of genealogical value. The site's content is variously targeted to beginners, intermediate researchers, and experts, and at present it is available in 11 languages. The other language wikis are found via links at the bottom of the wiki homepage. The wiki in English currently has over 75,000 articles.

You don't search for individuals in the Wiki – instead, search for places and topics to discover the records that could contain your ancestors' information. It is helpful to know a possible location and a time period. In the Wiki, you will find:

Links to record collections where your ancestor's information could be found.

Research advice for how to approach research problems.

staff and community. You can...

ask your research questions

collaborate on your research, and

share knowledge you have gained as you've done your own research in a specific area.

Choose from the **List of Genealogy Research Communities** (categorized by country, state, ethnicity, etc.). In addition, there are other locality-specific genealogy research sites, *Pages and Groups and Surname Pages and Groups*, that can also be of assistance to you in your research. Simply click on the links provided on the page or here... https://familysearch.org/learn/wiki/en/Pages_and_Groups_on_Facebook.

FamilySearch Research Help - FREE

https://familysearch.org/learn/wiki/en/FamilySearch_Communities

A place where you can get assistance with your research questions. You are invited to join any of the communities. You can get a Live Research Assistance by calling 866-237-2067 or you can click to chat, and ask a volunteer specialist your research question online.

Surname Pages & Groups on Facebook - FREE

https://familysearch.org/learn/wiki/en/Surname_Pages_and_Groups_on_Facebook

New surname or family organization Pages and Groups are being created by the community of genealogists around the world. The main topic of either a Page or a Group of this type will typically be about doing research on a family or surname.

Unlocking the Granite Vault

FamilySearch and The Family History Library are in the process of a new massive project called the *Scanstone Project*. They are scanning, digitizing and indexing their extensive collection of genealogical records held in the Granite Mountain Records Vault, and seeking volunteer help for the project (see *You Can Make a Difference on page 313*). This is a climate-controlled, underground storage facility to safeguard master copies of all their microfilm records. The storage facility, built literally into a mountainside, is located about 25 miles from downtown Salt Lake City, Utah.

Community Trees is an exceptionally valuable website that not many people know about.

Search the FamilySearch Community Trees - FREE
http://histfam.familysearch.org

www.familysearch.org/learn/wiki/en/Community_Trees_Project

Community Trees is an effort to gather and publish an exhaustive genealogy for a whole town or community. These are lineage-linked genealogies from specific time periods and geographic localities around the world. The information also includes supporting sources, photos, and documents. Most of the genealogies are joint projects between FamilySearch and others who live locally or have expertise in the area or records used to create the genealogies. Each Tree is a searchable database with views of individuals, families, ancestors and descendants, as well as printing options.

The scope of partner projects may be a small, grass roots village or township working together to form a family tree of all the known residents of its community for a given time period. Some are genealogical and historical societies working with FamilySearch to index several sources of data to link them to common, lineage-linked genealogies of a targeted geographic area of interest.

The scope could also be focused on a particular record set and locality. The goal is to identify and reconstitute all families of a particular place from a village, county, or even a country. Many of the current projects were produced by FamilySearch's Family Reconstitution team and date back to the medieval times.

If you share any ancestors with any of the trees, it will be enormously helpful for you. Currently there are 93 different trees containing over 8.3 million people, and growing. You may or may not find information on your ancestors, but you need to check it out from time to time. GEDCOM downloads may be available depending on any records restrictions.

You might want to check out the following trees:

Europe: Royal and Noble Houses of Europe -

Check out these cool videos on YouTube about using FamilySearch.

FamilySearch YouTube - FREE
www.youtube.com/familysearch

There are 60-70 short videos on YouTube to assist you. They range from About FamilySearch, and Honoring Ancestors, to Genealogy for Beginners, and more. You should check them out.

contains 297,942 individuals ranging from A.D. 100 to the 1800s

Mexico: Yucatan - contains 2.73 million merged civil and church records of birth and marriage, with a few death records

Pacific Islands - contains over 73,000 individuals with oral genealogies and genealogical information collected from the Polynesian peoples and from the Pacific Islands.

US: Early Utah Families - Merges the 1850-1880, 1900, and 1920 US Census records for Utah with extracted Utah Vital Records (births 1892 to 1941, marriages 1887 to 1966, deaths and burials 1880's to 1956) to create families and extended lineages of 1.73 million people.

Wales: Welsh Medieval Database Primarily of Nobility and Gentry - contains approximately 350,000 individuals living from about A.D. 100 to the 1800s

The Family History Library has an extensive collection of over 100,000 published family histories and is digitizing more everyday – even faster.

Check Out FamilySearch Searchable Maps Project
http://maps.familysearch.org FREE

www.familysearch.org/learn/wiki/en/England_Jurisdictions_1851

Continued on page 260

5 Best of the **Internet**

FamilySearch certifies minimum requirements for product features, processes, or services from other vendors programs to make it easier for you to understand what they offer to be able to synchronize your records with FamilyTree.

FamilySearch Certified Affiliates (FREE)

http://www.familysearch.org/eng/affiliates/index.html

https://familysearch.org/products

In order for any independent family history software to be compatible with FamilySearch.org and Family Tree, it needs to make some enhancements or adaptations. FamilySearch certifies 3rd party vendors products when they conform to FamilySearch's strict standards of quality. Vendors are then licensed to use the

FamilySearch Certified Logo on the product packaging, website, and marketing literature.

For a current list and description of the certified software affiliates (third-party companies) that provide products and services with features that are compatible with FamilySearch programs, click on https://familysearch.org/products. These products and services are independently developed and supported by their respective organizations.

Product	Function	Windows	Mac	Web	Mobile	Cost
Advanced Tree Inspector - www.usfamilytree.com	Navigate and analyze your family tree					**FREE** or $19.99/yr
AGES-Online - www.ages-online.com	Internet family tree builder					$39.95-$59.95/yr
All My Cousins - www.allmycousins.com	Searches and reads family tree; displays LDS ordinance status					**FREE**
Ancestral Quest - www.ancquest.com	Full-featured family tree program					**FREE** or $29.95
AncestorSplit - www.ancestorsplit.com	Publishes/combines data into FamilyTree					**FREE** to subscribers
AncestorsWaiting - www.ancestorswaiting.com	Combs your family tree to identify ancestors needing LDS ordinances					$24.95/yr
Archives - www.archives.com	A comprehensive resource for researching your family history					$7.95/mth **Free Trial**
BillionGraves - www.billiongraves.com	A database for records and images from the world's cemeteries					**FREE**
Branches - www.branchesgenealogy.com	Full featured desktop genealogy program					$14.95
BrowseHero www.muddyheroes.com	Provides extensive tree analysis capabilities					$39.95/yr **Free trial**
Celebrating My Family Tree and Me - http://celebratingfamilyhistory.com	Helps organize your genealogy and family history projects					assorted products
Charting Companion - http://progenygenealogy.com	View, customize, print and publish your family history					$29.95
Family ChartMasters - www.familychartmaster.com	Comprehensive, easy-to-use genealogy chart printing service					$
Family ChArtist - www.familychartmasters.com	Print Free 8.5x11" custom charts from your printer					**FREE**
FamilyHero - www.muddyheroes.com	View and analyze your family tree					$39.95/yr **Free trial**
FamilyInsight - www.ohanasoftware.com	Synchronize your files with FamilyTree					$25.00
Family Photoloom - www.photoloom.com	Free web app to tag and link pictures, and archive and share images					**FREE** or $39/year

Product	Function	Windows	Mac	Web	Mobile	Cost
FamilySeek - www.treeseek.com	Easily find people and calculate relationship in FamilyTree					**FREE**
Get My Ancestors - www.ohanasoftware.com	Download records from new.FamilySearch.org					**FREE**
iLived - www.ilived.com	Upload photos and memories to your family tree from your mobile device.					**FREE**
Leaf https://leaf.byu.edu	Finds the leaves in your tree that need your attention					**FREE**
Legacy FamilyTree - www.legacyfamilytree.com	Free genealogy software to organize, research, and publish your family's tree					**FREE** or $29.95
Legacy Mobile - www.apple.com/itunes www.android.com/apps	Take a picture of a gravestone and learn more about your ancestor buried there.					**FREE**
Legacy Stories - www.legacystories.org	Stories, photos, audio or video can be tied with persons in Family Tree					**FREE** or $49/year
MacFamilyTree - www.syniumsoftware.com	Modern genealogy application for the Mac					$59.99
MagiKey FamilyTree - www.themagikey.com	Basic family tree software and GEDCOM translator.					**FREE**
MobileTree - www.mobiletree.me	View your family tree on your iOS mobile device					**FREE**
Names in Stone - www.namesinstone.com/family-search.aspx	Searches and displays cemetery and burial information; geo-mapping					**FREE** or $39.99/yr
Ordinance Tracker - www.ohanasoftware.com	Easy way to work with LDS reserved ordinances					$12.50
OurFamily-ology - www.family-genealogy.com	Saves photos, images, documents, slides, audio and video in FamilyTree.					$9.99/yr **Free Trial**
RecordSeek - http://recordseek.com	Submit a web page or upload an image as a source to FamilyTree					**FREE**
RootsMagic - www.rootsmagic.com	Free full-featured family tree program					**FREE** or $29.95
Sharing Time - www.sharingtime.com	Helps you team up with others about your ancestors with many tools					$15/yr
TenGenChart - www.tengenchart.com	Create large circular 10- generation pedigree charts					**FREE**
TreeSeek - www.treeseek.com	Creates unique high quality genealogy charts from FamilyTree					**FREE**
Zap The Grandma Gap www.gapthegrandmagap.com	A collection of resources to help you connect with the youth in your family					assorted products

The Granite Mountain Records Vault currently holds 132 times more data than the U.S. Library of Congress which is considered the world's largest library.

Billions of New Records

Records contained in the Family History Library and in FamilySearch databases (which are safeguarded in the mountain vault) have been gathered from a wide variety of sources worldwide in an ongoing collection and preservation effort that has been under way for more than a century. Most of the microfilm collection has been produced by microfilming original sources worldwide. FamilySearch has 6.875 billion historic records on microfilm that are currently being digitized and indexed. These records contain an estimated 20.6 billion names.

In cooperation with legal custodians of records worldwide, FamilySearch currently has about 200 digital cameras photographing records in 45 countries who produce more than 100 million new digital images for free online publication each year.

As part of this project, they are currently scanning over 32 million images per month or approximately 370,000 rolls of microfilm per year from their vault, *the equivalent of about 6 million 300-page volumes.* Volunteers extract family history information from

digital images of historical documents to create indexes that assist everyone for free in finding their ancestors.

With volunteer help, each and every name and word in every record will be indexed so that we can find particular ancestors quickly. The indexing project is expected to be completed within the next 5-10 years, but the newly indexed records are added to the FamilySearch records collection monthly. This gives you the ability to search millions of newly indexed genealogy records at your finger tips instantly.

Continued from page 257

Maps can be used to locate the places where your ancestors lived. They identify political boundaries, names of places, geographical features, cemeteries, churches, and migration routes. Historical maps are especially useful for finding communities and political boun-

daries that no longer exist.

FamilySearch is experimenting with searchable maps. Check out the England Jurisdictions 1851 Project at the above links. It is a powerful Internet based Geographic Information System showing parish maps of the 40 counties in England. This mapping system simplifies research by consolidating data from many finding aids into a single searchable repository that can be accessed just by clicking in a parish boundary. This is a research tool provided by FamilySearch using Google Maps to visually display maps

You Can Make a Difference

http://familysearchindexing.org *FREE*

Over one billion records have been indexed by volunteers. You can help and its easy.

FamilySearch Indexing is a non-profit volunteer effort to transcribe and index records of genealogical significance worldwide. Indexing unlocks access to the world's records by making them searchable for free. FamilySearch is enlisting the help of thousands to index digitized records to create free public access to records all around the world.

The key life events of billions of people are being preserved and shared through the efforts of people like you. Using their online indexing system, volunteers from around the world are able to quickly and easily transcribe the records – all from and information. For tips on using the website, look beneath the two blue buttons on the left side of the home page and click the "Find out here" link.

Just above the map is a drop-down menu where you can select various map layers, such as: Parish, County, Civil Registration District, Diocese, Rural Deanery, Poor Law Union, Hundred, or Province. Use the drop-down menu to view any of the layers.

the convenience of your home. The indexes are then posted for free on FamilySearch.

Once indexed, people from anywhere in the world can search to find the records that document the lives of their ancestors, providing an invaluable link between generations. The availability of a single record is often the key that allows someone to discover an ancestor – or an entire branch of a family tree. Every record you index is important because it helps document someone's life, and everyone deserves a legacy.

Governments, churches, societies, and commercial companies are also working to make more records available. You can help by joining the army of volunteers to index one of the current U.S. immigration or census projects, or any project of your choice. It's easy, you can work on your own time, and they train you. You can get more info on their web site http://family-searchindexing.org, or on their Facebook page at www.facebook.com/familysearchindexing.

FamilySearch is indexing ancestor's names, the places where your ancestors are found, and the map reference. So with a click you can view and print the actual locality where your ancestors lived. This one feature alone will save you hours of research time. Then you can retrieve a copy of the record images to document your genealogy at a fraction of the time we spend today.

MyHeritage

The Most Popular Family Network on the Web

My Heritage has free iPad, iPhone and Android apps where you can view and edit your family trees, research share photos and do Celebrity-Look-A-Likes.

www.myheritage.com **FREE** **$**

A family-oriented social network service and genealogy website. It allows you to create your own family website, share pictures and videos, organize family events, create family trees, and search for ancestors. With over 75 million users, MyHeritage is one of the largest sites in the social networking and genealogy field. It hosts 1.5 billion profiles, over 4 billion historical records, 27 million family trees, 200 million photos, and is accessible in 40 languages.

One of its primary services is its free, personal family websites that allow you to connect and stay in touch with relatives, build an online family tree, share photos, events, messages and videos. Members can invite other family members to join their site to stay in touch with family. MyHeritage is able to automatically tag the faces of people in photos that members upload onto their family pages. If the person in the photo is in the family tree, then the software can also identify them automatically.

Their genealogy research allows you to search for your ancestors online with an online database, *SuperSearch*, of over 4 billion historical records worldwide including birth, marriage, death, census, military, and immigration records. SuperSearch also contains one of the world's largest collection of historical newspapers.

Their *SmartMatching* technology intelligently matches each family tree to hundreds of millions of profiles in other family trees. You will be notified about new matches and compare profiles in family trees to lead to new family discoveries.

MyHeritage allows you to automatically generate timelines and timebooks from your family data. Timelines show an interactive story of your family, displaying births, marriages, deaths, as well as photographs and videos that are stored on the site. Timebooks show the life and story of individuals in the tree through pictures and information.

A new key feature is *Record Matching*–a technology that automatically compares billions of historical records to the 1 billion profiles on MyHeritage, and alerts you whenever a match is found for a relative in your family tree. It also provides *Family Tree Builder* - its popular free genealogy software - with new features including sync, unicode and Record Matches.

Their *Record Detective* feature is the first technology of its kind to automatically extend the paper trail from a single historical record to other related records and family tree connections. It generates new leads and discoveries by turning a single record into a door to more by automatically including a summary of additional records and individuals in family trees relating to it.

MyHeritage has 3 types of subscriptions.

1. Free basic: limited to 250 people in tree, limited storage.

2. Premium: up to 2500 people in tree, increased storage, Smart Matching, Priority support, and some power features, $6.25/month for the first year (25% off).

3. PremiumPlus: unlimited people in tree,

unlimited storage, Search trees, and some additional power features, $9.95/month for the first year (25% off). Subscribe for more years and save:

2 years - save 40%, 5 years - save 47%.

Here are the other MyHeritage brands.

Geni.com - FREE

www.geni.com

Geni is a genealogy and social networking website with the goal of creating a family tree of the world. While family profiles are private, Geni's mission is to create a shared family tree of common ancestors. By combining research into a single tree that you work on together, you can focus on verifying information and on new avenues of research, rather than spending time duplicating research that others have already done. It features over 100 million profiles from over 6 million users. MyHeritage acquired Geni in November 2012.

Family Tree Builder - FREE $

www.myheritage.com/family-tree-builder

A genealogy software to create family trees. The free download version is distributed as freeware, with no restrictions, although registration is required to run the software. Users may pay a fee to "unlock" the additional features in the Premium version for $75.

FamilyLink.com - www.familylink.com

WorldVitalRecords.com - $

www.worldvitalrecords.com

A wonderful resource that provides access to a large database of historical content including census, birth, marriage and death records, as well as a sizeable archive of historical newspapers. It has a well-organized interface that places an emphasis on finding information narrowed down by specific locations. This works particularly well for anyone who knows their family lived in a part of Ireland for generations, for example, but does not know much beyond that.

The emphasis on place gives a nice bit of context as you get to know your ancestors and can help highlight additional records you might not have thought to search for in the first place. When you click on a specific state, for instance, you are given a list of records available for that state. Every state's collection is different. If you go looking for a birth or death record you may notice a historical book that mentions your relative too, which can offer information about much more than just important dates.

This site uses avant-garde technology called Geo-coding. Geo-coding identifies the latitude and longitude of a geographical location. The location is then displayed on an interactive map that has zooming and planning features. The main purpose of this technology is to see the geographic location in comparison to surrounding areas. It also follows migrations over time. This can be handy in analyzing the communities of your distant family members.

MyHeritage acquired U.S. based FamilyLink.com and WorldVitalRecords.com in November 2011. Free 3-day trial, $16.25/month, or $89.99/year.

BackupMyTree - FREE

www.backupmytree.com

Fast, automatic backup and off-site storage for all of your family tree files. All of the popular family tree file formats are supported. Download your files at any time. Free, simple, easy, safe and secure.

GenealogyBank

www.genealogybank.com

Find the facts in four centuries of fragile, rare newspapers, books and documents. GenBank makes it easy to discover exciting details about ancestors with unlimited access to: Over 1 billion names, more than 6,500 newspapers from all 50 States from 1690 to today, over 215 million obituaries and death records appearing in American newspapers that document and give the details of our ancestor's lives.

More Newspapers

It contains a ton of newspapers from across the US, 95% of which are exclusive — including Colonial pre-1860, Hispanic (over 360), and African American newspapers (over 280). You will find perspectives on notable African Americans from Frederick Douglass to Martin Luther King, Jr., as well as obituaries, advertisements, editorials and illustrations. New newspapers are added every day, and give a host of family history records.

You can also learn about the triumphs, troubles and everyday experiences of your American ancestors. The unique primary documents go beyond just names and dates. They provide first-hand accounts that simply aren't available from the census or vital records alone.

Newspapers often add crucial details that tell the rest of the story, the actual images of our ancestors, and the homes where they lived. Who knew it would be this easy to find them after all these years.

Books, Documents, & More

A unique source that provides you with complete text of over 286,000 historical books and documents, including: U.S. genealogies, biographies, funeral sermons, local histories, cards, charts, and more published 1789-1994.

Find military records, casualty lists, Revolutionary and Civil War pension requests, widow's claims, orphan petitions, land grants and much more, including all of the American State Papers, and all genealogical content carefully selected from the U.S. Serial Set (1817-1980).

It contains the comprehensive SSDI (Social Security Death Index). It's updated weekly, and it's free to search. Contains full text and digital images of: Senate Journal; House Journal; War of the Rebellion Record; DAR Reports: Graves of Soldiers of the Revolution; Army Register, Navy Register, Air Force Register and much more.

These annual service registers give genealogical information about military personnel. The format and specific information has varied over the years, but generally the entries include the person's name, rank, birth date/place; death date/place and details of their military service. New content added daily. $9.95/30-day trial. $19.95/month or $69.95/year.

DC Thomson Family History

The British-based Leader in Online Family History

This family of websites (formerly called Brightsolid) hosts more than 850 million U.S. records, and 1.7 billion international family history records from the U.S., Canada, UK, Australia, New Zealand and beyond with records going back to 1200. New collections are added every month.

FindMyPast - $

www.findmypast.com (US)
www.findmypast.co.uk (UK)
www.findmypast.ie (Ireland)
www.findmypast.com.au
(Australia/New Zealand)

Hosts exclusive family history records and newspapers only found on these sites. They offer more than 1,000 exclusive collections that you will not find online anywhere else. For example:

- British newspaper archives from England, Wales and Scotland
- Parish records, including 40 million baptisms, marriages and burials from across England and Wales dating back to 1538
- Passenger lists of ships leaving the UK 1890-1960 to the U.S., Canada and Australia
- British Army Records 1760-1915
- Rapidly growing collection of local English,

Welsh, Irish and Scottish records dating back to 1700, including school admissions, workhouse registers and apprenticeships records.

Irish court records

They added more than 30 million records in the past year and will continue to add more core and rare U.S. records and Canadian family history. Their U.S. and World newspapers cover 21 countries, all 50 states and Canada. They offer one billion records from the British Isles – a treasure chest of records from England, Wales, Scotland and Ireland going back to 700. These collections are being added to constantly with new additions being announced monthly.

They partner with societies and provide excellent indexing in order to give you the most accurate search results to simply find your ancestors. Their search filters narrow your results saving time and resulting in more results for your family tree.

Their payment flexibility offers you to view records with credits through their pay-as-you-go option. You decide which records you want to purchase without a commitment. It's always free to search and see what records you need. 14-day free trial, $23.96/month, $14.93/month - 6 months, $159.96/year.

Genes Reunited $

www.genesreunited.co.uk

British site to build your family tree investigate which ancestors you share with other members. You can also search historical records, such as census records from England, Wales and Scotland and birth, marriage and death records dating from 1837 to 2006. Online community boards give members the opportunity to chat and share advice. You can also upload and share family photos and documents. Acquired by DC Thomson in 2009. Standard membership: £15/6 months, Platinum £19.95/month.

British Newspaper Archives

www.britishnewspaperarchive.co.uk $

 Contains most of the runs of newspapers published in the UK since 1800 – currently over 7 million pages. In partnership with the British Library to digitize up to 40 million newspaper pages from the British Library's vast collection. Pay-as-you-go credits. 7-days £9.95, 30-days £29.95.

CensusRecords.com

www.censusrecords.com

 Provides essentially the complete US census records 1790-1940. The 1940 census is free, otherwise Pay-as-you-go credits. $7.95/1000 credits, $9.99/month, $34.95/6-month.

Scotlands People

www.ScotlandsPeople.gov.uk

 A pay-as-you-go e-commerce site as a partnership between the National Records of Scotland and the Court of the Lord Lyon operated by DC Thomson. The site allows searches of 50 million names, has more than 30 million images and over one million registered customers. Hosted by DC Thomson but owned independently.

More of the Top Websites

Mocavo - www.mocavo.com *FREE*

A free genealogy website and family tree search engine. It includes billions of names, dates and places worldwide, seeking to index all free online genealogy information. It searches hundreds of thousands of genealogy web sites, looking for the words that you specify.

Web sites searched on Mocavo include thousands of genealogy message boards, society web pages, genealogy pages uploaded by individuals, state historical societies, family societies, Find-A-Grave, the Internet Archive (mostly scanned genealogy books from the Allen County Public Library), the Library of Congress, Rootsweb, Archive.org, Allen County Public Library, National Archives, Ellis Island, various U.S. state archives, several sites containing scanned images of old photographs, and tens of thousands of distinct sites that contain various transcribed records of genealogical interest.

As with any other search engine, you can search for towns, states, occupations, relatives, or any other text information you think might be included with an ancestor's name. You can browse by category (vital records, directories, histories, military, etc.), location, or date.

Mocavo also has some functional tools to speed up research and connect with others. You can organize your sources for easy reference later. You can build your family tree and make it completely private or public. And you can share your story with family and friends.

Mocavo Plus (subscription option) gives you additional research tools to help you make discoveries faster. Turn fuzzy clues into crystal-clear leads with advanced search. Discover more connections faster by setting custom alerts. Fill the gaps in your family tree with smart trees. And bookmark your results for quicker access with browsing history. 7-day free trial, $59.95/year.

Genealogy in Time - *FREE*

www.genealogyintime.com

A free, popular online genealogy magazine, weekly newsletter, and genealogy website with tools and resources to help you find your ancestors. The most popular feature is their 3 dedicated search engines:

- The Genealogy Search Engine searches for free ancestral records. This very popular search engine covers over 3.0 billion ancestral records across over 1,000 websites in the United States, Canada, UK, Ireland, Europe, Australia and New Zealand.

- The Family Tree Search Engine searches online family trees and genealogy forums. It covers 3.8 billion records.

- The Rare Book Search Engine can be used to track down and purchase second-hand, rare and out-of-print books about your ancestors. It covers 250 million books.

They also maintain a complete list of new genealogy records from around the world which can be search by date and by country. They offer a free toolbar for direct link to their search engines, listings of the newest genealogy records on the internet, and to the top 100 most popular genealogy websites.

They offer a Twitter gadget that provides real-time

updates the current time anywhere in the world relative to your location. This is a great map to use if you are of all genealogy tweets, and a genealogy news gadget that provides real-time updates on genealogy news from hundreds of sources. They also have a world time zone map to help you find corresponding with someone in another time zone. They also provide great educational articles on many subjects.

U.S.GenWeb - World GenWeb - *FREE*

www.usgenweb.org

http://usgwarchives.net

www.usgwtombstones.org

www.worldgenweb.org

These free, sprawling, all-volunteer sites are packed with how-to tips, queries and records such as censuses, tombstones, family group sheets, cemetery surveys and marriage indexes for every U.S. state and virtually every U.S. county. They are more of a resource than a database as they serve as gateways to state-level, regional and country GenWeb sites, and is an excellent tool to begin your search if you want to know information about a particular region in which your family lived. Organization for the US is by county and state, so it provides links to all the state genealogy websites (which includes historical information on the county and geographical boundaries) which, in turn, provide gateways to the counties. They often provide abstracts of actual records on file (such as cemetery, marriage, birth, death, census, tax, probate, or military records). They also sponsor important special projects at the national level and links to all those pages, as well.

Their United States Digital Map Library project includes US maps, State and County maps, and Indian Land Cessions at http://usgwarchives.net/maps/. The Pension Project provides transcriptions of Pension related materials for all Wars prior to 1900 at http://usgwarchives.net/pensions/.

World GenWeb provides genealogical and historical records and resources for world-wide access. Begin your search by exploring the Regional and Country Websites.

US National Archives - FREE

www.archives.gov

The National Archives and Records Administration (NARA) is the nation's record keeper. It's a treasure trove of records and documents to trace your family roots. This site increasingly lets you tap its treasures from home. Access to Archival Databases encompasses more than 85 million historical records, including extracts from WWII Army enlistment papers and 19thcentury arrivals of German, Italian, Irish and Russian immigrants. For historical photos and maps and American Indian records, try the *Archival Research Catalog*.

The archival descriptions include information on traditional paper holdings, electronic records, and artifacts. As of December 2012, the catalog consisted of about 10 billion logical data records describing 527 thousands artifacts and encompassing 81% of NARA's records.

Most of the documents in the care of NARA are in the public domain, as works of the federal government are excluded from copyright protection. Many of NARA's most requested records are frequently used for research in genealogy. This includes census records from 1790 to 1940, as well as ships passenger lists and naturalization records. Other records that are most commonly

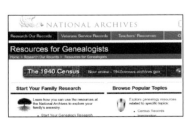

used by genealogists include: Military, immigration and land records which are not online, but there are finding aids, such as microfilm indexes, and information on how to conduct research in the different types of records.

NARA offers numerous resources for genealogists at http://www.archives.gov/research/genealogy/index.html.

National Archives Virtual Genealogy Fair -

www.ustream.tv/usnationalarchives

http://www.ustream.tv/recorded/38250975

The National Archives occasionally hosts a Virtual Genealogy Fair with live lectures via the website Ustream. The programs feature Federal records of genealogical interest. Lectures are designed for experienced genealogy professionals and novices alike. Check out the archived sessions.

In an effort to make its holdings more widely available and more easily accessible, the National Archives has entered into public-private partnerships. Google will digitize and offer NARA video online. Fold3.com www.fold3.com is digitizing historic documents. NARA's collection of Universal Newsreels from 1929 to 1967 is available for purchase through CreateSpace, an Amazon.com subsidiary. https://www.createspace.com/

NARA offers a YouTube channel to showcase popular archived films, inform the public about upcoming events around the country, and bring National Archives exhibits to the people at www.youtube.com/user/usnationalarchives.

It also offers a Flickr photostream to share portions of its photographic holdings.

http://www.flickr.com/photos/usnationalarchives/collections/

Accessing Family Treasures In The National Archives

www.archives.com/experts/brandt-kathleen/accessing-family-treasures-in-the-national-archives.html

A worthwhile article by Kathleen Brandt about retrieving research materials and family treasures from NARA.

NARA Blog

To stay abreast of National Archive news and activities, visit the NARAtions blog at http://blogs.archives.gov/online-public-access. Check out the Genealogy / Family History category.

Internet Archive - FREE

https://archive.org

 A non-profit digital library offering free universal access to books, papers, recordings, music, movies, Internet sites, as well as 364 billion archived web pages. It provides free access to researchers, historians, scholars, and the general public, and is a great resource for genealogists.

It has thousands of documents of interest to genealogists, including every surviving page of the U.S. Census records from 1790 through 1940. These census records are all available free of charge, as is everything else. The census records are not indexed, however, and can only be searched by manually going through the records, one page at a time like most any other traditional library. Thousands of other records of genealogy interest are also available, including many military records, local, state, and federal records, and much more. Many of these documents do not exist elsewhere online.

A variety of other great collections of genealogical interest can be found under Ebook and Texts Archive > Additional Collections > Genealogy, which includes vital statistics, parish records, and other historical and biographical documents. Due to the vast amount of data available on Internet Archive, learning how to effectively focus your search can often be critical to finding content relevant to your research. Learn more about the types of content that can be found here, plus the search methods that provide the best results in Kimberly Powell's Guide to Research in the Internet Archive at http://genealogy.about.com/od/history_research/a/internet-archive.htm.

American Ancestors -

www.americanancestors.org

 The New England Historical Genealogical Society research library provides access to some of the most important and valuable genealogical resources available anywhere in the world that are not available anywhere else. This online repository is home to more than 200 million searchable names covering New England, New York, and beyond.

It provides access to more than 200,000 published genealogies, biographies, family and local histories, as well as many other helpful books. Access to more than 100,000 microfilm reels, including vital records, probate records, administrations, wills, city directories, and other primary resources for New England and eastern Canada. And access to their special collections, which includes more than 28 million original artifacts, manuscripts, documents, family papers, records, photographs, diaries, journals, and other items that document more than 400 years of family and local history. $79.95/year

Godfrey Memorial Library -

www.godfrey.org

 The Godfrey Memorial Library has long been a valuable resource for genealogists. This private library houses over 200,000 books and periodicals in its collection including: state and local histories, international resources, family histories, biographies, records by religious organizations, church records, funeral records, cemetery records, military records, maps, and collection of hand-written material, much of which is not available elsewhere. The majority of the library's material is focused on New England families and history, but there are a great deal of books and periodicals relevant to those researching other states as well as internationally. It's an especially good resource for historic newspapers, including the London Times, 19th century U.S. newspapers,

and early American newspapers.

In addition, the Godfrey Library produces the *American Genealogical-Biographical Index*, an index of more than 4 million names from the more than 800 books in their original collection and the Boston Transcript genealogy query column. $45/year (without the newspaper databases), $80/year complete resources.

Genealogy.About.com - FREE

http://genealogy.about.com

 This extensive website provides you with the guidance you need to break down your genealogy 'brick walls' through how-to articles, free genealogy lessons, the latest news and product reviews and an extensive list of excellent online genealogical resources. Founded in 1996 as The Mining Company, they slowly transformed into the About you know and love today. Starting with nearly 700 Experts and 50 employees, they changed their name to About.com in 1999 and became one of the premiere search and information sites following the mid 90's dot-com boom.

Today, they are one of the most visited sites on the Internet with approximately 25% of the U.S. visiting them each month. they help their users find the answers they need and take action in their lives. They focus on providing high-quality information specifically tailored to their users' interests.

Hosted by Kimberly Powell, a professional genealogist and blogger. She is the author of "Everything Family Tree, 2nd Edition", the Everything Guide to Online Genealogy and the Everything Guide to Online Genealogy, 2nd Edition. She also serves as webmaster for the Western Pennsylvania Genealogical Society.

GeneaNet - FREE $

www.geneanet.org
www.facebook.com/Geneanet.en

 A popular international genealogy database that holds over 135 million family trees –

equivalent to over 400 million individuals. It's especially useful if you have ancestors from Europe. It's a free collaborative genealogy social-networking site to build your family tree, share your family history and improve your genealogy research with the ability to contact the submitters. They send you alerts on any surnames you choose when new stuff becomes available. It houses a community that includes forums, a wiki and a blog. You can post discussions, ask questions or make suggestions to others who are also searching through family history. A free app is available for iPad, iPhone, and Android in 10 languages. There is a cost to upgrade to the Privilege Club which offers enhanced search options and other functions. 40 Euros/year.

Ancient Faces -

www.ancientfaces.com
www.facebook.com/AncientFaces
www.pinterest.com/search/?q=ancientfaces

 A free online vintage photograph sharing service which aims to build a "portrait of our past" by offering members the opportunity to share and view vintage photographs of their ancestors. Historic family photographs are a component of genealogy research that can show shared family physical characteristics, traditions, and insight into the "portrayal of the lives of our ancestors".

Genealogical Research Library -

www.grlresearch.com

 This site searches globally to locate the best genealogical and historical resources for you, including eBooks and databases. They offer access to 835,000 genealogical and historical research resources (currently) in more than 150 countries. It offers some unique resources, including antique maps, historical books and a collection of family trees. With 5,000 databases currently, this genealogy search site is bound to help you unearth information about your ancestors that you didn't know before.

They rate each resource on a 5-star system (based on how useful they think it will be to most researchers) and summarize what they have. They categorize each resource alphabetically by geographical location, and group resources into categories, such as births, marriages, deaths, wills, probate records, directories, census records, cemetery lists, local histories, and so on. They also list thousands of newly discovered resources every month. By arranging resources in this way, it is now possible to search much easier and faster than ever before possible. Everything is arranged logically. $20/month, 6 months - $10/month, 12 months - $7.50/month.

Canadian Genealogy Centre - *FREE*

www.collectionscanada.gc.ca/genealogy

Library and Archives Canada collects and preserves Canada's documentary heritage including publications, archival records, sound and audio-visual materials, photographs, artworks, and electronic documents such as websites. It offers genealogical content, services, advice, research tools and searchable databases for vital, census, immigration and naturalization, military, land and people records, all in both official languages.

HeritageQuest - *FREE* www.heritagequestonline.com

You can't subscribe to this website yourself, but your local library can. If your library subscribes, you can use your library card at home to access the complete U.S. Census (1790-1940), over 24,000 family and local histories, Revolutionary War Pension and Bounty-Land Applications, Freedman's Bank records index (1865-1874), the PERSI index to 2.1 million genealogy articles, and part of the U.S. Serial Set of Memorials, Petitions and Private Relief Actions of Congress.

Genealogy Today - www.genealogytoday.com

This site offers a unique collection of family history records and photos. It's a specialized

portal providing unique databases, search tools and original articles, along with links to the newest sites and online resources. They track new and exciting resources, and host some features and unique databases themselves. It utilizes *Genealogist's Index to the World Wide Web* which is a combined index for family history research that contains over 10 million names across 5,000 sites. You'll also find hundreds of articles on a variety of family history topics, a community of amateur and professional genealogists.

Some of the Special Collections include: a searchable index of funeral cards, the largest online WW2 ration book index, a criminal records collection of original mug shots and wanted posters, and railroad employees compiled from various sources. $14.95/quarter, $32.95/year.

MyTrees.com - www.mytrees.com

This site (formerly Kindred Konnections) has been completely reorganized and now offers an attractive option for researching your family's story. It provides a strong sense of community, and it's database of existing family trees, Ancestry Archive, contains over 562 million names. You can browse the Family Tree Ancestry Archive and their newsletter archive totally free, but you need to subscribe to utilize their full features. A search also helps you tap into census, naturalization and Social Security Death Index information. The learning center and their newsletter are good. The newsletter covers a wide range of topics, and everything is well organized so you can find answers to common questions and information on up-to-the-minute genealogy developments. $10/10 days, $20/month, or $120/year. You get a one-time free-month when you submit a GEDCOM of your family history with at least 15 families and 60 individuals.

OneGreatFamily -
www.onegreatfamily.com

An online genealogical service which allows everyone to combine their knowledge and data to build one huge, shared database. It's more than a simple collection of different family trees. Using breakthrough technology, it is linking all of the family trees together into one great family – currently over 230 million names. With everyone working together on one database, everyone is able to leverage the effort and research of all the users rather than wasting time duplicating research that others have already done. It notifies you whenever new information impacting your family tree becomes available. So it may help you find your names and trace your roots further back than you have been able to go before.

The family tree software allows you to view hundreds of family trees with data entries attached. You can zoom in on an individual name to examine the entry and documents associated. There could be photos, birth certificates, video clips, or anything else the original research has collected. All users contribute to the database, and the materials added by other users to your common ancestors will automatically be added to your tree. There is also a surname index that is categorized alphabetically.

It has a tools section which provides you with resources other than the site databases. This section includes the surname index, a genealogy learning center, a newsletter archive, and genealogy resource page. 7-day free trial, $14.95/month, $79.95/year. Or you can buy a package for consultation with a specialist, or 4 hours of genealogical research.

Census.gov - *FREE*
www.census.gov

The US Census Bureau provides quality data about America's people and economy. It provides an overview of all of the censuses which you can access at http://www.census.gov/history/www/through_the_decades/overview.

It even has a specific section for Genealogy at http://www.census.gov/history/www/genealogy.

The site includes the lists of questions for every U.S. Census, and a list of all the

State Censuses, at www.census.gov/history/www/genealogy/other_resources/state_censuses.html.

Check out their references and links to other genealogical sources, such as National Archives, Immigration Records, and Military Records at

www.census.gov/history/www/genealogy/other_resources/other_genealogical_sources.html

SearchSystems - *$*
www.searchsystems.net

A directory of public records and a resource for background checks and criminal records on the Internet – over 55,000 databases by type and location. A good resource of business information, corporate filings, property records, deeds, mortgages, criminal and civil court filings, inmates, offenders, births, deaths, marriages, unclaimed property, professional licenses, and much more. Offers a database of over 300 million state, national, and international criminal records, and a database of over 100 million bankruptcies, judgments, and tax liens. Easy access to billions of records. $9.95/month, $29.95/year

Tribal Pages - *FREE*
www.tribalpages.com

A genealogy service dedicated to helping you build, maintain and share your Family Tree online.

It is home for over 300,000 members with family tree websites containing over 250 million names and 4 million photos. You can store your family tree data here and generate charts and reports right from the site. It provides 10 MB of free Web space just for family history sites.

Nobody is a Nobody

"In God's eyes, nobody is a nobody. We should never lose sight of what we may become and who we are."
Marvin J. Ashton (1915-1994)

Marvin J. Ashton

Genealogy Trails - *FREE*

www.genealogytrails.com

A volunteer project, transcribing genealogical and historical records in the United States for the free use of all researchers.

UK National Archives -

www.nationalarchives.gov.uk

The official archive for England, Wales and the central UK government, containing 1,000 years of history. Provides searchable databases for vital, census, passenger lists, military, citizen ship and naturalization, wills records, and more.

Free BMD - *FREE*

www.freebmd.org.uk

An ongoing project to transcribe the Civil Registration index of births, marriages and deaths for England and Wales, and to provide free Internet access to the transcribed records. It is a part of the FreeUKGEN family. Currently contains about 300 million records.

Best Web Directories/ Portals

Many web sites are directories of where you can go to try and locate more information. They do not contain actual records, but direct you or link you to them.

Cyndi's List - *FREE*

www.cyndislist.com

Perhaps the best known of the comprehensive web directories that serve as a list or catalog to the entire Internet to help you find other family history web sites.

It contains a categorized and cross-referenced index of over 328,000 genealogical online resources; a list of links listed in over 203 different categories that point you to genealogical research sites. It receives more than 3 million visits each month.

Linkpendium - *FREE*

www.linkpendium.com

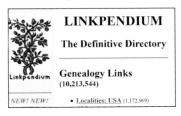

A huge directory of over 10 million genealogy web links categorized by U.S. localities and worldwide surnames.

AcademicGenealogy - *FREE*

www.academic-genealogy.com

A mega portal of key worldwide educational genealogical databases and resources. Professional, worldwide humanities and social sciences mega portal, connected directly to numerously related subsets, with billions of primary or secondary database family history and genealogy records.

Access Genealogy - *FREE*

www.accessgenealogy.com

With over 240,000 links and millions of records, it is one of the largest directories of genealogy websites. It's crowning achievement is the Native American History and Genealogy, providing you an avenue for research online. You cannot help but love Access Genealogy for their Native American records. They have an actual page devoted to a very respectable collection of them where information is divided by tribe and there are new documents added constantly. It also features access to African-American, cemetery, census, DNA, military and vital records. Even though it is a free site, much of the search database is from Ancestry.com. You will need to pay a subscription fee to view some of the information. Check out the free materials and online library.

GenealogySleuth - (FREE)

www.progenealogists.com/genealogysleuthb.htm

A list of web sites that professional genealogists use daily when conducting U.S. genealogy research. You can also link to the International Genealogy Sleuth.

OliveTreeGenealogy -

www.olivetreegenealogy.com (FREE)

Here you will find links to obscure genealogy databases, genealogy resources you can use offline to find ancestors, nuggets of information about a variety of subjects, explanations of genealogical terms, genealogy repositories, address and phone numbers of places and organizations you will need in your family tree search, and much more.

Genealogy Links - (FREE)

www.genealogylinks.net

It offers 4,500 pages of more than 50,000 Free Genealogy Links; for US, UK, England, Scotland, Wales, Ireland, Europe, Canada, Australia & New Zealand. The types of records you can find include parish registers, censuses, cemeteries, marriages, passenger lists, city directories, military records, obituaries and more.

GenealogyToolbox - (FREE)

www.genealogytoolbox.com

A searchable, categorized (by people, places, and topics) collection of tools to help you research your genealogy or family history. Provides links to hundreds of thousands of family history Web sites, as well as linking to content and digitized images of original documents.

AncestorHunt - (FREE)

www.ancestorhunt.com

Convenient genealogy search engines for Ellis Island, Census online, RootsWeb, Social Security Death Index, LDS Church records, Ancestry.com, United Kingdom Records, CensusDiggins, Genealogy.com and more.

To Know Our Heritage

Lloyd D. Newell

It's a hobby focused on obscure dates and places from hundreds of years ago. Yet it is so popular today it has eclipsed stamp collecting, coin collecting, and even gardening as one of the world's favorite pastimes. Whether you call it family history or genealogy, the pursuit of finding one's ancestry has filled libraries with earnest seekers willing to roll through miles of microfilm to find just one name. It has inspired Web sites, television programs, how-to books, classes, and conferences.

So we search and ponder about our ancestry. There's little bit of detective in most of us, and family history builds on that tendency. Birth and death dates are just a beginning. In the search, we may find that our lineage reaches back to royalty. More likely, we learn that our folk were a lot like us – the modest type who did their best to earn a living and loved their families.

They may have fought in wars, and perhaps they crossed the ocean by steamer or clipper with practically nothing in hand, hoping their children would someday have more. They may have joined the great westward migration and buried children along the way. Our ancestry may include preachers, cooks, farmers, gold miners, or mothers of 10. Regardless of their background and circumstances, we lay claim to some of their best characteristics – things like persistence, grit, goodwill, generosity, humor, loyalty, and faith.

All history is really family history, one generation after another. With each find comes a sense of belonging to something much bigger than this day, this time, this place. Indeed, with family history we find ourselves in what might just be called good company.

– Lloyd D. Newell, (1956-   ),
TV journalist, announcer, author
http://fans.musicandthespokenword.org/2010/07/25/to-know-our-heritage/

CHAPTER 6

Passport to the 'Old Country'

Best International Web Sites

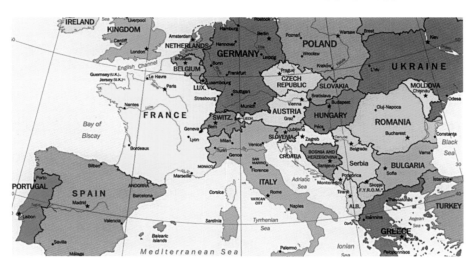

Most people want to find out where their ancestors came from, and search for their roots in the 'old country'. The ancestry of the people of the United States is widely varied and includes descendants of people from around the world.

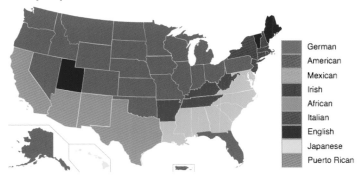

Ancestry with largest population in each state
http://en.wikipedia.org/wiki/File:Most_com
mon_ancestries_in_the_United_States.svg

The majority of the 300+ million people currently living in the United States (a 72% share of the U.S. population, according to the 2010 US Census) are descended from European immigrants who arrived in the past 400 years.

Major components of the European segment of the population are descended from immigrants from Germany (15.2%), Ireland (10.8%), England (7.7%), Italy (5.6%), Scandinavia (3.7%) and Poland (3.2%) with many immigrants also coming from other Slavic

countries. Other significant European immigrant populations came from eastern and southern Europe and French Canada.

Most Hispanic and Latino Americans (15% of population) have origins from Mexico and Central America of which about half are descended from indigenous peoples of those regions and Spaniards (Spain). Most African American people (nearly 13%) are descended from Africa.

You might think that unfamiliar records and language barriers could thwart your search for your family roots, but they don't have to. Many of the websites (containing the online records of the world's countries) are available in English, or can readily be translated to English using the Google translate app, which helps you access the original native language records easier.

I've done the pushups and leg-work for you. I've scoured the Internet to find the best tools and online resources to help you trace your ancestors in the 'old country'. These are searchable online databases and informative tools for most countries of the world where records are currently available online. Please note that new records and databases come online every day so if you don't find information today, check back regularly with these sites because new records may be available tomorrow.

Directory Resources

Directories are shortcuts to locate international records. See BEST WEB DIRECTORIES beginning on page 273 for more directories of the best international websites.

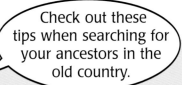

Check out these tips when searching for your ancestors in the old country.

Tips to Help Search the 'Old Country'

How to Find Your Ancestor's Birthplace – page 88

How to Find Your Ancestral Village – page 168

One of the most important things to discovering your heritage – besides your ancestors' name – is the precise place your family came from. Usually, you need more than just a country; you need the specific locale, district or village that they came from.

WorldGenWeb - FREE

www.worldgenweb.org

A non-profit, volunteer based organization

dedicated to providing genealogical and historical records and resources for worldwide access. Regional, country and ethnic sites here span the globe.

FamilySearch Wiki Browse by Country - FREE

https://familysearch.org/learn/wiki/en/Browse_by _Country

Getting started

with family history research. Browse alphabetically by country on a free Internet resource for researching your family tree; contains information on a wide variety of categories related to genealogy.

Research Communities on Facebook -

https://familysearch.org/learn/wiki/en/Research_C ommunities_on_Facebook FREE

The FamilySearch-sponsored Genealogy

Research Communities on Facebook help you connect with others who may be doing research in the same area as you. Currently there are 106 different Community pages with thousands of fans for many countries of the world, as well as US

states and some ethnic groups. You can ask your research questions, collaborate on your research, and share knowledge you have gained as you've done your own research in a specific area.

Ancestry.com Records - FREE

http://search.ancestry.com/search/CardCatalog.as px#ccat=hc%3D25%26dbSort%3D1%26sbo%3D 1%26

You can filter the database record collections on Ancestry.com by location in the world, language, and type of records using their Card Catalog. Membership is required to view most of the records. 14-day free trial, $19.99/month.

Family History Favorite Websites - FREE

www.fhlfavorites.info

A website using the bookmarks from the Family History Library for the best websites for each country. Other genealogy and family history links have been added to this site. Click on the map of each country to open a gateway to each country.

International Genealogy Sleuth - FREE

www.progenealogists.com/genealogysleuthi.htm

A directory of sites that ProGenealogist uses when conducting International genealogy research. These are all searchable online databases or informative tools.

ProGenealogists Country Specific - FREE

www.progenealogists.com/specialtysites.htm

Links to web sites that are focused on a particular country, with valuable data, articles, and help dealing with information from each unique region.

GenoPro Directory - FREE

www.genopro.com/genealogy-links/?cat=Databases

Links to searchable databases of genealogy records.

Africa

Ghana

FamilySearch Historical Records - FREE

https://familysearch.org/search/collection/list#page=1&region=AFRICA

https://familysearch.org/search/collection/list#page=1&countryId=1927065

Currently, FamilySearch contains the following records for Ghana: Census 1984, Marriages 1863-2003.

FamilySearch Wiki - FREE

https://familysearch.org/learn/wiki/en/Ghana

A free Internet resource for researching your African family tree; contains information on a wide variety of categories related to genealogy. Getting started with Ghana research. Similar to most of Africa, the history of pre-colonial Ghana is not known in complete details.

Research Guide - FREE

http://net.lib.byu.edu/fslab/researchoutlines/Africa/Ghana.pdf

This is a dated but still valuable 9-page PDF guide to doing research in Ghana.

African Genealogy Databases - FREE

www.freesurnamesearch.com/search/africa.html

A directory of links to records for all countries in Africa.

Cyndi's List Ghana - FREE

www.cyndislist.com/africa

Numerous links to records and resources for the countries of Africa.

Wikipedia Ghana - *FREE*

http://en.wikipedia.org/wiki/Ghana

The history, government, geography, economy, demographics, and culture of Ghana.

Ghana Genealogy - *FREE*

www.looking4kin.com/group/ghana-genealogy

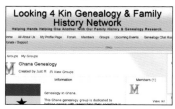

This Ghana genealogy group is dedicated to helping people with researching their ancestors in Ghana, offering a genealogy chatroom, Ghana genealogy links and a genealogy message forum.

Ivory Coast

Tribal Clusters

Cote d'Ivoire

FamilySearch Historical Records - *FREE*

https://familysearch.org/search/collection/list#page=1&region=AFRICA

Currently, they host the following records for Ivory Coast: Census 1975, Civil Registration 1920-2012, and Electoral Registers 1927-1960.

FamilySearch Wiki - *FREE*

http://familysearch.org/learn/wiki/en/Cote_d%27Ivoire

http://familysearch.org/learn/wiki/en/Ivory_Coast,_1975_Census_%28FamilySearch_Historical_Records%29

A free Internet resource for researching your African family tree; contains information on a wide variety of categories related to genealogy.

African Genealogy Databases - *FREE*

www.freesurnamesearch.com/search/africa.html

A directory of links to records for all countries in Africa.

Genealogy.com Links - *FREE*

www.genealogy.com/links/c/c-places-geographic,africa,ivory-coast.html

The Library of Congress has prepared this country study which is available online. The study provides information about political, economic, social, and national security systems.

Cyndi's List Ivory Coast - *FREE*

www.cyndislist.com/africa

Numerous links to records and resources for the countries of Africa.

Wikipedia Articles - *FREE*

http://en.wikipedia.org/wiki/Ivory_Coast

http://en.wikipedia.org/wiki/Portal:Ivory_Coast

Provides information on the history, geography, governance, economy and society of the Ivory Coast.

South Africa

Research Guide - *FREE*

http://web.archive.org/web/20081208085144/http:/
www.genealogyworld.net/Tracing/tracing_2.html

A free guide to South African research by Rosemary Dixon-Smith.

FamilySearch Wiki - *FREE*

https://familysearch.org/learn/wiki/en/South_Africa

Information on how to research your genealogy and family history in South Africa, including links to key websites. Check out the many Wiki pages detailing the South African record collections.

FamilySearch Historical Records - *FREE*

https://familysearch.org/search/collection/list#pag
e=1&region=AFRICAhttps://familysearch.org/searc
h/collection/list#page=1&countryId=1927115

Currently hosts 12 database collections for South Africa featuring Civil Deaths 1895-1972, Western Cape Archives Records 1792-1992, various Church records, Civil Marriages 1845-1955, and Estate Files.

Ancestry24 - $

www.ancestry.com/ancestry24

Ancestry.com has acquired over four million South African records from Ancestry24, the

South African family history website and will be available in the future on Ancestry.com. Click 'Search' on the top bar, then 'Card Catalog', and filter by location to find the records from Africa.

African Genealogy Databases - *FREE*

www.freesurnamesearch.com/search/africa.html

A directory of links to records for all countries in Africa.

Wikipedia South Africa - *FREE*

http://en.wikipedia.org/wiki/South_Africa

All about the Republic of South Africa.

Cyndi's List South Africa - *FREE*

www.cyndislist.com/south-africa/

Numerous links to records and resources for South Africa.

South African Research - *FREE*

http://home.global.co.za/~mercon

Links to research helps about conducting genealogical research in South Africa by Conrod Mercer of South Africa.

South African Genealogy - *FREE*

www.sagenealogy.co.za/

A directory of useful specialist websites covering important aspects of South African family history research by Sharon Warr.

Mole's Genealogy Blog - *FREE*

www.molegenealogy.blogspot.com/

South African genealogy research procedures and sources blog by Mole.

Zimbabwe

FamilySearch Wiki - *FREE*

https://familysearch.org/learn/wiki/en/Zimbabwe

A free Internet resource for researching your African family tree; contains information on a wide variety of categories related to genealogy.

FamilySearch Historical Records - *FREE*

https://familysearch.org/search/collection/list#page=1&region=AFRICAhttps://familysearch.org/search/collection/list#page=1&countryId=1927049

Currently hosts Death Registers (1892-1977) and Death notices (1904-1976).

African Genealogy Databases - *FREE*

www.freesurnamesearch.com/search/africa.html

A directory of links to records for all countries in Africa.

Wikipedia Zimbabwe - *FREE*

http://en.wikipedia.org/wiki/Zimbabwe

The history, government, geography, economy, demographics, and culture of Zimbabwe.

> Much of the record keeping in some parts of the world was done by the Church.

Treasures from the Past -

Vital records and some types of censuses were the domain of the church for centuries.

Fortunately for us, FamilySearch has photographed and microfilmed tons of these records around the entire world for over a century. You access these unique records for free using the library catalog and the Historical Records Collection at FamilySearch.

And with the advent of technology, FamilySearch is currently in the process of digitizing and indexing the gigantic vault of billions of records originally archived on microfilm and making them available for free on their web site as they become available.

And you can volunteer to help index these billions of records and make them available to everyone for free. Go to http://indexing.familysearch.org for more information. Join thousands of others, and index records from home at your leisure.

Cyndi's List Zimbabwe - *FREE*

www.cyndislist.com/africa

Numerous links to records and resources for Africa.

> Good maps and a gazetteer are essentials. Check out the map resources beginning on page 172.

Asia and Middle East

Features dated but valuable Research Guides for East Asian Researchers.

China

FamilySearch Wiki - *FREE*

https://familysearch.org/learn/wiki/en/China

https://familysearch.org/learn/wiki/en/China_Genealogy

https://familysearch.org/learn/wiki/en/Chinese_Research_Helps

https://familysearch.org/learn/wiki/en/Hong_Kong

A community website to help you learn how to find your Chinese ancestors with articles, information and links to key web sites. In the history of the Chinese people, there are three important elements that are significant. They are China's history, the local gazette, and a clan's genealogy. Among these three elements, genealogy has the longest history and is the most influential; Clan or lineage genealogies constitute the major source material.

Old Research Guides - *FREE*

http://net.lib.byu.edu/fslab/researchoutlines/Asia/HongKong.pdf

Features a dated guide to Hong Kong research.

http://net.lib.byu.edu/fslab/researchoutlines/Asia/Asia.pdf

FamilySearch Historical Records - *FREE*

https://familysearch.org/search/collection/list#page=1&region=ASIA_MIDDLE_EASThttps://family-search.org/search/collection/list#page=1&countryId=1927073

This collection currently includes records from 1239 to 2011 acquired from various archives and libraries in China, Japan, Hong Kong, Taiwan, other areas in Southeast Asia and the Untied States. The records are mostly about families who have lived in various provinces in China for several generations. It also provides Cemetery Records (1820-1983).

Hong Kong Libraries - *FREE*

http://lib.hku.hk/fpslib/collections.html

Provides over 1.03 million volumes, more than 14,000 periodicals titles and some 170 Chinese newspapers from Mainland China, Taiwan, Japan and Southeast Asian countries. Its collections also consisted of 5,400 titles of microfilm, more than 1,000 microfiche titles and 20,000 items of audio-visual materials. About 400 titles, most of them from clans in Guangdong and Hong Kong, are available. These are highly valuable primary sources for studying the history of Hong Kong and the region. Of growing importance is its digital collection, comprising key Chinese online databases.

Asia

6 Passport to the Old Country

Cyndi's List China - *FREE*

www.cyndislist.com/china

Numerous links to records and resources for China.

Wikipedia China - *FREE*

http://en.wikipedia.org/wiki/China

http://en.wikipedia.org/wiki/Chinese_language

The language, history, government, geography, economy, demographics, and culture of China.

GenWeb China - *FREE*

www.rootsweb.ancestry.com/~chnwgw/

Provides national genealogy resources from the Peoples Republic of China and links to its provinces; part of the AsiaGenWeb Project.

DistantCousin Links - *FREE*

www.distantcousin.com/Links/Ethnic/China/Province.html

Provides links to Chinese Province and City Genealogy Pages.

India

FamilySearch Wiki - *FREE*

https://familysearch.org/learn/wiki/en/India

https://familysearch.org/learn/wiki/en/India_Websites

Genealogy records about individuals and families in India are free online and stored in archives and libraries around the world. Information on this page will help you discover your family history in India.

FamilySearch Historical Records - *FREE*

https://familysearch.org/search/collection/list#page=1&countryId=1927063

Currently provides Deaths/Burials (1719-1948), Births and Baptisms (1786-1947), Church Records (1854-2012), Hindu Pilgrimage Records (1194-2013), Marriages (1792-1948), and Land Ownership Pedigrees (1887-1958).

National Library - *FREE*

www.nationallibrary.gov.in

The National Library is the apex body of the library system of India. Serving as a public library, it is a permanent repository of all documents published in India.

Indian Cemeteries - *FREE*

www.bacsa.org.uk/
www.indian-cemeteries.org/

Provides images of British and other European cemeteries, isolated graves and monuments in South Asia.

Tracing South Asian Roots - *FREE*

www.movinghere.org.uk/galleries/roots/asian/tracingasianroots/tracingasianroots.htm

There is no central-ised archive for South Asian family history and infor-mation must be pieced together from various sources, as described in the different sections of this site.

India Genealogy Forum - *FREE*

http://genforum.genealogy.com/india/

An active forum for Indian family history.

Wikipedia India - *FREE*

http://en.wikipedia.org/wiki/India

The history, govern-ment, geography, economy, demo-graphics, and culture of India.

Interactiva.org - *FREE*

http://regional.interactiva.org/Asia/India/Society_and_Culture/Genealogy/

This page provides links to some websites concerning genealogy and the study of family histories, including specific family surnames and genealogy related to India.

IndiaMan Magazine - $

www.indiaman.com/

Genealogical and history magazine about the British in India and South Asia from 1600 to the 20th century. They also offer an online database and provide a UK Genealogical Research Service for a flat fee. £29.95 per month.

Families in British India - $

www.new.fibis.org/

Search a database of more than 1,140,000 individual names, and connect with other people searching for ancestors. The data-base search is free but the social network requires a membership. £15.00-18.00/year.

Indonesia

Cyndi's List Indonesia - *FREE*

www.cyndislist.com/asia

Numerous links to records and resources for Indonesia.

FamilySearch Wiki - *FREE*

https://familysearch.org/learn/wiki/en/Indonesia

A free Internet resource for researching your Indonesian family tree; contains information on a wide variety of categories related to genealogy.

FamilySearch Historical Records - *FREE*

https://familysearch.org/search/collection/list#page=1&countryId=1927029

Currently hosts databases for the following: Naturalization and Citizenship Records (1960-2012), Misc-ellaneous Government Records (1950-2012), and District Court Records (1925-2013).

Wikipedia Indonesia - *FREE*

http://en.wikipedia.org/wiki/Indonesia

The history, government, geography, economy, demographics, and culture of Indonesia.

Japan

National Archives of Japan - *FREE*

www.archives.go.jp/english/index.html
www.digital.archives.go.jp/index_e.html

Provides an online catalog database with some images.

Cyndi's List Japan - *FREE*

http://www.cyndislist.com/chinawww.cyndislist.com/japan

Numerous links to records and resources for Japan.

FamilySearch Wiki - *FREE*

https://familysearch.org/learn/wiki/en/Japan

A community website to help you learn how to find your Japanese ancestors with extensive articles, information and links to key web sites. If you have Japanese ancestors who emigrated out of Japan, this guide may help you. The four top sources for Japanese genealogical research are: koseki (household registers), kakocho- (Buddhist death registers), Shumoncho- (Examination of Religion Register), and kafu (compiled family sources).

FamilySearch Historical Records - *FREE*

https://familysearch.org/search/collection/list#page=1&countryId=1927172

Currently features databases for Genealogies (1700-1900), and Village Records (709-1949).

Wikipedia Japan - *FREE*

http://en.wikipedia.org/wiki/Japan

The history, govern-ment, geography, economy, demo-graphics, and culture of Japan.

Genealogy.About.com - *FREE*

http://genealogy.about.com/od/japan/

Discover your Japanese ancestors with these genealogy and family history resources for Japan including Japanese koseki, nikkei, surname meanings, tutorials, culture and history.

Japanese Genealogy Resources - *FREE*

www.distantcousin.com/Links/Ethnic/Japan.html

Provides links for surname searches, general sources, societies, and Japanese search engines (in Japanese).

Japanese Genealogy Blog - *FREE*

www.advantagegenealogy.com/blog/

Family history research help for Japanese ancestry by Valerie Elkins.

Korea

FREE E-BOOK GUIDE
Korea Genealogy - *FREE*

http://koreangenealogy.org/

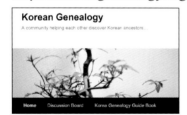

A community helping each other discover Korean ancestors. Check out the free Korean Genealogy Guide ebook by Jason Howard, a resource to help English speakers discover Korean ancestors. The author is making an electronic version of the book available for free for personal use at

http://koreangenealogy.org/wp-content/uploads/2012/08/KoreanGenealogyGuide.pdf

Cyndi's List Korea - *FREE*

www.cyndislist.com/asia

Numerous links to records and resources for Korea.

FamilySearch Wiki - *FREE*

https://familysearch.org/learn/wiki/en/South_Korea

A community website to help you learn how to find your Korean ancestors with extensive articles, information and links to key web sites. Getting started with South Korea research.

FamilySearch Historical Records - *FREE*

https://familysearch.org/learn/wiki/en/Korea,_Collection_of_Genealogies_%28FamilySearch_Historical_Records%29

https://familysearch.org/search/collection/list#page=1&region=ASIA_MIDDLE_EAST

This collection includes records from 1500 to 2012 on family biographies, genealogies, and histories. Ancestors are based on the male family line. The text is in Korean and Chinese.

Wikipedia Korea - *FREE*

http://en.wikipedia.org/wiki/Korea

The history, government, geography, economy, demographics, and culture of Korea.

Russell M. Nelson
© by Intellectual Reserve, Inc.

Power to Bless

"Family history work has the power to bless those beyond the veil, [and] it has an equal power to bless the living. It has a refining influence on those who are engaged in it. ...

Russell M. Nelson, internationally renowned cardiothoracic surgeon and religious leader

Philippines

FamilySearch Wiki - *FREE*

https://familysearch.org/learn/wiki/en/Philippines

Featured Content – Beginning in the late 1500s, the Spaniards took various censuses known as vecindarios (local censuses), padrón de almas (head census), or estado de almas (people status). The latter two were religious censuses conducted by parish clergy. Check out the free 28-page Philippines Research Outline under research tools.

FamilySearch Historical Records - *FREE*

https://familysearch.org/search/collection/list#page=1&countryId=1927042

Check out the various Wiki articles above that describe these online historical records collections.

Features the following database collections: Deaths/Burials (1726-1957), Births and Baptisms (1642-1994), Civil Registration (1706-1994), Court Records (1838-1936), Parish Registers (1615-1982), and Marriages (1723-1957).

Filipinas Heritage Library - *FREE*

www.filipinaslibrary.org.ph/

A one-stop electronic research center on the Philippines. They provide access to the wealth of Filipino heritage through the latest in information technology and telecommunications.

WorldVitalRecords - $

http://philippines.worldvitalrecords.com/

This search engine currently searches 90 websites related to doing genealogy in Philippines.

$16.25/month, $89.99/year.

Cyndi's List Philippines - *FREE*

www.cyndislist.com/philippines

Numerous links to records and resources for Philippines.

Wikipedia Philippines - *FREE*

http://en.wikipedia.org/wiki/Philippines

The history, government, geography, economy, demographics, and culture of Philippines.

Australia and New Zealand

Australia

Australian Family History Compendium - *FREE*

http://afhc.cohsoft.com.au

A free Internet resource for researching your Australian family tree; contains information on a wide variety of categories related to genealogy.

National Archives - *FREE*

www.naa.gov.au

A step-by-step guide to research at the Australian National Archives is available.

FindMyPast - $

www.findmypast.com.au

A family history and genealogy website with millions of records covering Australia, New Zealand, Papua New Guinea and the Pacific Islands. You will also find social, biographical and historical information, which provides a background to the records and helps you gain a deeper understanding of how your family lived.

FamilySearch Historical Records - *FREE*

https://familysearch.org/search/collection/list#page=1&region=AUSTRALIA_NEW_ZEALAND

Currently provides 12 different search-able database collections of Australian records: Deaths and Burials (1816-1980), Births and Baptisms (1792-1981), Cemetery Inscriptions (1800-1960), Marriages (1810-1980), Index to Newspaper Cuttings (1841-1987), Index to Bounty Immigrants (1828-1842), Cemetery Records (1802-1990), Public Records (1847-1989), and Civil Registration (1803-1933).

Ancestry.com Australia - $

http://search.ancestry.com/search/CardCatalog.aspx#ccat=hc%3D25%26dbSort%3D1%26sbo%3D1%26filter%3D1*5027%26www.ancestry.com.au/

Provides 133 search-able databases of Australian records. You can also access 800 million records including UK, New Zealand, and Ireland. AU $24.95/month, $249.95/year. Or you can pay-as-you-go: 10 record views for 14 days: AU $10.95

FamilySearch Wiki - *FREE*

https://wiki.familysearch.org/en/Australia

A community website to help you learn how to find your Australian ancestors with extensive articles, information and links to key web sites. To get started with Australian research, it is helpful to know where one's family or ancestors lived in Australia and to know when they died. Australian states' civil death certificates give a great deal of valuable information which will help you in your research.

Emigration and Immigration - *FREE*

https://familysearch.org/learn/wiki/en/Australia_Emigration_and_Immigration

Sources list names and other details about individuals leaving (emigration) or coming into (immigration) Australia. Between 1788 and 1900 over 1,000,000 people immigrated to Australia. Most of them were from the British Isles, but some were from Europe and Asia.

Cyndi's List Australia - *FREE*

www.cyndislist.com/australia

Numerous links to records and resources for Australia.

Wikipedia Australia - *FREE*

http://en.wikipedia.org/wiki/Australia

The history, government, geography, economy, demographics, and culture of Australia.

New Zealand

Archives New Zealand - *FREE*

http://archway.archives.govt.nz

Contains descriptive information only of over 1.5 million records; it does not yet provide on-line access to the text of the records themselves.

New Zealand Civil Registration - *FREE*

www.bdmhistoricalrecords.dia.govt.nz/search

In the searchable database there are about 5.7 million births, 2.4 million deaths, and 2.1 million marriages.

FamilySearch Historical Records - *FREE*

https://familysearch.org/search/collection/list#page=1&region=AUSTRALIA_NEW_ZEALAND

Currently hosts the following records: Cemetery Gravestones (1861-2009), Passenger Lists (1855-1973), and Probate Records (1848-1991).

FamilySearch Wiki - *FREE*

https://familysearch.org/learn/wiki/en/New_Zealand

A community website to help you learn how to find your New Zealand ancestors with extensive articles, information and links to key web sites.

FREE 23-MINUTE VIDEO *FREE*
Births, Deaths, and Marriages Online -

https://familysearch.org/learningcenter/lesson/new-zealand-births-deaths-and-marriages-online/34

Learn how to use New Zealand's online birth, death, and marriage records.

Cyndi's List New Zealand - *FREE*

www.cyndislist.com/new-zealand

Numerous links to records and resources for New Zealand.

Wikipedia New Zealand - *FREE*

http://en.wikipedia.org/wiki/New_Zealand

The history, government, geography, economy, demographics, and culture of New Zealand.

Canada

FREE RESEARCH GUIDE
How to Locate Your
Ancestor in Canada - *FREE*

https://familysearch.org/learn/wiki/en/How_to_Locate_Your_Ancestor_in_Canada

A Familysearch guide that will give you suggestions on how to find where your ancestor lived in

Canada. Many records in Canada are kept by the province. Some records may be kept by county, district, township, or town agencies. To find the records, you need to determine where your ancestor lived.

FREE E-BOOK
The Canadian Genealogical Handbook - *FREE*

A Comprehensive Guide to Finding Your Ancestors in Canada

https://familysearch.org/s/catalog/show?uri=http%3A%2F%2Fcatalog.familysearch.org%3A8080%2Fwww-catalogapi-webservice%2Fitem%2F121547&hash=HloWXpZgU9zB10k5M56iYku8TUc%253D

You can access a digital version of this book by Eric Jonasson for free, but only one user can use this book at a time.

Canadian Genealogy Centre - *FREE*

www.genealogy.gc.ca

This Web site facilitates the discovery of your Canadian heritage roots and family histories. Collections include published histories of Canadian families and communities, transcriptions and indexes of parish registers, census, cemetery, immigration, military and land records, newspapers and directories, journals of Canadian genealogical and historical societies, genealogical reference tools, government publications including genealogical data, and much more.

Ancestry.com Canada - $

www.ancestry.ca/

Offers members access to 129 million searchable Canadian family history records. Their historical record collection reflects Canada's multicultural heritage and enables

members to explore their family's history using Canadian and international records including the Canadian censuses, passenger lists, English, Welsh and Scottish censuses, birth, marriage and death records as well as user-contributed family trees, and by connecting to millions of other members making their own discoveries.

Key Canadian collections exclusive online access to the complete and fully indexed Censuses of Canada from 1851 to 1916, The Drouin Collection – the complete set of French-Canadian vital records from 1621 to 1947, Ontario and British Columbia vital records from as early as 1813 and U.S./Canada Border Crossings from 1895 to 1956. Annual membership is $9.95/month.

Cyndi's List Canada - *FREE*

www.cyndislist.com/canada

Provides links to sites for provinces and territories; military, census, cemeteries, land, obituaries, and vital records, general resource sites, government and cities, history and culture, libraries, archives and museums; mailing lists and newsgroups; maps, gazetteers and geographical information; newspapers; and queries, message boards and surname lists.

FamilySearch Wiki - *FREE*

https://familysearch.org/learn/wiki/en/Canada

Offers research strategies and tools for Canadian research.

FamilySearch Historical Records - *FREE*

https://familysearch.org/search/collection/list#page=1&region=CANADA

Offers 80 searchable database collections, including the British Columbia Death Registrations (1872-1986), and census records (1851-1916), Passenger Lists (1881-1922),

Births and Baptisms (1661-1959), Marriages (1661-1949), Ontario and Quebec Census, Deaths, Marriages, Births and Baptisms, and Marriages, among many others.

Canada - ProGenealogists - *FREE*

www.progenealogists.com/canada

This web site's aim is to educate and inform about the crucial resources that exist in Canada. They have province-specific pages that outline resources specific to those locations. You may wish to peruse their Canadian Sleuth page that contains links to hundreds of resources.

Wikipedia Canada - *FREE*

http://en.wikipedia.org/wiki/Canada

The history, government, geography, economy, demographics, and culture of Canada.

Canada - GenWeb.org - *FREE*

www.canadagenweb.org

This is the gateway to free Canadian genealogy organized into regional sites for each of the provinces and territories. From these sites you can get closer to your area of research. Contains resources and read/post queries.

Expert Genealogy - *FREE*

http://expertgenealogy.com/free/Canada.htm

How to find family records using the best free Internet resources.

Quebec Family History Society - *FREE*

www.qfhs.ca

A Canadian non-profit organization to foster the study of genealogy among the English speaking peoples of Quebec.

Canada Places - *FREE*

www.johncardinal.com/ca

This site includes place information and mapping resources for 28,898 places in Canada. You can review a list of place names by province or territory. From there, you can navigate to a link to locate a place using Google Maps, Live Local, MapQuest, or Yahoo! Maps.

Canadian Geographical Names - *FREE*

http://geonames.nrcan.gc.ca/index_e.php

Toponyms, or geographical names, are used by us all every day to describe our surroundings and to tell others where we have been or where we plan to go. When we use maps we expect the names to help us identify features of the landscape, and perhaps even to throw light on the local history of an area. This site is the national data base to provide official names of mapping and charting, gazetteer production, and World Wide Web reference, and other geo-referenced digital systems.

Genealogy Helplist Canada - *FREE*

www.rootsweb.ancestry.com/~canghl/

A list of volunteers willing to lookup specific information related to genealogy in Canada using reference materials at institutions near them, or otherwise easily accessible to them.

Caribbean, Mexico, Central and South America

Also see the Hispanic / Latino section beginning on page 134.

Argentina

FamilySearch Wiki - *FREE*

https://familysearch.org/learn/wiki/en/Argentina

A community website to help you learn how to find your Argentina ancestors with extensive articles, information and links to key web sites. Argentina is politically divided into 23 provinces and 1 autonomous city. Understanding political divisions is essential to doing family history, because these divisions determine where records are recorded and archived.

FamilySearch Historical Records - *FREE*

https://familysearch.org/search/collection/list#page=1&countryId=1927135

There are 28 genealogy database collections here. The most important include Baptisms

(1645-1930), various Catholic Church Records (1537-1981), National Census 1869 and 1895, and Marriages (1722-1911).

Cyndi's List Argentina - *FREE*

www.cyndislist.com/central-and-south-america

Numerous links to records and resources for Argentina.

Wikipedia Argentina - *FREE*

http://en.wikipedia.org/wiki/Argentina

http://en.wikipedia.org/wiki/Provinces_of_Argentina

The history, government, geography, economy, demographics, and culture of Argentina.

Bahamas

FamilySearch Wiki - *FREE*

https://familysearch.org/learn/wiki/en/Bahamas

A community website to help

you learn how to find your Bahama ancestors with articles, information and links to key web sites.

FamilySearch Historical Records - *FREE*

https://familysearch.org/search/collection/list#page=1&countryId=1927082

Currently provides Births 1850-1891, and Civil Registration 1850-1959.

Candoo.com - FREE

www.candoo.com/genresources/

Provides links and resources for Caribbean genealogy research.

Cyndi's List Bahamas - FREE

www.cyndislist.com/caribbean

Numerous links to records and resources for Bahamas.

Wikipedia Bahamas - FREE

http://en.wikipedia.org/wiki/The_Bahamas

The history, government, geography, economy, demographics, and culture of Bahamas.

Barbados

Cyndi's List Barbados - FREE

www.cyndislist.com/caribbean

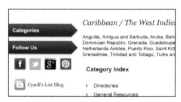

Numerous links to records and resources for Caribbean.

FamilySearch Wiki - FREE

https://familysearch.org/learn/wiki/en/Barbados

https://familysearch.org/learn/wiki/en/Barbados_Census

https://familysearch.org/learn/wiki/en/Barbados_Probate_Records

A community website to help you learn how to find your Barbados ancestors with articles,

information and links to key web sites. Many people throughout the world have early family connections to the Island of Barbados.

FamilySearch Historical Records - FREE

https://familysearch.org/search/collection/list#page=1&countryId=1927094

Currently provides records on Baptisms 1739-1891, Burials 1854-1885, Marriages, 1854-1879, and Church Records 1637-1887.

Your Archives - FREE

http://yourarchives.nationalarchives.gov.uk/index.php?title=Colonial_Ancestry

Provides interesting information on Colonial Ancestry.

Digital Library of the Caribbean - FREE

www.dloc.com/

Provides access to digitized versions of Caribbean cultural, historical and research materials currently held in archives, libraries, and private collections.

Wikipedia Barbados - FREE

http://en.wikipedia.org/wiki/Barbados

The history, government, geography, economy, demographics, and culture of Barbados.

Brazil

Cyndi's List Brazil - FREE

www.cyndislist.com/central-and-south-america

Numerous links to records and resources for Brazil.

FamilySearch Wiki - FREE

https://familysearch.org/learn/wiki/en/Brazil

https://familysearch.org/learn/wiki/en/Brazil_Census

A community website to help you learn how to find your Brazilian ancestors with articles, information and links to key web sites. Brazil is the largest country by both land area and population on the continent of South America.

FamilySearch Historical Records - FREE

https://familysearch.org/search/collection/list#page=1&countryId=1927159

Features many searchable and browseable database collections for Brazil, including: Church records, Civil Registration, Marriages, Immigration Cards, and Death/Burial Records.

Brazil Research Outline - FREE

http://net.lib.byu.edu/fslab/researchoutlines/Latin America/Brazil.pdf

A dated but still valuable 62-page PDF guide to research in Brazil.

Wikipedia Brazil - FREE

http://en.wikipedia.org/wiki/Brazil

The history, government, geography, economy, demographics, and culture of Brazil.

Caribbean

FamilySearch Historical Records - FREE

https://familysearch.org/search/collection/list#page=1&region=CENTRAL_SOUTH_AMERICA

Currently provides records for Caribbean Births and Baptisms 1590-1928, Deaths and Burials 1790-1906, and Marriages 1591-1905.

Digital Library of the Caribbean - FREE

www.dloc.com/

Provides access to digitized versions of Caribbean cultural, historical and research materials currently held in archives, libraries, and private collections.

Cyndi's List Caribbean - FREE

www.cyndislist.com/caribbean

Numerous links to records and resources for the Caribbean.

Wikipedia Caribbean - FREE

http://en.wikipedia.org/wiki/Caribbean

The history, government, geography, economy, demographics, and culture of Caribbean.

Central America

FamilySearch Historical Records - *FREE*

https://familysearch.org/search/collection/list#page=1&region=CENTRAL_SOUTH_AMERICA

Currently provides some Colonial Records for Central America.

Wikipedia Central America - *FREE*

http://en.wikipedia.org/wiki/Central_America

The history, government, geography, economy, demographics, and culture of Central America.

Cyndi's List Central America - *FREE*

www.cyndislist.com/central-and-south-america

Numerous links to records and resources for Central America.

Chile

FamilySearch Historical Records - *FREE*

https://familysearch.org/search/collection/list#page=1&countryId=1927143

Currently provides records for Chile Baptisms 1585-1932, Civil Registration 1885-1903, Deaths 1700-1920, Marriages 1579-1930, and Santiago Cemetery Records 1821-2011.

FREE PDF GUIDE
Research Outline - *FREE*

http://net.lib.byu.edu/fslab/researchoutlines/LatinAmerica/Chile.pdf

A dated but still valuable 57-page PDF guide to doing research in Chile.

FamilySearch Wiki - *FREE*

https://familysearch.org/learn/wiki/en/Chile

A community website to help you learn how to find your Chilean ancestors with articles, information and links to key web sites.

Cyndi's List Chile - *FREE*

www.cyndislist.com/central-and-south-america

Numerous links to records and resources for Chile.

Wikipedia Chile - *FREE*

http://en.wikipedia.org/wiki/Chile

The history, government, geography, economy, demographics, and culture of Chile.

Costa Rica

FamilySearch Historical Records - *FREE*

https://familysearch.org/search/collection/list#page=1&countryId=1927128

Currently hosts records for Costa Rica Baptisms 1700-1915, Catholic Church Records 1595-1992, Civil Registration 1860-1975, Deaths 1787-1900, and Marriages 1750-1920.

Research Outline - FREE

http://net.lib.byu.edu/fslab/researchoutlines/Latin America/CostaRica.pdf

A dated but still valuable 22-page PDF guide to research in Costa Rica, in English and Spanish.

FamilySearch Wiki - FREE

https://familysearch.org/learn/wiki/en/Costa_Rica

A community website to help you learn how to find your Costa Rica ancestors with articles, information and links to key web sites.

Cyndi's List Costa Rica - FREE

www.cyndislist.com/central-and-south-america

Numerous links to records and resources for South America.

Wikipedia Costa Rica - FREE

http://en.wikipedia.org/wiki/Costa_Rica

The history, government, geography, economy, demographics, and culture of Costa Rica.

Ecuador

Cyndi's List Ecuador - FREE

www.cyndislist.com/central-and-south-america

Numerous links to records and resources for South America.

FamilySearch Wiki - FREE

https://familysearch.org/learn/wiki/en/Ecuador

A community website to help you learn how to find your Ecuadorean ancestors with articles, information and links to key web sites. Being a Spanish colony since 1532, Ecuador became independent in 1822 as part of the federation of Gran Colombia. It seceded in 1830.

FamilySearch Historical Records - FREE

https://familysearch.org/search/collection/list#page=1&countryId=1927138

Currently provides Ecuador Baptisms 1680-1930, Catholic Church Records 1565-1996, Deaths 1800-1920, and Marriages 1680-1930.

Research Outline - FREE

http://net.lib.byu.edu/fslab/researchoutlines/Latin America/Ecuador.pdf

A dated but still valuable PDF 17-page guide to research in Ecuador.

Wikipedia Ecuador - FREE

http://en.wikipedia.org/wiki/Ecuador

The history, government, geography, economy, demographics, and culture of Ecuador.

El Salvador

FamilySearch Wiki - FREE

https://familysearch.org/learn/wiki/en/El_Salvador

A community website to help you learn how to find your El Salvadorean ancestors with articles, information and links to key web sites.

FamilySearch Historical Records - FREE

https://familysearch.org/search/collection/list#page=1&region=CENTRAL_SOUTH_AMERICA

Offers databases for Baptisms 1750-1940, Catholic Church Records 1655-1977, Civil Registration 1704-1977, and Marriages 1810-1930.

GenForum - FREE

http://genforum.genealogy.com/elsalvador/

Queries and messages for family information about El Salvador.

Cyndi's List El Salvador - FREE

www.cyndislist.com/central-and-south-america

Numerous links to records and resources for South America.

Wikipedia El Salvador - FREE

http://en.wikipedia.org/wiki/El_Salvador

The history, government, geography, economy, demographics, and culture of El Salvador.

Guatemala

FamilySearch Wiki - FREE

https://familysearch.org/learn/wiki/en/Guatemala

A community website to help you learn how to find your Guatemalan ancestors with articles, information and links to key web sites.

FamilySearch Historical Records - FREE

https://familysearch.org/search/collection/list#page=1&countryId=1927125

Currently provides records for Guatemala Baptisms 1730-1917, Catholic Church Records 1581-1977, Ciudad de Guatemala Census 1877, Civil Registration 1877-2008, Deaths, 1760-1880, and Marriages 1750-1930.

Research Outline - FREE

http://net.lib.byu.edu/fslab/researchoutlines/Latin America/Guatemala.pdf

A dated but still valuable 20-page PDF guide to doing research in Guatemala.

Cyndi's List Guatemala - FREE

www.cyndislist.com/central-and-south-america

Numerous links to records and resources for South America.

Wikipedia Guatemala - FREE

http://en.wikipedia.org/wiki/Guatemala

The history, government, geography, economy, demographics, and culture of Guatemala.

Haiti

Cyndi's List Haiti - FREE

www.cyndislist.com/caribbean

Numerous links to records and resources for the Caribbean.

FamilySearch Wiki - FREE

https://familysearch.org/learn/wiki/en/Haiti

A community website to help you learn how to find your Haitian ancestors with articles, information and links to key web sites. Haiti is a country occupying the western third of Hispaniola Island in the West Indies which it shares with the Dominican Republic.

FamilySearch Historical Records - FREE

https://familysearch.org/search/collection/list#page=1&region=CENTRAL_SOUTH_AMERICA

Currently offers records for Port-au-Prince Civil Registration 1794-1843.

Candoo.com - FREE

www.candoo.com/genresources/

Provides links and resources for Caribbean genealogy research.

Wikipedia Haiti - FREE

http://en.wikipedia.org/wiki/Haiti

The history, government, geography, economy, demographics, and culture of Haiti.

Jamaica

Cyndi's List Jamaica - FREE

www.cyndislist.com/caribbean

Numerous links to records and resources for the Caribbean.

Jamaica Genealogy - FREE

http://jamaicagenealogy.org/

A blog with links to Jamaican resources.

Jamaican Family Search - FREE

http://jamaicanfamilysearch.com/

This is a virtual genealogy library for those researching family history for Jamaica, West Indies, especially for people born before 1920. The site contains transcriptions from various documents including nineteenth century Jamaica Almanacs (which list property owners and civil and military officials), Jamaica Directories for 1878, 1891 and 1910, extractions from Jamaican Church records, Civil Registration, Wills, Jewish records, and excerpts from newspapers, books, and other documents. There is information on immigration and on slavery.

FamilySearch Wiki - FREE

https://familysearch.org/learn/wiki/en/Jamaica

A community website to help you learn how to find your Jamaican ancestors with articles, information and links to key web sites.

FamilySearch Historical Records - *FREE*

https://familysearch.org/search/collection/list#page=1&countryId=1927006

Currently provides records for Jamaica Births and Baptisms 1752-1920, Church of England Parish Register Transcripts 1664-1880, and Civil Registration 1880-1999.

Wikipedia Jamaica - *FREE*

http://en.wikipedia.org/wiki/Honduras

The history, government, geography, economy, demographics, and culture of Jamaica.

Mexico

Also see the Hispanic / Latino section beginning on page 134.

FamilySearch Wiki - *FREE*

https://familysearch.org/learn/wiki/en/Mexico

https://familysearch.org/learn/wiki/en/Mexico_Locating_Place_of_Origin

A community website to help you learn how to find your Mexican ancestors with articles, information and links to key web sites.

FamilySearch Historical Records - *FREE*

https://familysearch.org/search/collection/list#page=1&region=MEXICO

Currently offers 66 database collections including Mexico Baptisms 1560-1950, Deaths 1680-1940, Civil Registration 1832-2005, Catholic Church Records 1546-1971, Marriages 1570-1950, and National Census 1930, among others.

Cyndi's List Mexico - *FREE*

www.cyndislist.com/mexico

Numerous links to records and resources for Mexico.

Wikipedia Mexico - *FREE*

http://en.wikipedia.org/wiki/Mexico

The history, government, geography, economy, demographics, and culture of Mexico.

Panama

Cyndi's List Panama - *FREE*

www.cyndislist.com/central-and-south-america

Numerous links to records and resources for Panama.

FamilySearch Wiki - *FREE*

https://familysearch.org/learn/wiki/en/Panama

A community website to help you learn how to find your Panama ancestors with articles, information and links to key web sites.

FamilySearch Historical Records - *FREE*

https://familysearch.org/search/collection/list#page=1&countryId=1927175

Currently provides records for Panama Baptisms 1750-1938, Catholic Church Records 1707-1973, Deaths 1840-1930, and Marriages 1800-1950.

Wikipedia Panama - FREE

http://en.wikipedia.org/wiki/Panama

The history, government, geography, economy, demographics, and culture of Panama.

Wikipedia Puerto Rico - FREE

http://en.wikipedia.org/wiki/Puerto_Rico

The history, government, geography, economy, demographics, and culture of Puerto Rico.

Puerto Rico

Virgin Islands

Cyndi's List Puerto Rico - FREE

www.cyndislist.com/caribbean

Numerous links to records and resources for the Caribbean.

Cyndi's List Virgin Islands - FREE

www.cyndislist.com/us/territories/us-virgin-islands

Numerous links to records and resources for the Caribbean.

FamilySearch Wiki - FREE

https://familysearch.org/learn/wiki/en/Puerto_Rico

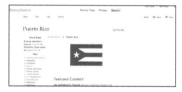

A community website to help you learn how to find your Puerto Rico ancestors with articles, information and links to key web sites.

FamilySearch Wiki - FREE

https://familysearch.org/learn/wiki/en/U.S._Virgin_Islands

A community website to help you learn how to find your Caribbean ancestors with articles, information and links to key web sites.

FamilySearch Historical Records - FREE

https://familysearch.org/search/collection/list#page=1&countryId=5931730

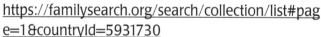

Currently provides records for Puerto Rico Catholic Church Records 1645-1969, Civil Registration 1836-2001, and Records of Foreign Residents 1815-1845.

FamilySearch Historical Records - FREE

https://familysearch.org/search/collection/list#page=1&countryId=5931733

Currently provides US Virgin Islands Church Records 1765-2010.

Puerto Rico GenWeb - FREE

www.rootsweb.ancestry.com/~prwgw/index.html

Provides numerous links to websites and information for research in Puerto Rico.

Wikipedia Virgin Islands - FREE

http://en.wikipedia.org/wiki/Virgin_Islands

The history, government, geography, economy, demographics, and culture of Virgin Islands.

Europe
CONTINENTAL

East European

Family History - FREE

http://feefhs.org

The Federation of East European Family History Societies is a very large collection of materials for people with ancestry in Eastern Europe. Contains links to: Albania, Armenia, Austria, Banat, Belarus, Bosnia, Bukovina, Carpatho-Rusyn, Croatia, Czech Republic, Denmark, Estonia, Finland, Georgia, Galicia, Germans/Russia, Germany, Hungary, Jewish, Kosovo, Latvia, Lithuania, Macedonia, Moldova, Montenegro, Norway, Poland, Romania, Russia, Serbia, Slovakia, Slovenia, Sweden, Switzerland, and Ukraine.

Cyndi's List Eastern and Western Europe - FREE

www.cyndislist.com/eastern-europe
www.cyndislist.com/western-europe
www.cyndislist.com/scandinavia
www.cyndislist.com/baltic

Numerous links to records and resources for Eastern and Western Europe, including Scandinavia and the Baltic States.

WorldGenWeb - FREE

www.worldgenweb.org

Links to European (and other regional) country's websites.

European Historical Documents - FREE

http://eudocs.lib.byu.edu/index.php/Main_Page

These free links from BYU library connect to European primary historical documents– ancient, medieval, renaissance, and modern times–that shed light on key historical happenings within the respective countries and within the broadest sense of political, economic, social and cultural history.

Albania

DistantCousin.com - FREE

www.distantcousin.com/Links/Ethnic/Albanian/

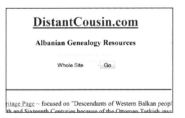

Provides links to some websites and information about Albanian genealogy resources.

Albania Genealogy Links - FREE

www.genealogylinks.net/europe/albania/

Provides links to some websites and information about Albanian research.

FamilySearch Wiki - FREE

https://familysearch.org/learn/wiki/en/Albania

A community website to help you learn how to find your Albanian ancestors with articles, information and links to key web sites.

Wikipedia Albania - FREE

http://en.wikipedia.org/wiki/Albania
http://en.wikipedia.org/wiki/Virgin_Islands

The history, government, geography, economy, demographics, and culture of Virgin Islands.

Austria

The boundaries of Austria have changed over time. Your ancestor may have said he was from Austria, but actually he may have come from any of the countries that once belonged to the Hapsburg Monarchy or Austro-Hungarian Empire.

Austrian Genealogy Pages - FREE

www.rootsweb.ancestry.com/~autwgw/

Find answers to family history related questions concerning Austria.

FamilySearch Wiki - FREE

https://familysearch.org/learn/wiki/en/Austria

A community website to help you learn how to find your Austrian ancestors with articles, information and links to key web sites.

FamilySearch Historical Records - FREE

https://familysearch.org/search/collection/list#page=1&countryId=1927070

Hosts records for Austria Burials 1768–1918, Births and Baptisms 1651-1940, Military Personnel Records 1846-1897, Evangelical-Lutheran Church Records 1848-1900, Marriages 1722-1898, Seigniorial Records 1537-1888, Austria, Tirol, Parish Register Index 1578-1970, Catholic Church Records 1581-1910, Citizen Rolls 1658-1937, Death Certificates 1818-1899, Census Records 1613-1900, Vienna Population Cards, 1850-1896, and Jewish Registers of Births, Marriages, and Deaths 1784-1911.

Cyndi's List Austria - FREE

www.cyndislist.com/austria

Numerous links to records and resources for Austria.

Wikipedia Austria - FREE

http://en.wikipedia.org/wiki/Austria

The history, government, geography, economy, demographics, and culture of Austria.

Belgium

Cyndi's List Belgium - FREE

www.cyndislist.com/belgium

Numerous links to records and resources for Belgium.

Europe

6 Passport to the Old COuntry

FamilySearch Wiki - *FREE*

https://familysearch.org/learn/wiki/en/Belgium

 A community website to help you learn how to find your Belgium ancestors with articles, information and links to key web sites.

FamilySearch Historical Records - *FREE*

https://familysearch.org/search/collection/list#page=1&countryId=1927071

 Contains Belgium Deaths and Burials 1564-1900, Police Immigration Index 1840-1930, Civil Registration 1582-1912, Births and Baptisms 1560-1890, and Marriages 1563-1890.

Wikipedia Belgium - *FREE*

http://en.wikipedia.org/wiki/Belgium

 The history, government, geography, economy, demographics, and culture of Belgium.

Czech Republic and Slovakia

Slovakia became an independent state in 1993 when Czechoslovakia peacefully split into the Czech Republic and Slovakia.

Czech Genealogy for Beginners - *FREE*

http://czechgenealogy.blogspot.com/2011/09/czech-archives.html

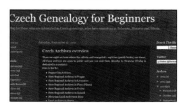 A Blog for those who are interested in Czech genealogy, who have ancestors in Bohemia, Moravia and Silesia.

Cyndi's List - *FREE*

www.cyndislist.com/czech

 Numerous links to records and resources for Czech Republic and Slovakia.

FamilySearch Wiki - *FREE*

https://familysearch.org/learn/wiki/en/Czech_Republic

https://familysearch.org/learn/wiki/en/Slovakia

https://familysearch.org/learn/wiki/en/Slovakia_Online_Genealogy_Records

https://familysearch.org/learn/wiki/en/Slovakia_Accessing_Slovak_Vital_Records

https://familysearch.org/learn/wiki/en/Slovakia_Websites

 A community website to help you learn how to find your Czech and Slovakian ancestors with extensive articles, information and links to key web sites. Most of the records are now available online.

Free Tutorials and Classes - *FREE*

https://familysearch.org/learningcenter/results.html?fq=place%3A%22Czech%20Republic%22

 FamilySearch offers a variety of free classes online and in person to help you discover your family tree. Introduction to the Using Online Czech Records series will teach you how to use the Czech digitized records.

FamilySearch Historical Records - *FREE*

https://familysearch.org/search/collection/list#page=1&region=EUROPE

 Currently offers searchable databases for Czech Republic Births and Baptisms 1637-1889,

Europe

Censuses 1843-1921, Church Books 1552-1948, Civil Registers 1874-1937, Land Records 1450-1889, Marriages 1654-1889, and Nobility Seignorial records 1579-1859. Currently only contains a couple of databases for Slovakian research: Census 1869, and Church and Synagogue Books, 1592-1910.

Wikipedia Czech Republic - FREE

http://en.wikipedia.org/wiki/Czech_Republic

http://en.wikipedia.org/wiki/Slovakia

The history, government, geography, economy, demographics, and culture of Czech Republic and Slovakia.

Denmark

Danish Demographic Database - FREE

www.ddd.dda.dk/ddd_en.htm

http://ddd.dda.dk/kiplink_en.htm

Created by the Danish State Archives, it is designed to be an every name index for searching the Danish censuses. It is not linked to the original census images. Although the census database does not include all parishes for every year of national census yet, the 1801, 1834, 1840,and 1845 are complete for the entire kingdom. The next year to be complete for the entire kingdom is the 1880 census.

Danish Data Archive - FREE

www.sa.dk/content/us/about_us/danish_data_archive

The DDA is the national data bank used by researchers wanting access to data materials created by Danish researchers, especially transcribed historical censuses.

Danish Emigration Archives - FREE

www.emiarch.dk

The archive has an extensive database where relevant emigration information can be searched. Holds a large collection of private letters, manuscripts, diaries, biographies, newspaper clippings, photographs, portraits, etc.

ProGenealogists Denmark - FREE

www.progenealogists.com/denmark/articles/

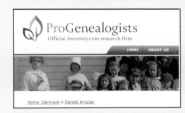

Links to websites and articles on advanced research strategies and records, including in-depth guides to Copenhagen and Bornholm.

Cyndi's List Denmark - FREE

www.cyndislist.com/scandinavia

www.cyndislist.com/denmark

Provides links to sites for General Resources, Government & Cities, History & Culture, How To, Language & Names, Libraries, Archives & Museums, Locality Specific, Mailing Lists, Newsgroups & Chat, Maps, Gazetteers & Geographical Information, Military, Newspapers, People & Families, Volunteers & Other Research Services, Publications, Software & Supplies, Queries, Message Boards & Surname Lists, Records (Census, Cemeteries, Land, Obituaries, Personal, Taxes and Vital), and Religion and Churches.

FamilySearch Wiki - FREE

https://familysearch.org/learn/wiki/en/Denmark

The Denmark portal page has many helpful articles that can help you learn how to find, use, and analyze Danish records of genealogical value. There are also sections on the page that can help simplify the research process.

FamilySearch Historical Records - FREE

https://familysearch.org/search/collection/list#page=1&region=EUROPE

https://familysearch.org/search/collection/list#page=1&countryId=1927025

Features database collections including: Burials (1640-1917), Civil Marriages (1851-1961), Baptisms (1618-1923), Church Records (1484-1941), Estate Records (1436-1964), and Marriages (1635-1916).

Expert Genealogy - FREE

http://expertgenealogy.com/free/Scandinavia.htm

How to find family records using the best free Internet resources.

Denmark - Distant Cousin.com - FREE

www.distantcousin.com/Links/Ethnic/Danish.html

A directory of links to Danish genealogy.

Wikipedia Denmark - FREE

http://en.wikipedia.org/wiki/Denmark

The history, government, geography, economy, demographics, and culture of Denmark.

Danish-American Genealogical Society - FREE

www.danishgenealogy.org

A branch of the Minnesota Genealogical Society offering Danish immigration, genealogy books, photography, history, etc.

Finland

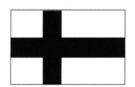

Finland GenWeb - FREE

www.rootsweb.ancestry.com/~finwgw/index.html

Provides numerous links to websites and resources for Finland genealogical information.

FamilySearch Wiki - FREE

https://familysearch.org/learn/wiki/en/Finland

A community website to help you learn how to find your Finnish ancestors with articles, information and links to key web sites.

FamilySearch Historical Records - FREE

https://familysearch.org/search/collection/list#page=1&region=EUROPE

Offers records for Finland Burials 1725-1909, Baptisms 1657-1890, and Marriages 1682-1892.

Expert Genealogy - FREE

http://expertgenealogy.com/free/Scandinavia.htm

How to find family records using the best free Internet resources.

Cyndi's List Finland - *FREE*

www.cyndislist.com/finland

Numerous links to records and resources for Finland.

Wikipedia Finland - *FREE*

http://en.wikipedia.org/wiki/Finland

The history, government, geography, economy, demographics, and culture of Finland.

France

FamilySearch Wiki - *FREE*

https://familysearch.org/learn/wiki/en/France

https://familysearch.org/learn/wiki/en/France_Websites

A community website to help you learn how to find your French ancestors with extensive articles, information and links to key web sites. Learn how to find, use, and analyze French records of genealogical value. Here you will find helpful research tools and research guidance, and link to websites.

FamilySearch Historical Records - *FREE*

https://familysearch.org/search/collection/list#page=1&region=EUROPE

Provides record databases for Catholic Parish Records 1533-1906, Inquiries of Consanguinity 1597-1818, Protestant Church Records 1612-1906, Catholic Parish Records 1772-1910, and Indexes to Church Records 1680-1789.

France Archive - *FREE*

http://fr.geneawiki.com/index.php/Archives_en_ligne#Archives_d.C3.A9partementales

The archives of most of the départements (states) in France and 60 French cities have digitized a wide range of historical records and made them available online. Additional French archives are coming online monthly. Records available often include birth, marriage, and death records, cadastral and other land records, military records, censuses, and more.

Cyndi's List France - *FREE*

www.cyndislist.com/france

Numerous links to records and resources for France.

GenWeb France - *FREE*

www.francegenweb.org

Excellent guide to French family history research includes sections for each department and region. Most links in French. Links to most if not all online French records.

Wikipedia France - *FREE*

http://en.wikipedia.org/wiki/France

The history, government, geography, economy, demographics, and culture of France.

French Family History - *FREE*

http://genealogy.about.com/od/france/French_Genealogy_Family_History.htm

Search for your French and French-Canadian ancestors in this collection of family history

databases and resources for France. Includes tutorials for researching French ancestors, suggestions for writing to France and translating French records, and information on civil records, parish registers and other French genealogical records.

American-French Genealogical Society - $

www.afgs.org

A genealogical and historical organiza-tion for French-Canadian research. Cemeteries, Head-stone and Obit Database Indexes with a total of over 600,000 listings. $35/year.

Germany

See also 'European Passenger Departure Lists' beginning on page 93.

FREE VIDEOS
German Research Tutorials - FREE

https://familysearch.org/learningcenter/results.html?fq=place%3A%22Germany%22

You should view the German Research online tutorials from FamilySearch Learning Center.

FamilySearch Historical Records - FREE

https://familysearch.org/search/collection/list#page=1&countryId=1927074

Currently offers 53 database collections; the most important include Births and Baptisms 1558-1898, Deaths and Burials 1582-1958, and Marriages 1558-1929, among others.

FamilySearch Wiki - FREE

https://familysearch.org/learn/wiki/en/Germany

www.facebook.com/GermanyGenealogy?ref=ts&fref=ts

http://familysearch.org/learn/wiki/en/Germans_from_Russia_Historical_Geography

A community website dedicated to helping people throughout the world learn how to find their ancestors.

Through the Germany pages you can learn how to find, use, and analyze Germanic records of genealogical value. The content is variously targeted to beginners, intermediate, and expert researchers. FamilySearch also has a Facebook page for this country that you should consider when doing your research.

Germany Historical Geography - FREE

https://familysearch.org/learn/wiki/en/Germany_Historical_Geography

As a result of wars and political realign-ments, the internal and external boun-daries of Germany have changed several times. Compare Germany Maps to see how the boundaries have changed.

German Research Websites - FREE

https://familysearch.org/learn/wiki/en/German_Research_Websites

Provides links to websites for archives, churches, colonies, concentration camps, culture, databases, digital libraries, directories, gazetteers, genealogy, historical geography, language helps, maps, military records, newspapers, research guides, and more.

Ancestry.com Germany $

http://search.ancestry.com/Places/Europe/Germany/

Hosts over 1700 database collections for Germany. US $19.99/month, World $34.99/month.

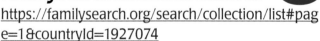

German Church Records Online - (FREE)

www.kirchenbuchportal.de/inhalt.htm

 The new Kirchen-buchportal (church book portal in German) has been created by the Association of Church Archives to facilitate access to German-language church records.

Genealogy Internet Portal - (FREE)

http://compgen.de

 The German genealogy Internet portal, including: links to local German genealogical societies, a GEDCOM based database (German language only), a Place gazetter (Austria, Swiss and Germany), newspapers, books, passenger lists, etc.

German Genealogy - (FREE)

www.daddezio.com/germgen.html

 Provides original articles and valuable links to information on German genealogy.

German Roots - (FREE)

www.germanroots.com

 Resources and guides for German genealogy by Joe Beine.

Cyndi's List Germany - (FREE)

www.cyndislist.com/germany

 Numerous links to records and resources for Germany.

German Interest Group - (FREE)

http://www.scgsgenealogy.com/interest-groups/german-group.html

 The German Research Team of the Southern California Genealogical Society and Family Research Library can help you navigate the unique challenges of researching your German ancestors. The specialized German Collection includes over 3,000 books, CDs, maps, manuscripts, and databases.

German Family History - (FREE)

http://feefhs.org/links/germany.html

 The Federation of East European Family History Societies is a very large collection of materials for people with ancestry in Eastern Europe, including Austria, Germans/ Russia, Germany, and Hungary, among others.

Targeted German Genealogy - (FREE)

www.sggee.org

 Focuses on the genealogy of Germans from Russian, Poland, Volhynia, and related regions.

Germans from Russia - (FREE)

https://familysearch.org/learn/wiki/en/Germans_from_Russia

 A FamilySearch Wiki page that discusses and links to sources to find ancestors who were Germans from Russia.

Germany GenWeb - (FREE)

www.rootsweb.ancestry.com/~wggerman

 Provides databases, resources, maps, ship lists, etc. as part of World GenWeb.

Wikipedia Germany - *FREE*

http://en.wikipedia.org/wiki/Germany

The history, government, geography, economy, demographics, and culture of Germany.

German Genealogical Society - $

www.palam.org

An American German genealogy society dedicated to the study of ancestors from all German speaking lands. Check out their interactive map. Membership required $35/year.

German Ancestry - *FREE*

www.businessinsider.com/german-american-history-2013-10#ixzz2kdNsNDAB

A worthwhile article about Why There Are So Many German-Americans In The US. It briefly covers the interesting history of German immigration to the US.

Hungary

ProGenealogists Hungary - *FREE*

http://www.progenealogists.com/hungary/links.htm

Links to websites and articles on Hungarian research.

FamilySearch Wiki - *FREE*

https://familysearch.org/learn/wiki/en/Hungary

A community website to help you learn how to find your Hungarian ancestors with articles, information and links to key web sites.

FamilySearch Historical Records - *FREE*

https://familysearch.org/search/collection/list#page=1&countryId=1927145

Currently hosts Catholic Church Records 1636-1895, Funeral Notices 1840-1990, Reformed Church Christenings 1624-1895, Baptisms 1734-1895, and Civil Registration 1895-1980.

Cyndi's List Hungary - *FREE*

www.cyndislist.com/eastern-europe

Numerous links to records and resources for Hungary.

Wikipedia Hungary - *FREE*

http://en.wikipedia.org/wiki/Hungary

The history, government, geography, economy, demographics, and culture of Hungary.

Iceland

Cyndi's List Iceland - *FREE*

www.cyndislist.com/iceland

Numerous links to records and resources for Iceland.

FamilySearch Wiki - *FREE*

https://familysearch.org/learn/wiki/en/Iceland

A community website to help you learn how to find your Iceland ancestors with articles, information and links to key web sites.

FamilySearch Historical Records - *FREE*

https://familysearch.org/search/collection/list#page=1&region=EUROPE

Currently provides Iceland Baptisms 1730-1905, and Marriages 1770-1920.

Wikipedia Iceland - *FREE*

http://en.wikipedia.org/wiki/Iceland

The history, government, geography, economy, demographics, and culture of Iceland.

Italy

Most Italian emigrants were from southern Italy and settled in New York, Chicago, and along the East Coast. Many emigrants from northern Italy settled in the coal and mineral mining towns across the United States. Other northerners later settled in northern California where a climate similar to their own existed.

From 1870 to 1880, an estimated 55,000 Italians came to the United States. From 1880 to 1890, more than 300,000 others arrived. As word arrived in Italy of the opportunities in

> Join a worldwide effort to make Italian civil registration records searchable online for free.

Calling all Italian Descendants

Help millions of Italian descendants worldwide discover their family history. Italy civil registration records from 1800-1940 are becoming available for genealogical and academic research.

Your help is needed to make them easily searchable. Become one of thousands of online volunteers from around the world who are indexing photographs of these records to make them searchable and free online for all. It's easy to index, and you decide how much time you want to contribute.

Volunteer today to help make Italian ancestry records come to life. Invite your family and friends to participate. Visit https://familysearch.org/indexing/ and volunteer today at www.familysearch.org/italian-ancestors.

America and as economic problems increased in Italy, nearly 4 million Italians came to America between 1890 and 1914.

FamilySearch Wiki - *FREE*

https://familysearch.org/learn/wiki/en/Italy

https://familysearch.org/learn/wiki/en/Italy_Emigration_and_Immigration

www.facebook.com/ItalyGenealogy?ref=tn_tnmn

A community website dedicated to helping people throughout the world learn how to find their ancestors.

Through the Italy pages you can learn how to find, use, and analyze Italian records of genealogical value. The content is variously targeted to beginners, intermediate, and expert researchers. FamilySearch also has a Facebook page for this country that you should consider when doing your research.

FREE VIDEO
Basic Italian Research -

https://familysearch.org/learningcenter/lesson/basic-italian-research/246

View the 59-minute Italian tutorial at FamilySearch. Researching your Italian heritage can be both fun and rewarding. It isn't difficult to do, and there are many resources to help you along. This video and slides will give you an overview of the research process and the records and resources available to you.

FamilySearch Historical Records -

https://familysearch.org/search/collection/list#page=1&countryId=1927178

https://familysearch.org/learn/wiki/en/Italian_Records_Available_Through_FamilySearch

Currently provides 133 databases of family history records, the most important of which are Deaths and Burials 1809-1900, Civil Registration, Church Records, and Census.

Italy Military Records -

https://familysearch.org/learn/wiki/en/Italy_Military_Records

Military records identify individuals who served in the military or who were eligible for service. From 1865 on, all young men were required to serve in or register for military service in Italy. These wiki pages describe the military records that are most useful to family history researchers.

Italy Websites - FREE

https://familysearch.org/learn/wiki/en/Italy_Websites

Provides numerous links to websites containing records, information, maps, and resources for Italian genealogy anywhere on the Web.

Research Guide for Italy - FREE

http://net.lib.byu.edu/fslab/researchoutlines/Europe/Italy.pdf

A valuable 122-page PDF guide to research for Italian family history from FamilySearch.

Italy GenWeb - FREE

www.italywgw.org

A self-help resource to assist you in finding your Italian ancestors in your genealogical research of Italy.

Italian Genealogy - FREE

www.daddezio.com

A resource for Italian genealogical research that provides articles, research services, passenger lists and information on archives in Italy.

Italian Heritage - FREE

www.theitalianheritage.it/?&lang=english

Provides useful information on Italian emigrants, but is also a virtual site were Italians of the world can meet and exchange opinions and information.

Cyndi's List Italy - FREE

www.cyndislist.com/italy

Numerous links to records and resources for Italy.

Wikipedia Italy - FREE

http://en.wikipedia.org/wiki/Italy

The history, government, geography, economy, demographics, and culture of Italy.

ItalyLink.com - FREE

www.italylink.com/genealogy.html

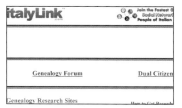

A social network for people of Italian heritage, and people who love Italy. Provides links to Italian genealogy related resources. Check out their forum, person locator.

Italian Genealogical Society of America - $

www.italianroots.org

A non-profit educational organization to promote Italian genealogy. Membership $15/year.

Anglo-Italian Family History Society - $

www.anglo-italianfhs.org.uk/default.shtml

Offers an Index of all the records that the Society's volunteers have transcribed. The Index contains approximately 600,000 names extracted from a miscellany of census, birth, baptism, marriage, and death records together with war, military,

directories and occupational records. Most of the records are not available on commercial genealogy sites. Membership £15.00 ($24).

ItalianGenealogy.com - FREE

www.italgen.com

Explains the research process and conditions in Italy. Also includes resources to locate other researchers who may be researching your places or surnames of interest.

Italian Ancestry.com - FREE

www.ItalianAncestry.com

A portal or jumpsite for all things Italian.

Italia Mia - FREE

www.italiamia.com/gene.html

Provides selected Italian genealogical links, and a guide on how to search for your Italian ancestors.

Italian American Culture - FREE

www.casaitaliachicago.net/

Casa Italia is a home for all Italian-American organizations in the Chicago area. They meet to 'pursue common goals, preserve our past, celebrate our heritage and ensure passage of values to future generations'. Donations accepted.

Netherlands

Dutch Civil Registration - FREE
www.wiewaswie.nl

The official website (in Dutch) for Dutch civil registration records. More than 85 million names have been indexed.

FamilySearch Wiki - FREE
https://familysearch.org/learn/wiki/en/The_Netherlands

A community website to help you learn how to find your Dutch ancestors with extensive articles, information and links to key web sites. When you have Dutch ancestors you are one lucky person as many records have been put on web-sites which are available to all without cost.

FamilySearch Historical Records - FREE
https://familysearch.org/search/collection/list#page=1&countryId=1927059

There are 31 database collections, the most important of which to date include Births and Baptisms 1564-1910, Deaths and Burials 1668-1945, and Marriages 1565-1892.

Dutch GenWeb -
www.rootsweb.ancestry.com/~nldwgw/ FREE

Hasn't been updated for several years, but offers good resources for research in The Netherlands.

Cyndi's List Netherlands - FREE
www.cyndislist.com/netherlands

Numerous links to records and resources for Netherlands.

Dutch Genealogy - FREE
www.dutchgenealogy.nl

Maintained by Yvette Hoitink, a professional genealogist in the Netherlands. Established in 1993, this website provides information to help you find your ancestors from the Netherlands. Read the articles to find out more about common Dutch sources, terms, emigration and tips per province.

Wikipedia Netherlands - FREE
http://en.wikipedia.org/wiki/Netherlands

The history, government, geography, economy, demographics, and culture of Netherlands.

Norway

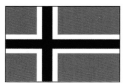

Cyndi's List Norway - FREE
www.cyndislist.com/norway

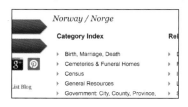

Numerous links to records and resources for Norway.

FamilySearch Wiki - FREE

https://familysearch.org/learn/wiki/en/Norway
https://familysearch.org/learn/wiki/en/Bergen,_Norway
https://familysearch.org/learn/wiki/en/Category:Norway

A community website to help you learn how to find your Norwegian ancestors with extensive articles, information and links to key web sites. You can learn how to find, use, and analyze Norwegian records of genealogical value.

FamilySearch Historical Records - FREE

https://familysearch.org/search/collection/list#page=1&countryId=1927171

Currently contains 4 databases providing: Norway Burials (1666-1927), Census 1875, Baptisms (1634-1927), and Marriages (1660-1926).

Norway DigitalArkivet - FREE

http://arkivverket.no/Digitalarkivet

http://arkivverket.no/eng/content/view/full/629 (English)

The Digital Archives offer online access to digital archive material. Here you can search databases/tables, read transcripts and browse digital images as well as listen to digitized sound from the archives.

It offers the following digitized census records online: 1664-1666, 1701, 1801, 1865, 1870, 1885, 1891, and 1910. They offer 1.85 million pages of parish registers, and real estate registers (mortgage books). The parish images are indexed at page level, meaning that you can easily find the first page of a register, as well as the start of a list of records, or the start of each year in this list allowing you to browse through the pages in the register or through a list of records.

National Archives Norway - FREE

http://fylkesarkiv.no/en

Provides database of the oldest church registers, population censuses, census registrations, shift register, register of mortgages and land registers. In conjunction with the remainder of the historical documents such as photos, emigration records and the farm name encyclopaedia, these archive series constitute rich source materials well suited for biographical and genealogical research.

Ancestry.com Norway - $

http://search.ancestry.com/search/CardCatalog.aspx#ccat=hc%3D25%26dbSort%3D1%26sbo%3D1%26filter%3D1*1652381|1*5173%26http://search.ancestry.com/Places/Europe/Norway/

Hosts 35 database collections for Norway, Including: Norway Burial Index, DIS-Norge, 1700-2010, Norway Births and Christenings, 1600s-1800s, and Norway Marriages, 1600s-1800s, among others.

Norway Genealogy - FREE

www.rootsweb.ancestry.com/~wgnorway/

This is part of the WorldGenWeb and CenEuroGenWeb. It offers links to Norwegian bygde-boker, census, emigration, farm and parish listings, history, lookup volunteers, message (query) boards, and a variety of other useful links.

Expert Genealogy - FREE

http://expertgenealogy.com/free/Scandinavia.htm

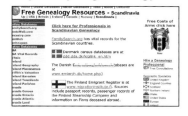

How to find family records using the best free Internet resources.

Wikipedia Norway - FREE

http://en.wikipedia.org/wiki/Norway

The history, government, geography, economy, demographics, and culture of Norway.

Church Photos - FREE

http://kirkefoto.blogspot.com/2009/06/fylkesvis-oversikt-over-kirker-som-er.html

Photo album of Norwegian Protestant churches.

Photo album of Farms - FREE

http://digitalarkivet.uib.no/cgi-win/WebFront.exe?slag=vis&tekst=album-eng.htm&spraak=e

Digitized photographs of farms in the 1900 census. Farm names are very important in locating people in Norway. Through these names you can find parishes and then your ancestors in the parish registers. Check out the Farm Books wiki page at https://familysearch.org/learn/wiki/en/Norway_Farm_Books.

Norwegian-American Genealogical Center - FREE $

www.nagcnl.org/links.php

An educational non-profit research center that offers many valuable links to Norwegian resources and a newsletter. Their Naeseth Library is open to all who are interested in learning more about their Norwegian and Norwegian-American roots. Basic membership $40/year.

Norway Heritage - FREE

www.norwayheritage.com/

Especially useful for finding passenger lists and ships leaving from Norway during the period 1825-1925.

DIS-Norway - $

www.disnorge.no/cms/

Norway's largest association for genealogists, with over 9,000 members. The Association's purpose is to create a national forum for genealogy and personal history in which computing and the Internet is used as an aid, spread knowledge about this and also encourage genealogical research in Norway. (Norwegian language only)

Poland

Polish Genealogy - FREE

www.polishroots.com

Covers all areas that were historically part of the Polish Commonwealth.

Poland GenWeb - FREE

www.rootsweb.ancestry.com/~polwgw/polandgen.html

A self-help resource to assist you in finding your Polish ancestors; part of the World GenWeb.

ProGenealogists Poland - FREE

www.progenealogists.com/poland/links.htm

Provides links to recommended Polish genealogy websites.

Ancestry.com Poland - $

http://search.ancestry.com/Places/Europe/Poland/

Provides 239 searchable databases related to Polish records. $19.99/month

FamilySearch Wiki - FREE

https://familysearch.org/learn/wiki/en/Poland

https://familysearch.org/learn/wiki/en/Poland_Beginning_Research

https://familysearch.org/learn/wiki/en/Poland_Websites

A community website to help you learn how to find your Polish ancestors with extensive articles, information and links to key web sites. Provides numerous links to Polish research and Polish ancestors' homeland.

FamilySearch Historical Records - FREE

https://familysearch.org/search/collection/list#page=1&countryId=1927187

Provides the Catholic Diocese Church Books, 1587-1976.

Cyndi's List Poland - FREE

www.cyndislist.com/poland

Numerous links to records and resources for Poland.

Wikipedia Poland - FREE

http://en.wikipedia.org/wiki/Poland

The history, government, geography, economy, demographics, and culture of Poland.

Research Community on Facebook - FREE

www.facebook.com/PolandGenealogy

This FamilySearch-sponsored Genealogy Research Community on Facebook helps you connect with others who may be doing research in the same area as you. You can ask your research questions, collaborate on your research, and share knowledge you have gained as you've done your own research in a specific area.

Polish Genealogical Society of America - $

www.pgsa.org

Produces a quarterly publication which provides helpful information. $25/year.

Portugal

Portugal National Archives - FREE

http://antt.dgarq.gov.pt/

In Portugese language only.

Etombo - FREE

www.etombo.com/

A list of links and resources for Portuguese genealogy, primarily a Directory of Parish Records, in Portuguese.

Azores GenWeb - FREE

www.rootsweb.ancestry.com/~azrwgw/

The Azore Islands site of the World GenWeb Project.

FamilySearch Wiki - FREE

https://familysearch.org/search/collection/list#page=1&countryId=1927058https://familysearch.org/learn/wiki/en/Portugal

A community website to help you learn how to find your Portugese ancestors with extensive articles, information and links to key web sites.

FamilySearch Historical Records - FREE

https://familysearch.org/search/collection/list#page=1&countryId=1927058

Currently provides 33 database collections for Portugese research, including: Church records, passport registers, baptisms, civil registration, and marriages.

Cyndi's List Portugal - FREE

www.cyndislist.com/portugal

Numerous links to records and resources for Portugal.

Wikipedia Portugal - FREE

http://en.wikipedia.org/wiki/Portugal

The history, government, geography, economy, demographics, and culture of Portugal.

About.com Portugal - FREE

http://genealogy.about.com/od/portugal/

Explore online Portuguese databases, photographs, maps, and other genealogical records for tracing your Portuguese ancestors. Plus, guidance for tracing your family tree in Portugal.

My Portuguese Gen Blog - FREE

http://myportuguesegen.blogspot.com/2012/10/researching-in-azores-useful-links.html

Some useful links for researching in Azores and Portugal by Baltar Family.

Romania

GenWeb Romania - FREE

www.rootsweb.ancestry.com/~romwgw/

A self-help resource to assist you in finding your Romanian ancestors through maps, surnames, queries, etc.

Romania Genealogy Resources - *FREE*

www.feefhs.org/links/romania.html

This is the Federation of European Family History Societies which is providing only a few links to websites and maps.

FamilySearch Wiki - *FREE*

https://familysearch.org/learn/wiki/en/Romania

https://familysearch.org/learn/wiki/en/Romania_Beginning_Research

A community website to help you learn how to find your Romanian ancestors with extensive articles, information and links to key web sites. The earliest vital records were kept by churches. To determine whether the records you need have been microfilmed, check the Family History Library Catalog.

Ancestry.com Romania - $

http://search.ancestry.com/Places/Europe/Romania/

Provides some databases for Romanian research.

Wikipedia Romania - *FREE*

http://en.wikipedia.org/wiki/Romanians

http://en.wikipedia.org/wiki/Demographics_of_Romania

The history, government, geography, economy, demographics, and culture of Romania.

Russia

Russia is now known as the Russian Federation since the dissolution of the Soviet Union in December 1991.

FamilySearch Wiki - *FREE*

https://familysearch.org/learn/wiki/en/Russia

https://familysearch.org/learn/wiki/en/Russia_Beginning_Research

A community website to help you learn how to find your Russian ancestors with extensive articles, information and links to key web sites. This article is intended to provide the background needed to pursue an ancestry that extends back into the Russian Empire.

FamilySearch Historical Records - *FREE*

https://familysearch.org/search/collection/list#page=1&countryId=1927021

Currently hosts 14 collections for Russian research: Deaths and Burials (1815-1917),

Church Books (1721-1939), Poll Tax Census (1719-1874), Births and Baptisms (1755-1917), Marriages (1793-1919), and Civil Registers (1918-1922), among others.

ArcheoBiblioBase - *FREE*

www.iisg.nl/abb

http://online.eastview.com/projects/ticfia/index.html

The Russian Federal Archives and major federal agencies, universities and libraries.

RussianArchives Online.com - FREE

www.russianarchives.com

Collections of Russian archival collections of photographs and films, audio, clips and transcripts from the 15 republics of the former Soviet Union, including Russia, Ukraine, Georgia and many more.

Cyndi's List Russia - FREE

www.cyndislist.com/eastern-europe

Numerous links to records and resources for Russia.

Wikipedia Russia - FREE

http://en.wikipedia.org/wiki/Russia

The history, government, geography, economy, demographics, and culture of Russia.

Research Community on Facebook - FREE

www.facebook.com/RussiaGenealogy

The FamilySearch-sponsored Genealogy Research Community on Facebook helps you connect with others who may be doing research in the same area as you. You can ask your research questions, collaborate on your research, and share knowledge you have gained as you've done your own research in a specific area.

Spain

FamilySearch Wiki - FREE

https://familysearch.org/learn/wiki/en/Spain

A community website to help you learn how to find your Spanish ancestors with extensive articles, information and links to key web sites.

FamilySearch Historical Records - FREE

https://familysearch.org/search/collection/list#page=1&countryId=1927167

Currently features 40 genealogy databases for Spanish research. Deaths 1600-1920, Baptisms 1502-1940, Catholic Church Records 1500-1987, Consular Records of Emigrants 1808-1960, Testaments 1531-1920, Catholic Parish Records 1550-1930, Marriages 1565-1950, Municipal Records 1387-1951, Civil Registration 1870-1960, Passports 1810-1866, and Records of Widows and Orphans 1833-1960, among others.

GenWeb Spain - FREE

www.genealogia-es.com/

A self-help resource to assist you in finding your Spanish ancestors through maps, surnames, queries, etc. Provides links, resources, databases and discussions related to genealogy research in Spain. Web site in Spanish only.

Cyndi's List Spain - FREE

www.cyndislist.com/spain

Numerous links to records and resources for Spain.

Wikipedia Spain - FREE

http://en.wikipedia.org/wiki/Spain

The history, government, geography, economy, demographics, and culture of Spain.

Directory of Royal Genealogical Data -

www.hull.ac.uk/php/cssbct/genealogy/royal/ FREE

Contains the genealogy of the British Royal family and those linked to it via blood or marriage relationships.

Research Community on Facebook -

www.facebook.com/SpainGenealogy FREE

The FamilySearch-sponsored Genealogy Research Community on Facebook helps you connect with others who may be doing research in the same area as you. You can ask your research questions, collaborate on your research, and share knowledge you have gained as you've done your own research in a specific area.

Sweden

To research your Swedish roots, you need the name of the person you are researching, the parish where the person lived in Sweden and a date of birth, death, marriage or emigration.

Tracing Your Swedish Ancestry - FREE

www.swedenabroad.com/SelectImage/15063/tracingyourswedishancestry.pdf FREE

A very nice 40-page reference guide on how to trace your immigrant Swedish ancestor, written by Nils William Olsson.

Ancestry Sweden - $

http://search.ancestry.com/Places/Europe/Sweden

Genline's Swedish Church Records (nearly 21 million) are now available on Ancestry's World Explorer Membership collection. You can find the records in the collection titled, "Sweden, Church Records 1500-1941".

It also provides 7.3 million Swedish Indexed Birth Records (1880-1930). You get access to 6 billion historical records. U.S. census records, vital records, obituary collections and much more. You can trace your ancestors emigration from Sweden with the popular Swedish databases Emigranten Populär and passenger lists from Göteborg, and find dates of birth in Sveriges Dödbok 1947-2006. And various Swedish emigration records from 1783-1951. World membership $34.99/month, $149/6-months

www.ancestry.se/ (in Swedish)

Ancestry offers both their regular Ancestry.com site which offers 55 database collections related to Swedish genealogy records, plus their Swedish website (in Swedish).

Genline - www.genline.com/ $

This site offers over 20 million Swedish Church Records from 1500-1937 which are now also available on Ancestry.com (world membership subscription). They are quality images scanned from microfilm of the original church records by the LDS Church. The archive records consist of birth/baptismal, confirmation, marriage, death/burial, church ledgers and household examination rolls. About $21 for 20 days, $85/quarter.

FamilySearch Wiki - *FREE*

https://familysearch.org/learn/wiki/en/Sweden

https://familysearch.org/learn/wiki/en/Swedish_Research_Websites

https://familysearch.org/learn/wiki/en/Sweden_Emigration_and_Immigration

https://familysearch.org/learn/wiki/en/Orphanages_in_Sweden

 A community website to help you learn how to find your Swedish ancestors with extensive articles, information and links to key web sites.

FamilySearch Historical Records - *FREE*

https://familysearch.org/search/collection/list#page=1&countryId=1927041

 It offers 27 different database collections of Swedish genealogical records. The largest collections are for Baptisms (1611-1920, 9.3 million), Marriages (1630-1920, 1.1 million), Death records (1649-1920, 1.2 million), and numerous Swedish Church records.

Tips for Swedish Research - *FREE*

https://familysearch.org/learn/wiki/en/Swedish_Research:_Tips_for_Swedish_American_Researchers

 The best thing you can do, when you start your Swedish research project is to start at home. You need to do your "basement and attic archeology" because in order to find your Swedish ancestor, you will eventually need to find the name of the village or parish where they were born, married, or lived in at some point in time.

Swedish National Archives - *FREE*

www.nad.riksarkivet.se/

 Offers all public records of the agencies of the central government,

including regional archives, census records, and military records. You can search both the National Archives Database and the Digital Research Room's numerous online collections, such as: Birth records, census, court, death, marriages, title deeds, army rolls, muster rolls, navy archive, church archives, property records, parish extracts, among others. There are some databases and images that require a subscription. 50 krona/3 hours (about $7).

ArkivDigital - *$*

www.arkivdigital.net/

 The largest private provider of Swedish Church Records and other Historical Records online. All images are newly photographed images of the original document. Hosts about 44 million color images covering various kinds of historical documents such as church records, court records and inventory of estates. 1 week 75 SEK ($11), 1 month 195 SEK ($29)

DDSS - *FREE*

www.ddss.nu/%28S%28lvjljk22ordad345gfmvhpfa%29%29/swedish/default.aspx

 Birth, Marriage, and Death Record Database for Southern Sweden (in Swedish).

Demographic Data Base - *FREE*

www.ddb.umu.se/ddb-english/?languageId=1

 The statistical study of the population, its size, distribution and change.

Nordiska Museet - *FREE*

www.nordiskamuseet.se/en

 Sweden's largest museum of cultural history. Discover exhibitions on Swedish trends and traditions in areas such as home interiors, fashion, celebrations and festivals. The museum's

image collections comprise approximately seven million photographs, while the library holds more than 250,000 books and journals, as well as brochures, maps and product catalogues.

Cyndi's List Sweden - *FREE*

www.cyndislist.com/sweden

Numerous links to records and resources for Sweden.

Wikipedia Sweden - *FREE*

http://en.wikipedia.org/wiki/Sweden

http://en.wikipedia.org/wiki/Swedish_emigration_to_the_United_States

The history, government, geography, economy, demographics, and culture of Sweden. During the Swedish emigration to the United States in the 19th and early 20th centuries, about 1.3 million Swedes left Sweden for the United States.

Swenson Swedish Immigration Research Center - *FREE*

www.augustana.edu/general-information/swenson-center-

A national archives and research institute providing resources for the study of Swedish immigration to North America.

Donations accepted.

Swedish Immigration - *FREE*

http://web.comhem.se/~u31263678/genealogy/Emigration-eng.pdf

A free 8-page guide to Swedish immigration to America.

www.spartacus.schoolnet.co.uk/USAEsweden.htm

Worthwhile articles on a description and history of Swedish emigration to America.

Genealogy Resources - *FREE*

www.feefhs.org/links/sweden.html

The East European Family History Societies resource page.

www.genealogylinks.net/europe/sweden/

A small directory of Swedish genealogy links.

www.looking4kin.com/group/swedenswedishgenealogy

The Looking 4 Kin Swedish genealogy forum.

http://expertgenealogy.com/free/Scandinavia.htm

Links to some records using free Internet resources.

Switzerland -

Cyndi's List Switzerland - *FREE*

www.cyndislist.com/switzerland

Numerous links to records and resources for Switzerland.

FamilySearch Wiki - *FREE*

https://familysearch.org/learn/wiki/en/Switzerland

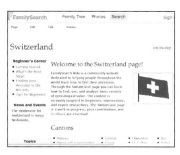

A community website to help you learn how to find your Swiss ancestors with extensive articles, information and links to key web sites.

FamilySearch Historical Records - *FREE*

https://familysearch.org/search/collection/list#page=1&region=EUROPE

Provides 21 database collections, the most important include: Switzerland Baptisms 1491-1940, Burials 1613-1875, Marriages 1532-1910, Church and Census records.

Wikipedia Switzerland - *FREE*

http://en.wikipedia.org/wiki/Switzerland

The history, government, geography, economy, demographics, and culture of Switzerland.

Ukraine

FamilySearch Wiki - *FREE*

https://familysearch.org/learn/wiki/en/Ukraine

A community website to help you learn how to find your Ukraine ancestors with articles, information and links to key web sites.

FamilySearch Historical Records - *FREE*

https://familysearch.org/search/collection/list#page=1&region=EUROPE

Currently offers Ukraine Births and Baptisms 1784-1879, and Church Book Duplicates 1600-1937.

Wikipedia Ukraine - *FREE*

http://en.wikipedia.org/wiki/Ukraine

The history, government, geography, economy, demographics, and culture of Ukraine.

Cyndi's List Ukraine - *FREE*

www.cyndislist.com/eastern-europe

Numerous links to records and resources for Ukraine.

United Kingdom and Ireland

England, Scotland, Wales, N. Ireland, Ireland, Channel Islands, Isle of Man

United Kingdom

The United Kingdom is a unitary state consisting of four countries: England, Northern Ireland, Scotland and Wales.

FindMyPast UK - $

www.findmypast.co.uk

Their family of websites hosts more than 1.7 billion international family history records from the UK, Australia, New Zealand, U.S., Canada and beyond with records going back to 1200. New collections are added every month.

It was the first website to put the UK's England and Wales birth, marriage and death records online. It now is one of the most wide-ranging collections of UK data. Databases include censuses (1841, 1851, 1861, 1871, 1881, 1891, 1901), 38 military datasets, migration and passport records, and government birth, marriage and death indexes (1837 to 2006).

It hosts exclusive family history records and newspapers only found on these sites. They offer more than 1,000 exclusive collections that you will not find online anywhere else. For example:

- British newspaper archives from England, Wales and Scotland
- Parish records, including 40 million baptisms, marriages and burials from across England and Wales dating back to 1538
- Passenger lists of ships leaving the UK 1890-1960 to the U.S., Canada and Australia
- British Army Records 1760-1915
- Rapidly growing collection of local English, Welsh, Irish and Scottish records dating back to 1700, including school admissions, work-house registers and apprenticeships records.
- Irish court records

Some records can be searched for free, but you'll need to pay for full access. Subscription rates:

Britain Foundation - birth, marriage, death and census records £79.95/year

Britain Full - all family history records £109.95/year

World - all records, including collections from Ireland, USA, Australia and New Zealand £159.95

Pay-as- you-go £6.95/60 credits (about $11)

Ireland - €59.95 EUR/year

Ancestry UK - $

www.ancestry.co.uk

This site maintains an extensive archive of over 1 billion searchable records from England, Ireland, Scotland and Wales, including England, Wales and Scotland Censuses. Their extensive collection enables you to explore your family history using censuses, the fully indexed birth,

marriage and death records, passenger lists, the British phone books, military and parish records. You can also explore names in other family trees and upload photographs of your own, and in doing so connect to millions of other members making their own discoveries. 14-day free trial, £12.95/month, £107.40/year.

FamilyRelatives - $

www.familyrelatives.com

An award-winning UK-based site that offers access to over 850 million records of which 400 million have been fully indexed. It's unique in a number of ways: it has more than 150 million indexed records from the General Register Office (GRO) Civil Registrations Indexes for Births, Marriages and Deaths for England and Wales (1866- 920 and 1984-2005) which is more than any other existing website. There are 150 million records which are also searchable on surname and forename (1837- 1865 and 1921-1983). Military and Parish records are also fully indexed. You can connect with fellow researchers and upload your own data.

They offer worldwide records from US, Australia, Canada, England, Scotland, Wales, Ireland and many others. $40/year. $10/60 units.

GenUKI - UK and Ireland - FREE

www.genuki.org.uk

Free resources for the UK (England, Scotland, Wales, Channel Islands and the Isle of Man) and Ireland. It serves as a "virtual reference library" of genealogical information provided by volunteers in cooperation with the Federation of Family History Societies. In the main, the information relates to primary historical material, rather than material resulting from genealogists' ongoing research, such as GEDCOM files.

Linkpendium Genealogy-UKI - *FREE*

http://genealogy-uki.linkpendium.com/

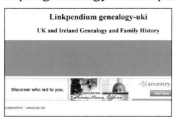

Provides over 10,000 links to UK and Ireland genealogy sites.

Origins.net - $

www.origins.net

Search over 80 million British and Irish genealogy records. A rich source of British genealogy online, featuring marriages, censuses, wills, and many more record collections, most not available anywhere else in digital form. £7.50/ 72 hours (about $12), £10.50/ month (about $16).

FamilySearch Wiki - *FREE*

https://familysearch.org/learn/wiki/en/United_Kingdom

https://familysearch.org/learn/wiki/en/England
https://familysearch.org/learn/wiki/en/Scotland
https://familysearch.org/learn/wiki/en/Wales
https://familysearch.org/learn/wiki/en/Northern_Ireland

A community website to help you learn how to find your British and Irish ancestors with extensive articles, information and links to key web.

FamilySearch Historical Records - *FREE*

https://familysearch.org/search/collection/list#page=1&region=UNITED_KINGDOM_IRELAND

They host numerous database collections, including: England Births and Christenings (1538-1975), Deaths/Burials (1538-1991), Marriages (1538–1973), England and Wales Census 1841-1911, Scotland Census (1841-1891), Parish Registers, and Merchant Navy Seamen Records (1835-1941), among many others.

UK National Archives -

www.nationalarchives.gov.uk/ $

As the official public archive of the United Kingdom government, they hold records covering more than 1,000 years of history. Provides links to census records for England and Wales from 1841 to 1911, military records, and much more. The work of putting these records online was done by their commercial partners. It is free to search their websites, but there may be a charge to view and download documents. £3.36 / digital download.

UK BMD -

http://www.uk *FREE* rg.uk/index.php?form_action=censuswww.ukbmd.org

An extensive gateway to numerous online databases for countries and counties throughout the United Kingdom. It links to web sites that offer on-line transcriptions of UK births, marriages, deaths and censuses. A wide range of other indexes and transcriptions are also available for most counties, these may include parish records, wills, monumental inscriptions, etc.

Free BMD - *FREE*

www.freebmd.org.uk

An ongoing project to transcribe the Civil Registration index of births, marriages and deaths for England and Wales, and to provide free Internet access to the transcribed records. It is a part of the FreeUKGEN family. Currently contains about 300 million records.

Deceased Online - *FREE*

www.deceasedonline.com/

The central database for UK burials and cremations. Search registers by Country, Region, County, Burial Authority or Crematorium free of charge.

Geograph - *FREE*

www.geograph.org.uk/

A project which aims to be a widely appealing web site that will produce a freely accessible archive of information educationally useful, and geographically located photographs of all of the British Isles. Donations accepted.

Cyndi's List UK and Ireland - *FREE*

www.cyndislist.com/uk

Numerous links to records and resources for UK and Ireland.

Expert Genealogy - *FREE*

http://expertgenealogy.com/free/Britain.htm
http://expertgenealogy.com/free/Ireland.htm

How to find family records using the best free Internet resources.

Emerald Ancestors - $

www.emeraldancestors.com/

Provides instant access to one of the largest collections of Northern Irish genealogy records available, containing birth, marriage, death and census records for over 1 million Irish ancestors. They specialize in Northern Ireland genealogy and our extensive Ulster ancestry database covers Irish Family records from civil registration indexes, church registers and historical sources in Counties. Membership £9.99.

Wikipedia United Kingdom - *FREE*

http://en.wikipedia.org/wiki/United_Kingdom

The history, government, geography, economy, demographics, and culture of United Kingdom.

International Society for British Genealogy - $

www.isbgfh.org/

Helps members overcome the challenges of researching British Isles roots from a distance. $25/year

British Isles Family History Society - $

www.rootsweb.ancestry.com/~bifhsusa

If your ancestors came from the British Isles this US society offers to help you in your quest; featuring a "guide to research". $35/year membership.

Scotland

Scotlands People - $

www.scotlandspeople.gov.uk

The official online source of parish register, civil registration, census and wills and testaments records for Scotland. Containing over 90 million records providing a fully searchable index of Scottish births (1553-2006), marriages (1553-2006) and deaths (1855-2006). In addition, indexed census data (1841-1901) as well as Scottish Wills & Testaments (1513-1901) and Coats of Arms records (1672-1907).

To respect privacy of living people, internet access has been limited to birth records over 100 years old, marriage records over 75 years, and death records over 50 years. You may view, save and print images of many of the original documents, and order extracts of any register entries by mail. Credits are required to search for a specific record and to view details and digitized images of records. Viewing images costs 5 credits per image. Searching the index of testaments (wills) and the index for a Coat of Arms is free.

Scottish Archive Network - *FREE*

www.scan.org.uk
Provides access to the National Archives of Scotland offering more than 20,000 collections of historical records held by 52 Scottish archives.

FamilySearch Wiki - *FREE*

https://wiki.familysearch.org/en/Scotland

https://familysearch.org/learn/wiki/en/Category:
Scotland

A community website to help you learn how to find your Scottish ancestors with extensive wiki pages, articles, information and links to key web sites.

FamilySearch Historical Records - *FREE*

https://familysearch.org/search/collection/list#pag
e=1&region=UNITED_KINGDOM_IRELANDhttps://
familysearch.org/search/collection/list#page=1&c
ountryId=1986318

They host the following database collections: Scotland Census 1841-1891, Births and Baptisms (1564-1950), and Marriages (1561-1910).

Church Records Union Lists - *FREE*

https://familysearch.org/learn/wiki/en/Scotland_
Church_Records_Union_Lists

The purpose of the union list is to bring together and list all known church records of Scotland (particularly pre-1855), regardless of denomination, to briefly tell their history when possible, and to identify their existing records of genealogical interest.

ScottishDocuments - *FREE*

www.scottishdocuments.com

Scottish historical records, including wills and testaments (from 1500 to 1901), kirk sessions, presbyteries, synods and the General Assembly of the Church of Scotland.

Research Guide for Scotland - *FREE*

http://net.lib.byu.edu/fslab/researchoutlines/Europe/Scotland.pdf

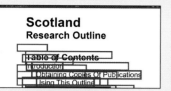

A 212-page guide to discovering your Scottish ancestors hosted by BYU.

Some of the valuable information has been updated and available on FamilySearch Wiki, but this guide puts it all together in one PDF guide.

Cyndi's List Scotland - *FREE*

www.cyndislist.com/uk/sct/

Provides numerous links to websites and resources for Scotland.

GenWeb Scotland - *FREE*

www.scotlandgenweb.org

A self-help resource to assist you in finding your Scottish ancestors.

Wikipedia Scotland - *FREE*

http://en.wikipedia.org/wiki/Scotland

The history, government, geography, economy, demographics, and culture of Scotland.

Wales

FamilySearch Wiki - *FREE*

https://wiki.familysearch.org/en/Wales

Extensive information and links to doing Welsh genealogy. Check out the other wiki

pages providing detailed information and links on birth, baptisms, deaths, marriages, and probate.

FamilySearch Historical Records - *FREE*

https://familysearch.org/search/collection/list#page=1&region=UNITED_KINGDOM_IRELANDhttps://familysearch.org/search/collection/list#page=1&countryId=1986311

They host over 30 database collections for Wales, including: England and Wales Census 1841-1911, Wales Births and Baptisms (1541-1907), Parish Registers, and Non-Conformist Record Indexes, among others.

National Library of Wales - *FREE*

www.llgc.org.uk/index.php?id=2

A mountain of knowledge about Wales and the world – millions of books on every subject, thousands of manuscripts and archives, maps, pictures and photographs, films and music, and electronic information. Their Digital Mirror database features hundreds of thousands of electronic copies of books, manuscripts, archives, pictures and photographs. You can also access Welsh newspapers containing 4.5 million articles and 420,000 pages at http://welshnewspapers.llgc.org.uk/en/.

Many manuscript pedigrees at The National Library of Wales have been microfilmed and are available through the Family History Library and the FamilySearch Centers. Visit the wiki pagse at https://familysearch.org/learn/wiki/en/National_Library_of_Wales_Manuscript_Pedigrees_on_Microfilm and https://familysearch.org/learn/wiki/en/National_Library_of_Wales.

1911 Census - *$*

www.1911census.co.uk/

A record of everyone who lived in England and Wales in 1911. £6.95 per 60 credits.

UK/Ireland

6 Passport to the Old Country

GenUKI Wales - FREE

www.genuki.org.uk/big/wal

Directory provides links to individual county family history resources, including surname lists, official archives, maps, and history profiles.

Cyndi's List Wales - FREE

www.cyndislist.com/uk/wls

A range of information and links.

Wikipedia Wales - FREE

http://en.wikipedia.org/wiki/Wales

The history, government, geography, economy, demographics, and culture of Wales.

Wales History BBC - FREE

www.bbc.co.uk/wales/history

Articles and links to Welsh family history.

Wales National Gazetteer - FREE

http://homepage.ntlworld.com/geogdata/ngw/home.htm

Comprehensive index and maps of Wales.

Ireland

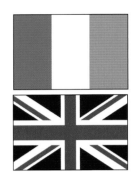

Prior to 1922 the island of Ireland was one country. Today the island is divided into two countries: The Republic of Ireland, also known as Éire, is made up of 26 counties, and is not a part of the United Kingdom. Northern Ireland, a constituent part of the United Kingdom, made up of six of the counties of the Province of Ulster.

FindMyPast Ireland - $

www.findmypast.ie

Search millions of Irish family history records; they offer over 3 million records to help you fill the gaps left by the loss of pre-1901 Irish censuses. Land and estates records in particular make for excellent census substitutes. Their collection contains the largest and most detailed records available including the Landed Estate Court rentals and 1.4 million names in Griffith's Valuation.

They work with all the major stakeholders in Irish genealogy, such as Eneclann, the National Archives of Ireland and the National Library of Ireland. They help you to understand your Irish heritage and make amazing discoveries about your ancestors. €59.95 EUR/year

FamilySearch Historical Records - FREE

https://familysearch.org/search/collection/list#page=1&region=UNITED_KINGDOM_IRELAND

Perhaps the most important resource for Irish genealogy research here is the searchable Civil Registration Indexes

(1845-1958) currently containing over 23 million records. Other valuable databases include: Ireland Births and Baptisms (1620-1881), Marriages (1619-1898), Calendar of Wills and Administrations (1858-1920), Deaths (1864-1870), Landed Estate Court Files (1850-1885), Prison Registers (1790-1924), and Tithe Applotment Books (1814-1855).

Among its data are census records for the US, England and Wales Census (1841-1911) and Canada, which can be extremely useful for those seeking family who had left Ireland by that date. For general information about all of these records and how to use them, visit the FamilySearch Wiki pages.

FamilySearch Wiki - *FREE*

https://familysearch.org/learn/wiki/en/Ireland

https://familysearch.org/learn/wiki/en/Counties_of_Ireland

A community website to help you learn how to find your Irish ancestors with extensive articles, information and links to key websites.

GenUKI - *FREE*

www.genuki.org.uk/big/irl

Free resources with links for all of Ireland. It serves as a virtual reference library of genealogical information provided by volunteers in cooperation with the Federation of Family History Societies. Provides links to hundreds of sites that will be useful in your ancestry research, such as: the availability and location of church records, sites dedicated to specific surname interests, historical events, and locations, etc.

Ireland GenWeb - *FREE*

www.irelandgenweb.com

The resource index page for Ireland research. They have a wonderful genealogy list which covers

the genealogy, history and the culture of Ireland. It covers all the counties and is a great place for you to learn new research methods and make connections.

National Archives of Ireland - *FREE*

www.genealogy.nationalarchives.ie/

The most popular resources on this free Irish genealogy site are the fully digitize 1901 and 1911 census returns.

In addition to a searchable index, you can download images. Other resources are the Tithe Applotment Books, a collection of World War One Soldiers' Wills, and the calendars of Wills and Administration 1858–1922.

National Library of Ireland - *FREE*

www.nli.ie/

Library material used by family history researchers includes the micro-films of Catholic parish registers, copies of the important nineteenth century land valuations (the Tithe Applotment Books and Griffith's Valuation), trade and social directories, estate records and newspapers. They also offer a reference enquiry service, provision of advice to those engaging in family history research and a range of copying services.

Wikipedia Ireland - *FREE*

http://en.wikipedia.org/wiki/Ireland

http://en.wikipedia.org/wiki/Republic_of_Ireland

The history, government, geography, economy, demographics, and culture of Ireland.

Cyndi's List Ireland - *FREE*

www.cyndislist.com/uk/irl

Numerous links to records and resources for Ireland and Northern Ireland.

Irish Genealogy - *FREE*

www.irishgenealogy.ie

Relaunched by the Department of Arts, Heritage and the Gaeltacht with search functionality for the following records: Church records, 1901/1911 Census records, Tithe Applotments, Soldier's Wills, Griffith's Valuations, Ireland-Australia Transportation database, Military Archives, US immigration records of Ellis Island.org Ellis Island, and the National Photographic Archive from the National Library of Ireland, amongst others.

Roots Ireland - $

www.rootsireland.ie/

This website was created by the Irish Family History Foundation, an all Ireland not-for-profit organization, which features a database of Irish genealogical sources to assist those who wish to trace their Irish ancestry. It contains a unique set of over 20 million online Irish family history records including Birth, Death, Marriage and Gravestone records the majority of which are only available online on this website and cannot be found online elsewhere. It provides access to an index of Irish records and digitized versions of the original source material; it does not contain images of original documents.

Its county genealogy centre members are based in local communities and work with local volunteers, historical societies, clergy, local authorities, county libraries and government agencies to develop and preserve a database of genealogical records for their county. It does not contain images of original documents. Searching is free (limited to 100 searches); to view each record will cost you about $6.50.

Irish Origins.net - $

www.irishorigins.com

Offers online access to some of the richest ancestral information available to help you research your family history. Includes subscription access to exclusive genealogy related collections on British Origins, Irish Origins, National Wills Index, plus free Scots Origins services. Includes censuses, marriage registers, wills, passenger lists, court, burial, militia, and apprentice records, as well as downloadable images of original maps and plans used in 19th surveys. Most of this information is not available anywhere else on the internet. £8/3 days (about $11)

Genealogical Society of Ireland - $

www.familyhistory.ie/index.php/en/

An independent, not-for-profit voluntary heritage organization with an Irish and international membership. It publishes a monthly newsletter and an annual journal, and has a growing Archive and a Research Centre. Check out Their Irish Family Names Map. €40.00 per annum.

AncestryIreland.com - $

www.ancestryireland.com/

A non-profit family history research organization with over 50 years experience tracing your Irish and Scots-Irish ancestors. Search over 2 million Irish family history records including Birth, Marriage & Death (BMD) records for Antrim and Down. 1 Year Guild Membership - £31

Check out the free search for Surnames in Ireland in 1890 at www.ancestryireland.com/family-records/distribution-of-surnames-in-ireland-1890-mathesons-special-report/. It provides an indication as to the parishes and counties in the province of Ulster (includes counties Antrim, Armagh, Cavan, Donegal, Down, Fermanagh, Londonderry/Derry, Monaghan and Tyrone) where the above surname is most concentrated.

From Ireland - FREE
www.from-ireland.net/

Features Free Gravestone Records, Free Gravestone Photographs, and Dr. Jane Lyons' Genealogy Blog.

Ireland Reaching Out - FREE
www.irelandxo.com/

A reverse genealogy program that entails the tracing and recording of all the people who left Ireland and seeking out their (est. 70 million) living descendants worldwide. Those identified or recognized as persons of Irish heritage or affiliation are invited to become part of a new extended Irish society. Currently has over 500 parishes engaged with active volunteers assisting in answering questions and queries.

Looking 4 Kin - FREE
www.looking4kin.com/group/ireland

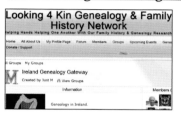

Provides an active, caring genealogy chat room in which all with an interest in Irish genealogy feel at home for sharing knowledge, ideas, resources and making of friendships.

Your History
It's not just history. It's your history.

anonymous

Connecting With the Generations

Lloyd D. Newell

Something deep within us wants to connect with those who went before us: our parents, grandparents, great-grandparents, and other family members. When we know who they are—their life stories, their triumphs and failures, their strengths and weaknesses—we gain a better sense of who we are. In a sense, their stories become our stories. We not only learn from them, we feel strengthened and inspired by their lives and experiences. We may even find ourselves thinking, "If they could do difficult things, so can I."

But what if we never knew our ancestors? What if their stories were never recorded? How can we begin to reconnect with past generations? Start with those who are still living. Talk with them. Listen to their stories and write down their thoughts, feelings, and memories. What you learn might lead to information about more distant ancestors. If nothing else, you can record your own story.

One teenage girl wanted to know more about her grandmother, so over the course of several months she sat down with her, asked questions, and recorded her grandmother's answers. Those answers taught her, made her laugh, and deepened her love for her grandma. She then sent out copies of their conversations to her extended family. They all felt they had received a great treasure, and each learned something new about Grandma.

We don't have to be experienced genealogists to begin researching our family history. Malachi spoke anciently of children's hearts turning to their fathers. [Malachi 4:6] That's all we really need—a sincere desire to connect. With a little effort, we can come to know and love those whose lives flow directly into ours.

– Lloyd D. Newell, (1956-), TV journalist, announcer, author
http://fans.musicandthespokenword.org/2009/05/03/connecting-with-the-generations/

Family History Insights - 6

Gordon B. Hinckley
© by Intellectual Reserve, Inc.

Increases Sense of Identity

As I learn more about my own ancestors who worked so hard, sacrificed so much, it increases my sense of identity and deepens my commitment to honor their memory. Perhaps there has never been a time when a sense of family, of identity and self worth has been more important to the world. Seeking to understand our family history can change our lives and helps bring unity and cohesion to the family." Gordon Hinckley, *Deseret News,* 17 Apr 2001

Woodrow Wilson

Know Where You Came From

"A nation [or family] which does not remember what it was yesterday, does not know what it is today, nor what it is trying to do. We are trying to do a futile thing if we do not know where we came from or what we have been about." Woodrow Wilson, 28th President of the United States (1913-1921)

Boyd K. Packer
© by Intellectual Reserve, Inc.

A Feeling of Inspiration

"[Inspiration] comes to individual[s]... as they are led to discover their family records in ways that are miraculous indeed. And there is a feeling of inspiration attending this work that can be found in no other. When we have done all that we can do, we shall be given the rest. The way will be opened up." Boyd K. Packer

Frederick Douglass

No Progress Without Struggle

"If there is no struggle, there is no progress. Those who profess to favor freedom and yet renounce controversy are people who want crops without ploughing the ground." – Frederick Douglass (1818-1895), Abolitionist, author, statesman & reformer

John H. Widtsoe
© by Intellectual Reserve, Inc.

Help From the Other Side

"Those who give themselves with all their might and main to this work...receive help from the other side, and not merely in gathering genealogies. Whosoever seeks to help those on the other side receives help in return in all the affairs of life." John A. Widtsoe, *Utah Genealogical and Historical Magazine,* July 1931, p. 104

Lee Iacocca

Love Your Family

"No matter what you've done for yourself or humanity, if you can't look back on having given love and attention to your family, what have you really accomplished?" Lee Iacocca (1924-), former Chrysler CEO

Abraham Lincoln

Shall Not Have Died in Vain

"...from these honored dead we take increased devotion to that cause for which they gave the last full measure of devotion – that we here highly resolve that these dead shall not have died in vain – that this nation, under God, shall have a new birth of freedom – and that government of the people, by the people, for the people, shall not perish from the earth." Abraham Lincoln, (1809-1865) Gettysburg Address

Family History Insights - 7

Finding Your Roots

Simone Weil

"To be rooted is perhaps the most important and least recognized need of the human soul."
— Simone Weil (1909-1943), Philosopher

Consider the Past

"Consider the past and you shall know the future." — Chinese Proverb

Forces Working With Us

Harold B. Lee
© by Intellectual Reserve, Inc.

"I have a conviction born of a little experience...that there are forces beyond this life that are working with us. ... I have the simple faith that when you do everything you can, researching to the last of your opportunity, the Lord will help you to open doors to go further with your genealogies, and heaven will cooperate, I am sure." Harold B. Lee

Our Noble Heritage

Ezra Taft Benson
© by Intellectual Reserve, Inc.

Fifty-six men signed the [Declaration of Independence] on August 2, 1776, or, in the case of some, shortly thereafter. They pledged their lives!—and at least nine of them died as a result of the war. If the Revolution had failed, if their fight had come to naught, they would have been hanged as traitors. They pledged their fortunes!—and at least fifteen fulfilled that pledge to support the war effort. They pledged their sacred honor!—best expressed by the noble statement of John Adams. He said: "All that I have, and all that I am, and all that I hope, in this life, I am now ready here to stake upon it; and I leave off as I begun, that live or die, survive or perish, I am for the Declaration. It is my living sentiment, and by the blessing of God it shall be my dying sentiment, Independence, now, and INDEPENDENCE FOR EVER." (Works of Daniel Webster, Boston: Little, Brown & Co., 1877, 17th ed., 1:135.)

How fitting it is that we sing: O beautiful for heroes proved, In liberating strife, Who more than self their country loved, And mercy more than life!

("America the Beautiful" Hymn)

...[Our forefathers] came—with indomitable faith and courage, following incredible suffering and adversity. They came—with stamina, with inspired confidence for better days. We live amid unbounded prosperity—this because of the heritage bequeathed to us by our forebears, a heritage of self-reliance, initiative, personal industry, and faith in God, all in an atmosphere of freedom. Though they did not possess our physical comforts, they left their posterity a legacy of something more enduring—a hearthside where parents were close by their children, where daily devotions, family prayer, scripture reading, and the singing of hymns was commonplace. Families worked, worshipped, played, and prayed together. ...

There should be no doubt what our task is today. If we truly cherish the heritage we have received, we must maintain the same virtues and the same character of our stalwart forebears—faith in God, courage, industry, frugality, self-reliance, and integrity. We have the obligation to maintain what those who pledged their lives, their fortunes, and sacred honor gave to future generations. Our opportunity and obligation for doing so is clearly upon us. As one with you, charged with the responsibility of protecting and perpetuating this noble heritage, I stand today with bowed head and heart overflowing with gratitude. May we begin to repay this debt by preserving and strengthening this heritage in our own lives, in the lives of our children, their children, and generations yet unborn." Ezra Taft Benson

Continuation of Your Ancestors

Thich Nhat Hanh

"If you look deeply into the palm of your hand, you will see your parents and all generations of your ancestors. All of them are alive in this moment. Each is present in your body. You are the continuation of each of these people." Thich Nhat Hanh, Vietnamese Zen Buddhist monk, teacher, author, poet and peace activist. *A Lifetime of Peace*, 2003, 141

Here's a nice glossary for you.

Family History Glossary

Ahnentafel chart - An ancestor table that lists the name, date, and place of birth, marriage, and death for an individual and specified number of his or her ancestors; an alternative to a pedigree chart. The first individual on the list is number one, the father is number two, the mother is number three, the paternal grandfather is number four, and so forth. Ahnentafel is a German word that means ancestor chart or ancestor table.

Ancestral File - A computer database file located at www.familysearch.org containing names and often other vital information (such as date and place of birth, marriage, or death) of millions of individuals who have lived throughout the world. Names are organized into family groups and pedigrees. To allow you to coordinate research, the file also lists names and addresses of those who contributed to the file.

Ancestral File Number (AFN) - A number used to identify each record in Ancestral File on FamilySearch.

Ancestry chart - A pedigree chart that contains only names and limited information about the people on it.

Archive - A place in which public records or historical documents are preserved and researched. Unlike a Library, archived records cannot be checked out but can be used in the building.

Blog (or web log) - A website consisting of entries appearing in reverse chronological order with the most recent entry appearing first. They typically are free-style, interactive web sites containing news, commentary, photos, web links, etc.

Bookmark - A saved link to a Web site that has been added to a list of saved links so that you can simply click on it rather than having to retype the address when visiting the site again.

Browser - An Internet tool for viewing the World Wide Web. Some of the Web browsers currently available for personal computers include Internet Explorer, Opera, Mozilla Firefox, Safari, Google Chrome, and AOL Explorer.

Bulletin Board - Refers to online message systems to read and post messages.

Call number - The number used to identify a book, microfilm, microfiche, or other source in a library or archive. Library materials are stored and retrieved by call number.

Cascading family group record - An option that allows you to print family group records for a specified number of generations in a family. If you printed a cascading pedigree you could select the same starting person and number of generations to print a family group record for each couple in the pedigree charts.

Cascading pedigree - An option that allows you to print pedigree charts for a specified number of generations. Each page is numbered, which allows you to keep the pages in order.

Census - Official enumeration, listing or counting of citizens.

CD-ROM (Compact Disk Read Only Memory) - A computer disk that can store large amounts of information and is generally used on computers with CD-ROM drives.

Chat Room - A location on an online service that allows users to communicate with each other about an agreed-upon topic in "real time" (or "live"), as opposed to delayed time as with email.

Chat - When people type live messages to each other using a network.

Collateral line - A family that is not in your direct ancestral line but in the same genealogical line.

Compiled Record - A record (usually in book form) consisting of information that has been gathered from original records, other compiled records and verbal testimony.

Database - Information for computer search, storage, and retrieval.

Date calculator - A feature in family history programs that allows you to determine the days, months, and years elapsed between two dates or to determine a date based on the amount of time elapsed before or after a date. For example, this is useful to approximate a birth date for a person who appears in a census.

Default - A computer term for "normal" settings of a program.

Descendency chart - A report that lists an individual and his or her children and their spouses and children.

Domain name - The Internet's way to find unique addresses on the World Wide Web.

Download - The process of retrieving information from another computer to yours.

E-mail - Short for electronic mail messages that are sent from one person to another.

End of line - The last known person in a line of ancestry. An end-of-line person has no parents listed in the database file.

Export - A feature in many family history programs that allows you to save or send information to use in another genealogical program. Information is usually saved in GEDCOM format.

Facebook.com - Connect and share with the people in your life. A free social networking website where you can add friends and send them messages. Anyone can join.

Family group record - A printed form that lists a family—parents and children—and gives information about dates and places of birth, marriage, and death. This is also called a family group sheet.

Family History Center (FHC) - Local branches of the Family History Library in Salt Lake City, Utah. There are currently more than 4,500 around the world.

Family History Computer Software Program - A computer family history program for home use. Users enter family history information electronically, thus allowing information to be printed as a pedigree chart, family group record, descendency chart, or many other formats. Information can also be given to others as a GEDCOM file for instant transfer of family history data.

Family History Library - The main family history library in Salt Lake City, Utah used by genealogical researchers worldwide. It has the world's largest collection of genealogical holdings and has both printed sources and microfilmed records.

FamilySearch - A web site and a term that refers to computer products that help people learn about their ancestors.

Freenet - A community network that provides free online access, usually to local residents, and often includes its own forums and news.

Forum - A set of messages on a subject, usually with a corresponding set of files.

FTP (File Transfer Protocol) - Enables an Internet user to transfer files electronically between computers.

GEDCOM - The acronym for "GEnealogical Data COMmunications." GEDCOM is a computer data format for storing genealogical information so that many computer programs can use it. It is the standard file format worldwide for exchanging family information between genealogical databases. If you choose, your family history software program can save your family information as a GEDCOM file.

Genealogy - The study of how individuals and their families are descended from their ancestors. It often includes learning about family histories and traditions.

Given name - A person's first name(s).

Gregorian calendar - The calendar commonly used in Western and Westernized countries. It corrected the Julian calendar, which, because of miscalculated leap years, fell behind the solar year by several days.

Hardware - A term for the nuts, bolts, and wires of computer equipment and the actual computer and related machines.

Home page - A web page that serves as the table of contents or title page of a web site.

Home person - A feature in family history programs that allows you to return to the individual record that is designated to be the home person. The term "home" can also refer to the first person in a file.

HTML - Acronym for HyperText Markup Language, the coding language of the World Wide Web.

Hyperlink Link - Highlighted text that allows you to jump to other information in a file or to another web page or web site.

Hypertext Transfer Protocol - A standard used by World Wide Web servers to provide rules for moving text, images, sound, video, and other multimedia files across the Internet.

ICON - A small picture on a Web page that represents the topic or information category of another Web page. Frequently, the icon is a hypertext link to that page.

IGI (The International Genealogical Index) - A database of names located at www.FamilySearch.org.

IM (Instant Message) - A type of chat program that allows users to send and receive text messages instantly and requires users to register with a server. Users build "buddy lists" of others using the same program and are notified when people on their list are available for messages.

Import - A feature on the menu in family history programs that allows you to add information that is stored in a GEDCOM file into your database.

Immigrant - One moving into a country from another.

Internet - A system of computers joined together by high-speed data lines. It is a repository for vast amounts of data, including family history data, that is accessed by computer through an Internet Service Provider and Web Browser. It includes data in various formats (or protocols) such as HTML, e-mail (SMTP), File Transfer Protocol (FTP), and Telnet.

ISP (Internet Service Provider) - A company that has a continuous, fast and reliable connection to the Internet and sells subscriptions to use that connection.

Julian calendar - A calendar introduced in Rome in 46 B.C. This calendar was the basis for the Gregorian calendar, which is in common use today. The Julian calendar specified that the year began on 25 March (Lady's Day) and had 365 days. Each fourth year had a leap day, so it had 366 days. The year was divided into months. Each month had 30 or 31 days, except February, which had 28 days in normal years and 29 days in leap years. This calendar was used for several centuries (until the mid 1500s) but was eventually replaced by the Gregorian calendar because leap years had been miscalculated.

LDS - An abbreviation for The Church of Jesus Christ of Latter-day Saints, also known as the Mormons.

Legacy Contributor - A person who originally submitted information to Ancestral File or the Pedigree Resource File in FamilySearch.

Link - To define family relationships between individual records or to attach a source or multimedia file to an individual or marriage record.

Living - A person who is still alive. Some family history programs define a living person as someone who was born within the last 110 years whose individual record contains no death or burial information.

Lossless Compression - A digital file where the original and the decompressed data are identical.

Lossy Compression - Digital file formats that suffer from *generation loss*: repeatedly compressing and decompressing the file causes it to progressively lose quality. It produces a much smaller compressed file which in some cases still meets the requirements of the application. For example, a JPG image file, and MP3 or WMA (music) audio files.

Maiden name - A female's surname at birth.

Match/Merge - A feature on the Tools menu in some family history programs that allows you to find duplicate records in a file and combine them into one record.

Maternal Line - The line of descent on a mother's side.

Modem - A device that allows computers to communicate with each other over telephone lines or other delivery systems by changing digital signals to telephone signals for transmission and then back to digital signals. Modems come in different speeds: the higher the speed, the faster the data is transmitted.

Modified register - A report that lists an individual and his or her descendants in a narrative form. The first paragraph identifies the individual and explains birth and other event information in complete sentences. The next paragraph describes the person's first spouse. Children and spouses are listed next. If the person had more than one spouse, those spouses and any children appear after that.

Mouse - A small device attached to the computer by a cord which lets you give commands to the computer. The mouse controls an arrow on the computer screen and allows you to point and click to make selections.

MRIN - An abbreviation that stands for "Marriage Record Identification Number." PAF software assigns each marriage record a unique MRIN and uses it to distinguish one marriage record from another.

Multimedia - A term used to refer to electronic pictures, sound clips, and video clips for use in your family history program or website. To create video and sound clips, you must already have the required computer hardware and software. Multimedia features may include: *Video Clips* - portions of digitized video images that can be displayed through various programs via the Internet. *Sound Clips* - portions of digitized sound clips that can be heard through various programs via the Internet. *Digital Images* - picture (images) that can be displayed on computers or via the Internet. These images can be displayed using various image formats, such as JPEG, GIFF, BITMAP, etc.

Multiple parent indicator - A symbol used on reports that indicate that a person is linked to more than one set of parents.

Navigation bar - Words or images on website pages with links to other sections or pages of the same website

Netiquette - Rules or manners for interacting courteously with others online (such as not typing a message in all capital letters, which is equivalent to shouting).

NGS - National Genealogical Society.

Notes - Information about an individual, marriage, or set of parents that does not fit in the individual record, the marriage record, or sources. Notes can contain additional information, research notes, or other narrative information. Also a feature on the Edit menu that allows you to add or edit the notes

associated with the selected individual or marriage.

Offline - Not being connected to an Internet host or service provider.

Online - Refers to computer connection to the Internet. Made possible through the use of an internet service provider and web browser.

Original Record - A record created at or close to the time of an event by an eyewitness to the event. (e.g., a birth record by the doctor who delivered the baby.)

PAF (Personal Ancestral File) - A free family history program available from www.familysearch.org.

Parent Link - The type of relationship selected for an individual and his or her parents. The options are biological, adopted, guardian, sealing, challenged, and disproved. If a person is linked to only one set of parents, the relationship is assumed to be biological unless you change it. On the Family screen, the parent link appears only if it is something other than biological.

Password - A set of characters that you can use to prevent another individual from inadvertently changing information.

Paternal Line - The line of descent on a father's side.

PDF (Portable Document Format) - A file format that allows a document to be saved in a certain way, no matter what kind of computer is used to display it. The machine must have Adobe's Acrobat Reader (a free program available at www.adobe.com) to display the file.

Pedigree - An ancestral line or line of descent.

Pedigree chart - A chart that shows an individual's direct ancestors—parents, grandparents, great-grandparents, and so forth. This is the traditional way to display a genealogy or 'family tree'. A pedigree chart may contain birth, marriage, and death information.

Pedigree Resource File (PRF) - A computer file containing names and often other vital information (such as date and place of birth, marriage, or death) of individuals who have lived throughout the world. Names are organized into family groups and pedigrees. The information will appear as it was originally submitted and will not be merged with information submitted by others. Available at www.familysearch.org.

Person Identifier (PID) - A number that identifies people in FamilySearch. An individual's person identifier does not change over the life and death of the individual.

Query - An online request for family history information which usually includes a name, date, location and your contact information.

RAM (Random Access Memory) - The working memory of a computer used for storing data temporarily while working on it, or running application programs, etc.

Relationship calculator - A feature on menu in family history programs that allows you to determine how two individuals are related.

Repository - The place where records are stored, such as an archive or library.

Restore - A feature on the menu of some family history programs that allows you to use a backup copy to return a certain file to its state when the backup copy was made.

RIN - An abbreviation that stands for "Record Identification Number" in the PAF program. PAF assigns a unique RIN to each individual record. This number is used to distinguish that individual record from others in a .paf file.

RSS (Really Simple Syndication) - A Web feed format used to publish frequently updated works—such as blog entries, news headlines, audio, and video—in a standardized format. They benefit readers who want to subscribe to timely updates from favored websites or to aggregate feeds from many sites into one place.

Search Engine - A tool designed to search for information on the World Wide Web. The search results are usually presented in a list and are commonly called *hits.* The information may consist of web pages, images, information and other types of files. Some search engines also mine data available in newsbooks, databases, or open directories. Unlike Web directories, which are maintained by human editors, search engines operate algorithmically or are a mixture of algorithmic and human input. Some of the major search engines are Google, Yahoo, Dogpile, Live, Ask, etc. (Note that Yahoo is a directory, not a search engine.) A web directory does not display lists of web pages based on keywords; instead, it lists web sites by category and subcategory.

Server - A computer that allows other computers to log on and use its resources.

Shareware - The try-before-you-buy concept in computer software where the author expects to receive compensation after a trial period. For example, *Brother's Keeper* is shareware.

Slide Show - A presentation that displays all of the multimedia that is attached to an individual. It displays each item for a specific amount of time, in a sequential fashion.

Software - A computer program or set of instructions. System software operates on the machine itself and is invisible to you. Application software allows you to carry out certain activities, such as word processing, family history, spreadsheets, etc.

Soundex - A type of index that groups surnames that sound similar but are spelled differently. Each surname is assigned a code that consists of the first letter of the name. The next three consonants are assigned a number. Vowels are ignored. Soundex has been used to index the 1880, 1900, 1910, and 1920 United States censuses and some other types of records, such as naturalization records and passenger lists.

Sources & Notes - This is a feature in a family history program that displays: The sources used to obtain genealogical data for a specific individual and the notes of those who entered the information to give additional helpful information. This will increase your ability to collaborate and verify your genealogical information with others doing work on your same line.

Surname - A person's last name or family name.

Sync / Synchronize - Ensuring that data is the same in two or more databases or locations. To sync two computers means to copy the data from one computer to the other.

Tag - A word or phrase used to classify the information in a note. Tags should be typed in all uppercase letters at the beginning of the note and be followed by a colon.

Tagged notes - A type of note that uses a keyword to identify the type of information contained in a note in PAF. The keyword is typed in all uppercase letters at the beginning of a paragraph and followed by a colon. For example, in the following note, "NAME:" is the tag: "NAME: This person changed her name."

Twitter - A social networking and micro-blogging service for friends, family, and co-workers to stay connected through the exchange of quick, frequent answers (known as tweets) to one simple question: What are you doing? Answers must be under 140 characters in length and can be sent via mobile texting, instant message, or the web. Located at www.twitter.com.

Upload - The process of sending a file or message from your computer to another.

URL (Uniform Resource Locator) - The World Wide Web address of a site on the Internet. For example, the URL for the White House is http://www.whitehouse.gov.

Usenet Newsgroups - A system of thousands of special interest groups to which readers can send or "post" messages; these messages are then distributed to other computers on the network. Usenet registers newsgroups, which are available through Internet Service Providers.

Virus - A program that installs itself secretly on your computer by attaching itself to another program or e-mail. It duplicates itself when the e-mail is opened and is usually intended to erase important files in your system

Vital Records - The official records of birth, death, marriage, and other events of a persons life.

Web browser - A software program that lets you find, see, and hear material on the World Wide Web, including text, graphics, sound, and video. Popular browsers are Explorer, Netscape, and AltaVista. Most online services have their own browsers.

Web page - A multimedia document that is created and viewable on the internet with the use of a world wide web browser.

Web site - Refers to one or more World Wide Web pages on the internet.

Worm - A computer program that makes copies of itself and spreads through connected systems, using up resources or causing other damage.

www (World Wide Web) - The portion of the Internet that is written in HTML. A hypertext-based system that allows you to browse through a variety of linked Internet resources organized by colorful, graphics-oriented home pages.

Index

Other Books / eBooks by Author
The Perfect Companion Books

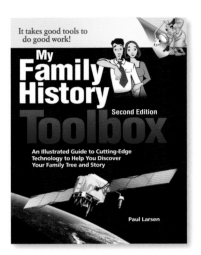

My Family History Toolbox
An Illustrated Guide to Cutting-Edge Technology to Help You Discover Your Family Tree and Story

The perfect guidebook about how to use the latest tools, gadgets and apps to help you plant, nourish, and grow your family tree, and connect to your ancestors. It enables easier and faster ways of searching and organizing your family tree, and collaborating with others. Includes using your iPad for family history.

www.easyfamilyhistory.com/store?page=shop.browse&category_id=3

Softcover 160 pages Reg. $24.95 **Special offer $19.99 – SAVE 20%**

Digital eBook Reg. $19.95 **Special offer $14.99 – SAVE 25%**

Using Google Power to Connect to Your Ancestors
An illustrated guide to harnessing 'the full Power of Google' to help you locate data, fill-in missing information, and add richness to your family story.

www.easyfamilyhistory.com/store?page=shop.browse&category_id=3

Digital eBook Reg. $9.95 **Special offer $7.99 – SAVE 20%**

Bring Your Ancestors to Life Using Newspapers

This digital book is a full-color, illustrated guide to the best free archived newspapers. Newspapers allow you to tap into a reliable source of hundreds of years of history, and give you the remarkable ability to see history through eyewitness accounts. You can easily explore your family tree and bring your family history to life for *free* using historical newspapers... *if you know where to look.*

www.easyfamilyhistory.com/store?page=shop.product_details&flypage=flypage.tpl&product_id=20&category_id=3

Digital eBook Reg. $14.95 **Special offer $11.99 – SAVE 20%**

Family History Power Tools
Essential Tools and Apps to Discover and Share Your Own Family Roots and Story

A premium set of 4 powerful family history eBooks that provides a wealth of invaluable resources, ideas, tips and techniques using today's technology to help you discover your family tree and story: Crash Course, Google Power, Newspaper, Toolbox. 4 eBook Set – Reg. $75 **Special Offer $44.99 - SAVE 40%**

DNA GENEALOGY

Discover your deep ancestral roots, find out where your ancestors came from, and discover their ethnic background using genetic genealogy.

Who Are Your Ancestors?

About Genetic or DNA Genealogy

How did you end up where you are today? Genetic genealogy is the newest and an exciting addition to genealogy research, and allows you to trace the path of your ancestors and find out who they were, where they lived and how they migrated throughout the world.

What is DNA?

All living things, including humans, are made up of many different kind of cells.

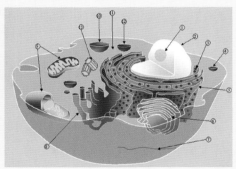

A Human Cell

Most of the cells in your body have a nucleus. The nucleus of all of your cells contains *chromosomes* which are responsible for storing your hereditary information. Chromosomes are made up of DNA (deoxyribonucleic acid). DNA is like a blueprint because it holds the informational code for all of the genetic information for you, and is unique to you. With the exception of the egg and sperm cell, all of the cells in your body contain 23 pairs of chromosomes, 46 in total.

DNA research is based on the 46 chromosomes that every human being has (with few exceptions). Each of the 23 pairs consists of one chromosome inherited from your mother and one from your father. In females, the 23rd chromosome pair consists of two X-chromosomes. Males, however, have an X-chromosome and a Y-chromosome. It is the Y-chromosome that determines male gender. The Y-chromosome can be traced from father-to-son-to-son and so on. Y-chromosome is only carried by men and is only inherited from your fathers. Men who share a common paternal ancestor will have virtually the same Y-DNA, even if that male ancestor lived my generations ago.

The male Y-chromosome is one of the most useful chromosomes in genealogical studies, because it has the unique property of being passed virtually unchanged from generation to generation. This means that a man and all his sons will have the same (or similar) Y-chromosome, and that males with a common paternal ancestor have similar Y-DNA. Unrelated males from a different family line will have a different Y-Chromosome code.

The mother has a Mitrochrondial DNA (mtDNA) which is something of an energy source for the cells. All children of one mother have the same mtDNA as do all children of that mother's daughters. MtDNA is only inherited from your mother. Mothers inherit their DNA from their Mothers, and so on back in time along one's maternal line. mtDNA can't be passed by men. The study of the *Y-chromosome* or the *mtDNA* trail forms the basis of the DNA genealogy. No